SPI
EGE
L&G
RAU

A

JEWISH

WOMAN'S

Prayer Book

EDITED BY

Aliza Lavie

SPIEGEL & GRAU

NEW YORK

2008

LIBRARY OF CONGRESS CATALOGING-IN-PRODUCTION DATA

Tefillat nashim. English
   A Jewish woman's prayer book / edited by Aliza
Lavie—1st ed.
       p. cm.
1. Jewish women—Prayers and devotions. 2. Jewish
women—Religious life. 1. Lavie, Aliza. 11. Title.
   BM667.W6T4613 2008
296.4'5082—dc22

                               2008013304

ISBN 978-0-385-52274-8

PRINTED IN THE UNITED STATES OF AMERICA

10 9 8 7 6 5 4 3 2 1

FIRST EDITION

Dedicated to the memory of my

DEVOUT AND SAINTLY GRANDMOTHER,

HANNAH MASHIAH,

TISHREI 5666–TISHREI 5762

May it be Your will, Lord my God and God of my forefathers, that this hour—as I stand to pray before You for my soul and the souls of my household—be a time of favor, a time of heeding, a time of hearing; that when I call out to You, You answer me; that I petition You and You grant my request.

FROM A HANDWRITTEN COLLECTION OF WOMEN'S PRAYERS DEDICATED TO SARA, WIFE OF K. HIZKIYA LEVI (ITALY, 1814)

Contents

II ✦ BARRENNESS AND FERTILITY

VI ✦ TIMES OF CRISIS

Notes on Transliteration and Hebrew Text

The transliteration of Hebrew terms generally follows the *Merriam-Webster's Collegiate Dictionary*, 11th edition. For transliteration of Hebrew words not found in *Merriam-Webster's*, *H* (or *h̲*) is used to indicate the Hebrew letter *h̲et*, while *Kh* (or *kh*) represents the Hebrew letter *khaf*. (For the Yiddish term *tekhines*, however, *kh* appears instead of *h̲*, in accordance with generally accepted rules for Yiddish transliteration.)

Words that are recognized by *Merriam-Webster's* have been set in roman typeface. For consistency, all names of Jewish holidays appear here in roman—even those, such as Shemini Atzeret, that do not appear in *Merriam-Webster's*. *Tish'a be-Av* and *Tu bi-Shevat*, however, are italicized because they are dates, rather than names, of festivals.

Words that end in silent *heh* in Hebrew (including names of biblical characters) are spelled here with a corresponding *h*.

Words that start with the *heh ha-yedi'a* in Hebrew are transliterated as, for example, *ha-Makom* rather than *hamakom*, to aid pronunciation and to better reflect the Hebrew grammar.

Prior to the publication of the original Hebrew version of this book, extensive discussion was devoted to the issue of Hebrew vowels. On the one hand, the book sought to present the prayers in their authentic form; on the other hand, some modifications of voweling would be necessary for the reader's convenience. The final Hebrew text is therefore not uniform in its orthography. Many of the prayers in this volume were originally composed in various languages of the Jewish Diaspora, and only later translated into Hebrew. In such instances, the Hebrew language and voweling follow the accepted grammatical rules.

Preface

"It is possible to live without hope; perhaps even without truth—but not without prayer, which is the quest for both ... If art is man's way of saying 'no,' prayer is his way of saying 'yes.' Yes to the universe and its Creator, yes to life and its meaning, yes to faith, to hope, to joy. A torch for the wanderer who has lost his way, a ladder for Jacob, who seeks dreams, a window onto the soul."
—ELIE WIESEL

On the eve of Yom Kippur in 2002 I read a newspaper interview with Hen Keinan, a woman who had lost her baby daughter, Sinai, and her mother, Ruthi Peled, in a terrorist attack in a shopping center in Petah Tikva, Israel. In an instant, Hen had become both a bereaved mother and an orphan. After the attack, Hen and her husband, Lior, left Israel and moved to the United States. This interview, I sensed, was a farewell to Israeli society. Hen was unable to contain her pain; staying in the country where she had sustained the loss of that which was most precious to her had become too difficult for her to bear.

The article shook me and stirred up a storm of emotions. Hen's pain and despair, her cry from the heart cut through me, leaving me bewildered and burdened with questions. I wanted to embrace her; I wanted to offer words of comfort, to strengthen her spirit. When I stood in the synagogue later that evening for the *Kol Nidrei* service, I could not pray. The words in the prayer book escaped me. The little that I read was blurred by my tears. Thoughts raced through my head and carried me beyond the synagogue walls and across the boundaries of time. I thought of the many Jewish women throughout history who had suffered losses similar to Hen's and had remained strong. I wanted to tell Hen about those women, whose merits are preserved forever by the Creator; women like our matriarchs, Sarah and Rachel. I wanted to tell her about Elisheva, daughter of Aminadab, who lost her sons Nadab and Abihu; about Ruth, the Moabite; and about Glückel of Hameln. I wanted to convey to her the strength and fortitude of Jewish women in Italy; to tell her about my own grandmother, Hannah Mashiah, who emigrated from Bukhara as a respected, wealthy woman and then endured bereavement and impoverishment in the Promised Land: she bore nine children, but by the age of thirty-six she had lost three of them and was a widow. I would whisper to Hen that my grandmother's steadfast and knowledgeable faith and her attendance at prayer services three times a day, every day, all year round, were the foundations of my own strong connection to Judaism.

As I stood there in the synagogue, grappling with Hen's questions and sensing that the prayer book in front of me could not provide the answers, I resolved to seek out the secret of my grandmother's legacy; to explore the eternal, powerful faith of Jewish women. At that moment I undertook a quest that could be fulfilled only with the publication of this collection in Hebrew and, now, in English.

I am sitting in Jerusalem, not far from the synagogue where this adventure began. My thoughts carry me to the prayers I have come to know, the life stories to which I have been exposed, the women I have met, and the imaginary conversations I have held with women long deceased. The publication of this book marks the culmination of a six-year journey that exposed me to a spiritual world that had nearly been lost to time. This collection reviews prayers that were passed down from mother to daughter and from daughter to granddaughter; they were whispered throughout the generations, in Israel and around the world, in Hebrew and in the many languages of the Jewish Diaspora, only rarely being set down in print. Here are prayers that were written three thousand years ago alongside prayers composed in the third millennium. The world I discovered, the age-old code of Jewish women that opened up before me, is preserved here in a single volume.

Significantly, Judaism's entire conception of prayer originated with a woman. After the destruction of the Temple, a fixed prayer formula was set down to replace the daily Temple sacrifices. Many of the laws and details pertaining to this prayer formula were derived from the biblical account of the supplication of Hannah, the mother of the prophet Samuel, for a son. Out of all the instances of prayer in the Bible, the rabbis chose this woman's heartfelt, personal appeal to God as the paradigm for the individual, whispered prayer that is at the heart of every public prayer service. In tribute to the importance of her contribution, the prayer books of many Jewish communities around the world open with the words, "Hannah prayed and she said."

Hannah knew how to pray without any external guidance. The pure expression of her pain and bitterness of spirit, together with her manifest faith in the power of the Creator of the universe, are together the essence of the power of her prayer. Hannah also understood that the act of praying is itself inspiring and empowering. Regardless of whether the request to God is ultimately granted, the prayer is spiritually fulfilling in and of itself. Hence, as the Hazon Ish (Rabbi Avraham Yeshayahu Karelitz, 1878–1953) points out, Hannah did not need an immediate response from God to alleviate her emotional suffering; her prayer itself was solace enough, and, by the end of it, "her countenance was no longer [sad]."

As my research for this book progressed, I discovered that Hannah's mode of prayer—an intimate, emotional, and personal dialogue with God—has lived on among Jewish women across the world and throughout history. I was able to trace a rich heritage of women's involvement in the creation and dissemination of prayers that has continued until the present day. I perceived a direct link between the intensely spiritual lives of fifteenth-century Italian Jewish women and Fanny Neuda, the nineteenth-century author of a bestselling book of prayers that she composed in German; I saw echoes of Hannah's private entreaty for a son in the Yiddish *tekhines* composed in the sixteenth century. I came across a letter that Rabbi Ovadia of Bartenura wrote to his father in 1488, and I was struck by his portrait of the Jewish women of Sicily. Though they had no formal Jewish education or textual knowledge and did not pray according to accepted custom, the women Rabbi Ovadia of Bartenura described lived their Judaism powerfully and emotionally. Their Judaism came from the heart, from the soul. It was a constant, unmediated dialogue with the Creator; it was an authentic Judaism that had been passed down, unadulterated, from generation to generation. Perhaps, I thought, it had always been so; Jewish women, it seemed, regardless of their background, had preserved a visceral, personal relationship with God, echoing the mood of Hannah's ancient prayer.

The quest to seek out the material included in this book exposed me to many different works, reflecting a fascinating feminine mosaic: prayers composed for the entire community, meant to be recited by men and women alike; prayers for worshippers in the "women's gallery" of the synagogue or for a separate women's prayer group; texts composed or gathered and collated by men for women, often by a father for his daughter, or by a groom for his bride. I viewed rare texts preserved around the world—in museums and libraries—but also in private collections, in forgotten archives, and in family settings. I found prayers tucked into books of family trees and in private siddurim that were handed down from mother to daughter.

Each prayer, each liturgy, had its own story. Often I was struck dumb by the beauty of a newly discovered prayer or brought to tears by its poignancy. In some cases it was the author herself who aroused my curiosity. The prayers, supplications, liturgies, and psalms that emerged are different from one another, but they share common themes: a dialogue with the Creator, hope for a better future, and concern for the welfare of the Jewish nation.

The many women I met and the stories I heard taught me about women's customs in worship, about forgotten ceremonies and unique versions of prayers. More than anything else, they proved to me that there was a common longing for *Bubbie*'s prayers, for Mamma's prayers, for the prayers of a women's circle that had been broken. In many Western countries, the catalyst for this disintegration was the quest to adopt gentile values and to assimilate socially. In modern Israel, the acceptance of a standardized prayer formula, as well as mass immigration and acculturation and an accelerated process of secularization, have led to the disappearance of the spiritual world and heritage of Jewish women from different parts of the Diaspora; their prayers, songs, ceremonies, customs, and special versions of blessings have been all but forgotten. In most instances, only a small portion of the communal customs and traditional modes of expression were documented. This volume retrieves many that had nearly been lost to time and preserves them for our daughters and granddaughters and the generations to come.

The prayers included in this book are the fruit of extensive research. The guiding principle was to include only prayers that were written by, for, or about women. In most cases the author of the prayer is named explicitly. Sometimes we have no definitive knowledge of his or her identity, but tradition attaches a certain name to the prayer. Most of the prayers in this volume are accompanied by some explanation or commentary. When information about the author of the prayer—the circumstances that brought her to set down her words, or her environment and living conditions—was unavailable, I have attempted to supply supplementary details about the prayer's origin. There are prayers here to commemorate every occasion and every passage in the cycle of life, from the mundane to the extraordinary. There are special prayers for Shabbat and holidays and important dates in the Jewish year; prayers to mark celebratory milestones, such as bat mitzvahs, marriage, pregnancy, and childbirth; and prayers for comfort and understanding in times of tragedy and loss.

The book is a political work, and it was received, at first, with wariness by some in the rabbinical establishment. I had to explain time and again my motives and intentions in publishing such a work. At the same time I understood that the prayers, with the conservative gender stereotypes that unquestionably pervade some of them, risked offending the modern and politically correct sensibilities of some readers. By way of contrast, there are several volumes of contemporary Jewish women's prayers that have been published in recent years, many of which have humanist, universalist appeal and convey a manifestly politically correct message. My book is not meant as a contribution to this genre. Despite its great diversity of geographical and historical sources, this collection evidences a remarkable degree of unity in the core perception of existential purpose. The real life of real Jewish women throughout the generations is what gave rise to the prayers that they created. The prayers reflect their customs, beliefs, norms, and values. We dare not ignore or distort their voices and their message. My aspiration has been to convey them in good faith, with the belief that their meaningful and compelling heritage is a treasure that neither contemporary universalistic texts, on the one hand, nor the traditional prayer book, on the other, can replace. For the sake of the identity and continuity of generations of Jewish women in the present and the future, it is this heritage—living on in dwindling numbers of hearts and minds—that I have sought to reclaim before it recedes beyond our grasp. Ultimately, the book and the lively, multifaceted discussion surrounding it have redeemed countless women— individuals and the communities around them—from oblivion, and restored them to their proper place in Jewish history, consciousness, tradition, and prayer.

The Hebrew version of this book, *Tefillat Nashim* (Women's Prayers), was published in Israel at the end of 2005. It has enjoyed enormous popularity among all sectors of the country's fragmented society. It has been embraced by members of every major religious denomination in Israel, from the ultra-Orthodox to the most secular, and, surprisingly, by Muslims and Christians, too. In fact, an entire cultural phenomenon has developed around it. The book has given rise to a great many critical reviews, academic conferences and debates, and cultural dialogues in the Israeli media. Liturgical poems and prayers have been set to music by Israeli musicians, and others have been dramatized. These prayers have gradually seeped into the heart of the cultural scene and, at the same time, have enriched the religious lives of individuals and communities. Groups and workshops have been set up to encourage the writing of personal prayers, inspired by the intimate, individual style of this volume's supplications. A particularly moving example of the courage and impetus that the book has provided is the "*Yizkor* Prayer for a Son," which Dalia Wertheim-Yohanan composed for her friend, Reena Robinson, whose son, Matanya, an IDF soldier, was killed in battle.

Through the response to the publication of the book in Hebrew, I have encountered many more women's prayers and ceremonies and have discovered more women writers whose names appear nowhere in the pages of Jewish history books. I have also continued to learn more about the dissemination of and popularity enjoyed by some of the prayers included in the book. Since *Tefillat Nashim*'s publication, I have come across accounts of women who recited "Prayer For a Son Serving in the Army" during World War I, as well as in modern-day Israel.

The flourishing contemporary research in the spheres of gender and Judaism brings some hope for the revelation of further information that will shed new light on this book—both by adding new insights into the material that appears here and by introducing additional prayers and authors who have yet to be discovered. In the meantime, I have attempted to present the prayers in such a way as to maintain their textual authenticity along with their relevance in the twenty-first century, to women as well as men and to Jews and gentiles alike.

The translation of the prayers, supplications, and liturgical poems into English posed a complex challenge. A prayer written in the Hebrew language, with its unique wealth of biblical and liturgical associations, cannot be "translated" in the conventional sense of the word. While every effort has been made to remain faithful to the Hebrew text, the English translation is, by definition, an approximation. It is a new creation inspired by the original one, aiming to capture the mood and the emotion of the appeal to God while also striving to retain the multilayered meanings of the words themselves. One of the most moving aspects of many of these prayers, and one that elicited a profound reaction from women of every background when the book was published in Hebrew, is their formulation in the feminine first person. While some of the prayers are quite similar in content to those found in the standard prayer book, the unusual sound of them uttered in the feminine voice is a sudden glimpse of a parallel world. Unfortunately, because English grammar does not differentiate between genders in the first person, that effect was virtually impossible to re-create in translation.

My hope for this collection is beautifully captured by this Hassidic legend:

> When the Ba'al Shem Tov foresaw some mortal danger threatening the Jewish people, he would go off to a certain place in the forest; there he would ignite a fire and utter a certain prayer in intense meditation, and the decree would miraculously be annulled.
>
> Later on, when his disciple Rabbi Dov-Ber, the Maggid of Mezritch, was faced with a similar matter of dire importance, he would go to the same place in the forest, where he would declare: "Master of the world: I know not how to ignite the fire, but I am able to offer the prayer"—and the same miraculous deliverance would occur.
>
> Another generation passed, and now it was Rabbi Moshe Leib of Sasov who sought to save his people. He went to the forest and said: "I am unable to ignite the fire; the secret meditations of the prayer, too, have been lost. But at least I can stand here at the place in the forest where it all happened." This alone was enough to avert the decree.
>
> Yet another generation went by, and it was Rabbi Yisrael of Ruzhin's turn to plead for divine mercy. He sat upon his stately seat, held his head in his hands, and spoke with the Holy One, blessed be He: "Master of the universe: Hear my voice. I cannot ignite the fire, nor do I know the prayer. I cannot even find the place in the forest. All that I am able to do is to tell the story. Please let that suffice."

And indeed, the fourth *tzaddik*'s telling was no less effective than the actions of the first three had been.

It is my hope that this volume will succeed in evoking and reviving the great heritage of Jewish women's faith—the story that this book as a whole aims to tell.

Aliza Lavie, Fall 2008

I

MOMENTS

in a

WOMAN'S

LIFE

Everyday Prayers

Though few Jewish prayers attributed to female authors have been preserved, historical evidence suggests that women have been composing prayers since the Middle Ages. During the second half of the tenth century, the wife of the Spanish rabbi and poet Dunash ben Labrat is said to have demonstrated a gift for liturgical composition, proficiency in the intricacies of the Hebrew language, and familiarity with biblical style. Similarly, the epitaph on the tombstone of Urania, who lived in the thirteenth century and was the daughter of a Rabbi Avraham of Worms, memorializes her as "Lady Urania … who also wrote and rendered prayer in song for women." Lady Dulcie, the wife of the famous liturgist Rabbi Elazar of Worms (1165–1238), also wrote prayers of her own. Following her martyrdom at the hands of the Crusaders, Rabbi Elazar delivered a eulogy that praised her for "singing sweet songs and prayers, and uttering supplications ... and in all the provinces she taught women to sing praises. She regularly attended morning and evening services, arriving early at the synagogue and leaving last." The contemporary scholar Avraham Grossman concludes from the eulogy that Dulcie would conduct a separate prayer service for women, accompanied with song.

The prayers of Dunash ben Labrat's wife, Lady Urania, and Lady Dulcie have unfortunately been lost to time; this section, however, brings together other prayers—from as early as the seventeenth century until the present day—that attest to a rich tradition of Jewish female liturgists. The prayers in this section are specifically intended for a woman's everyday routine, imbuing her ordinary consciousness with spiritual depth and religious purpose.

HEAR MY PRAYER
Italy

*M*ay it be Your will, Lord my God and God of my forefathers, that this hour—as I stand to pray before You for my soul and the souls of my household—be a time of favor, a time of heeding, a time of hearing; that when I call out to You—You answer me, that I petition You and You grant my request. Command Your angels who are appointed over mortal matters to be with me, to aid and to assist, to deliver and to save. Direct the hearts of people with whom I have dealings to whatever I desire, and turn their will to all that I want. Thwart all the plots of those who hate me and confound the counsel of my enemies. Fulfill all of my wishes for the good, as it is written, "He shall give you as your heart desires, and He shall fulfill all your counsel." Be with my heart as I deliberate [...]. Grant me sound judgment and guide me in all of my ways, make me successful in all my undertakings, and bless all my endeavors. Let me not be needful of

---

Jewish women in Italy, especially during the Renaissance, were well versed in Jewish law and tradition and held positions of religious authority. In the official records of the Jewish community of Lugo that date back to the sixteenth century, there are names of women who are listed as having been Torah teachers for children. In the registry of the community's deceased, there is an entry memorializing "the venerable matriarch, Mrs. Diana Pissarro ... knowledgeable in all matters, especially the ritual status of menstrual stains. Any woman who experienced irregular stains would go to her."

In the sixteenth and seventeenth centuries it was common for Italian Jewish women to receive both a secular and a religious education, and many worked as apothecaries and ritual slaughterers. The Venetian Jewish scholar Leon (Yehuda Aryeh) de Modena (1571–1648) wrote of a female relative, Fiorita (Bat-Sheva),

תפילת האשה שתתקבל תפילתה

איטליה

יְהִי רָצוֹן מִלְפָנֶיךָ יְיָ אֱלֹהַי וֵאלֹהֵי אֲבוֹתַי שֶׁתְּהֵא שָׁעָה זוֹ שֶׁאֲנִי עוֹמֶדֶת
לְהִתְפַּלֵּל לְפָנֶיךָ עַל נַפְשִׁי וְעַל נַפְשׁוֹת בֵּיתִי שְׁעַת רָצוֹן שְׁעַת הַקְשָׁבָה
שְׁעַת הָעֲנָיָה אֶקְרָאֶךָּ וְתַעֲנֵנִי אַעְתִּיר לָךְ וְתֵעָתֵר לִי וְצַוֵּה לְמַלְאָכֶיךָ
הַמְמוּנִים עַל עִנְיְנֵי בְנֵי אָדָם שֶׁיִּהְיוּ עִמִּי לַעֲזוֹר וּלְהוֹעִיל לְהוֹשִׁיעַ וּלְהַצִּיל
וְהַטֵּה לִבּוֹת בְּנֵי אָדָם שֶׁיֵּשׁ לִי עֵסֶק עִמָּהֶם לְכָל אֲשֶׁר אֶחְפּוֹץ וְהָשֵׁב רְצוֹנָם
לְכָל אֲשֶׁר אֶרְצֶה וּבַטֵּל כָּל מַחְשְׁבוֹת שׂוֹנְאַי וְהָפֵר כָּל עֲצַת אוֹיְבַי וּמַלֵּא
כָּל מִשְׁאֲלוֹתַי לְטוֹבָה כַּכָּתוּב יִתֶּן לְךָ כִלְבָבֶךָ וְכָל עֲצָתְךָ יְמַלֵּא וְתִהְיֶה עִם
לְבָבִי בְּעֵת מַחְשְׁבוֹתַי... וְתַשְׂכִּילֵנִי וְתוֹרֵנִי בְכָל דְּרָכַי וְתַצְלִיחֵנִי בְּכָל מַהֲלָכַי
וְתִשְׁלַח בְּרָכָה בְּכָל מַעֲשֵׂי יָדַי וְאַל תַּצְרִיכֵנִי לִידֵי מַתְּנַת בָּשָׂר וָדָם אֶלָּא
לְיָדְךָ הָרְחָבָה וְהַמְלֵאָה וּמֵעָפָר עָנְיִי תְּקִימֵנִי וּמֵאַשְׁפּוֹת דַּלּוֹתִי תְּרוֹמְמֵנִי
וְתִסְמְכֵנִי בִּימִין בִּרְכוֹתֶיךָ וְתִגְמְלֵנִי חֲסָדִים טוֹבִים, בָּרוּךְ הַגּוֹמֵל חֲסָדִים
טוֹבִים לְעַמּוֹ יִשְׂרָאֵל.

---

wife of Shelomo of Modena, who was knowledgeable in Torah, Talmud, rabbinic responsa, and Jewish mysticism. Another Italian Jewish woman whom Leon de Modena mentions, Estelina, wife of Avraham, son of Shelomo Kunat, was a typesetter who established one of the first·Hebrew printing presses in Italy. Similarly, the poet Devora Ascarelli, who lived at the end of the sixteenth century, composed and wrote poems in Italian. She also translated into Italian the second section of *Mikdash Me'at*, the book of liturgical work written by the fifteenth-century rabbi, poet, and physician Moshe di Rieti, who was known as the "Jewish Dante." The first translation of the Haggadah for Pesach into Italian is likewise attributed to a woman: Flora Randegger Freidenberg published it in 1851.

Even prior to the Renaissance, however, Italian Jewish women were composing prayers. At the end of the thirteenth century, for instance, a woman known as mortal gifts, but rather depend upon Your generous and open hand. Lift me up from the dust of my destitution; elevate me from the lowliness of my need. Draw me close with the blessings of Your right hand; render me beneficent kindness. Blessed is He Who renders beneficent kindness to His nation, Israel.

"Paula, daughter of Avraham" had extensive knowledge of halakhic literature and was by profession a copier of manuscripts. At the end of Rabbi Yishaya Detrani's *Sefer ha-Makhri'a*, which she copied by hand, she added a prayer of her own on behalf of all of Israel. Written in 1292, her prayer appears to have been composed against the background of the decrees forcing Jews to convert, leading to martyrdom, expulsion, and outward acceptance of Christianity: "May He, in His mercy, grant me the merit of seeing His honor and our honor / And take us out of the great darkness / In which we find ourselves today and which has come about in our times."

AT DAWN

Freiha, daughter of Rabbi Avraham

*T*urn to us in mercy / In the merit of the righteous Abraham
Have mercy on us from on High / Almighty; my Redeemer.
Hear me at dawn.

Have mercy upon Your chosen nation / For they are Your people
    and Your inheritance
Speedily gather Your congregation / to the mountains of the Galilee
Hear me at dawn.

One and only elevated, hidden One, / Redeem Your children, like
    mute sheep
Rebuild Your Temple and Sanctuary / and aid my destiny.
Hear me at dawn.

Freiha was an eighteenth-century Moroccan poet who wrote in Hebrew under the pen-name Bat Yosef. Respectfully referred to as *Rabbanit*, she was a Torah scholar and left a legacy of writings and poems, few of which have survived. Her extensive library, including kabbalistic works, testified to the breadth of her learning. Women in her community approached her as they would a saint, often invoking her name in times of distress.

    In the wake of unrest in Morocco, Freiha moved with her father and brother to Tunisia. Rabbi Avraham and his son moved on in 1756, when Tunisia was conquered by the Algerians, and contact with Freiha was lost. When they returned, they were unable to locate her; their extensive searches offered no clue as to her fate. Freiha's father established a synagogue in his home in her memory. At the spot where her

פנה אלינו ברחמים

פריחא בת רבי אברהם

פְּנֵה אֵלֵינוּ בְּרַחֲמִים / בִּזְכוּת אַבְרָהָם תָּמִים,
רַחֵם עָלֵינוּ מִמְּרוֹמִים, / הָאֵל גּוֹאֲלִי.
בֹּקֶר וְתִשְׁמַע קוֹלִי.

רַחֵם עַל עַם סְגֻלָּתֶךָ. / כִּי הֵם עַמְּךָ וְנַחֲלָתֶךָ;
מַהֵר קַבֵּץ קְהִלָּתֶךָ / אֶל הַר גְּלִילִי.
בֹּקֶר וְתִשְׁמַע קוֹלִי.

יָחִיד נִשָּׂא וְנֶעְלָם. / פְּדֵה בִּנְךָ כְּשֶׂה נֶאֱלָם.
וּבְנֵה דְּבִיר וְאוּלָם, / וְתָמֹךְ גּוֹרָלִי.
בֹּקֶר וְתִשְׁמַע קוֹלִי.

bed had stood, he dug a *mikveh*, and the Holy Ark was placed on the spot that had held her library. The synagogue remained there until 1936.

Of Freiha's writings, only two songs remain, both composed in Hebrew. One is called "Redemption Song"; it alludes to the suffering of the Jewish nation in exile as well as the personal tribulations of the composer's own family in Morocco, and expresses a powerful longing for personal and national redemption. "At Dawn" likewise interweaves communal and personal elements. It is a prayer for a hastening of the redemption, for ascent to the Land of Israel, for the rebuilding of the Holy Temple, and for forgiveness for sin. The recurring plea "Hear me at dawn" tells us that this is a prayer for weekdays, meant to be recited prior to the morning service, or together with *tikkun ḥatzot* (the "midnight prayer") that some recite in memory of the destruction of the Temple and for Israel's restoration.

Have mercy and compassion upon us / and take us up to Zion
Reestablish Your Temple for us / my Rock and Redeemer.
Hear me at dawn.

My God, hear my supplication / Lord, Who favors my song
God—my shield, my portion / my cup, my lot.
Hear me at dawn.

Bat Yosef waits expectantly / Asking of Your goodness
That she speedily inherit her land / From the hand of the
    Ishmaelites.
Hear me at dawn.

My Father, in Your great mercy / Hasten Your nation's savior,
Act for Your Name's sake, / Forgive all my sins.
Hear me at dawn.

My Creator, have mercy upon my soul / my Rock, strengthen my
    assembly
Lead me up to the land that I desire / that I may offer fragrant
    sacrifices.
Hear me at dawn.

Among the masses I praise Him / May He raise His banner in our
    tents
Perform Your wondrous kindnesses toward us / and accept my
    words with favor.
Hear me at dawn.

חוּס וַחֲמֹל עָלֵינוּ, / וּלְצִיּוֹן הַעֲלֵינוּ,
וְהָקֵם דְּבִירָךְ אֵלֵינוּ, / צוּרִי וְגוֹאֲלִי.
בֹּקֶר וְתִשְׁמַע קוֹלִי.

אֵלִי, שְׁמַע תְּחִנָּתִי, / אָדוֹן בּוֹחֵר רְנָתִי,
הָאֵל מָגִנִּי וּמְנָתִי, / כּוֹסִי וְחֶבְלִי.
בֹּקֶר וְתִשְׁמַע קוֹלִי.

בַּת יוֹסֵף מְיַחֶלֶת, / הַטּוֹב מִמְּךָ שׁוֹאֶלֶת,
מַהֵר אַרְצָהּ תְּהִי נוֹחֶלֶת / מִיַּד הַיִּשְׁמְעֵלִי.
בֹּקֶר וְתִשְׁמַע קוֹלִי.

אָבִי, בְּרֹב רַחֲמֶיךָ, / הָחֵשׁ מוֹשִׁיעַ עַמֶּךָ,
וַעֲשֵׂה לְמַעַן שְׁמֶךָ, / כָּל חֵטְא מְחוֹל לִי.
בֹּקֶר וְתִשְׁמַע קוֹלִי.

בּוֹרְאִי, רַחֵם יְחִידָתִי, / צוּרִי, חַזֵּק קְהִלָּתִי,
וְהַעֲלֵנִי לְאֶרֶץ חֶמְדָּתִי / וְאַקְטֵר כְּלִילִי.
בֹּקֶר וְתִשְׁמַע קוֹלִי.

בְּתוֹךְ רַבִּים אֲהַלֶלֶנּוּ, / דְּגָלוֹ יָרִים בְּאָהֳלֵינוּ.
הַפְלֵא חַסְדְּךָ אֵלֵינוּ, / וּרְצֵה חֵן זֶה קוֹלִי.
בֹּקֶר וְתִשְׁמַע קוֹלִי.

A MOTHER'S EARLY MORNING PRAYER

Hava Pinhas-Cohen

As I stand ready to prepare porridge

Remove all other thoughts from my mind

And when I touch the baby's back to check for fever

Let all worries leave me

Lest they confuse my thinking

And grant me courage to soften my expression

So that each of my children may

See his face within my face

As in a mirror polished for a holiday

And the darkness that is ingrained within

My face—cover it with light,

That my patience not run out, nor my throat grow hoarse

Hava Pinhas-Cohen is a poet and a lecturer in literature and art. This prayer is an expression of the fears and uncertainties that she felt as a young wife and a new mother, and a request for comfort and strength at a time of doubt. "On that early morning," she recounts, recalling the origins of this special prayer, "I got up before everyone else in the house, hoping for a little time to myself before nursing the baby. Unthinkingly I lifted the prayer book that was lying on the table, and I happened upon a 'Prayer Prior to the Morning Service.' I was not taught to pray as a child, nor am I particularly familiar with the standard prayer book. I have

תפילה לאם בטרם שחרית

חוה פנחס כהן

בְּשָׁעָה שֶׁאֲנִי עוֹמֶדֶת לְבַשֵּׁל דַּיְסַת סֹלֶת
הָסֵר מִמֶּנִּי כָּל מִינֵי מַחְשָׁבוֹת זָרוֹת
וּכְשֶׁאֲנִי נוֹגַעַת בְּגֵו הַתִּינוֹק וּמַדָּה חֻמּוֹ
שֶׁיֵּלְכוּ מִמֶּנִּי כָּל מִינֵי טְרָדוֹת
שֶׁלֹּא יְבַלְבְּלוּ מַחְשְׁבוֹתַי.
וְתֵן לִי אֹמֶץ לְזַכֵּךְ פָּנַי
שֶׁיּוּכַל כָּל אֶחָד מִילָדַי,
לִרְאוֹת פָּנָיו בְּתוֹךְ פָּנַי
כְּמוֹ בְּמַרְאָה רְחוּצָה לִקְרַאת חַג

וְאֶת הַחֹשֶׁךְ הַמֻּשְׁקָע מִפְּנִים
פָּנַי – כַּסֵּה בָּאוֹר.

fought conscientiously to make prayer part of my life." On this occasion, however, the words burst forth from inside her, "challenging the solid security offered by the canonical prayer book: security in the face of almost every human anxiety, with unequivocal faith." As a young wife and mother, Hava's faith was "riddled with fears." This prayer, unlike the one that she found that morning in the siddur, voiced her hope that from the gaps in her faith "words can emerge with the power to weld the cracks together, to teach that the consort of fear is love, and that faith is the prayer that the two of them may be able to live together."

From shouting—despite myself—that thickens;

That I not become helpless

In the face of the unknown

And that there be no break even for a moment

In the closeness of flesh to flesh between my children and me

Imbue me with Your love, that I might have enough to stand

at the front door and to share it out

With the simplicity of slicing bread and spreading butter every

   morning

Anew the aroma of milk boiling and overflowing and the

fragrance of the coffee in lieu

Of the thanksgiving sacrifice and the daily sacrifice

That I know not how to offer.

שֶׁלֹּא תִּפָּקַע סַבְלָנוּתִי וְלֹא יִחַר גְּרוֹנִי
מִצְּעָקָה מִתְחַבֶּטֶת וּמִתְעַבָּה
שֶׁלֹּא יִהְיֶה לִי רִפְיוֹן יָדַיִם
מוּל הַבִּלְתִּי נוֹדָע
וְשֶׁלֹּא יִפָּסֵק אַף לֹא לְרֶגַע
מַגַּע בָּשָׂר בְּבָשָׂר בֵּינִי לְבֵין יְלָדַי

תֵּן בִּי אַהֲבָתְךָ שֶׁיְהֵא בִּי דֵּי לַעֲמֹד בְּפֶתַח הַבַּיִת וּלְחַלְּקָהּ
בְּפַשְׁטוּת בָּהּ פּוֹרְסִים לֶחֶם וּמוֹרְחִים חֶמְאָה כָּל בֹּקֶר
מֵחָדָשׁ נִיחוֹחַ חָלָב רוֹתֵחַ וְגוֹלֵשׁ וְרֵיחַ הַקָּפֶה מְכַסִּים
עַל קָרְבַּן תּוֹדָה וְקָרְבַּן תָּמִיד
שֶׁאֵינִי יוֹדַעַת אֵיךְ נוֹתְנִים.

THREE ALTERNATIVE RENDERINGS FOR THE BLESSING "... WHO HAS MADE ME IN ACCORDANCE WITH HIS WILL"

*B*lessed are You, Lord our God, King of the universe,
Who has made me a woman.

*B*lessed are You, Lord our God, King of the universe,
that you have made me a woman and not a man.

*B*lessed are You, Lord our God, King of the universe, Who has
made me according to His will and has not made me a man.

———————————————— ✦ ————————————————

The morning blessings were instituted by the Sages to praise and thank the Creator at the start of each new day. In the original version, one of the blessings expresses thanks to God "... for not making me a woman." The blessing usually appears in the standard prayer book followed by a note in small script that reads: "Women say: '... Who made me according to His will.'"

Many women are understandably uncomfortable with the formulation of this blessing. Various explanations have been proposed in an attempt to alleviate their unease. The main idea that emerges from the body of rabbinic discussion on this issue has been that the blessing expresses a man's thanks for the multiplicity of divine commandments that he is privileged to be obligated to fulfill by virtue of his being male. According to this view, a man's spiritual state is lower than that of a woman, and therefore he requires more commandments in order to perfect himself. A woman, on the other hand, having been created intrinsically more perfect, offers thanks to God for having been made closer to the ideal of "His will."

Nevertheless, despite such attempts to justify its seemingly sexist formulation, the blessing has historically been perceived as problematic by some women and men, as evidenced by the various alternative renderings that have been proposed over the course of the generations.

The first alternative version that appears here, "Who made me a woman," was found in a women's siddur from Provence that dates back to the fourteenth or

שָׁלוֹשׁ בְּרָכוֹת חֲלוּפִיּוֹת לְבִרְכַּת "שֶׁעָשַׂנִי כִּרְצוֹנוֹ"

בָּרוּךְ אַתָּה ה׳ אֱלֹהֵינוּ מֶלֶךְ הָעוֹלָם שֶׁעָשַׂנִי אִשָּׁה.

בָּרוּךְ אַתָּה ה׳ אֱלֹהֵינוּ מֶלֶךְ הָעוֹלָם שֶׁעֲשִׂיתַנִי אִשָּׁה וְלֹא אִישׁ.

בָּרוּךְ אַתָּה ה׳ אֱלֹהֵינוּ מֶלֶךְ הָעוֹלָם שֶׁעָשַׂנִי כִּרְצוֹנוֹ וְלֹא עָשַׂנִי אִישׁ.

---

fifteenth century. The cover of the prayer book bears the inscription, "My sister—may you become thousands of tens of thousands."

The second alternative version comes from a siddur that Avraham Farissol of Avignon wrote for his wife in 1471.

The third alternative was proposed by Rabbi Shlomo Riskin, a prominent Modern Orthodox rabbi, at the Kolech International Congress of Orthodox Women held in 1999 in Jerusalem. He proposed that men recite the corresponding blessing: "Who has not made me a woman, and who has made me according to His will." This solution preserves the formulation of the blessing as conceived by the Sages, while both men and women acknowledge the uniqueness of their gender and give thanks for it, using the same words as each other.

In addition to the three alternatives here, there are others that originated many centuries earlier. For instance, Rabbi Yisrael ben Petahia Isserlin's mother (c. 1400) recited yet a different formulation: "Who did not make me a beast." In the Karaite tradition, the blessing "Who did not make me a woman" was omitted entirely, out of consideration and love for women.

Rabbi Yehuda Henkin, another contemporary Orthodox scholar, has proposed a solution that accords with halakhic tradition: that the morning blessings—or, at the very least, this one particular blessing—should be recited by the entire congregation in a whisper, rather than out loud by the prayer leader.

PRAYER FOR ALL OCCASIONS
Ben Ish Hai

This prayer encompasses the essential themes and is suitable for all occasions.

*M*ay Your Name be praised, Lord our God and God of our fathers, and may Your remembrance be glorified and exalted, our King— the King Who is great and holy in the heavens and on earth—without Whom we have no King, Redeemer or Helper, Liberator, and Savior; Who answers and is merciful at all times of trouble and distress; we have no King Who helps and supports except for You.

Conducting Your world with kindness and Your creations with mercy, You are the God of righteousness; You neither slumber nor sleep. You revive the dead and heal the sick, cause the blind to see, and the bowed to be upright; the wordless to speak, and the secret things to be revealed. You clothe the naked, free the imprisoned, and help the needy.

I am Your maidservant, My Maker; I call out to You, my eyes look to You.

Rabbi Yosef Haim of Baghdad, the leading nineteenth-century Sephardic rabbi known as the "Ben Ish Hai," composed a book of teachings, parables, and prayers exclusively for women called *Laws of Women*. In his introduction, the Ben Ish Hai asks that readers study and revise the book at least once every six months. In nineteenth-century Baghdad, it was customary for women to read the book to-

תְּפִילָה לְכָל עֵת

ה"בֶּן אִישׁ חַי"

וְזוֹ הַתְּפִלָּה הַנֶּאֱמֶרֶת בְּכָל זְמַן, וּבָהּ דְּבָרִים הַנְּחוּצִים:

שֶׁתִּתְבַּח שִׁמְךָ יְהֹוָה אֱלֹהֵינוּ וֵאלֹהֵי אֲבוֹתֵינוּ, וְיִתְפָּאֵר וְיִתְעַלֶּה זִכְרְךָ מַלְכֵּנוּ, הַמֶּלֶךְ הַגָּדוֹל וְהַקָּדוֹשׁ בַּשָּׁמַיִם וּבָאָרֶץ, וּמִבַּלְעָדֶיךָ אֵין לָנוּ מֶלֶךְ גּוֹאֵל וְעוֹזֵר, פּוֹדֶה וּמַצִּיל, וְעוֹנֶה וּמְרַחֵם, בְּכָל עֵת צָרָה וְצוּקָה, אֵין לָנוּ מֶלֶךְ עוֹזֵר וְסוֹמֵךְ אֶלָּא אָתָּה.

מַנְהִיג עוֹלָמְךָ בְּחֶסֶד, וּבְרִיּוֹתֶיךָ בְּרַחֲמִים, אַתָּה אֱלֹהֵי הַצֶּדֶק, לֹא תָנוּם וְלֹא תִישָׁן. מְחַיֶּה מֵתִים, וְרוֹפֵא חוֹלִים, פּוֹקֵחַ עִוְרִים, וְזוֹקֵף כְּפוּפִים, מֵשִׂיחַ אִלְּמִים, וּמְפַעֲנֵחַ הַנֶּעֱלָמִים, מַלְבִּישׁ עֲרֻמִּים, וּמַתִּיר אֲסוּרִים, וְעוֹזֵר דַּלִּים.

אֲנִי אֲמָתְךָ, קוֹנִי, אֲנִי אֵלֶיךָ אֶקְרָא, וְעֵינַי לְךָ תְּצַפֶּה.

מִן הַמֵּצַר קָרָאתִי יָהּ, עֲנֵנִי בַמֶּרְחָב יָהּ. כְּעֵינֵי עֲבָדִים אֶל יַד אֲדוֹנֵיהֶם, כְּעֵינֵי שְׁפָחוֹת אֶל גְּבִירוֹתֵיהֶן, כֵּן עֵינַי אֵלֶיךָ יְהֹוָה אֱלֹהֵינוּ, עַד אֲשֶׁר תְּחָנֵּנוּ עָלֵינוּ.

gether every Shabbat, as well as on the intermediate days of Pesach and on Suk-kot. They would gather in private houses, and the participants would take turns reading a chapter or page aloud to a melody until they completed reciting the entire book. From the Ben Ish Hai's responsa, it is clear that Jewish women in Iraq could read the Bible in Hebrew and even scheduled regular sessions for Torah study.

From the depths I call to God; God answers me with expansiveness. As servants look to the hand of their masters, as maidservants look to their mistresses, so I look to You, Lord our God, that You may take pity on us.

I pray You, Lord—forgive me my sin.

I pray You, Lord—purify my heart.

I pray You, Lord—help me to perform Your will.

I pray You, Lord—give me strength to fulfill Your commandments.

My Lord: I am Your maidservant, and my sins are many; You are the great All-Powerful One, Your mercy is great; You are there for those who call upon You, possessing great mercy, pardoning and forgiving their many sins.

My Lord, I am Your handmaid, and I have no righteousness in the merit of which I can ask, nor good deeds that I may use as support. Rather, I place my trust in Your manifold mercies, trust in Your manifold kindnesses, and rely upon Your great Name—You, Who lifts the destitute from the dust and the needy from lowliness. Hear, in Your mercy, my prayer and supplication; answer me, Lord; answer me.

My Lord: Have mercy upon Your servant, my husband, and bless him from the provisions of Your full hand. Let him not depend on human generosity, nor let him be embarrassed or confounded; let him not borrow or ask from others and not sigh or worry. Bless the work of his hands; deliver him from all trouble and distress, and save him from all injury and loss. Steer him clear of all obstacles; deliver him from all evil and from sudden setbacks; save him from all harm and ruin; and spare him all illness and affliction. Bless all of his endeavors and grant him success in all his transactions so that he may earn great blessing from his dealings. Lengthen his days with goodness and grant him a life of tranquillity. Let him hear joyous and happy tidings; help him to perform Your will and to fulfill Your commandments.

אָנָּא יְהֹוָה מְחַל לִי עֲוֹנִי.

אָנָּא יְהֹוָה טַהֵר לִבִּי.

אָנָּא יְהֹוָה עָזְרֵנִי לַעֲשׂוֹת רְצוֹנֶךָ.

אָנָּא יְהֹוָה חַזְּקֵנִי לְקַיֵּם מִצְוֹתֶיךָ.

אֲדֹנָי, אֲנִי אֲמָתְךָ וַעֲוֹנוֹתַי רַבִּים, וְאַתָּה הַיָּכוֹל הַגָּדוֹל, רַחֲמֶיךָ רַבִּים, מָצוּי לְקוֹרְאָיו, בַּעַל הָרַחֲמִים הַגְּדוֹלִים, מוֹחֵל וְסוֹלֵחַ הָעֲוֹנוֹת הָרַבִּים.

אֲדֹנָי, אֲנִי שִׁפְחָתְךָ, וְאֵין לִי מִצְוֹת אֲשֶׁר אֲבַקֵּשׁ בְּזְכוּתָם, וְלֹא טוֹבוֹת אֲשֶׁר אֶסָּמֵךְ בָּהֶם. אֶלָּא בָּטַחְתִּי עַל רֹב רַחֲמֶיךָ, וְסָמַכְתִּי עַל רֹב חֲסָדֶיךָ, וְנִשְׁעַנְתִּי בְּשִׁמְךָ הַגָּדוֹל, אַתָּה הַמַּעֲלֶה מֵעָפָר דַּלִּים, וּמֵאַשְׁפּוֹת תָּרִים אֶבְיוֹן, שְׁמַע בְּרַחֲמֶיךָ תְּפִלָּתִי וּתְחִנָּתִי, עֲנֵנִי ה' עֲנֵנִי.

אֲדֹנָי, רַחֵם עַל עַבְדְּךָ בַּעֲלִי וּתְבָרְכֵהוּ, מִנִּתְנַת יָדְךָ הַמְּלֵאָה. וְלֹא תַצְרִיכֵהוּ לְמַתְּנוֹת בָּשָׂר וָדָם, וְלֹא יֵבוֹשׁ וְלֹא יִכָּלֵם, וְלֹא יִלְוֶה וְיִשְׁאַל מֵהַבְּרִיּוֹת וְלֹא יֵעָנֵחַ וְלֹא יִדְאַג. וּתְבָרֵךְ מַעֲשֵׂה יָדָיו, וְתַצִּילֵהוּ מִכָּל צָרָה וְצוּקָה, וְתַצִּילֵהוּ מִכָּל נֶזֶק וְהֶפְסֵד, וְתַצִּילֵהוּ מִכָּל מִכְשׁוֹל, וְתַצִּילֵהוּ מִכָּל רַע וּמַכַּת פִּתְאֹם, וְתַצִּילֵהוּ מִכָּל נֶזֶק וַאֲבַדּוֹן, וְתַצִּילֵהוּ מִכָּל חֳלִי וּמַכָּה. וּתְבָרֵךְ כָּל עִנְיָנָיו, וְיַצְלִיחַ בְּכָל מִקָּח וּמִמְכָּר, וְיַרְוִיחַ בַּעֲסָקָיו בְּרָכָה רַבָּה, וְיַאֲרִיךְ יָמָיו בְּטוֹב, וְתִתֶּן לוֹ חַיִּים בְּנַחַת, וְתַשְׁמִיעֵהוּ שָׂשׂוֹן וְשִׂמְחָה, וּתְעַזְּרֵהוּ לַעֲשׂוֹת רְצוֹנֶךָ וּלְקַיֵּם מִצְוֹתֶיךָ.

אֲדֹנָי, רַחֵם בְּרַחֲמֶיךָ הַגְּדוֹלִים, וּבַחֲסָדֶיךָ הַמְרֻבִּים עַל עֲבָדֶיךָ בָּנַי, וְתַצִּילֵם מִכָּל חֳלִי וּמַחֲלָה, וְתַצִּילֵם מִכָּל צָרָה וּמְצוּקָה, וְתַצִּילֵם מִכָּל נֶזֶק וּמִכְשׁוֹל, וְתַצִּילֵם מִכָּל צַעַר. וְתַאֲרִיךְ יְמֵיהֶם בְּטוֹב וּבְרִיאוּת וּמְנוּחָה, וְשָׁלוֹם וְשָׂשׂוֹן וְשִׂמְחָה, וַאֲנִי וּבַעֲלִי נִשְׂמַח בָּהֶם, וּבִבְנֵיהֶם וּבִבְנֵי בְנֵיהֶם.

אֲדֹנָי, רַחֵם עָלַי, וְרַחֵם עַל עַבְדְּךָ בַּעֲלִי, וְתִשְׁמַע תְּחִנָּתִי. וּתְקַבֵּל בְּרָצוֹן תְּפִלּוֹתֵינוּ, וְתַשְׁכִּין אַהֲבָה בְּאֹהָלֵינוּ, וְתַרְבֶּה הָאַהֲבָה בֵּינֵינוּ, וְיִרְבּוּ בָנֵינוּ, וְנִפְרֶה וְנִרְבֶּה כְּאִילָן שָׁתוּל עַל פַּלְגֵי מַיִם, אֲשֶׁר עָלָיו יָפִים וְרַבִּים, וּפֵרוֹתָיו טוֹבִים.

My Lord: Take pity, in Your great mercies and in Your manifold kindnesses, upon your servants—my children. Spare them all disease and illness; deliver them from all trouble and distress; steer them clear of all harm and obstacles; save them from all suffering. Lengthen their days with goodness, health, and calm, peace, joy, and happiness; and may my husband and I rejoice in them and their children and grandchildren.

My Lord: Have mercy upon me and have mercy upon Your servant, my husband; hear my supplication and accept our prayers with favor. Cause love to dwell in our home, and cause the love between us to grow. Let our children multiply; let us be fruitful and multiply like a tree planted by streams of water, possessing beautiful and plentiful leaves, and producing fine fruit.

SECRET PSALMS
Crypto-Jewish Women of Portugal

The following psalm draws on verses from several different chapters from the book of Psalms:

G od—fill my mouth with laughter and my mouth with song

Fulfill my wishes, bless me from Zion

Hear, Lord, the prayer of Your servant

Let my heart not be proud, nor my eyes be arrogant

Grant me, my God, that I should understand [simple things]

Until I find a place for God; dwelling places for the Mighty One of
   Jacob

For there God commanded the blessing—life unto eternity,

There I shall spread my hands to [these].

I shall bless You, Lord, for You judge Your nation

The story of the crypto-Jews of Spain and Portugal (also known as conversos or *anusim*) is one of the most fascinating chapters of Jewish history. At the end of the fifteenth century, the Jewish aristocracy of pre-expulsion Spain, followed by a large majority of Portuguese Jewry, were forced to choose between expulsion and conversion to Christianity. In order to avoid expulsion, they outwardly assumed a Christian identity but continued practicing the tenets of Jewish faith in secret.

These two psalms, originally written in Old Spanish and based on various chapters of the book of Psalms, belong to the oral tradition of crypto-Jewish

מזמורי נשים אנוסות מפורטוגל

ה' מַלֵּא פִּי שְׂחוֹק וּלְשׁוֹנִי רַנָּה

קַיֵּם חֲפָצַי בְּרִכֵּי מִצִּיּוֹן

שְׁמַע אֲדֹנָי אֶת תְּפִלַּת עַבְדֶּךָ

לֹא יִגְבַּהּ לִבִּי וְלֹא יָרוּמוּ עֵינַי

הַעֲנֵק לִי אֱלֹהַי כִּי אֶשְׁמַע [דְּבָרִים פְּשׁוּטִים]

עַד אֶמְצָא מָקוֹם לַה' מִשְׁכָּנוֹת לַאֲבִיר יַעֲקֹב

כִּי שָׁם צִוָּה ה' אֶת הַבְּרָכָה חַיִּים עַד הָעוֹלָם

שָׁם אֶפְרֹשׂ כַּפַּי ל [דְּבָרִים אֵלּוּ]

אֲבָרֶכְךָ ה' כִּי אַתָּה שׁוֹפֵט עַמְּךָ

---

women and have been passed down from generation to generation since the fifteenth century. These psalms were included in the testimony that was delivered by Isabelle de la Vega before the Inquisition in 1590. Yitzhak Hamitovsky, who translated them into Hebrew for a paper by the researcher Rina Levin Melammed, notes that the practice of borrowing fragments of verses from Psalms, evident in these samples, was also prevalent among regular Jewish communities throughout the Sephardic Diaspora.

And Your servants accompany You

Hear my cry in Your Sanctuary.

The following psalm is based upon Psalm 121:

A song of ascents:

I shall raise my eyes to the Lord and to the mountains

From whence comes my help

My help is from God, Maker of the heavens and the earth

Guardian of Israel Who neither slumbers nor sleeps

God watches over me more than my right hand does

By day, the sun shall not strike me

Nor shall the moon make shadows for me at night

Lord, watch over my life and my soul

My going out and my coming in

From every sort of evil, danger, and enemy.

וּמְשָׁרְתֶיךָ מְלַוִּים אוֹתְךָ
שְׁמַע שַׁוְעָתִי בְּהֵיכָלְךָ.

מזמור על־פי תהלים קכא:

שׁיר לַמַּעֲלוֹת
אֶשָּׂא עֵינַי אֶל הָאָדוֹן וְאֶל הֶהָרִים
מֵאַיִן יָבוֹא עֶזְרִי
עֶזְרִי מֵעִם ה׳ עוֹשֵׂה שָׁמַיִם וָאָרֶץ
שׁוֹמֵר יִשְׂרָאֵל שֶׁלֹּא נָם וְלֹא יָשֵׁן
ה׳ שׁוֹמְרִי יוֹתֵר מֵאֲשֶׁר יַד יְמִינִי
יוֹמָם הַשֶּׁמֶשׁ לֹא יַכֵּנִי
וְלֹא הַיָּרֵחַ בַּלַּיְלָה יְעַרְפִּלֵנִי
שְׁמֹר אֲדֹנָי אֶת חַיַּי וְנַפְשִׁי
צֵאתִי וּבוֹאִי
מִכָּל רַע, סַכָּנָה וְאוֹיֵב.

BEDTIME PRAYER

Ladino

I entrust my soul to the Most High God

That I may lie down in goodness

And awaken in goodness.

Protect us from an evil acquaintance,

From an evil neighbor, from evil times,

From evil decrees,

And from evil illnesses.

I lie down to sleep

I lock my doors

With the keys of

Miriam the prophetess,

And with King Solomon

Peace be upon him.

Ladino, often referred to as "Judeo-Spanish," is a written and spoken language that developed in the wake of the Spanish Expulsion in 1492, when many of the expelled Jews lost their connection with the original Castilian-Spanish language and began speaking a blend of the local vernacular and their language of study, Hebrew. Much like Yiddish, Ladino was heavily influenced by its surrounding languages. It eventually developed into two principal dialects: the Eastern dialect (in Turkey and in Rhodes), based on Castilian Spanish, and the Western dialect (in Greece, Macedonia, Bosnia, Serbia, and Romania), which was influenced by the language of northern Spain and Portugal. The Ladino vocabulary includes many words that have disappeared from modern Spanish, as well as words borrowed from Hebrew and the local languages in the areas where it was spoken: Arabic, Turkish, Greek, French, Portuguese, and Italian.

תפילה על המיטה לנשים

לדינו

לְאֵל עֶלְיוֹן אַפְקִיד נִשְׁמָתִי	**א** ל דייו אלטו אינקומינדו מי אלמה
בְּטוֹב אָלִין	בואינה סיאה מי איג׳אדה
אַשְׁכִּים בְּטוֹב	מאס מיזור מי אליב׳אנטארי
שְׁמֹר נָא עָלֵינוּ מֵחָבֵר רַע,	גודראמוס די חבר מאלו
מִשָּׁכֵן רַע מִשָּׁעוֹת רָעוֹת.	די ב׳יזינו מאלו די אוראס מאלאס
מִגְּזֵרוֹת רָעוֹת	די סיטינסייאס מאלאס
וּמִמַּחֲלוֹת רָעוֹת.	אי די חאזינוראס מאלאס
אֶשְׁכַּב לִישֹׁן	אה איג׳אר מי איג׳ו
אָגִיף דַּלְתוֹתַי	סירו מיס פואירטאס
עִם מַפְתְּחוֹת	קון לאס ייאב׳יס
מִרְיָם הַנְּבִיאָה	די מרים לה פרופ׳יטה
וְעִם הַמֶּלֶךְ שְׁלֹמֹה	אי קון סינייור שלמה המלך
עָלָיו הַשָּׁלוֹם.	עליו השלום.

Due to immigration, assimilation, and the annihilation of Ladino-speaking communities during the Holocaust, the number of Ladino speakers alive today is dwindling. Currently, Israel is home to the largest community still in existence, with approximately 200,000 speakers of the language.

The custom of reading the three sections from the Torah that together comprise the *Shema* dates back to the Second Temple period, when the priests would recite it in the Temple. Since the destruction of the Temple, the *Shema* has remained a central element of the morning and evening prayer services, and at least the first paragraph is also recited before going to bed. This version is a shortened, alternative version of the bedtime *Shema*, originally written in Ladino and intended for women who may not have been familiar with Hebrew. The prayer in this form is recalled by Allegra ben-Melekh of Netanya, who was born in Turkey in 1920.

Bat Mitzvah

The term *bat mitzvah* means "one who is commanded." According to the Mishnah, at the age of twelve a girl becomes obligated in the commandments of the Torah. At this point she takes her place among the Jewish people; henceforth, this affiliation will mold all of her experiences as a woman—both as an individual and as a member of a community.

Historically, it was not customary to celebrate the occasion of a girl reaching maturity. Only with the approach of the twentieth century was attention given, in various forms, to the bat mitzvah girl's need for a ceremonial celebration of her entry into Jewish adulthood. In the absence of any standard collection of traditional prayers, blessings, and customs, each Jewish community in the Diaspora and in Israel has adopted its own manner of celebration. Some of the prayers that have been composed for the occasion are written in a personal, feminine style, whereas others follow the more formal conventions of the traditional prayers.

Over the course of the years, rabbinical authorities have addressed the issue of bat mitzvah celebrations. Around a century ago, the Ben Ish Hai ruled that even though it had not been customary until then, a festive meal should be held in honor of the bat mitzvah girl. He recommended that she should wear a new dress for the occasion and recite the *Sheheheyanu* blessing, intending it also for the assumption of her new status.

Rabbi Yitzhak Nissim (1896–1981), a former Sephardic chief rabbi of Israel, wrote about bat mitzvah in three of his responsa. He repeats the Ben Ish Hai's recommendations and adds that the girl should pray in the synagogue and deliver a speech on a subject pertinent to the occasion—such as the Song of Deborah or Hannah's prayer. The father of the girl should recite the blessing, "… Who has exempted me … ," and the participants should offer the celebrant the blessing, "Our sister—may you become thousands of tens of thousands."

Ashkenazi rabbis also have encouraged the custom of celebrating a girl's bat mitzvah. Following World War II, sensitive to the spirit of the times and the devastated state of the Jewish nation, Rabbi Yehiel Yaakov Weinberg, one of the greatest Lithuanian halakhic authorities, wrote: "Now our responsibility is to focus all of our energies on girls' education … logic and pedagogic principle render it almost obligatory that we celebrate for a girl, too, her reaching the age of being commanded; the discrimination that is practiced between boys and girls with regard to the celebration of maturity causes grave offense to the human emotion of the adolescent girl."

BAT MITZVAH PRAYER
Italy

*B*lessed are You, our God, King of the universe, Who has rendered me all manner of good, and has given me life and sustained me until this time, so as to be counted among adults and to accept the yoke of Your commandments. Lord, Lord, merciful and gracious God, slow to anger and abundant in kindness and truth: Behold, today I have begun to visit Your holy Sanctuary, with awe of You, to become part of Your inheritance. Though I am but a young girl with no word that my tongue can offer in the face of Your exalted glory, please do not reject me, for from the mouths of babies and infants You have established Your might, and You cause the tongue of those weaned from milk and long parted from the breast to speak Your praises with adoration. Lord God of the spirits of all flesh: Who is like You, instructing and teaching knowledge to Israel? From the heavens You have pronounced law: Moses commanded us the Torah, an

---

In the Italian Jewish communities of Torino and Milan, it is customary to hold a communal bat mitzvah ceremony for all of the twelve-year-old girls in the congregation. Accompanied by family members, friends, community members, and the chief rabbi, the girls stand before the open Ark, facing the Torah scrolls, and

32

תפילה לבת־מצווה

איטליה

בָּרוּךְ אַתָּה אֱלֹהֵינוּ מֶלֶךְ הָעוֹלָם שֶׁגְּמָלַנִי כָּל טוֹב וְהֶחֱיַנִי וְקִיְּמַנִי לַזְּמַן הַזֶּה לָבוֹא בַּאֲנָשִׁים וּלְקַבֵּל עוֹל מִצְוֹתֶיךָ: ה׳ ה׳ אֵל רַחוּם וְחַנּוּן אֶרֶךְ אַפַּיִם וְרַב חֶסֶד וֶאֱמֶת. הִנֵּה הַיּוֹם הַחִלּוֹתִי גֶּשֶׁת אֶל הֵיכַל קָדְשְׁךָ בְּיִרְאָתְךָ לְהִסְתַּפֵּחַ בְּנַחֲלָתְךָ: גַּם כִּי נַעֲרָה אָנֹכִי וְאֵין מִלָּה בִּלְשׁוֹנִי מוּל כְּבוֹד רוֹמְמוּתֶךָ אַל נָא תִמְאָסֵנִי. כִּי מִפִּי עוֹלָלִים וְיוֹנְקִים יָסַדְתָּ עֹז. וַתְּנוֹבֵב לְשׁוֹן גְּמוּלֵי חָלָב וַעֲתִיקֵי מִשָּׁדַיִם לְהִשְׁתַּבֵּחַ בִּתְהִלָּתְךָ: אֵל אֱלֹהֵי הָרוּחוֹת לְכָל בָּשָׂר מִי כָמוֹךָ מוֹרֶה הַמְלַמֵּד לְיִשְׂרָאֵל דַּעַת: מִשָּׁמַיִם הִשְׁמַעְתָּ דִּין. תּוֹרָה צִוָּה לָנוּ מֹשֶׁה מוֹרָשָׁה קְהִלַּת יַעֲקֹב. הִיא חַיֵּינוּ וְאֹרֶךְ יָמֵינוּ: וּבַמֶּה תְזַכֶּה נַעֲרָה אָרְחָהּ לִשְׁמֹר כִּדְבָרֶךָ: יַחֵד לְבָבִי לְיִרְאָה אֶת שְׁמֶךָ וְהַדְרִיכֵנִי בַּאֲמִתָּךְ לְהִשְׁתַּעֲשֵׁעַ בְּחֻקֵּי צִדְקֶךָ וּבְדִבְרֵי קָדְשְׁךָ וּבְלִמּוּדֵי חָכְמָתֶךָ: אֲדַבְּרָה נֶגֶד הַמִּתְעַתְּעִים וְלֹא אֵבוֹשׁ. בְּשֵׁם אֱלֹהֵי אֲבוֹתַי אֶדְגַּל וְלֹא תִכְבַּדְנָה יָדָי.

---

take turns reciting the verses of this prayer (which is also recited by Italian boys on the occasion of their bar mitzvah). The chief rabbi then offers his blessing to the girls and their families. At the conclusion of the ceremony, festive meals are held in the girls' homes.

inheritance for the community of Jacob; it is our life and the length of our days. How shall a young girl then refine her path, so as to observe as You have spoken? Direct my heart to fear Your Name and guide me, in Your truth, to rejoice in Your righteous statutes, Your holy words, and the study of Your wisdom. Let me speak out against those who lead others astray, and not be ashamed. May I uphold the Name of the God of my forefathers, and may my arms not grow weary. May my lips pronounce praise, to spread Torah and to bring it glory, and may I not grow silent. May I glory in the name Israel and not betray my faith. My life is in Your hands; I entrust my spirit to You. Make me healthy and give me life, that I may walk in Your ways wholeheartedly and willingly, to perform righteousness and kindness. Strengthen me and give me courage to be among Your servants who cleave to You, to make known Your great and awesome Name among the many, that the earth may be full of it, and that Your House may be called a house of prayer for all the nations. Blessed are You, Lord; teach me Your statutes.

תַּבַּעְנָה שְׂפָתַי תְּהִלָּה לְהַגְדִּיל תּוֹרָה וּלְהַאֲדִירָהּ וְלֹא אֵחֵשָׁה: אֶתְפָּאֵר בְּשֵׁם יִשְׂרָאֵל וְלֹא אֲשַׁקֵּר בֶּאֱמוּנָתִי: בְּיָדְךָ עִתּוֹתַי וּבְיָדְךָ אַפְקִיד רוּחִי: הַחֲלִימֵנִי וְהַחֲיֵנִי לָלֶכֶת בִּדְרָכֶיךָ בְּלֵב שָׁלֵם וּבְנֶפֶשׁ חֲפֵצָה לַעֲשׂוֹת צְדָקָה וָחֶסֶד: חַזְּקֵנִי וְאַמְּצֵנִי לִהְיוֹת מֵעֲבָדֶיךָ הַדְּבֵקִים בָּךְ לְהוֹדִיעַ בָּרַבִּים שִׁמְךָ הַגָּדוֹל וְהַנּוֹרָא: וּמָלְאָה הָאָרֶץ וּבֵיתְךָ יִקָּרֵא בֵית־תְּפִלָּה לְכָל־הָעַמִּים: בָּרוּךְ אַתָּה ה' לַמְּדֵנִי חֻקֶּיךָ:

DEBORAH'S SONG
Judges 5

There were two women who uttered praise to the Holy One, such that no man had ever uttered. Who were they? Deborah and Hannah. And all of these verses spoken by Deborah are illuminated with Supreme wisdom.

[THE ZOHAR, 3, 19]

*T*hen Deborah sang, and Barak, son of Abinoam, on that day, saying:

At a time of tumult in Israel, when the people willingly offered themselves—bless the Lord.

Hear, O kings; give ear, O princes: As for me, I will sing to the Lord, I will sing praise to the God of Israel.

Lord, when You went forth from Se'ir, when You marched out of the field of Edom, the earth trembled; the heavens also rained, the clouds, too, dropped water.

In the Italian Jewish communities of Torino and Milan, Deborah's song is recited by each celebrant at the communal bat mitzvah ceremony.

According to the Bible, the prophetess Deborah recruited Barak, son of Abinoam, to wage war against the kingdom of Ḥatzor. Not only was the war initiated by a woman; it was also won thanks to a woman: Jael, "wife of Heber the

שירת דבורה

וַתָּ֣שַׁר דְּבוֹרָ֔ה וּבָרָ֖ק בֶּן־אֲבִינֹ֑עַם בַּיּ֥וֹם הַה֖וּא לֵאמֹֽר:

בִּפְרֹ֤עַ פְּרָעוֹת֙ בְּיִשְׂרָאֵ֔ל בְּהִתְנַדֵּ֖ב עָ֑ם בָּרֲכ֖וּ יהוה:

שִׁמְע֣וּ מְלָכִ֔ים הַאֲזִ֖ינוּ רֹֽזְנִ֑ים אָֽנֹכִ֗י לַֽיהוה֙ אָנֹכִ֣י אָשִׁ֔ירָה אֲזַמֵּ֕ר לַֽיהוה אֱלֹהֵ֥י יִשְׂרָאֵֽל:

יהוה בְּצֵאתְךָ֤ מִשֵּׂעִיר֙ בְּצַעְדְּךָ֙ מִשְּׂדֵ֣ה אֱד֔וֹם אֶ֣רֶץ רָעָ֔שָׁה גַּם־שָׁמַ֖יִם נָטָ֑פוּ גַּם־עָבִ֖ים נָ֥טְפוּ מָֽיִם:

הָרִ֥ים נָזְל֖וּ מִפְּנֵ֣י יהוה זֶ֣ה סִינַ֔י מִפְּנֵ֕י יהוה אֱלֹהֵ֥י יִשְׂרָאֵֽל:

בִּימֵ֞י שַׁמְגַּ֤ר בֶּן־עֲנָת֙ בִּימֵ֣י יָעֵ֔ל חָדְל֖וּ אֳרָח֑וֹת וְהֹלְכֵ֣י נְתִיב֔וֹת יֵלְכ֕וּ אֳרָח֖וֹת עֲקַלְקַלּֽוֹת:

חָדְל֧וּ פְרָז֛וֹן בְּיִשְׂרָאֵ֖ל חָדֵ֑לּוּ עַ֤ד שַׁקַּ֙מְתִּי֙ דְּבוֹרָ֔ה שַׁקַּ֥מְתִּי אֵ֖ם בְּיִשְׂרָאֵֽל:

יִבְחַר֙ אֱלֹהִ֣ים חֲדָשִׁ֔ים אָ֖ז לָחֶ֣ם שְׁעָרִ֑ים מָגֵ֤ן אִם־יֵֽרָאֶה֙ וָרֹ֔מַח בְּאַרְבָּעִ֥ים אֶ֖לֶף בְּיִשְׂרָאֵֽל:

לִבִּי֙ לְחֽוֹקְקֵ֣י יִשְׂרָאֵ֔ל הַמִּֽתְנַדְּבִ֖ים בָּעָ֑ם בָּרֲכ֖וּ יהוה:

Kenite," who drove a tent peg into the head of Sisera. The inclusion of Deborah and her song of praise as part of the bat mitzvah ceremony is no accident. It conveys a clear statement to the bat mitzvah girl: Deborah—political leader, judge, and prophetess—is a worthy model for emulation.

The mountains melted before the Lord, [even] that Sinai, before the Lord God of Israel.

In the days of Shamgar, son of Anat, in the days of Jael, the highways ceased, and travelers followed crooked byways.

Those of valor ceased, they ceased in Israel, until I, Deborah, arose, arising as a mother in Israel.

They chose new gods, then there was war in the gates; was any shield seen, or any spear, among the forty thousand in Israel?

My heart is with the governors of Israel, who offered themselves willingly among the people—bless the Lord.

You who ride upon white asses, who sit upon couches, and you who walk by the way—tell of it.

Louder than the voice of the archers by the watering troughs—let them recite there the righteous acts of God, the righteous acts of His valiant ones in Israel, when the people of the Lord went down to the gates.

Awake, awake, Deborah; awake, awake, utter a song; arise, Barak, and lead away your captives, O son of Abinoam.

Then He caused a remnant to have dominion over the nobles of the people; the Lord caused me to have dominion over the mighty ones.

They came from Ephraim, but were rooted in Amalek, beyond you, Benjamin, with your hordes; from Makhir there came down governors, and from Zebulun—those who handle the marshal's staff.

And the princes of Issachar were with Deborah; as was Issachar, so was Barak; into the valley they rushed forth at his feet. Among the divisions of Reuben there was great resolve of heart.

Why did you remain among the sheepfolds, to hear the pipings

רֹכְבֵי אֲתֹנוֹת צְחֹרוֹת יֹשְׁבֵי עַל־מִדִּין וְהֹלְכֵי עַל־דֶּרֶךְ שִׂיחוּ:

מִקּוֹל מְחַצְצִים בֵּין מַשְׁאַבִּים שָׁם יְתַנּוּ צִדְקוֹת יְהוָה צִדְקֹת פִּרְזוֹנוֹ בְּיִשְׂרָאֵל אָז יָרְדוּ לַשְּׁעָרִים עַם־יְהוָה:

עוּרִי עוּרִי דְּבוֹרָה עוּרִי עוּרִי דַּבְּרִי־שִׁיר קוּם בָּרָק וּשֲׁבֵה שֶׁבְיְךָ בֶּן־אֲבִינֹעַם:

אָז יְרַד שָׂרִיד לְאַדִּירִים עָם יְהוָה יְרַד־לִי בַּגִּבּוֹרִים:

מִנִּי אֶפְרַיִם שָׁרְשָׁם בַּעֲמָלֵק אַחֲרֶיךָ בִנְיָמִין בַּעֲמָמֶיךָ מִנִּי מָכִיר יָרְדוּ מְחֹקְקִים וּמִזְּבוּלֻן מֹשְׁכִים בְּשֵׁבֶט סֹפֵר:

וְשָׂרַי בְּיִשָּׂשכָר עִם־דְּבֹרָה וְיִשָּׂשכָר כֵּן בָּרָק בָּעֵמֶק שֻׁלַּח בְּרַגְלָיו בִּפְלַגּוֹת רְאוּבֵן גְּדֹלִים חִקְקֵי־לֵב:

לָמָּה יָשַׁבְתָּ בֵּין הַמִּשְׁפְּתַיִם לִשְׁמֹעַ שְׁרִקוֹת עֲדָרִים לִפְלַגּוֹת רְאוּבֵן גְּדוֹלִים חִקְרֵי־לֵב:

גִּלְעָד בְּעֵבֶר הַיַּרְדֵּן שָׁכֵן וְדָן לָמָּה יָגוּר אֳנִיּוֹת אָשֵׁר יָשַׁב לְחוֹף יַמִּים וְעַל מִפְרָצָיו יִשְׁכּוֹן:

זְבֻלוּן עַם חֵרֵף נַפְשׁוֹ לָמוּת וְנַפְתָּלִי עַל מְרוֹמֵי שָׂדֶה:

בָּאוּ מְלָכִים נִלְחָמוּ אָז נִלְחֲמוּ מַלְכֵי כְנַעַן בְּתַעְנַךְ עַל־מֵי מְגִדּוֹ בֶּצַע כֶּסֶף לֹא לָקָחוּ:

מִן־שָׁמַיִם נִלְחָמוּ הַכּוֹכָבִים מִמְּסִלּוֹתָם נִלְחֲמוּ עִם סִיסְרָא:

נַחַל קִישׁוֹן גְּרָפָם נַחַל קְדוּמִים נַחַל קִישׁוֹן תִּדְרְכִי נַפְשִׁי עֹז:

אָז הָלְמוּ עִקְּבֵי־סוּס מִדַּהֲרוֹת דַּהֲרוֹת אַבִּירָיו:

אוֹרוּ מֵרוֹז אָמַר מַלְאַךְ יְהוָה אֹרוּ אָרוֹר יֹשְׁבֶיהָ כִּי לֹא־בָאוּ לְעֶזְרַת יְהוָה לְעֶזְרַת יְהוָה בַּגִּבּוֹרִים:

תְּבֹרַךְ מִנָּשִׁים יָעֵל אֵשֶׁת חֶבֶר הַקֵּינִי מִנָּשִׁים בָּאֹהֶל תְּבֹרָךְ:

מַיִם שָׁאַל חָלָב נָתָנָה בְּסֵפֶל אַדִּירִים הִקְרִיבָה חֶמְאָה:

יָדָהּ לַיָּתֵד תִּשְׁלַחְנָה וִימִינָהּ לְהַלְמוּת עֲמֵלִים וְהָלְמָה סִיסְרָא מָחֲקָה

for the flocks? For the divisions of Reuben there were great
searchings of heart.

Gilad dwells beyond the Jordan; as for Dan—why does he sojourn
by the ships? Asher remained by the seashore, remaining by its
bays.

Zebulun is a people that endangered itself to the death, also
Naphtali, on the high places of the field.

The kings came and fought; then fought the kings of Canaan at
Taanakh, by the waters of Megiddo; they took no gain of silver.

They fought from heaven; the stars in their courses fought against
Sisera.

The wadi of Kishon swept them away—that ancient brook, the
brook of Kishon; O my soul, tread with strength.

Then the hoofs of the horses beat down with the galloping,
galloping of his mighty ones.

Curse Meroz, says the angel of the Lord; curse bitterly its
inhabitants, for they did not come to the side of the Lord; to
the side of the Lord against the mighty ones.

Blessed above women is Jael, wife of Heber the Kenite; she is
blessed above women in the tent.

He asked for water, [but] she gave him milk; she offered cream in a
lordly bowl.

She put her hand to the tent-peg and her right hand to the
workmen's hammer; and she hammered Sisera, breaking his head;
she crushed and pierced his temple.

He sank at her feet, he fell, he lay; he sank and fell at her feet.
Where he sank, there he fell down dead.

The mother of Sisera looked through the window, through the

רֹאשׁוֹ וּמָחֲצָה וְחָלְפָה רַקָּתוֹ׃

בֵּין רַגְלֶיהָ כָּרַע נָפַל שָׁכָב בֵּין רַגְלֶיהָ כָּרַע נָפָל בַּאֲשֶׁר כָּרַע שָׁם נָפַל שָׁדוּד׃

בְּעַד הַחַלּוֹן נִשְׁקְפָה וַתְּיַבֵּב אֵם סִיסְרָא בְּעַד הָאֶשְׁנָב מַדּוּעַ בֹּשֵׁשׁ רִכְבּוֹ לָבוֹא מַדּוּעַ אֶחֱרוּ פַּעֲמֵי מַרְכְּבוֹתָיו׃

חַכְמוֹת שָׂרוֹתֶיהָ תַּעֲנֶינָּה אַף־הִיא תָּשִׁיב אֲמָרֶיהָ לָהּ׃

הֲלֹא יִמְצְאוּ יְחַלְּקוּ שָׁלָל רַחַם רַחֲמָתַיִם לְרֹאשׁ גֶּבֶר שְׁלַל צְבָעִים לְסִיסְרָא שְׁלַל צְבָעִים רִקְמָה צֶבַע רִקְמָתַיִם לְצַוְּארֵי שָׁלָל׃

כֵּן יֹאבְדוּ כָל־אוֹיְבֶיךָ יְהוָה וְאֹהֲבָיו כְּצֵאת הַשֶּׁמֶשׁ בִּגְבֻרָתוֹ וַתִּשְׁקֹט הָאָרֶץ אַרְבָּעִים שָׁנָה׃

lattice, and cried: Why is his chariot so long in coming? Why do the sounds of his chariots tarry?

The wisest of her ladies answer her, she even gives answer to herself:

Are they not finding and sharing the booty? A maiden, two maidens, to each man; a booty of dyed garments for Sisera, a booty of dyed garments of needlework; dyed doubled embroidery for the necks of each of the spoilers.

So may all your enemies perish, O Lord, but let those who love Him be like the sun at its zenith.

And the land was quiet for forty years.

A YOUNG GIRL'S PRAYER

Fanny Neuda

> *Grace is deceiving and beauty is transient; a woman*
> *who fears God—she shall be praised.*
>
> [PROVERBS 31:30]

Our God Who is in heaven and on earth, God Who is good: You attend to all of Your creatures; faithful Father, all of Your creations take refuge under Your wings.

You have called me, too, Your daughter; to me, too, You extend Your love—an eternal love. My childhood has passed in green pastures; I thank you for my happy youth; I thank You for what I am. You have given me all kinds of goodness: a dear mother and father at my side, guiding me with gentleness and love, with advice and help, caring for me and sustaining me, enhancing my life with sweet and heartwarming joys.

Fanny Neuda (1819–1894) was born to a rabbinical family in Moravia, Czechoslovakia. Her brother, Dr. Avraham (Adolph) Schmidl, was a rabbi in Vienna and a well-known scholar of the philosophy of religion. Like her brother, Fanny was educated in both Jewish and secular studies, and she married Rabbi Avraham Neuda—one of the first rabbis in Moravia to have received a secular education. When he died at a young age, Fanny created a prayer book in his memory. As far as we are able to ascertain, she was the first Jewish woman to write a book of her own prayers in German.

In the nineteenth century, Hebrew, the traditional language of Jewish prayer, was familiar to learned men who frequented the synagogue and study hall but was foreign and incomprehensible to women and laymen. In the wake of the Enlightenment, many Jews in Yiddish-speaking countries had abandoned Yiddish

תפילת הנערה הצעירה

פאני נוידא

"שֶׁקֶר הַחֵן וְהֶבֶל הַיֹּפִי אִשָּׁה יִרְאַת ה' הִיא תִתְהַלָּל"
[משלי לא 30]

אֱלֹהֵינוּ שֶׁבַּשָּׁמַיִם וּבָאָרֶץ, הָאֵל הַטּוֹב. אַתָּה דּוֹאֵג לְכָל בְּרוּאֶיךָ. אָב נֶאֱמָן, בְּצֵל כְּנָפֶךָ חוֹסִים כָּל יְצוּרֶיךָ.

גַּם לִי קָרָאתָ בִּתְּךָ, גַּם אוֹתִי מְלַוָּה אַהֲבָתְךָ, אַהֲבַת עוֹלָם. בִּנְאוֹת דֶּשֶׁא מוֹרִיקִים חָלְפוּ עָלַי יְמֵי יַלְדוּתִי, אוֹדְךָ עַל נְעוּרַי הַמְאֻשָּׁרִים, אוֹדְךָ עַל מַה שֶּׁאֲנִי. נָתַתָּ לִי מִכָּל טוֹב, אֵם וְאָב יְקָרִים לְצִדִּי, מַנְחִים אוֹתִי בֶּרֶךְ וּבְאַהֲבָה, בְּעֵצָה וּבְעֶזְרָה, מְטַפְּלִים וּמְפַרְנְסִים אוֹתִי, מְעַטְּרִים אֶת חַיַּי בִּשְׂמָחוֹת מְתוּקוֹת וְרַבּוֹת חֵן.

בַּעֲנָוָה, אֵלִי, אֲנִי קְרֵבָה אֵלֶיךָ, פּוֹרֶשֶׂת צְפוּנוֹת לִבִּי וּמוֹדָה לְךָ.

---

in favor of the local language. Fanny Neuda's prayer book, written in Old German, answered the needs of women of her time: It was written by a woman, for women, in a familiar language. Her touching supplications address the needs and problems of women throughout the ages, and include prayers for all hours of the day, prayers for weekdays and for festivals, prayers for special occasions, for the New Year, and for religious holidays.

Fanny's book, *Prayers and Supplications: Intimate Devotions, A Book of Prayer and Ethics for Jewish Women and Girls, for Prayer in Public and in Private, for All Occasions in a Woman's Life*, immediately became a bestseller among German-speaking Jewish communities. The work "migrated" together with the thousands of Jewish families that moved to America in the early twentieth century and was also popular in its English translation, which was first published in the United States in 1866.

With humility, my Lord, I approach You, revealing the hidden secrets of my heart, and offering thanks to You.

You see into my soul; my innermost being is before You as an open book. No emotion that moves my heart, no breath, no utterance of my voice, no thought that animates my soul—none is hidden from Your eyes. If only all my emotions, my thoughts, and my actions might find favor and grace before You. Deliver me from the evil inclination and imbue my heart with submission and humility.

Our Father Who is in heaven: Guide my heart to choose the way that is good and not to deviate from the straight path. Wherever I—lacking experience—am unable to distinguish between good and evil, grace me with Your wisdom, teach me to recognize the truth, that I may maintain modesty and good traits, that I may punctiliously observe Your words and Your commandments with faith and with love, and walk before You wholeheartedly and with devotion.

Let my heart not follow vanity and emptiness, and let the pleasures of the world not cloud my vision, that I not waste my precious life—the life given to me to fulfill my obligations. May it be Your will that I not turn,

Fourteen of Fanny's prayers were translated into Hebrew for the first time, by Katya Manor, for inclusion in the Hebrew volume *Tefillat Nashim.* The Hebrew translation aims to preserve the style and language of the period when it was written. The three years that have passed since the publication of *Tefillat Nashim* in Israel have witnessed two interesting developments. First, women's prayer in general, and the prayers of Fanny Neuda in particular, have aroused extraordinary cultural and

אַתָּה רוֹאֶה לְנַפְשִׁי, כַּסֵּפֶר הַפָּתוּחַ מָנֶּחַ תּוֹכִי לְפָנֶיךָ. כָּל סַעֲרַת רוּחַ
הַמְּנִיעָה אֶת לִבִּי, כָּל נְשִׁימָה, כָּל הֶבֶל-פֶּה הַמַּרְעִיד מֵיתָרִים, כָּל מַחֲשָׁבָה
הַמַּסְעִירָה אֶת נַפְשִׁי, אֵינָם נִסְתָּרִים מִנֶּגֶד עֵינֶיךָ. לוּ יִהְיוּ כָּל רִגְשׁוֹתַי,
מַחְשְׁבוֹתַי וּמַעֲשַׂי נוֹשְׂאִים חֵן וְחֶסֶד מִלְּפָנֶיךָ, וְתַצִּילֵנִי מִיֵּצֶר הָרָע וְתֵן בְּלִבִּי
הַכְנָעָה וַעֲנָוָה.

אָבִינוּ שֶׁבַּשָּׁמַיִם, הַנְחֵה אֶת לִבִּי לִבְחֹר בַּדֶּרֶךְ הַטּוֹבָה וְלֹא לִסְטוֹת מִדֶּרֶךְ
הַיָּשָׁר. בְּמָקוֹם שֶׁבּוֹ אֲנִי, הַחֲסֵרָה נִסָּיוֹן, לֹא אֵדַע לְהַבְחִין בֵּין טוֹב וָרַע, חָנֵּן
אוֹתִי בְּחָכְמָתֶךָ, לַמְּדֵנִי לְהַכִּיר בֶּאֱמֶת, לְמַעַן אֶשְׁמֹר עַל צְנִיעוּת וּמִדּוֹת
טוֹבוֹת, עַל דְּבָרֶיךָ וּמִצְווֹתֶיךָ אַקְפִּיד בֶּאֱמוּנָה וּבְאַהֲבָה, וּבְנִקְיוֹן כַּפַּיִם
וּבְאֲדִיקוּת אֶתְהַלֵּךְ לְפָנֶיךָ.

אַל נָא תִּתֵּן אֶת לִבִּי לְהֶבֶל וּלְרִיק, וְלַהֲנָאוֹת עוֹלָם אַל תִּתֵּן לְעַרְפְּלֵנִי,
שֶׁלֹּא אוֹצִיא לַשָּׁוְא אֶת עִתּוֹתַי הַיְקָרוֹת, הָעִתִּים שֶׁעָלַי לְקַיֵּם בָּהֶן אֶת
חוֹבוֹתַי. יְהִי רָצוֹן, שֶׁלֹּא אָסוּר בְּשָׁעָה שֶׁל קַלּוּת-דַּעַת מֵאִמְרֵי פִּיךָ, שֶׁכְּבוֹד
הַבְּתוּלָה וְהַלֵּב הַזַּךְ יִהְיוּ לִי לַעֲדִי יְקַר עֵרֶךְ.

בָּרְכֵנִי, אֵלִי, בְּבִינָה וּבִתְבוּנָה, בִּבְרִיאוּת גּוּף וָנֶפֶשׁ, בְּלֵב שָׂמֵחַ וּשְׂבַע-
רָצוֹן. תֵּן שֶׁלְּעוֹלָם לֹא אָסוּר מִמִּצְוַת כִּבּוּד אָב וָאֵם, שֶׁלֹּא אֶפְגַּע וְלֹא אַכְעִיס

---

religious interest and are being integrated into various personal ceremonies as well
as communal initiatives. Second, the response to the appearance of Neuda's prayers
in Hebrew has included testimonies as to the centrality of her prayers in the lives of
women in Europe, the United States, and Israel. Indeed, Neuda's moving words may
hold the key to the "code" of women's prayer. The power of her expression reflects
knowledge, faith, hope, and intimate dialogue with God.

in a moment of frivolity, from the words of Your mouth; that virginal honor and a pure heart be a precious adornment for me.

Bless me, my Lord, with understanding and insight, with a healthy body and soul, with a heart that is joyful and content. May I never deviate from the commandment of honoring one's father and mother, and not offend or anger my dear parents, so that I may succeed in bringing them happiness through my actions. Bestow Your blessing, my God, upon my loved ones; that illness, trouble, and anxiety never be their lot; that they may enjoy success in their endeavors and fulfillment of their hearts' wishes; and may their occupations and work bear abundant fruit. Bless them, my God, with long life, that they may rejoice in their lifetimes with strength and good health of body and soul. Amen.

אֶת הוֹרַי הַיְקָרִים, שֶׁיַּעֲלֶה בְּיָדִי לְשַׂמֵּחַ אוֹתָם בְּמַעֲשַׂי. שִׂים בִּרְכָתְךָ,
אֱלֹהַי, עַל יַקִּירַי, שֶׁלְּעוֹלָם אַל יִהְיוּ חֹלִי, צָרָה וַחֲרָדָה מְנָת חֶלְקָם, שֶׁיִּשְׂאוּ
בְּרָכָה בַּעֲמָלָם וּבְמִשְׁאֲלוֹת לִבָּם, וּבְמִשְׁלַח יָדָם וּבְעִסּוּקָם יִשְׂאוּ פֵּרוֹת לָרֹב.
בָּרֵךְ אוֹתָם, אֵלִי, בַּאֲרִיכוּת יָמִים, שֶׁבְּכֹחַ וּבִבְרִיאוּת הַגּוּף וְהַנֶּפֶשׁ יִשְׂמְחוּ
בְּחַיֵּיהֶם, אָמֵן.

PRAYER FOR A FIRST PERIOD

Ruth Lazare

*B*lessed are You, Lord, for having made me a woman

For having created my body with wisdom

Such that each organ knows its time

And You gather my organs together

Bringing maturity and fertility to ripeness within me.

Now I am a complete woman

Recognizing all the wisdom of Creation.

You have graciously granted me Your blessed gift;

You have included me among all the women of Israel

And here I am before You

Full of joy and thanks.

Ruth Lazare grew up on a religious kibbutz and is active in the Israeli educational system. "I never saw myself as an author of prayers," she said, recalling her decision to compose prayers of her own. "I regarded the very idea that a 'regular person' could write prayers as a sort of cheapening of prayer. But my encounter with women's *tekhines* (personal supplications) gave me a different perspective. The genre aroused mixed feelings in me: Some of the texts made me smile, while others made me scornful, even angry. I couldn't identify with the image of the

תחינה לבת עם קבלת המחזור

רות לזר

בָּרוּךְ אַתָּה ה' שֶׁעֲשִׂיתָנִי אִשָּׁה
שֶׁבָּרֵאתָ אֶת גּוּפִי בְּחָכְמָה
שֶׁכָּל אֵבֶר יוֹדֵעַ אֶת עִתּוֹ
וְאַתָּה כּוֹלֵל אֶת אֵבָרַי יַחַד
וּמַבְשִׁיל בִּי בַּגְרוּת וּפִרְיוֹן.
עַתָּה אֲנִי אִשָּׁה שְׁלֵמָה
הַמַּכִּירָה אֶת מְלֹא חָכְמַת הַבְּרִיאָה.
חָנַנְתָּ אוֹתִי בְּמַתְּנָתְךָ הַבְּרוּכָה
כָּלַלְתָּ אוֹתִי עִם כָּל נְשֵׁי יִשְׂרָאֵל
וְהִנֵּה אֲנִי לְפָנֶיךָ
מְלֵאַת שִׂמְחָה וְהוֹדָיָה.

---

woman that emerged from them, and I couldn't see myself incorporating these texts into my prayer book. On the other hand, the simplicity—even innocence—of the *tekhines* made it easier for me to regard their composition as something that could be attempted by anyone. My dissatisfaction with the existing *tekhines*, along with the sense that I, too, was capable of writing them, motivated me to propose alternatives for existing texts, as well as prayers for times and life-cycle events that had never yet had words composed specifically for them."

Finding a Spouse

"Enjoy life with a wife whom you love."

[ECCLESIASTES 9:9]

"A Roman matron once asked the Talmudic Sage Rabbi Yose ben Ḥalafta what God has been doing since He completed the Creation of the world. The Sage replied that God has been busy making matches. The matron was astounded: 'Is that what God does? Why, even I can do that! I have many menservants and maidservants; I could pair them up in a second!'

The Sage told her, 'It may seem simple to you, but for God it is as complex a task as splitting the Red Sea!'

The matron went and lined up a thousand menservants and a thousand maidservants. Then she announced, 'This man will marry this woman; that woman will marry that man.'

The next day, they all arrived—beaten and wounded, for this man wasn't happy with his wife, and that woman wasn't happy with her husband.

The matron sent for Rabbi Yose and said to him: 'Rabbi, your Torah is true.'"

[BEREISHIT RABBAH 68, 4]

PRAYER TO FIND A WORTHY MATCH

Rabbi Salman Mutzafi

$\mathcal{M}$ay it be Your will, Lord our God and God of our forefathers, that You be filled with compassion for me and appoint me a spouse who is pleasant, God-fearing, a learned scholar, intelligent and of good character, and successful and blessed in his study and in his dealings. For thereby we shall be able to establish a Jewish home, as You have commanded us in Your holy Torah—"And you shall be fruitful and multiply." When the young man who is proposed to me is worthy, when he is God-fearing and has good traits and good luck and is right for me, then in Your great compassion be gracious to me and incline my heart and the heart of my parents to complete the matter, that it may be well for us in this world and in the World to Come.

God Who is full of compassion, merciful, and gracious; Who protects, supports, delivers, is upright, and redeems.

Rabbi Salman Mutzafi (1900–1975) was born in Baghdad, moved to Palestine in 1935, and was among the disciples of the kabbalist Rabbi Yehuda Fetaya. He established a yeshiva adjacent to Rachel's Tomb in Bethlehem that remained active up until Israel's War of Independence in 1948, when the area fell under Jordanian

תְּפִילָה לְבַת לִמְצוֹא חָתָן הָגוּן

המקובל הרב סלמן מוצפי

יְהִי רָצוֹן מִלְפָנֶיךָ יְהֹוָה אֱלֹהֵינוּ וֵאלֹהֵי אֲבוֹתֵינוּ שֶׁתִּתְמַלֵּא רַחֲמִים עָלַי
וְתַזְמִין לִי בֶּן זוּג נָאֶה יְרֵא הַשֵּׁם וְתַלְמִיד חָכָם, וּבַעַל שֵׂכֶל וּמִדּוֹת טוֹבוֹת,
וּמֻצְלָח וּמְבֹרָךְ בְּלִמּוּדוֹ וּבְעִנְיָנָיו, כִּי בָזֶה נוּכַל לְהָקִים בַּיִת בְּיִשְׂרָאֵל כְּמוֹ
שֶׁצִּוִּיתָ אוֹתָנוּ בְּתוֹרָתְךָ הַקְּדוֹשָׁה וְאַתֶּם פְּרוּ וּרְבוּ. וְהָיָה הַבָּחוּר אֲשֶׁר
יְדַבְּרוּ לִי עָלָיו וְהוּא רָאוּי, וְיֵשׁ לוֹ יִרְאַת הַשֵּׁם וּמִדּוֹת טוֹבוֹת וּמַזָּל טוֹב וְהָגוּן
לִי. בְּרַחֲמֶיךָ הָרַבִּים תָּחוֹן עָלַי וְתַטֶּה לִבִּי וְלֵב הוֹרַי לִגְמֹר הַדָּבָר וְטוֹב לָנוּ
בָּעוֹלָם הַזֶּה וּבָעוֹלָם הַבָּא.

אֵל מָלֵא רַחֲמִים רַחוּם חַנּוּן שׁוֹמֵר תּוֹמֵךְ מַצִּיל יָשָׁר פּוֹדֶה.

---

control. Rabbi Salman Mutzafi explored the depths of kabbalistic wisdom and composed prayers for the welfare of the nation of Israel, including this one on behalf of single women.

COMPLETION

Based on the teachings of Rabbi Naḥman of Breslov

*L*oving God:

So numerous are

Those devoid of true love;

So many

fail to find their match.

Have mercy upon them.

Source of love—

Allow

Every solitary, lonely soul

To experience the completion

That comes

with finding one's match.

Rabbi Naḥman of Breslov was born in 1772 in the town of Medzhibozh in the Ukraine. He was the great-grandson of the Ba'al Shem Tov, the founder of Hassidism. Before the age of twenty, Rabbi Naḥman already led a group of Hassidim and had instituted a unique religious approach that met with disapproval on the part of other Hassidic leaders who suspected him of Sabbateanism. Their disfavor was further aroused by his young age, his manner of leadership, and his sharp style of expression.

In 1798, at the time of Napoleon's war against the Turks, Rabbi Naḥman left his family, traveled to the Holy Land, and remained there for an entire winter, spending most of his time in Safed and Tiberias. His stay in the Holy Land influenced him deeply. Later he would say, "All the vitality that I have is only from my stay in *Eretz Yisrael*." Four years later, in 1802, he arrived in the city of Breslov,

זיווג

על־פי רבי נחמן מברסלב

אֵל אוֹהֵב,
כֹּה רַבִּים הֵם
חַסְרֵי אַהֲבַת הָאֱמֶת;
כֹּה רַבִּים
אֵינָם מוֹצְאִים אֶת זוּגָם.
רַחֵם עֲלֵיהֶם.
מְקוֹר הָאַהֲבָה,
תֵּן
לְכָל נְשָׁמָה בּוֹדְדָה וְגַלְמוּדָה,
לַחֲווֹת אֶת הַשְּׁלֵמוּת
הַנּוֹבַעַת
מִמְּצִיאַת זוּג.

---

where the essence of his philosophy was consolidated and where he established his circle of followers: the Breslov Hassidim.

Rabbi Na<u>h</u>man loved to commune with God, his heart pouring forth prayers that he composed himself at times of inspiration. He experienced enormous tragedy in his life, losing his wife and several of his children to illnesses. At the end of his life, suffering from tuberculosis and sensing that his own death was not far off, he moved to the city of Uman, where he died in 1810 and where he was buried.

Rabbi Na<u>h</u>man of Breslov authored only two books himself; one was burned at his orders, and the other remains hidden among his followers. Natan Sternhartz, his closest disciple, recorded the rest of his teachings.

This beautiful matchmaking prayer is taken from *The Gentle Weapon: Prayers for Great Occasions and Small Moments* (1999), a work authored by M. Mykoff and S. H. Mizra<u>h</u>i and based on Rabbi Na<u>h</u>man's teachings.

PRAYER FOR SINGLE WOMEN
Rabbi Yoel Bin-Nun

I pray You, Lord God—

Hear the cry of the single women seeking to be married, and
   provide them with spouses,

That they may set up their homes with joy and in purity

And raise their children with love, in good health, and with God's
   blessing

("Shabbat—for ceasing to cry out, and salvation is close at hand"),

and let us say: Amen.

Rabbi Yoel Bin-Nun was born in 1946 in Haifa. After studying at the Merkaz
Ha-Rav yeshiva, he fought in the battle for Jerusalem in the Six-Day War. In
1968, he moved to Gush Etzion, and with the establishment of the Har Etzion
yeshiva, he joined its staff, headed by Rabbi Yehuda Amital and Rabbi Aharon
Lichtenstein. In 1974 he was one of the founders of the Gush Emunim movement

תְּפִילַת הָרְוְוקָה

הרב יואל בן־נון

אָנָּא ה' אֱ־הִים,
שְׁמַע שַׁוְעַת הַנָּשִׁים הָרְוָוקוֹת הַמְחַפְּשׂוֹת אֶת פִּרְקָן, וְהַמְצֵא לָהֶן
זִווּגָן,
וְיִזְכּוּ לִבְנוֹת אֶת בֵּיתָן בְּשִׂמְחָה וּבְטָהֳרָה,
וּלְגַדֵּל צֶאֱצָאֵיהֶן בְּאַהֲבָה, בִּבְרִיאוּת וּבְבִרְכַּת ה',
[שַׁבָּת הִיא מִלִּזְעֹק וִישׁוּעָה קְרוֹבָה לָבוֹא], וְנֹאמַר: אָמֵן.

---

and among the pioneers of the settlement of Ofra, where he established a religious high school for girls. Rabbi Bin-Nun is a well-known public figure who has worked extensively to promote mutual respect and understanding among different sectors of Israeli society. He is the head of the Religious Kibbutz movement's yeshiva in Ein-Tzurim.

The Wedding Day

"... I found him whom my soul loves; I held him and would not let him go ..."

[SONG OF SONGS 3:4]

Judaism regards the formalization of the connection between
a couple as a creation in and of itself. Some opinions view the
bride's immersion in rainwater, on the night prior to the wedding,
as symbolic of the birth of the bride and groom as a couple. The
bride's immersion, as part of her preparation for unification with
her groom, is also of historical religious significance: As part of the
preparations for accepting the Torah at Mount Sinai, the Israelites
were required to sanctify and purify themselves, and to keep
separate from their spouses. The prolonged process of preparation
contributed toward the impact and intensity of the encounter
between God and His creation—like the moment of unification
of a couple seeking to proceed together toward a joint future.
Some four hundred years ago, the Maharal (Rabbi Yehuda Loew,

1525–1609) elaborated on this parallel as follows: "Prior to the giving of the Torah, the nation of Israel had not yet achieved the most supreme level; when they received the Torah, then they achieved it. And this is so because there are two aspects to the unification between man and woman: One aspect is the coming together for the purpose of reproduction, as is the case concerning the mating of all species of animals, whose mating is for the sake of reproduction— for 'God did not create [the world] to be a wasteland, but rather formed it to be settled' [...] The second aspect [...] is that it is proper that the human being, representing the pinnacle of creation in this lower world, should be complete, and the creation of man can be completed only by a wife. This is the second aspect—that their joining together is the completion of the human being."

PRAYER FOR THE WEDDING DAY
Rabbi Dr. Rafael Mildola

It is good and right and proper that a woman recite this prayer on her wedding day, for it is a time of supplication to the Creator:

God brings the lonely ones to their home.

And God said: Let us make man

In Our form, according to Our image.

And God created man in His image;

In the image of God He created him.

And the Lord God formed the side

Which had been taken from man

By God, into a woman, and He brought her to the man.

And God blessed them

And God said to them:

The descendant of a family of rabbis and doctors, Rabbi Dr. Rafael Mildola (1754–1828) was born in Livorno, Italy. He, too, was both a rabbi (having been ordained by Rabbi Haim Yosef David Azoulay, known as the "Hidda") and a doctor. Rabbi Mildola served as the rabbi of the Sephardic community in England, where he worked to ameliorate tensions between the local Sephardic and Ashkenazic congregations. His teachings were characterized primarily by two elements:

תפילה לאשה ביום כניסתה לחופה
הרב ד״ר רפאל מילדולה

טוב ונכון והגון שתאמר האשה ביום כניסתה לחופה זו התפילה וזו
תוארה כי הוא עת לחננה לבורא עולם:

אֱלֹהִים מוֹשִׁיב יְחִידִים בַּיְתָה.
וַיֹּאמֶר אֱלֹהִים נַעֲשֶׂה אָדָם
בְּצַלְמֵנוּ כִּדְמוּתֵנוּ.
וַיִּבְרָא אֱלֹהִים אֶת הָאָדָם בְּצַלְמוֹ
בְּצֶלֶם אֱלֹהִים בָּרָא אוֹתוֹ.
וַיִּבֶן יְיָ אֱלֹהִים אֶת הַצֵּלָע
אֲשֶׁר לָקַח מִן הָאָדָם
אֱלֹהִים לְאִשָּׁה וַיְבִיאֶהָ אֶל הָאָדָם.
וַיְבָרֶךְ אוֹתָם אֱלֹהִים

---

the integration of halacha (law) and kabbala (mysticism), and an openness to secular culture, as long as it was not opposed to the spirit of Judaism.

This prayer is taken from his book, *Huppat Hatanim: Laws and Customs, Liturgical Poems and Prayers for the Groom and the Bride*, published in Livorno in 1797. The book was immensely popular and was reprinted in several editions.

Be fruitful and multiply, and fill the earth.

You are the Lord God,

The Almighty Who is great, mighty, and awesome;

You created the heavens and the earth.

It is You Who

Formed man and breathed into him

Spirit and soul

And created man and woman

And inscribed them with Your holy Name;

yod in man [in the Hebrew word ish], and heh in woman [in the
   word isha],

For the sake of knowledge, and to teach them, that

If they merit it, the divine presence rests with them.

Therefore I, the woman standing before You this day

Lord God, holy God—

Prepared and ready, in sanctity and purity

In accordance with the law of Moses and Israel, Your servants,

To enter the wedding canopy with the groom, my husband—

Hereby pour forth prayer and supplication

Before the Throne of Your glory

At this time and occasion,

That You forgive my groom and me for all of our iniquities,
   transgressions, and sins

As it is written: He who has found a wife, has found goodness,

And finds favor from God.

And may our iniquities be dissolved

Through repentance and good deeds and the wedding canopy.

וַיֹּאמֶר לָהֶם אֱלֹהִים

פְּרוּ וּרְבוּ וּמִלְאוּ אֶת הָאָרֶץ.

אַתָּה הוּא יְיָ הָאֱלֹהִים

הָאֵל הַגָּדוֹל הַגִּבּוֹר וְהַנּוֹרָא

אַתָּה עָשִׂיתָ אֶת הַשָּׁמַיִם וְאֶת הָאָרֶץ.

אַתָּה הוּא

יוֹצֵר הָאָדָם וְנָפַחְתָּ בּוֹ

רוּחַ וּנְשָׁמָה

וּבָרָאתָ אִישׁ וְאִשָּׁה

וְרָשַׁמְתָּ בָּהֶם שִׁמְךָ הַקָּדוֹשׁ

יוֹ"ד בְּאִישׁ וה"א בְּאִשָּׁה.

לְמַעַן דַּעַת וּלְלַמֵּד אוֹתָם לֵאמֹר

זְכוּ שְׁכִינָה בֵּינֵיהֶם.

לָכֵן אֲנִי הָאִשָּׁה הַנִּצֶּבֶת לְפָנֶיךָ הַיּוֹם

יְיָ הָאֱלֹהִים אֱלֹהִים קְדוֹשִׁים

הַמּוּכֶנֶת וּמְזוּמֶנֶת בִּקְדוּשָׁה וּבְטַהֲרָה

כְּדָת מֹשֶׁה וְיִשְׂרָאֵל עֲבָדֶיךָ

לִיכָּנֵס לְחֻפָּה עִם הֶחָתָן בַּעֲלִי.

הִנְנִי מַפֶּלֶת תְּפִלָּה וְתַחֲנוּנִים

לִפְנֵי כִּסֵּא כְבוֹדֶךָ

בָּעֵת וּבָעוֹנָה הַזֹּאת

שֶׁאַתָּה מוֹחֵל לִי וּלְבַעֲלִי עַל כָּל עֲווֹנוֹתֵינוּ וְחַטֹּאתֵינוּ וְאַשְׁמוֹתֵינוּ

כַּכָּתוּב מָצָא אִשָּׁה מָצָא טוֹב

וַיָּפֶק רָצוֹן מֵיְיָ.

וַעֲווֹנוֹתֵינוּ מִתְפַּקְּקִין

עַל יְדֵי תְּשׁוּבָה וּמַעֲשִׂים טוֹבִים וְחֻפָּה.

BRIDE'S PRAYER ON HER WEDDING DAY

Fanny Neuda

"A wise woman builds her house, but one who is foolish destroys it with her own hands."

[PROVERBS 14:1]

*M*y Lord—a great and fateful hour approaches and draws close; the hour in which I shall enter the covenant of betrothal and marriage with the man whom You, Knower of hidden matters, have appointed to be the spouse who will be my companion through life. I am full of emotion and agitation in anticipation of the momentous hour. At this time I seek Your closeness, merciful and compassionate God, in order that You—Master of all the world—may grant me guidance and blessing.

What the future holds for me—who can, who dares, question? Who can dispel its mists? Will joy or sadness be my portion? Will the path of my life be drenched with light or be gloomy? Into Your hands, my Lord, I entrust my future; I give over my fate to Your beneficence. I shall not fear nor be afraid, "For You will do all with goodness and with wisdom; in Your right hand are kindness and love." My God, this day I assume obligations, both sweet and bitter. A new page is starting in the story of my life; a new cycle of tasks is opening up before me. It is easy to walk the roads of life with the loving and concerned hand of a beloved mother and father supporting one, but now I must pave my way by myself, and bear with dignity the yoke of the dual and blessed role—the role of wife and homemaker. I cleave to the person who, from now, will be my everything. I shall consider the fulfillment of his wishes a great and exalted task.

תפילת הכלה ביום חתונתה

פאני נוידא

"חַכְמוֹת נָשִׁים בָּנְתָה בֵיתָהּ וְאִוֶּלֶת בְּיָדֶיהָ תֶהֶרְסֶנּוּ"

[משלי יד ו]

אֵלִי, שָׁעָה גְדוֹלָה וַהֲרַת־גּוֹרָל קְרֵבָה וּבָאָה, הַשָּׁעָה שֶׁבּוֹא אָבוֹא
בִּבְרִית הַנִּשּׂוּאִין בְּקִדּוּשִׁין עִם הָאִישׁ אֲשֶׁר אַתָּה, בּוֹחֵן כְּלָיוֹת וָלֵב, יָעַדְתָּ
לִהְיוֹת לִי לְבֶן־זוּג שֶׁיְּלַוֶּה אוֹתִי בְּאָרְחוֹת הַחַיִּים. נַפְשִׁי רוֹגֶשֶׁת וְסוֹעֶרֶת
לִקְרַאת הַשָּׁעָה הַגְּדוֹלָה. בְּשָׁעָה זוֹ אֲבַקֵּשׁ קִרְבָתְךָ, אֵל רַחוּם וְחַנּוּן, כְּדֵי
שֶׁאַתָּה, אֲדוֹן כָּל הָעוֹלָמוֹת, תִּתֵּן לִי עֵצָה וּבְרָכָה.

מַה צוֹפֵן לִי הֶעָתִיד, מִי יוּכַל, מִי יָעֹז לַחְקֹר? מִי יָסִיר מֵעָלָיו אֶת
הָעֲרָפֶל? הַאִם שִׂמְחָה אוֹ עֶצֶב יִהְיוּ מְנָת חֶלְקִי? הַאִם שְׁטוּף אוֹר אוֹ קוֹדֵר
יִהְיֶה נְתִיב חַיָּי? בְּיָדְךָ אֵלִי, אַפְקִיד דַּרְכִּי, לַטּוֹב לְבַד אֶמְסֹר גּוֹרָלִי. לֹא
אִירָא וְלֹא אֶפְחַד "יַעַן אַתָּה תַּעֲשֶׂה הַכֹּל בַּטּוֹב וּבְחָכְמָה. בִּימִינְךָ חֶסֶד
וְאַהֲבָה." אֱלֹהַי, הַיּוֹם אֲנִי מְקַבֶּלֶת עַל עַצְמִי חוֹבוֹת, מְתִיקוּת וּמָרוֹת.
דַּף חָדָשׁ נִפְתָּח בְּסֵפֶר חַיַּי, מַעְגַּל מְלָאכוֹת חָדָשׁ נִפְרָשׂ לְפָנַי. כָּל לְצַעֹד
בִּנְתִיבוֹת הַחַיִּים כְּשֶׁיַּד אוֹהֶבֶת וְדוֹאֶגֶת שֶׁל אֵם וְאָב יְקָרִים תּוֹמֶכֶת בָּךְ;
אַךְ עַתָּה עָלַי לְסַלֵּל אֶת דַּרְכִּי בְּעַצְמִי וְלָשֵׂאת בִּכְבוֹד בְּעַל הַתַּפְקִיד
הַכָּפוּל הַמְבֹרָךְ, תַּפְקִיד הָרַעְיָה וַעֲקֶרֶת הַבַּיִת. אֲנִי דְבֵקָה בָּאָדָם שֶׁמֵּעַתָּה
יִהְיֶה לִי הַכֹּל בַּכֹּל. לְהַשְׂבִּיעַ אֶת רְצוֹנוֹ יֵחָשֵׁב לִי תַּפְקִיד רָם וְנַעֲלֶה.
אַשְׁרוֹ הוּא קִנְיָנִי הַיָּקָר מִכֹּל – כָּל חֶפְצִי וְיִשְׁעִי. בִּשְׁעוֹתָיו הַקָּשׁוֹת אֶהְיֶה
לוֹ נֶחָמָה, בְּיָמִים טוֹבִים – אֹשְׁרוֹ הָעִלָּאִי. בְּכָל עֲמָלוֹ וּתְלָאוֹתָיו אֶהְיֶה לוֹ

67

His happiness will be my most precious attainment; his love—all that I desire and wish for. At times of difficulty I shall be his comfort; in good times—his highest joy. In all of his labors and tribulations I shall be his companion and helper: an aid throughout an eventful life; a soft and gentle support, imbued with loyalty and devotion, so that our marriage may be a fulfillment of the verse, "I am my beloved's, and my beloved is mine."

My Lord in heaven, with all my heart and soul I sense and know the magnitude and sanctity of these obligations; will I have the strength, the wisdom, and the courage to carry them out in full, under all circumstances?

O my Lord; You—Who, from my childhood, have guided me with words of love and with much kindness, through the gentle voices of my parents and teachers, through mighty emotions and the even mightier sounds of actions—take up my prayer, offered wholeheartedly and in submission. Do not forsake me; grant me grace that will accompany me in my new life, in whose gateway I enter this day. Guide me in Your wisdom; stand by my side with counsel and warning. Grant me gentleness, patience, and tranquillity; let my husband's heart be bound up with me in love and honor, that I may always appear to him adorned with wisdom, grace, and kindness, and that I may never experience fear and anxiety that his love toward me may be extinguished, that his affection may wane.

Bless our covenant with strength, longevity, and peace all the days of our lives, that we may proceed jointly on the straight path to the exalted destiny that life holds in store for us. Let our home be like the homes of Sarah, Rebecca, Rachel, and Leah—full of love and faith, blessed by all who come and go.

And since I come in supplication for my future happiness, how can I not also pray for those who are most dear to me—my mother and father, who cared for me in my childhood, who led me and guided me in my youth, who molded my heart with careful artistry—the ministering

חֶבְרָה וּמְסִיעַת. סְעַד בְּחַיִּים רַבֵּי מַעֲלָלִים, מִשְׁעֶנֶת רַכָּה וַעֲדִינָה חֲדוּרָה נֶאֱמָנוּת וּמְסִירוּת, וְיִתְגַּשֵּׁם בְּנִשּׂוּאֵינוּ הַפָּסוּק: "אֲנִי לְדוֹדִי, וְדוֹדִי לִי."

אֵלִי שֶׁבַּשָּׁמַיִם, בְּלֵב וָנֶפֶשׁ אֲנִי חָשָׁה וְיוֹדַעַת אֶת גָּדְלָן וּקְדֻשָּׁתָן שֶׁל חוֹבוֹת אֵלֶּה; הַאִם יַעַמְדוּ לִי הַכֹּחַ, הַחָכְמָה וְהָאֹמֶץ לְמַלֵּא אוֹתָן בִּמְלוֹאָן בְּכָל תְּנַאי?

הוֹ, אֵלִי, אַתָּה שֶׁמִּיַּלְדוּת הִנְחִיתָ אוֹתִי בִּמְלוֹא אַהֲבָה וּבְרֹב חֶסֶד, בְּקוֹלָם הָרַךְ שֶׁל הוֹרַי וּמוֹרַי, בְּרַחֲשֵׁי לֵב אַדִּירִים, בְּקוֹלוֹת הָרָמִים עוֹד יוֹתֵר שֶׁל הַמַּעֲשִׂים, שָׂא תְּחִנָּתִי הַכֵּנָה וְהַכְּנוּעָה. אַל תִּטְּשֵׁנִי, תֵּן לִי חֶסֶד שֶׁיְּלַוֶּה אוֹתִי בְּחַיַּי הַחֲדָשִׁים שֶׁבְּשַׁעֲרָם אֲנִי בָּאָה הַיּוֹם; הַנְחֵנִי בְּחָכְמָתְךָ, עֲמֹד לְצִדִּי בְּעֵצָה וּבְאַזְהָרָה; תֵּן לִי עֶדְנָה, סַבְלָנוּת וְשַׁלְוָה; נְצֹר לִי אֶת לֵב בַּעֲלִי בְּאַהֲבָה וּבִיקָר, שֶׁלְּעַד אוֹפִיעַ לְפָנָיו בַּעֲדִי הַחָכְמָה, הַחֵן וְהַחֶסֶד, שֶׁהַפַּחַד וְהַחֲרָדָה שֶׁמָּא תִּכְבֶּה אַהֲבָתוֹ אֵלַי, שֶׁמָּא תִּיבַשׁ חִבָּתוֹ, לְעוֹלָם לֹא יִהְיוּ מְנָת חֶלְקִי.

בָּרֵךְ אֶת בְּרִיאֻתֵנוּ בְּחֹזֶק, בַּאֲרִיכוּת־יָמִים וּבְשָׁלוֹם לְכָל יְמֵי חַיֵּינוּ; שֶׁבְּעֵצָה אַחַת נִצְעַד בַּדֶּרֶךְ הַיָּשָׁר אֶל הַגּוֹרָל הַנַּעֲלֶה שֶׁהוֹעַדְתָּ לָנוּ הַחַיִּים. תֵּן שֶׁיִּהְיֶה בֵּיתֵנוּ כְּבֵיתָן שֶׁל שָׂרָה, רִבְקָה רָחֵל וְלֵאָה, מָלֵא בְּאַהֲבָה וּבֶאֱמוּנָה, מְבֹרָךְ עַל־יְדֵי כָּל יוֹצֵא וּבָא.

וּבַאֲשֶׁר אֲנִי בָּאָה בִּתְחִנָּה עַל אָשְׁרִי לֶעָתִיד, הֵיאַךְ לֹא אֶתְפַּלֵּל גַּם עַל אֵלֶּה הַיְּקָרִים לִי מִכֹּל – אִמִּי וְאָבִי, שֶׁשָּׁמְרוּ עָלַי בְּיַלְדוּתִי, שֶׁהוֹבִילוּ וְהִנְחוּ אוֹתִי בִּנְעוּרַי, שֶׁיָּצְקוּ אֶת לִבִּי מַעֲשֵׂה־חוֹשֵׁב, מַלְאֲכֵי שָׁרֵת הַמְּגִנִּים עַל חַיָּי. דַּלָּה שְׂפָתִי מִלְּבַטֵּא אֶת עֹשֶׁר הָאַהֲבָה, הַטּוֹב וְהַמְּסִירוּת שֶׁהִרְעִיפוּ עָלַי אִמִּי וְאָבִי. אֵיךְ אוּכַל לְהוֹדוֹת לָהֶם עַל כָּל אֵלֶּה. יְהִי רָצוֹן מִלְּפָנֶיךָ, אָבִינוּ שֶׁבַּשָּׁמַיִם, שֶׁתִּגְמֹל לָהֶם בְּרֹב אַהֲבָתְךָ עַל נֶאֱמָנוּתָם, וְעַל רֹאשָׁם שָׂא בְּרָכוֹת. הַרְחֵק דְּאָגָה מִלִּבָּם, יִהְיוּ הָעֶצֶב וְהַתּוּגָה זָרִים לָהֶם, תֵּן שֶׁיִּהְיֶה לִבָּם שָׂמֵחַ וְטוֹב עֲלֵיהֶם לָעַד.

angels who have protected my life. My lips are not worthy of expressing the wealth of love, goodness, and devotion that my mother and father have showered upon me. How can I thank them for all of this? May it be Your will, our Father in heaven, that You repay them, in Your great love, for their faithfulness, and place blessings upon their heads. Remove worry from their hearts, let sadness and grief be foreign to them; let their hearts be joyful and content forever.

II

BARRENNESS

and

FERTILITY

Fertility Prayers

Three of the four matriarchs of the Jewish nation—Sarah, Rebecca, and Rachel—originally were unable to conceive, and each responded to her infertility in her own way. Abraham and Sarah were accepting of their inability to bear children and were prepared to regard the offspring of Hagar, the handmaid, as their successors; Sarah laughed at the idea that she herself would bear a child. Isaac and Rebecca, on the other hand, prayed together for a child. In the case of Jacob and Rachel, tension and anger developed between the couple as a result of Rachel's barrenness. Her cry, "Give me children; if not—I shall die," along with Jacob's disturbing response, "Jacob grew angry with Rachel and he said, Am I in place of God Who has withheld children from you?"(Genesis 30:1–2), are thought provoking. Some commentators understand this dialogue as the manifestation of two different perspectives on the existential role of woman: Jacob represents the view that she has two purposes, as summed up by the author of *Sefer Akedat Yitzhak*: "'Woman' (*isha*)—representing knowledge and wisdom, and 'Eve' (Hava)—representing motherhood. And the negation of one aspect does not affect the other." Neḥama Leibowitz, a leading biblical scholar of the twentieth century (who happened to be childless herself), explains: "Jacob's anger is to be understood here [as resulting] from Rachel forgetting her true and primary role—which, according to the author of *Sefer Akedat Yitzhak*, is no different from his own role [as a man] ... She, in her longing for a child, viewed as her entire purpose ... to be a mother ... This was a betrayal of her role, a fleeing from her destiny, an evasion of the obligations placed upon her—not as a woman, but as a human being. It was her summing up of her entire life—all of its substance, all of its purpose—in terms of the one thing that she lacked (motherhood) that aroused his anger."

The Midrash questions, "Why were the matriarchs barren? Because the Holy One desires their prayers and desires their words." Infertility, according to this view, though tragic and emotionally debilitating, can also be a catalyst for intense prayer and supplication to God, as evidenced in the pages that follow.

PRAYER FOR CHILDLESS COUPLES
Rabbi Salman Mutzafi

*M*ay it be Your will, Lord our God and God of our forefathers, that You act for the sake of Your mercy and graciousness, and grant holy progeny, viable progeny, to all those amongst Your nation, Israel, who are childless (and especially for … [insert the man's name and the name of his mother, and the woman's name and the name of her mother]). Grant them children who are righteous and pious, occupied with Torah, and God-fearing; with good traits, straight sense, and good deeds; and complete in every positive aspect: whole in body, in their organs, in their strength and in their minds; with wealth, success, and comfortable sustenance.

As You granted children and heard the prayers of our holy matriarchs—Sarah, Rebecca, Rachel, and Leah; and Hannah the prophetess and all the righteous women of each generation, so may You grant healthy children and righteous offspring to all the women of Your nation, Israel. In the merit of the holy Names that emerge from the verses: "God remembered Sarah as He had promised, and God did to Sarah as He had spoken"; and "God blessed them and God said to them: Be fruitful and multiply," fulfill in them the verses: "The Lord granted her a pregnancy and she bore a son"; "I am the Almighty God: Be fruitful and multiply"; "Blessed be the fruit of your womb and the fruit of your land: You shall be blessed more than all the nations, there shall be among you no man or woman who is barren, nor among your livestock."

May the words of my mouth and the thoughts of my heart find favor before You, Lord, my Rock and Redeemer.

תפילה לזכות בבנים

המקובל הרב סלמן מוצפי

יְ֒הִי רָצוֹן מִלְּפָנֶיךָ יְהוָה אֱלֹהֵינוּ וֵאלֹהֵי אֲבוֹתֵינוּ שֶׁתַּעֲשֶׂה לְמַעַן רַחֲמֶיךָ וַחֲסָדֶיךָ וְתִפְקוֹד בְּזֶרַע קוֹדֶשׁ זֶרַע שֶׁל קַיָּמָא לְכָל חֲשׂוּכֵי בָנִים מֵעַמְּךָ יִשְׂרָאֵל, [וּבִפְרָט לְ... שְׁמוֹ וְשֵׁם אִמּוֹ, שְׁמָהּ וְשֵׁם אִמָּהּ], בְּבָנִים צַדִּיקִים וַחֲסִידִים, עוֹסְקִים בַּתּוֹרָה וִירֵאֵי שָׁמַיִם. בַּעֲלֵי מִדּוֹת טוֹבוֹת, שֵׂכֶל יָשָׁר וּמַעֲשִׂים טוֹבִים, וּמוּשְׁלָמִים בְּכָל דָּבָר טוֹב. שְׁלֵמִים בְּגוּפָם, בְּאֵיבַרֵיהֶם, בְּכוֹחוֹתֵיהֶם וּבְדַעְתָּם. בְּעוֹשֶׁר וְהַצְלָחָה וְכַלְכָּלָה טוֹבָה.

וּכְשֵׁם שֶׁפָּקַדְתָּ בְּבָנִים וְשָׁמַעְתָּ תְּפִלַּת אִמּוֹתֵינוּ הַקְּדוֹשׁוֹת שָׂרָה רִבְקָה רָחֵל וְלֵאָה וְחַנָּה הַנְּבִיאָה, וְכָל הַנָּשִׁים הַצַּדְקָנִיּוֹת שֶׁבְּכָל דּוֹר וָדוֹר, כֵּן תִּפְקוֹד בְּזֶרַע שֶׁל קַיָּמָא בָּנִים זְכָרִים וְצַדִּיקִים לְכָל נְשׁוֹת עַמְּךָ יִשְׂרָאֵל. בִּזְכוּת שְׁמוֹת הַקּוֹדֶשׁ הַיּוֹצְאִים מֵהַפְּסוּקִים: וַיהוָה פָּקַד אֶת שָׂרָה כַּאֲשֶׁר אָמָר וַיַּעַשׂ יְהוָה לְשָׂרָה כַּאֲשֶׁר דִּבֵּר. לְמַעַן שְׁמֶךָ הַקָּדוֹשׁ הַמְמוּנֶּה עַל הַפְּקִידָה [יוד, יוד הי, יוד הי ויו, יוד הי ויו הי, = פקד], וּפָסוּק: וַיְבָרֶךְ אֹתָם אֱלֹהִים וַיֹּאמֶר לָהֶם אֱלֹהִים פְּרוּ וּרְבוּ.

אֲשֶׁר שֵׁם שַׁדַּי הַמְסוּגָּל לְהֵרָיוֹן, נִרְמָז בְּמִילּוּאוֹ בְּתֵיבוֹת פְּרוּ וּרְבוּ [שִׁין דָּלֶת יוֹד יָ‫ן‬ לָת וָד גִּימַטְרִיָּא פרו ורבו]. וּתְקַיֵּים בָּהֶם אֶת הַפְּסוּקִים: וַיִּתֵּן יְהוָה לָהּ הֵרָיוֹן וַתֵּלֶד בֵּן. אֲנִי אֵל שַׁדַּי פְּרֵה וּרְבֵה. בָּרוּךְ פְּרִי בִטְנְךָ וּפְרִי אַדְמָתֶךָ. בָּרוּךְ תִּהְיֶה מִכָּל הָעַמִּים לֹא יִהְיֶה בְךָ עָקָר וַעֲקָרָה וּבִבְהֶמְתֶּךָ. יִהְיוּ לְרָצוֹן אִמְרֵי פִי וְהֶגְיוֹן לִבִּי לְפָנֶיךָ יְהוָה צוּרִי וְגוֹאֲלִי.

77

PRAYER OF A CHILDLESS WOMAN
Yiddish

Sovereign of all worlds; Master of all souls, my Molder and Creator: You formed me from dust and suffused me with a holy soul, giving me life in this world—all through Your great kindness and mercy. But to my great sorrow and grief, I have but little good in this world, for You have granted me no progeny. Woe to me! My life is bitter! I am like a withered tree that bears no fruit. I suffer great anguish; I know not where to turn in my pain, nor where to flee for relief.

To the heavens and the earth I cast my eyes that they may plead on my behalf; for my years are drifting by like smoke, and I am repairing nothing in my existence. May my deep sorrow be the atonement for my sins, such that I may merit the World to Come. Woe is me; woe is my life! My eyes flow with tears and my heart is grieved. There is no joy in my world; only weeping, keening, and lamentation for my years and for my youth. Woe to

In contrast to formal prayers, which are usually said at set times and prescribed occasions, *tekhines* are personal supplications that are uttered in response to one's particular situation or needs. *Tekhines* were composed by Jewish Sages throughout history, from the time of the Talmud onward; but during the past few centuries

תחינה לאשה חשוכת בנים

אידיש

רִבּוֹן כָּל הָעוֹלָמִים, אֲדוֹן כָּל הַנְּשָׁמוֹת. יוֹצְרִי וּבוֹרְאִי! אַתָּה יְצַרְתַּנִי מֵעָפָר וְנָפַחְתָּ בִּי נְשָׁמָה קְדוֹשָׁה לָתֵת לִי חַיִּים בָּעוֹלָם הַזֶּה, הַכֹּל בְּגֹדֶל חֲסָדֶיךָ וְרַחֲמֶיךָ. אַךְ, לְרֹב צַעֲרִי וְדַאֲבוֹנִי, טוּבִי בָּעוֹלָם הוּא אַךְ מְעַט, כִּי לֹא זִכִּיתַנִי בִּפְרִי בָטֶן. אוֹי לִי! חַיַּי מָרִים עָלַי! אֵינִי יוֹדַעַת אָנָה אֶפְנֶה לְעֵץ יָבֵשׁ שֶׁאֵינוֹ עוֹשֶׂה פְּרִי. יְגוֹנִי גָּדוֹל עָלַי! אֵינִי יוֹדַעַת אָנָה אֶפְנֶה בִּיגוֹנִי וְאֶל מִי אָנוּס לְעֶזְרָה.

אֶל שָׁמַיִם וָאָרֶץ אֶשָּׂא עֵינַי שֶׁיִּתְחַנְנוּ עֲבוּרִי, כִּי שְׁנוֹתַי כָּלוּת כְּעָשָׁן, וְאֵינִי מְתַקֶּנֶת מְאוּמָה בְּעוֹלָמִי. בִּגְלַל צַעֲרִי כִּי רָב, אֶתְכַּפֵּר עַל חֲטָאַי וְאֶזְכֶּה לָעוֹלָם הַבָּא. אוֹי וַי לִי, וַי לְחַיַּי! עֵינַי דּוֹלְפוֹת כְּמַרְזֵב וְלִבִּי עָלַי דּוֹאֵב. שִׂמְחָה אֵין לִי בְּעוֹלָמִי, רַק בְּכִי יְלַל וְקִינָה עַל שְׁנוֹתַי וִימֵי נְעוּרַי. אוֹי לִי! מָה אֹמַר וּמָה אֲדַבֵּר? הָאֱלֹהִים מָצָא אֶת עֲוֹנִי כִּי רַב הוּא. יְיָ הַטּוֹב, הֵן אֵין בָּעוֹלָם אֲשֶׁר יוּכַל לְרַפְּאֵנִי, רַק אַתָּה שֶׁיְּצַרְתַּנִי כְּלִי לְעָבְדֶךָ, רַק אַתָּה תּוּכַל לְרַפֵּא

---

they have come to refer to prayers offered specifically by women, usually in Yiddish. Books of *tekhines* in Yiddish generally do not note names of authors; the prayers are simply organized by subject.

me! What shall I say, how shall I speak? God has found my iniquity, for it is great. Beneficent Lord—there is no one in the world who is able to heal me; only You, Who formed me as a vessel for Your service, only You can heal me. Therefore I set forth my wish before You: If I have no life in this world, grant me good life in the World to Come, that my soul not be shamed in the World to Come.

Master of the world, let me voice the bitterness of my heart before You. I wonder to myself: At whom shall I be angry; whom shall I accuse? Perhaps my mother, who bore me—but her intention was for the sake of heaven, to perform Your holy will, as You commanded; "He did not create it a wasteland, He formed it to be inhabited." Shall I cast blame upon the star under which I was born? But the stars, too, are all obligated to fulfill Your commands, for all the hosts of the heavens prostrate themselves before You, as it was for this purpose that You created them and appointed them to their posts. Shall I blame the day I was born? But are not all of my days and years gloomy! Shall I blame the midwife for not tending my limbs properly at the time of my birth? Shall I blame the angel appointed over the pregnancy? All of these merely fulfilled Your mission and Your instruction; they were commanded by Your great Name, and their intention was that I should be good and healthy; to be Your handmaid and to serve You always, to bear sons and daughters to settle Your world, and to give praise to Your Name.

Thus, for my many sins, iniquity and blame rest with me alone—Your lowly maidservant—for I have sinned and transgressed before You, my Molder and Creator. Therefore I offer up myself to You—body and soul—before my time has come. May my great sorrow and anguish be an atonement for my soul, to deliver it from the punishment of *Geihinnom* and from descending to the depths, and may I be worthy of taking refuge in the hidden shelter of Your wings forever, Amen.

לִי, לָכֵן בַּקָּשָׁתִי שְׁטוּחָה לְפָנֶיךָ, אִם אֵין לִי חַיֵּי עוֹלָם הַזֶּה, זַכֵּנִי לְחַיִּים טוֹבִים בָּעוֹלָם הַבָּא, וְלֹא תִכָּלֵם נִשְׁמָתִי לָעוֹלָם הַבָּא:

רִבּוֹנוֹ שֶׁל עוֹלָם, בִּרְצוֹנִי לָשִׂיחַ לְפָנֶיךָ אֶת מַר לִבִּי! מְהַרְהֶרֶת אֲנִי בְּנַפְשִׁי: עַל מִי אֶכְעַס וְאֶת מִי אֲאַשִּׁים? אִם אֶת אִמִּי הוֹרָתִי אַאֲשִׁים – הֲלֹא כַּוָּנָתָהּ הָיְתָה לְשֵׁם שָׁמַיִם, לַעֲשׂוֹת אֶת רְצוֹנְךָ הַקָּדוֹשׁ וַאֲשֶׁר צִוִּיתָ: "לֹא תֹהוּ בְרָאָהּ, לָשֶׁבֶת יְצָרָהּ". הַאִם אֶתְלֶה אַשְׁמָה בַּמַּזָּלִי שֶׁבּוֹ נוֹלַדְתִּי? – הֲלֹא גַם הַמַּזָּלוֹת כֻּלָּם חַיָּבִים לְקַיֵּם פִּקּוּדֶיךָ, כִּי כָּל צְבָא הַשָּׁמַיִם לְךָ מִשְׁתַּחֲוִים, כִּי לְשֵׁם כָּךְ בְּרָאתָם וְהִפְקַדְתָּם עַל מִשְׁמַרְתָּם. הַאִם אַאֲשִׁים אֶת יוֹם לֵדָתִי? – הֲלֹא כָּל יָמַי וּשְׁנוֹתַי קוֹדְרִים עָלַי. הַאִם אֶת מְיַלַּדְתִּי אַאֲשִׁים, שֶׁמָּא לֹא עָרְכָה הֵיטֵב אֶת אֵבָרַי בְּעֵת לֵדָתִי? הַאִם בַּמַּלְאָךְ הַמְמֻנֶּה עַל הַהֵרָיוֹן אַשְׁלִיךְ אַשְׁמָה? – הֲלֹא כָּל אֵלֶּה רַק שְׁלִיחוּתְךָ וּפְקֻדָּתְךָ קִיְּמוּ, וְהֵם נִצְטַוּוּ בְּשִׁמְךָ הַגָּדוֹל, וְדַעְתָּם הָיְתָה שֶׁאֶהְיֶה טוֹבָה וּבְרִיאָה לִהְיוֹת לְךָ לְשִׁפְחָה וּלְעָבְדְךָ תָּמִיד, וְלָלֶדֶת בָּנִים וּבָנוֹת לְיִשּׁוּב עוֹלָמְךָ וּלְהוֹדוֹת לִשְׁמֶךָ:

עַל כֵּן, בַּעֲווֹנוֹתַי הָרַבִּים, חַטֹּאתַי וְאַשְׁמָתִי תְּלוּיוֹת אַךְ בִּי, שִׁפְחָתְךָ הַדַּלָּה, כִּי חָטָאתִי וּפָשַׁעְתִּי לְפָנֶיךָ, יוֹצְרִי וּבוֹרְאִי. לָכֵן מוֹסֶרֶת אֲנִי אֵלֶיךָ אֶת עַצְמִי, גּוּפִי וְנִשְׁמָתִי, בְּטֶרֶם יָבוֹא עִתִּי. וְרֹב צַעֲרִי וִיגוֹנִי יְכַפֵּר עַל נִשְׁמָתִי לְהַצִּילָהּ מִדִּינָהּ שֶׁל גֵּיהִנֹּם וּמֵרֶדֶת שַׁחַת, וְאֶזְכֶּה לַחֲסוֹת בְּסֵתֶר כְּנָפֶיךָ לְעוֹלָמִים, אָמֵן:

Pregnancy and Childbirth

"I give thanks with all my heart for having entered the nine months of pregnancy; thus far God has helped me and has faithfully delivered me from accidents that may harm a pregnant woman and her fetus. Beneficent One Whose mercies are not exhausted—therefore I ask further for His mercy, that He assist me and support me when it is time for labor, and give me strength to give birth to him ..."

[FROM A HANDWRITTEN COLLECTION OF WOMEN'S PRAYERS DEDICATED TO SARA, WIFE OF K. HIZKIYA LEVI, 5574 (1814), ITALY]

"And now, I pray, let the power of my Lord be great, as You have spoken ..."

[NUMBERS 14:17]

"THE SOUL OF ALL LIVING THINGS"

*L*et the soul of all living things bless Your Name, Lord our God, and let the spirit of all flesh continually glorify and exalt Your remembrance, our King. Since eternity and for eternity You are God, and other than You we have no king, redeemer, or savior. Liberator, Deliverer, Sustainer Who answers and is merciful at every time of trouble and distress—we have no king, helping and supporting, but You, God of the beginning and of the end, God of all creatures, Master of all generations, extolled in all manner of praises, Who guides His world with kindness and His creatures with mercy. The Lord God is truth; He neither slumbers nor sleeps. He Who rouses the sleepers and awakens the slumberers, resurrects the dead and heals the sick, causes the blind to see and those bent over to stand upright, the mute to speak and hidden things to be revealed—to You alone we give thanks. Were our mouth as full of song as the sea, and the joyful singing of our tongue as its multitude of waves, and the praise of our lips like the breadth of the sky, and our eyes as brilliant as the sun and the moon, and our hands outstretched like the eagles of the heavens, and our feet as light as deer—we could not thank You sufficiently, Lord our God and God of our forefathers, nor bless Your Name, our King, for any one of the thousand thousand, thousands of thousands, and myriad myriads of favors, miracles, and wonders that You have performed for us and for our forefathers. In ancient times You redeemed us from Egypt, Lord our God,

Some women follow the custom of reciting this prayer (which appears in the regular prayer book as part of the morning prayer service for Shabbat and festivals) throughout their pregnancy.

נִשְׁמַת כָּל חַי

נִשְׁמַת כָּל חַי תְּבָרֵךְ אֶת שִׁמְךָ יְיָ אֱלֹהֵינוּ וְרוּחַ כָּל בָּשָׂר תְּפָאֵר וּתְרוֹמֵם זִכְרְךָ מַלְכֵּנוּ תָּמִיד. מִן הָעוֹלָם וְעַד הָעוֹלָם אַתָּה אֵל. וּמִבַּלְעָדֶיךָ אֵין לָנוּ מֶלֶךְ גּוֹאֵל וּמוֹשִׁיעַ. פּוֹדֶה וּמַצִּיל וּמְפַרְנֵס וְעוֹנֶה וּמְרַחֵם בְּכָל עֵת צָרָה וְצוּקָה. אֵין לָנוּ מֶלֶךְ עוֹזֵר וְסוֹמֵךְ אֶלָּא אָתָּה: אֱלֹהֵי הָרִאשׁוֹנִים וְהָאַחֲרוֹנִים, אֱלוֹהַּ כָּל בְּרִיּוֹת, אֲדוֹן כָּל תּוֹלָדוֹת, הַמְהֻלָּל בְּכָל הַתִּשְׁבָּחוֹת. הַמְנַהֵג עוֹלָמוֹ בְּחֶסֶד וּבְרִיּוֹתָיו בְּרַחֲמִים. וַיְיָ אֱלֹהִים אֱמֶת לֹא יָנוּם וְלֹא יִישָׁן. הַמְעוֹרֵר יְשֵׁנִים וְהַמֵּקִיץ נִרְדָּמִים, מְחַיֶּה מֵתִים, וְרוֹפֵא חוֹלִים, פּוֹקֵחַ עִוְרִים, וְזוֹקֵף כְּפוּפִים, הַמֵּשִׂיחַ אִלְּמִים, וְהַמַּפְעֲנֵחַ נֶעֱלָמִים. וּלְךָ לְבַדְּךָ אֲנַחְנוּ מוֹדִים. וְאִלּוּ פִינוּ מָלֵא שִׁירָה כַּיָּם וּלְשׁוֹנֵנוּ רִנָּה כַּהֲמוֹן גַּלָּיו, וְשִׂפְתוֹתֵינוּ שֶׁבַח כְּמֶרְחֲבֵי רָקִיעַ, וְעֵינֵינוּ מְאִירוֹת כַּשֶּׁמֶשׁ וְכַיָּרֵחַ, וְיָדֵינוּ פְרוּשׂוֹת כְּנִשְׁרֵי שָׁמָיִם. וְרַגְלֵינוּ קַלּוֹת כָּאַיָּלוֹת, אֵין אֲנַחְנוּ מַסְפִּיקִין לְהוֹדוֹת לְךָ יְיָ אֱלֹהֵינוּ וֵאלֹהֵי אֲבוֹתֵינוּ וּלְבָרֵךְ אֶת שְׁמֶךָ מַלְכֵּנוּ. עַל אַחַת מֵאֶלֶף אֶלֶף אַלְפֵי אֲלָפִים וְרֹב רִבֵּי רְבָבוֹת פְּעָמִים הַטּוֹבוֹת נִסִּים וְנִפְלָאוֹת שֶׁעָשִׂיתָ עִמָּנוּ וְעִם אֲבוֹתֵינוּ. מִלְּפָנִים מִמִּצְרַיִם גְּאַלְתָּנוּ יְיָ אֱלֹהֵינוּ. מִבֵּית עֲבָדִים פְּדִיתָנוּ. בְּרָעָב זַנְתָּנוּ. וּבְשָׂבָע כִּלְכַּלְתָּנוּ. מֵחֶרֶב הִצַּלְתָּנוּ. מִדֶּבֶר מִלַּטְתָּנוּ. וּמֵחֳלָאִים רָעִים וְרַבִּים דִּלִּיתָנוּ.

עַד הֵנָּה עֲזָרוּנוּ רַחֲמֶיךָ וְלֹא עֲזָבוּנוּ חֲסָדֶיךָ וְאַל תִּטְּשֵׁנוּ יְיָ אֱלֹהֵינוּ לָנֶצַח. עַל כֵּן אֵבָרִים שֶׁפִּלַּגְתָּ בָּנוּ. וְרוּחַ וּנְשָׁמָה שֶׁנָּפַחְתָּ בְּאַפֵּנוּ. וְלָשׁוֹן אֲשֶׁר שַׂמְתָּ

and liberated us from the house of slavery. During famine You fed us and during plenty You sustained us. You saved us from the sword, snatched us from the plague, and spared us varied terrible illnesses.

Thus far Your mercy has helped us and Your kindness has not forsaken us; do not abandon us, Lord our God, forever. Therefore the organs that You have set within us, the spirit and soul that You have breathed into our nostrils, and the tongue that You have placed in our mouth—they themselves will thank and bless, praise, glorify, and extol Your Name, our King, continually. For every mouth will offer thanks to You, and every tongue will praise You; every eye will look to You, every knee will bow to you, and every upright stature will prostrate itself before You. Hearts will fear You; innermost thoughts and emotions shall sing praises to Your Name. As it is written: "All my bones shall say, Lord—who is like You, saving the poor man from one who is stronger than him, and the needy and the destitute from those who would rob them. You hear the cry of the poor; You hearken to the groan of the needy—and save them." As it is written:

> Sing joyfully, righteous ones, of God;
>
> for the upright, praise is becoming.
>
> By the mouths of the upright may You be exalted,
>
> by the lips of the righteous may You be blessed,
>
> by the tongues of the devout may You be sanctified,
>
> and among the holy may You be praised—

In the gatherings of the myriads of Your people, the house of Israel. For such is the duty of all creatures before You, Lord our God and God of our forefathers: to thank, to laud, to praise, to extol, to exalt, to honor, and to glorify; even beyond all the words of song and praises of David, son of Jesse; Your servant, Your anointed one.

בְּפִינוּ. הֵן הֵם יוֹדוּ וִיבָרְכוּ וִישַׁבְּחוּ וִיפָאֲרוּ וִישׁוֹרְרוּ אֶת שִׁמְךָ מַלְכֵּנוּ תָּמִיד.

כִּי כָל פֶּה לְךָ יוֹדֶה. וְכָל לָשׁוֹן לְךָ תִּשָּׁבַע. וְכָל עַיִן לְךָ תְּצַפֶּה. וְכָל בֶּרֶךְ לְךָ

תִכְרַע. וְכָל קוֹמָה לְפָנֶיךָ תִשְׁתַּחֲוֶה. וְהַלְּבָבוֹת יִירָאוּךָ וְהַקֶּרֶב וְהַכְּלָיוֹת יְזַמְּרוּ

לִשְׁמֶךָ. כַּדָּבָר שֶׁנֶּאֱמַר כָּל עַצְמוֹתַי תֹּאמַרְנָה יְיָ מִי כָמוֹךָ מַצִּיל עָנִי מֵחָזָק

מִמֶּנּוּ. וְעָנִי וְאֶבְיוֹן מִגֹּזְלוֹ: שַׁוְעַת עֲנִיִּים אַתָּה תִּשְׁמַע. צַעֲקַת הַדַּל תַּקְשִׁיב

וְתוֹשִׁיעַ. וְכָתוּב.

רַנְּנוּ צַדִּיקִים בַּיְיָ

לַיְשָׁרִים נָאוָה תְהִלָּה:

בְּפִי יְשָׁרִים תִּתְרוֹמָם:

וּבְשִׂפְתֵי צַדִּיקִים תִּתְבָּרַךְ:

וּבִלְשׁוֹן חֲסִידִים תִּתְקַדָּשׁ:

וּבְקֶרֶב קְדוֹשִׁים תִּתְהַלָּל:

בְּמַקְהֲלוֹת רִבְבוֹת עַמְּךָ בֵּית יִשְׂרָאֵל. שֶׁכֵּן חוֹבַת כָּל הַיְצוּרִים לְפָנֶיךָ

יְיָ אֱלֹהֵינוּ וֵאלֹהֵי אֲבוֹתֵינוּ לְהוֹדוֹת. לְהַלֵּל. לְשַׁבֵּחַ. לְפָאֵר. לְרוֹמֵם. לְהַדֵּר.

וּלְנַצֵּחַ. עַל כָּל דִּבְרֵי שִׁירוֹת וְתִשְׁבָּחוֹת דָּוִד בֶּן יִשַׁי עַבְדְּךָ מְשִׁיחֶךָ:

PRAYER FOR AN EASY PREGNANCY
Italy

*M*ay it be Your will, Lord my God and God of my forefathers, that You relieve me [insert the worshipper's name] of the pain of pregnancy and add to my vitality throughout the pregnancy; such that neither the strength of the fetus nor my own strength be exhausted through any cause at all. Deliver me from the punishment of Eve: When I give birth and the term of pregnancy is complete, let the birth pangs not overwhelm me; let the infant emerge into the world in an instant, and let me bear him effortlessly, as would a chicken, easily and with no injury either to me or to the infant. Let him be born at a propitious time and with good luck for life and peace, good health, favor and grace, wealth and honor.

May I not give birth on Shabbat, so that others will not need to desecrate Shabbat on my behalf. Fulfill all my wishes in the proper measure, for salvation and mercy, among all of Israel who need mercy; and do not turn me away from before You empty-handed, Amen, Selah. In

This prayer appears in a collection of women's prayers from eighteenth-century Italy and is based on the seventeenth-century work *Kitzur ha-Shela* by Rabbi Yehiel Mikhel Epstein. It is one of many examples of an age-old phenomenon whereby excerpts from classical works are interwoven in women's personal prayers.

תפילה להקלת צער העיבור

איטליה

יְהִי רָצוֹן מִלְפָנֶיךָ יְיָ אֱלֹקַי וֵאלֹקֵי אֲבוֹתַי שֶׁתָּקֵל מֵעָלַי [תֹאמַר
הַמִתְפַּלֶלֶת אֶת שְׁמָהּ] אֶת צַעַר עִבּוּרִי וְתוֹסִיף לִי כֹּחַ כָּל יְמֵי עִבּוּרִי אֶת
צַעַר עִבּוּרִי שֶׁלֹא יוּתַשׁ כֹּחַ הֶעָבָר וְלֹא כֹּחִי בְּשׁוּם דָּבָר שֶׁבָּעוֹלָם. וְתַצִיל
אוֹתִי מִפְּתָקָה שֶׁל חַוָּה. וּבְעֵת לִדְתִי כִּי יִמְלְאוּ יָמַי לָלֶדֶת לֹא יֵהָפְכוּ עָלַי
צִירֵי הַלֵּידָה וְיֵצֵא הַוָּלָד לַאֲוִיר הָעוֹלָם בְּרֶגַע קָטָן וְאֵלֵד בְּנָקֵל כְּתַרְנְגֹלֶת,
בְּקַלּוּת בְּלִי שׁוּם הֶזֵק לֹא לִי וְלֹא לַוָּלָד. וְיִהְיֶה נוֹלָד בְּשָׁעָה טוֹבָה וּמַזָּל טוֹב
לְחַיִּים וּלְשָׁלוֹם וְלִבְרִיאוּת לְחֵן וּלְחֶסֶד לְעֹשֶׁר וּלְכָבוֹד.

וְשֶׁלֹא אֵלֵד בְּשַׁבָּת וְיִצְטָרְכוּ לְחַלֵּל שַׁבָּת בִּשְׁבִילִי, וּתְמַלֵּא כָּל מִשְׁאֲלוֹתַי
בְּמִדָּה טוֹבָה יְשׁוּעָה וְרַחֲמִים בְּקֶרֶב כָּל יִשְׂרָאֵל הַצְּרִיכִים רַחֲמִים וְאַל
תְּשִׁיבֵנִי רֵיקָם מִלְפָנֶיךָ אָמֵן סֶלָה וָעֶד. וּבְיָדְךָ יְיָ אֱלֹקֵינוּ הַמַּפְתֵּחַ שֶׁל חַיָּה
וְהַלֵּידָה שֶׁלֹא נִמְסְרָה לְשׁוּם מַלְאָךְ לָכֵן זְכוֹר רַחֲמֶיךָ יְיָ וַחֲסָדֶיךָ וְזָכְרֵנִי
לְחַיִּים וּפָקְדֵנִי בִּישׁוּעָה וְרַחֲמִים וְאֵלֵד בְּרֶוַח זֶרַע שֶׁל קַיָּמָא מִסְטְרָא

Your hand, Lord our God, is the key to life and birth, which was never given over to any angel; therefore, remember Your mercy, Lord, and Your kindness; and remember me for life and grant me salvation and mercy, that I may give birth easily to a healthy child from the source of holiness. As David gave song in the Psalms: "From the straits I called to God; God answered me with expansiveness. The Lord is with me, I shall not fear; what can mortals do to me?" He Who heard David's prayer at the time of his distress—may He hear this, my prayer. And as He answered our holy matriarchs—Sarah, Rebecca, Rachel, Leah, and Hannah and all the righteous, pious, and worthy women—may He answer me. Amen. May the words of my mouth and the thoughts of my heart find favor before You, Lord, my Rock and Redeemer.

דְקֻדְשָׁא כְּמוֹ שֶׁזִּמֵּר דָּוִד בַּתְּהִילִים מִן הַמֵּצַר קָרָאתִי יָהּ עָנָנִי בַמֶּרְחַב יָהּ:
יְיָ לִי לֹא אִירָא מַה יַּעֲשֶׂה לִי אָדָם: מִי שֶׁשָּׁמַע תְּפִלַּת דָּוִד בְּעֵת צָרוֹתָיו
הוּא יִשְׁמַע אֶת תְּפִלָּתִי זֹאת וּכְמוֹ שֶׁעָנָה לְאִמּוֹתֵינוּ הַקְּדוֹשׁוֹת שָׂרָה רִבְקָה
רָחֵל וְלֵאָה וְחַנָּה וּלְכָל הַצַּדִּיקוֹת וְהַחֲסִידוֹת וְהַהֲגוּנוֹת הוּא יַעֲנֵנִי. אָמֵן: יִהְיוּ
לְרָצוֹן אִמְרֵי־פִי וְהֶגְיוֹן לִבִּי לְפָנֶיךָ יְיָ צוּרִי וְגֹאֲלִי:

UPON ADMISSION TO THE HOSPITAL
Yiddish

*M*aster of the universe: I believe with perfect faith that my salvation
is in Your hands and that no mortal doctor has the power to heal anything.
May it be Your will to save me from this mighty danger, and help me
so that the doctor who comes to deliver me at the proper time may be
Your faithful emissary; and that no mishap occur on his account, heaven
forefend, and that I may give birth with good fortune and with no injury
either to me or to the fetus.

For a lengthy period, Yiddish was the spoken language of most of European Jewry,
and over time Yiddish spawned a rich cultural world. The language reached its apogee in the period between the two world wars; however, since then—in the wake of
the Holocaust, the anti-Semitism of the Soviet regime, the establishment of the

תְּפִלַּת הָאִשָּׁה כְּשֶׁנִּכְנֶסֶת לְבֵית־הַחוֹלִים

אידיש

רִבּוֹנוֹ שֶׁל עוֹלָם, אֲנִי מַאֲמִינָה בֶּאֱמוּנָה שְׁלֵמָה שֶׁיְשׁוּעָתִי בְּיָדְךָ הִיא,
וְאֵין בְּיַד רוֹפֵא בָּשָׂר וָדָם לְרַפֵּא שׁוּם דָּבָר. וִיהִי רָצוֹן מִלְּפָנֶיךָ שֶׁתַּצִּילֵנִי מִן
הַסַּכָּנָה הָעֲצוּמָה הַזֹּו, וְעָזְרֵנִי שֶׁהָרוֹפֵא שֶׁיָּבֹא לְיַלֵּד אוֹתִי בְּשָׁעָה טוֹבָה
יִהְיֶה שָׁלִיחַ נֶאֱמָן מֵאִתְּךָ, וְשֶׁלֹא תָבֹא חַס וְשָׁלוֹם שׁוּם תְּקָלָה עַל יָדוֹ, וְאֵלֵד
בְּמַזָּל טוֹב בְּלִי שׁוּם הֶזֵּק לֹא לִי וְלֹא לַיֶּלֶד.

꧁ ꧂

State of Israel, and the revival of the Hebrew language—it has suffered a steady
decline.

The first woman known to have written in Yiddish was Raizel, daughter of
Fishel, who wrote an introduction to a translation of Psalms that was published in
Cracow in 1586 and dedicated to "righteous men, women, and girls."

MIDWIVES' PRAYER

Shemot Rabba

[C]oncerning the words] "And they let the children live"—Some were destined to be born crippled, blind, and so on. What did [the midwives] do? They stood in prayer and declared before the Holy One, blessed be He: "You know that we have not fulfilled the instructions of Pharaoh; it is Your word that we seek to fulfill. Master of the world: May the fetus emerge safely, so that the Israelites will find no reason to murmur against us, saying: '[The infants] emerged blemished, for [the midwives] sought to kill them.'" The Holy One, blessed be He, would acquiesce immediately, and the infants would emerge perfectly formed. Then they would stand in prayer and declare before Him: "Master of the universe; invest them and grant them their souls right away, so that the Israelites will not say, 'They killed them.'" And the Holy One, blessed be He, would accede to their prayers.

According to midrashic tradition, Shifra and Puah—the midwives who courageously defied Pharaoh's decree to kill all newborn Jewish boys in Egypt—are identified as Jochebed and Miriam.

תפילת המיילדות

שמות רבה

"וַתְּחַיֶּיןָ אֶת־הַיְלָדִים" – יֵשׁ מֵהֶם שֶׁרְאוּיִים לָצֵאת חִגְרִים אוֹ סוּמִין וְכוּ'. וּמָה הָיוּ עוֹשׂוֹת? עוֹמְדוֹת בִּתְפִלָּה וְאוֹמְרוֹת לִפְנֵי הקב"ה: אַתָּה יוֹדֵעַ שֶׁלֹּא קִיַּמְנוּ דְּבָרָיו שֶׁל פַּרְעֹה, דְּבָרֶיךָ אָנוּ מְבַקְשׁוֹת לְקַיֵּם. רִבּוֹן הָעוֹלָם יֵצֵא הַוָּלָד לְשָׁלוֹם שֶׁלֹּא יִמְצְאוּ יִשְׂרָאֵל יְדֵיהֶם לְהַשִׂיחַ עָלֵינוּ לוֹמַר הֲרֵי יָצְאוּ בַּעֲלֵי מוּמִים שֶׁבִּקְשׁוּ לַהֲרֹג אוֹתָם מִיָּד הָיָה הקב"ה שׁוֹמֵעַ קוֹלָן וְיוֹצְאִים שְׁלֵמִים. וְהָיוּ עוֹמְדוֹת בִּתְפִלָּה וְאוֹמְרוֹת להקב"ה, רִבּוֹנוֹ שֶׁל עוֹלָם תְּלֵה לָהֶם עַכְשָׁיו וְתֵן לָהֶם נַפְשׁוֹתֵיהֶם שֶׁלֹּא יֹאמְרוּ יִשְׂרָאֵל הֵן הָרְגוּ אוֹתָן, והקב"ה עוֹשֶׂה תְּפִילָתָן [שמות רבה, פרשה א'].

95

THE BIRTH

Rabbi Eliyahu ha-Kohen of Izmir

[Midwives] should offer the prayer attributed to the [biblical] Hebrew midwives, so that no accident takes place through them. As they go to the house of the woman who is ready to give birth, they should say:

*M*ay it be Your will—great, mighty, awesome God—that no mishap take place through me. And may the merit of this pitiable woman, writhing and shouting out in her travail, be remembered before You. If she bears any sin, forgive and erase it in view of her suffering in the pain of her travail, and let the sound of her cry rise up to the Throne of Your Glory. Seal the mouths of those who would accuse her, and may all who would testify on her behalf enter before You—in accordance with Your attribute of beneficence toward those who are worthy, as well as to those who are not. Take pity on her, for You answer at times of trouble; merciful King Who has mercy upon all, Who saves and delivers, hears and answers.

Shevet Musar, the seventeenth-century work by Rabbi Eliyahu ha-Kohen of Izmir, is a book of ethics that also includes a collection of prayers, liturgical poems, and texts gathered from other books of ethics. Published in more than sixty editions,

תפילת המיילדת על האשה היושבת על המשבר

רבי אליהו הכהן מאיזמיר

דברים השייכים למיילדות העבריות, שתתפללנה

שלא תבֹא תקלה על ידן ויאמרו בעת לכתן

לבית האשה היושבת על המשבר:

יְהִי רָצוֹן מִלְּפָנֶיךָ הַשֵׁם הַגָּדוֹל הַגִּבּוֹר וְהַנּוֹרָא שֶׁלֹּא תָבֹא שׁוּם תַּקָלָה עַל־יָדִי וְיִזָּכְרוּ לְפָנֶיךָ זְכוּת הָאִשָּׁה הָעֲנִיָּה הַזֹּאת אֲשֶׁר תַּחִיל וְתִזְעַק בַּחֲבָלֶיהָ. וְאִם יֵשׁ בָּהּ שׁוּם עָווֹן מְחֹל וּמְרֹק אוֹתוֹ בַּמֶּה שֶׁנִּצְטַעֲרָה בִּכְאֵב הַחֲבָלִים וְתַעֲלֶה קוֹל צַעֲקָתָהּ עַד כִּסֵּא כְבוֹדֶךָ. וּסְתֹם פִּי הַ[מְ]קַטְרְגִים עָלֶיהָ וְיִכָּנְסוּ לְפָנֶיךָ כָּל הַמְלִיצִים בַּעֲדָהּ טוֹב כְּמִדָּתְךָ לְהֵטִיב לְהָגוּן וּלְבִלְתִּי הָגוּן. וְיִכְמְרוּ רַחֲמֶיךָ עָלֶיהָ כִּי אַתָּה עוֹנֶה בְּעֵת צָרָה מֶלֶךְ הָרַחֲמָן וּמְרַחֵם עַל כֻּלָּם פּוֹדֶה וּמַצִּיל שׁוֹמֵעַ וְעוֹנֶה.

Shevet Musar is the only work by Rabbi Eliyahu ha-Kohen of Izmir that appeared during his lifetime, although he wrote over forty books. This prayer is to be recited by midwives prior to delivery.

The midwife should say to the woman:

*K*now, my daughter, that your salvation lies not in my hands, but rather in Him Who created you and formed you. Place your trust in Him, for the key of life has never been given over to any other creature. Therefore, arise, call to your God Who is your Master; worship Him and know that your salvation depends upon Him.

She should then say, before the woman settles onto the birthing stool:

*K*now, my daughter, that at this time a woman is remembered by God. If you have committed some transgression, repent for it; for He is a merciful God Who desires the repentance of the penitent and does not desire their death.

It is proper that before settling onto the birthing stool, the woman accept upon herself some commandment that she will perform with special zeal—such as Rosh Ḥodesh, which is observed by women, or to prepare the wicks for kindling the lamps in the synagogue and study halls, or to spin wool for tzitzit (ritual fringes), to wash *talitot* (prayer shawls), to purchase lanterns for the synagogue, or suchlike.

דְּעִי בִּתִּי שֶׁאֵין הַצְלָחָתֵךְ מְסוּרָה בְּיָדִי כִּי אִם בְּמִי שֶׁבְּרָאָךְ וִיצָרֵךְ וְשִׂימִי בִּטְחוֹנֵךְ בּוֹ שֶׁמַּפְתֵּחַ הַחַיָּה לֹא נִמְסַר לְשׁוּם בְּרִיָּה. לָכֵן קוּמִי קִרְאִי אֶל אֱלֹהַיִךְ שֶׁהוּא אֲדוֹנֵךְ וְהִשְׁתַּחֲוִי לוֹ וּדְעִי שֶׁהַצְלָחָתֵךְ מְסוּרָה בְּיָדוֹ.

וְעוֹד תֹּאמַר לָהּ קֹדֶם שֶׁתֵּשֵׁב עַל הַמַּשְׁבֵּר

דְּעִי בִּתִּי שֶׁבְּעֵת הַזֹּאת הָאִשָּׁה נִפְקֶדֶת וְאִם יֵשׁ אֵיזֶה עֲבֵרָה בְּיָדֵךְ חִזְרִי בָּךְ שֶׁהוּא אֵל רַחְמָן חָפֵץ בִּתְשׁוּבַת הַשָּׁבִים כִּי לֹא יַחְפֹּץ בְּמוֹת הַמֵּת.

וְטוֹב שֶׁתְּקַבֵּל הָאִשָּׁה קֹדֶם שֶׁתֵּשֵׁב עַל הַמַּשְׁבֵּר אֵיזֶה מִצְוָה לִהְיוֹת זְרִיזָה בָּהּ, רֹאשׁ־חֹדֶשׁ שֶׁמַּשְׁמְרוֹת הַנָּשִׁים אוֹ לְקַבֵּל עָלֶיהָ לַעֲשׂוֹת פְּתִילָה לְהַדְלִיק בְּבָתֵּי כְנֵסִיּוֹת וּמִדְרָשׁוֹת אוֹ לִטְווֹת צֶמֶר לְצִיצִית וּלְכַבֵּס טַלִּיתוֹת שֶׁל קֹדֶשׁ וְלִקְנוֹת עֲשִׁישׁוֹת שֶׁל ביהכ״נ וּדְבָרִים דּוֹמִים לָאֵלּוּ.

Thanksgiving After Birth

*"Prepare sufficient milk in my breasts that I may nurse him, and
grant me that I may raise him to fear You and serve You ..."*

[PRAYER BOOK OF YEHUDIT KUTSCHER COEN, ITALY, 1786]

Most standard prayer books include the blessings that are recited
at a circumcision ceremony, which marks the entry of a Jewish
baby boy into the covenant forged between God and Abraham.
It is rare, however, for a prayer book to make any mention of a
ceremony marking the birth of a daughter, though it is customary
for the father of a baby girl to be given an *aliyah* in the synagogue
(i.e., he is called up to the podium and given the honor of reciting
the blessings accompanying a reading from the weekly Torah
portion) on the Shabbat following her birth, and to announce the
baby's name as part of the *Mi Sheberakh* blessing. Among Bukharan
Jews, the congregation accompanies him with a rendition of the
liturgical poem *"Deror Yikra"* ("Freedom shall He proclaim to son
and daughter" by Dunash ben Labrat, 920–990 c.e.), with emphasis
on the recurring suffix *bat* (daughter).

The circumcision ceremony is inherently masculine in character.
Traditionally, its participants are all males: the baby boy, his
father, the *sandek* (godfather), and the mohel (the specially trained
professional who performs the procedure). The other major
participant is the prophet Elijah. This ancient tradition is based
upon a midrash that cites Elijah's apparent questioning of Israel's
loyalty to God: "For the children of Israel have abandoned Your

covenant" (1 Kings 19:10), and teaches that, in response, God decreed that Elijah would be present at every circumcision ceremony and thus witness firsthand the commitment to and continuity of the covenant throughout all generations.

The mother of the baby—along with all other women present—is usually somewhat removed from the actual ceremony. During the Middle Ages, however, various communities developed customs that integrated some degree of feminine participation: The baby was carried into the synagogue by the wife of the *sandek*, or would be passed from one grandparent to the next. Among Italian Jews—contrary to the Ashkenazic practice—it is customary, after the ceremony, to send the goblet of wine over which the blessing had been recited to the mother and the other women present.

The Jewish women of Tripoli observe an ancient custom of gathering at the home of the woman who has given birth on the night prior to her son's circumcision. While the men gather elsewhere to read from the book of the Zohar and recite the full Hallel service, the women crush spices and sing the "song of the book." The custom originated during the religious persecution following the failed Bar Kokhba revolt, when the Romans forbade the performance of Jewish religious ceremonies, including circumcision. The Jews, determined to maintain their custom and to let everyone know that a circumcision was to take place, would produce loud milling noises as a message to the community that a baby boy had been born. The women of Tripoli preserved this custom and to this day, they pound their mortars and pestles on the night preceding a circumcision.

PRAYERS FOLLOWING CHILDBIRTH

Rabbi Eliyahu ha-Kohen of Izmir

*M*ay it be Your will, Lord my God and God of my forefathers, merciful and compassionate King, that as You have saved me from this distress and from this great danger, so You will have pity and grant deliverance from this danger to all the daughters of Abraham, Isaac, and Jacob, the descendants of those who loved You. And as You have delivered me now, so may You grant me a favorable omen—and likewise each time that I shall give birth in the future. Amen; so may it be Your will.

Prayer upon rising from her bed:

*M*ay it be Your will that You prepare food for Your servant, this infant, with an abundance of milk in accordance with his need, and let my heart know the time to nurse in order to provide for him. Let me sleep lightly so that when he cries, my ears may be open and hear him immediately. Guard me that my arm not smother him while I sleep and he die, heaven forfend.

תפילות לאשה לאחר לידה

רבי אליהו הכהן מאיזמיר

יְהִי רָצוֹן מִלְּפָנֶיךָ יְיָ אֱלֹהַי וֵאלֹהֵי אֲבוֹתַי מֶלֶךְ רַחֲמָן וּמְרַחֵם. כְּשֵׁם
שֶׁהִצַּלְתַּנִי מֵהַצָּרָה הַזֹּאת וּמִן הַסַּכָּנָה הָעֲצוּמָה זוֹ כָּךְ יִכָּמְרוּ רַחֲמֶיךָ לְהַצִּיל
מִן הַסַּכָּנָה זוֹ לְכָל בְּנוֹת אַבְרָהָם יִצְחָק וְיַעֲקֹב זֶרַע אוֹהֲבֶיךָ וּכְשֵׁם שֶׁהִצַּלְתַּנִי
עַתָּה כָּךְ עֲשֵׂה עִמִּי אוֹת לְטוֹבָה וּבְכָל פַּעַם שֶׁאֵלֵד אָמֵן כֵּן יְהִי רָצוֹן.

תפילת היולדת בקומה מהמיטה:

יְהִי רָצוֹן שֶׁתַּזְמִין מָזוֹן לְעַבְדְּךָ הַתִּינוֹק הַזֶּה בְּרִבּוּי חָלָב דֵּי מַחְסוֹרוֹ
אֲשֶׁר יֶחְסַר לוֹ וְשִׂים בְּלִבָּבִי הָעֵת שֶׁצָּרִיךְ לְהֵנִיק כְּדֵי לָתֵת לוֹ. וְהָקֵל מֵעָלַי
הַשֵּׁנָה שֶׁבְּעֵת שֶׁיִּבְכֶּה פָּתַח אָזְנִי כְּדֵי לִשְׁמוֹעַ מִיָּד וְתַצִּילֵנִי שֶׁלֹּא תִפּוֹל יָדִי
עָלָיו בְּעֵת הַשֵּׁנָה וְיָמוּת חַס וְשָׁלוֹם.

Prayer of the nursing mother:

Sovereign of the universe: You hear the prayer of all who cry out to You with all their heart and all their soul, who fear and tremble at Your words. Lord, behold—I shall not hold back my lips from thanking and praising Your great Name for all the favors that You have performed for me, rather than repaying me in accordance with my actions. What am I, what is my life, that You should perform so many great deeds and miracles and wonders as You have done, Lord God: saving and delivering me from distress and the travail of the birth pangs of my pregnancy? And You have added further kindness and compassion and benevolence, filling my breasts with milk that will suffice to sustain and nourish the baby, and strength to arise from my bed to thank and praise and honor Your great Name.

At the time when the Holy Temple stood and we were engaged in Your service, I could have fulfilled Your will by bringing the sacrifices that You commanded us in Your Torah to offer and by which we would achieve atonement for our unknowing and knowing transgressions. Now, for our sins and the sins of our forefathers [...] Your holy and glorious Temple is destroyed, and we have neither altar nor priest to atone for us. Therefore, I rely upon Your great mercy by which You have promised to accept the words of our mouths as though they were sacrifices—as it is written: "We shall offer our words instead of calves." So I pour out before You my prayer and supplication and declare the teaching of my offering.

רִבּוֹן הָעוֹלָמִים אַתָּה שׁוֹמֵעַ תְּפִלַּת כָּל־פֶּה הַצּוֹעֲקִים אֵלֶיךָ בְּכָל לְבָבָם וּבְכָל נַפְשָׁם הַיְרֵאִים וְהַחֲרֵדִים אֶל דְּבָרֶיךָ. יְיָ הִנֵּה שְׂפָתַי לֹא אֶכְלָא מֵהוֹדוֹת וּלְשַׁבֵּחַ לְשִׁמְךָ הַגָּדוֹל עַל־כָּל־הַטּוֹבוֹת שֶׁעָשִׂיתָ עִמָּדִי וְלֹא כִּגְמוּלַי הֲשֵׁבוֹתָנִי. וּמָה אֲנִי וּמֶה חַיַּי שֶׁתִּתְעַשֶּׂה עִמִּי כַּמָּה גְדוֹלוֹת וְנִסִּים וְנִפְלָאוֹת כְּמוֹ שֶׁעָשִׂיתָ יְיָ אֱלֹקִים לְהַצִּילֵנִי וּלְמַלְּטֵנִי מִצַּעַר וּמִצִּירֵי חֶבְלֵי יוֹלֵדָה שֶׁל הֵרָיוֹן שֶׁלִּי. וְעוֹד הוֹסַפְתָּ לִי חֶסֶד עַל חֶסֶד וְחֶמְלָה וַחֲנִינָה עָלַי, לָתֵת לִי חָלָב בְּדַדַּי שֶׁיַּסְפִּיק לְהַחֲיוֹת וְלָזוֹן אֶת הַיֶּלֶד [אֶת הַיַּלְדָּה] וְכֹחַ שֶׁיָּכַלְתִּי לַעֲמוֹד מִמִּטָּתִי לְהוֹדוֹת וּלְשַׁבֵּחַ וּלְכַבֵּד אֶת שִׁמְךָ הַגָּדוֹל.

וּבִזְמַן שֶׁהָיָה בֵּית הַמִּקְדָּשׁ קַיָּם וְהָיִינוּ עוֹסְקִים בַּעֲבוֹדָתֶךָ הָיִיתִי יְכוֹלָה לְהַשְׁלִים רְצוֹנֶךָ בְּהַקְרִיב הַקָּרְבָּנוֹת שֶׁצִּוִּיתָנוּ בְּתוֹרָתֶךָ לְהַקְרִיב וּבָהֶם הָיִינוּ מִתְכַּפְּרִים עַל שְׁגָגוֹתֵינוּ וּזְדוֹנוֹתֵינוּ. וְעַתָּה בַּעֲוֹנוֹתֵינוּ וַעֲוֹנוֹת אֲבוֹתֵינוּ יְרוּשָׁלַיִם וְעַמְּךָ לְחֶרְפָּה לְכָל סְבִיבוֹתֵינוּ. וּבֵית קָדְשְׁךָ וְתִפְאַרְתֶּךָ חָרֵב. וְאֵין לָנוּ מִזְבֵּחַ וְלֹא כֹהֵן שֶׁיְּכַפֵּר בְּעַדֵנוּ. לָכֵן נִשְׁעַנְתִּי עַל רוֹב רַחֲמֶיךָ שֶׁאָמַרְתָּ לְקַבֵּל שִׂיחַ שְׂפָתוֹתֵינוּ כְּקָרְבָּנוֹת. כְּמוֹ שֶׁכָּתוּב וּנְשַׁלְּמָה פָרִים שְׂפָתֵינוּ. וְאֶשְׁפּוֹךְ לְפָנֶיךָ שִׂיחִי וְשַׁוְעָתִי וְאֶקְרָא תּוֹרַת קָרְבָּנִי.

OFFERING OF PRAYER
Yiddish

*M*aster of compassion and forgiveness!

I thank and praise You, Lord my God, for having delivered me from the travail of labor and retaining me among the living before You, and for filling me with strength and vigor to arise from my confinement and come before You.

At the time when Your Holy Temple stood in Your holy city, I would have been obligated to ascend to Your Sanctuary, to give thanks before You, and to offer the sacrifices of one who has given birth. Now, for our many sins, with the Holy Temple destroyed, the synagogue is considered our miniature Temple; our prayers substitute for the sacrifices, and our tears replace the wine offerings.

Therefore, I come to plead before You, Sovereign of the world: Accept my entreaty, my request, and my call to Your great Name from the depths of my heart as a meal offering and as a sacrifice. Guard me along with my

It is customary for a woman to recite a special prayer of thanksgiving, such as this *tekhineh*, when visiting the synagogue on Shabbat for the first time after giving birth.

תחינה ליולדת בבואה לבית־הכנסת

אידיש

אָדוֹן הָרַחֲמִים וְהַסְּלִיחוֹת!

מוֹדָה וּמְשַׁבַּחַת אֲנִי לְפָנֶיךָ יְיָ אֱלֹהַי עַל שֶׁהוֹשַׁעְתַּנִי מֵחֶבְלֵי הַלֵּדָה וְהוֹתַרְתַּנִי בֵּין הַחַיִּים לְפָנֶיךָ, וּמִלֵּאתַנִי כֹּחַ וְאוֹן לַעֲמֹד מִמִּטָּתִי וְלָבוֹא לְפָנֶיךָ:

בִּזְמַן שֶׁבֵּית מִקְדָּשְׁךָ הָיָה קַיָּם בְּעִיר קָדְשֶׁךָ, הָיָה מְחוֹבָתִי לַעֲלוֹת אֶל מִקְדָּשְׁךָ, לְהוֹדוֹת לְפָנֶיךָ וּלְהַקְרִיב קָרְבְּנוֹת הַיּוֹלֶדֶת.

וְעַתָּה, בַּעֲווֹנוֹתֵינוּ הָרַבִּים, כְּשֶׁחָרַב בֵּית הַמִּקְדָּשׁ, נֶחְשָׁב לָנוּ בֵּית הַכְּנֶסֶת לְמִקְדָּשׁ מְעַט, וְהַתְּפִילּוֹת חֵלֶף הַקָּרְבָּנוֹת, וְהַדְּמָעוֹת תְּמוּרַת נִסְכֵּי הַיַּיִן.

עַל־כֵּן בָּאתִי לְהִתְחַנֵּן לְפָנֶיךָ, רִבּוֹנוֹ שֶׁל עוֹלָם, קַבֵּל נָא עֲתִירָתִי וּשְׁאֵלָתִי וּקְרִיאָתִי בְּשִׁמְךָ הַקָּדוֹשׁ מֵעֹמֶק לִבִּי כְּמִנְחָה וּכְקָרְבָּן, וְשָׁמֹר אוֹתִי וְאֶת יַלְדִּי מִכָּל רָע, וְתֵן בִּי כֹּחַ וָאֹמֶץ לְגַדְּלוֹ וּלְחַנְּכוֹ בְּדַרְכֵי תּוֹרָתְךָ הַקְּדוֹשָׁה.

child from all evil; imbue me with strength and courage to raise him and educate him in the ways of Your holy Torah.

Bless my husband and me with a good and long life, health, and a good livelihood; and may we educate this child of ours, and our other children, to occupation with Your Torah and fear of Your Name, and to the marriage canopy, good deeds, wealth, and honor. May good fortune and blessing dwell in our home, with no illness, anguish, or sorrow; may only joy and happiness be heard in our midst.

I pray You, God Who formed and created me—accept my thanks and my blessing to You for Your kindness toward me and toward my husband and child thus far, and my plea for the future—that You always bestow kind favors upon us.

May it be Your will, Lord our God, that we soon merit to behold the rebuilding of Your Holy Temple, where we shall perform our obligatory sacrifices with song and praise to Your great Name. Amen, Selah.

וּתְבָרֵךְ אוֹתִי וְאֶת אִישִׁי בְּאֹרֶךְ יָמִים טוֹבִים, בִּבְרִיאוּת וּפַרְנָסָה טוֹבָה,
וְשֶׁנִּזְכֶּה לְחַנֵּךְ יַלְדֵּנוּ זֶה וּשְׁאָר יְלָדֵינוּ לַעֲסֹק תּוֹרָתְךָ וּלְיִרְאָה אֶת שְׁמֶךָ
וּלְחֻפָּה וּלְמַעֲשִׂים טוֹבִים, וּלְעֹשֶׁר וְכָבוֹד, וְיִשְׁכְּנוּ בְּבֵיתֵנוּ מַזָּל טוֹב וּבְרָכָה,
לְלֹא כָּל חֹלִי, יָגוֹן וַאֲנָחָה, וְיִשָּׁמַע בְּבֵיתֵנוּ אַךְ שָׂשׂוֹן וְשִׂמְחָה:
קַבֵּל נָא, יוֹצְרִי וּבוֹרְאִי, הוֹדָאָתִי וּבִרְכָתִי לְךָ עַל חֲסָדֶיךָ עִמִּי וְעִם אִישִׁי
וְיַלְדֵּי עַד הֵנָּה, וּבַקָּשָׁתִי עַל הֶעָתִיד לָבוֹא, שֶׁתִּגְמְלֵנוּ תָּמִיד חֲסָדִים טוֹבִים:
וִיהִי רָצוֹן מִלְּפָנֶיךָ יְיָ אֱלֹהֵינוּ, שֶׁנִּזְכֶּה לַחֲזוֹת בְּקָרוֹב בְּבִנְיַן בֵּית מִקְדָּשֶׁךָ,
וְשָׁם נַעֲשֶׂה לְפָנֶיךָ אֶת קָרְבְּנוֹת חוֹבוֹתֵינוּ בְּשִׁירָה וְהוֹדָיָה לְשִׁמְךָ הַגָּדוֹל,
אָמֵן סֶלָה.

MI SHEBERAKH PRAYER FOR A NEW DAUGHTER

Ashkenazic community of Ferrara

*H*e Who blessed Sarah, Rebecca, Rachel, and Leah, may He bless the daughter born to [insert father's name], whose name will be known in Israel as [insert daughter's name]. May God grant her a worthy spouse and may she merit to see children and grandchildren engaged in Torah, the commandments, and good deeds. May He lengthen her days in goodness and her years in pleasantness. May our Messiah come soon in her days and ours and redeem us, and let us say: Amen.

Many of the Jews expelled from Spain at the end of the fifteenth century found refuge in the Italian city of Ferrara. The welcoming attitude of the rulers of Ferrara toward Jews made it a major center of post-expulsion Jewry and conversos. In 1531, after the Inquisition was initiated in Portugal, an additional wave of Jewish refugees joined the community. Further reinforcements came in the form of the Italian Jews—the "Italino," headed by the Abarbanel family—who were expelled from Naples. Many of the wealthy Jews of Rome, Bologna, and Venice also moved to Ferrara around that time, as did a number of Jews from Germany.

The community of Ferrara developed into the spiritual center of Italian Jewry.

תפילת "מי שברך" לבת הנולדת
קהל האשכנזים בפיראודה

מִי שֶׁבֵּרַךְ שָׂרָה רִבְקָה רָחֵל וְלֵאָה, הוּא יְבָרֵךְ הַיַּלְדָּה שֶׁנּוֹלְדָה לְרַבִּי [פלוני] שֶׁתִּקָּרֵא בְּיִשְׂרָאֵל שְׁמָהּ [פלונית], הַשֵּׁם יְזַכֶּ(נָ)ה לְבֶן גִּילָהּ הָרָאוּי לָהּ וְתִזְכֶּה לִרְאוֹת בָּנִים וּבְנֵי בָנִים עוֹסְקִים בְּתוֹרָה וּבְמִצְוֹת וּמַעֲשִׂים טוֹבִים, יַאֲרִיךְ יָמֶיהָ בְּטוֹב וּשְׁנוֹתֶיהָ בַּנְּעִימִים וּבְיָמֶיהָ וּבְיָמֵינוּ יָבֹא מְשִׁיחֵנוּ בִּמְהֵרָה וְיִגְאָלֵנוּ וְנֹאמַר אָמֵן.

It was here that many of the conversos, including the famous Donna Gracia Nassi, returned to practicing their Judaism openly. In the mid-sixteenth century, Ferrara boasted ten synagogues, several study halls, and a Jewish printing press. The Renaissance atmosphere in Italy created comfortable conditions for Jews. Against the background of this cultural awakening, social and cultural ties between the Jews and their Christian neighbors were strengthened, and a culture of polemic developed between representatives of different religions and philosophies. Many Christians even visited the synagogue to hear sermons by the famous Jewish scholar Rabbi Yehuda Aryeh di Modena, which were delivered in Italian.

MOTHERHOOD CELEBRATION
Shlomit Kislev

Sheheheyanu blessing

A mother who has not yet recited the *Sheheheyanu* blessing following childbirth may do so at this point; the blessing is recited here over the fruit of the new season. Mothers who have not yet recited the *ha-Gomel* blessing also may avail themselves of this opportunity.

*B*lessed are You, Lord our God, King of the universe, Who has given us life and sustained us and allowed us to reach this time.

Kiddush (recited over wine or grape juice)

*B*lessed are You, Lord, sustaining the living with kindness, Who has imparted some of the power of Creation to mortals and has made us partners in the formation of man.

May it be Your will that You renew this life for goodness and blessing,

Gatherings in honor of a woman who has just given birth have existed for years in several different Jewish traditions, including communities in Tripoli, Yemen, Tunisia, and others. In Morocco, the new mother's relatives would gather in her home and hold a *tahdid* ceremony, which included liturgical poems and songs meant to ward off the evil eye. Since the nineteenth century, the *tahdid* ceremony has been elaborated upon and celebrated by groups of Jewish women in Holland, England, and Israel. The version that is presented here is a personal adaptation of a ceremony created by Shlomit Kislev and Ester Yisrael.

שלומית כסלו

ברכת "שהחיינו"

אם שלא ברכה "שהחיינו" לאחר הלידה יכולה לברך כאן.

נברך "שהחיינו" על פרי חדש. אמהות שטרם

ברכו "הגומל" יכולות גם הן להצטרף.

בָּרוּךְ אַתָּה ה' אֱלוֹקֵינוּ מֶלֶךְ הָעוֹלָם שֶׁהֶחֱיָנוּ וְקִיְּמָנוּ וְהִגִּיעָנוּ לַזְּמַן הַזֶּה.

קידוש

בָּרוּךְ אַתָּה ה', מְכַלְכֵּל חַיִּים בְּחֶסֶד, שֶׁחָלַק מִכֹּחַ הַבְּרִיאָה לְבָשָׂר וָדָם וְשִׁתֵּף אוֹתָנוּ בִּיצִירַת הָאָדָם.

"This ceremony," Shlomit Kislev explains, "is a prayer of thanksgiving, supplication, and love toward the Creator of the world, the Father of all mothers. We chose to hold this ceremony, in honor of the mother, specifically after the birth—a sensitive time for many women. We wanted to be partners at a time when mothers need strength and fortitude. This tradition, too, has a mother: in holding this ceremony, we relied upon ancient ceremonies that we had discovered."

for rejoicing and gladness, and for peace; and strengthen us in body and soul to enhance this life.

Blessed are You, Lord our God, King of the universe, Who creates the fruit of the vine.

Grandmother A

The first commandment given to the nation of Israel in the Torah—the sanctification of the months (Exodus 12:1–2), whose essence is the marking of a new beginning each month, may be connected to the first blessing given in the Torah—whose essence is likewise renewal: "Be fruitful and multiply and fill the earth and conquer it" (Genesis 1:28). Rabbi David Kimhi comments on that verse in Genesis as follows: "Being fruitful" means giving birth to children; "multiplying" refers to raising them. And although this is a blessing ... our Sages, of blessed memory, interpret this as a commandment to man. They teach: "A man is commanded to be fruitful and multiply; a woman is not commanded to be fruitful and multiply." The reason for the Hebrew formulation of the words "be fruitful and multiply" in the Torah in the plural, applying to both of them, is because it refers to the blessing.

Grandmother B

Rabbi Kimhi distinguishes two stages—giving birth and raising, and he emphasizes that whereas the woman is not actively commanded to have children, she receives this blessing. Some opinions suggest that the woman need not be commanded to have children because this is in fact her deepest and most profound inherent desire [...] But of course, there is a great need for Divine blessing, both in "being fruitful"—giving birth, and in

יְהִי רָצוֹן מִלְּפָנֶיךָ שֶׁתְּחַדֵּשׁ חַיִּים אֵלּוּ לְטוֹבָה וְלִבְרָכָה, לְשָׂשׂוֹן לְשִׂמְחָה
וּלְשָׁלוֹם.
וְחַזְּקֵנוּ בְּגוּף וּבְנֶפֶשׁ לְהֵיטִיב חַיִּים אֵלּוּ.
בָּרוּךְ אַתָּה ה׳ אֱלוֹקֵינוּ מֶלֶךְ הָעוֹלָם בּוֹרֵא פְּרִי הַגָּפֶן.

סבתא א'

את המצווה הראשונה בתורה, קידוש חודשים, שמהותה ציון
התחלה חדשה מידי חודש, ניתן לקשר לברכה הראשונה בתורה – שאף
היא מהותה התחדשות: "פְּרוּ וּרְבוּ וּמִלְאוּ אֶת הָאָרֶץ וְכִבְשֻׁהָ" [בראשית
א, 28]. אומר רבי דוד קמחי במקום: "הַפְּרִיָּה הִיא הַהוֹלָדָה וְהָרְבִיָּה הִיא
הַגִּדּוּל וְאַע"פ שֶׁהִיא בְרָכָה... רבותינו ז"ל סמכו שהיא מצוה לבני אדם
ואמרו: 'הָאִישׁ מְצֻוֶּה עַל פְּרִיָּה וּרְבִיָּה וְאֵין הָאִשָּׁה מְצֻוָּה עַל פְּרִיָּה וּרְבִיָּה'.
ומה שאמרו פרו ורבו שמשמעותו על שניהם, לענין ברכה נאמר."

סבתא ב'

הרד"ק דן כאן בשני שלבים – ההולדה והגידול – ומדגיש שהאשה
אומנם אינה מצווה כאיש אך היא מבורכת. יש המפרשים שאת האשה
אין צורך לצוות להוליד מכיוון שזהו רצונה היותר פנימי והיותר עמוק,
בבחינת "שתי כליותיה מורות לה". אך כמובן, יש צורך רב בברכת שמים
הן בפרייה בהולדה, והן ברבייה בגידול. ולשם כך בחרנו להתכנס כאן
הערב להיעצר ביחד כדי לברך. לברך אותך [שם האם] על הולדת בתך
החדשה, על שזכית לממש את הקצב הפנימי של חייך וללדת את [שם
התינוקת] לברך אותך – ודרכך גם את [שמות אבי התינוקת, אחיותיה

"multiplying"—raising one's children. And it is for this purpose that we are gathered here, to take a moment together to bless. To bless you, [name of the baby's mother] on the birth of your new daughter, for having merited to bring to realization the inner rhythm of your life and to give birth to [name of baby]; to wish you—and through you also [names of the baby's father, sisters, and brothers]—an easy rearing, with a strong connection to the nation of Israel, both in the rhythm of life and in its substance.

Symbols and blessings

Foods or other sensual stimulants related to and symbolizing motherhood are set out. All of the participants are invited to enjoy the foods, drinks, and spices and to express blessings and good wishes. As is customary on Rosh Hashanah, for each separate food the appropriate good wish is expressed, the relevant blessing is recited, and the food tasted and enjoyed.

Fish (fish-shaped cookies are distributed among all the participants, who recite the blessing):

May it be Your will that we be fruitful and multiply like fish.

Blessed are You, Lord our God, King of the universe, Who creates varied
   types of food.

Apples (slices of apple are distributed to all, who then recite):

"Sustain me with dainties, spread apples about me, for I am sick with love"
   (Song of Songs 2:5).

May it be Your will that love prevail in our house.

Blessed are You, Lord our God, King of the universe, Who creates the fruit
   of the tree.

ואחיה] בגידול טוב, בחיבור חזק לכלל ישראל, הן בקצב החיים והן בתוכנם.

ברכות "יהי רצון"

מניחים מאכלים או גירויים חושיים אחרים, השייכים ליולדת והמסמלים אותה. כל המשתתפים והמשתתפות מוזמנים ליטול חלק בהנאה ובאיחול. כנהוג בראש השנה, נאמר את האיחול ("יהי רצון"), נברך את ברכת הנהנין המתאימה ונהנה!

דגים (מחלקים עוגית קטנת בצורת דגים לכל המשתתפים והמשתתפות, ואומרים):

יְהִי רָצוֹן שֶׁנִּפְרֶה וְנִרְבֶּה כְּדָגִים. בָּרוּךְ אַתָּה ה' אֱלֹקֵינוּ מֶלֶךְ הָעוֹלָם בּוֹרֵא מִינֵי מְזוֹנוֹת.

תפוחים (מחלקים תפוח לכל אחד ואחת, ואומרים):

"סַמְּכוּנִי בָּאֲשִׁישׁוֹת, רַפְּדוּנִי בַּתַּפּוּחִים – כִּי חוֹלַת אַהֲבָה אֲנִי" [שיר השירים ב 5].

יְהִי רָצוֹן שֶׁתִּשְׁרֶה הָאַהֲבָה בְּבֵיתֵנוּ. בָּרוּךְ אַתָּה ה' אֱלֹקֵינוּ מֶלֶךְ הָעוֹלָם בּוֹרֵא פְּרִי הָעֵץ.

שקדים (מחלקים שקדים לכל המשתתפים והמשתתפות, ואומרים):

יְהִי רָצוֹן שֶׁיַּמְשִׁיךְ וְיִפְרְחוּ מַטּוֹתֵיכֶם וְיָנֵץ וְיִגְדַּל יַלְדְּכֶם וְיִשְׁקֹד ה' לְהַרְבּוֹתְכֶם וּלְחַזֶּקְכֶם בְּאַהֲבָתוֹ [על פי במדבר יז].

Almonds (almonds are distributed to all, who then recite):

May it be God's will that your staffs continue to blossom, and that your child grow and flourish, and that God continue [in Hebrew: *yishkod*, derived from the same root as the word for almond—*shaked*] to multiply you and strengthen you in His love (based on Numbers 17.)

Milk (milk is poured for each participant, and the following is recited:)

"Like an infant that must nurse each day—so one must toil in Torah" (Jerusalem Talmud Berakhot, 9).

May it be God's will that just as your child needs you, and you are the source of his sustenance, so may you cleave to the Torah, and may it be the nourishing breast in your life.

Blessed are You, Lord our God, King of the universe, through Whose word everything came into existence.

Spices

May this child be for you a restorer of life (based on Ruth 4:15).

Blessed are You, Lord our God, King of the universe, Who creates varied spices.

The company sings a selection of songs chosen by the new mother.

A discourse on the weekly Torah portion: grandfather.

A Torah insight: aunt.

Speech by the children of the family, the baby's siblings.

חלב (מחלקים חלב לכל אחד ואחת מהמשתתפים ואומרים):

"וּמַה תִּינוֹק צָרִיךְ לִינַק בְּכָל יוֹם, כָּךְ צָרִיךְ לִיגַּע בַּתּוֹרָה"
(ירושלמי, ברכות ט).

יְהִי רָצוֹן שֶׁכְּשֵׁם שֶׁבְּנֵךְ צָרִיךְ לָךְ וְאַת מְקוֹר חַיּוּתוֹ כָּךְ תִּדְבְּקִי בַּתּוֹרָה וְהִיא
תִּהְיֶה לְשַׁד חַיַּיךְ.

בָּרוּךְ אַתָּה ה' אֱלֹקֵינוּ מֶלֶךְ הָעוֹלָם שֶׁהַכֹּל נִהְיָה בִּדְבָרוֹ.

בשמים

בָּרוּךְ אַתָּה ה' אֱלֹקֵינוּ מֶלֶךְ הָעוֹלָם בּוֹרֵא מִינֵי בְשָׂמִים.
"וְהָיָה לָךְ הַיֶּלֶד הַזֶּה לְמֵשִׁיב נָפֶשׁ" (רות ד, 51).

מחרוזת שירים ישראליים

פרשת שבוע: סבא

דבר תורה: דודה

דברים: ילדי המשפחה - אֲחֵי התינוקת

ברכת השלום

ברכה זו נאמרת לאם על ידי כל הסבתות הנוכחות יחדיו [בלשון נקבה]:

יְבָרֶכְךָ ה' וְיִשְׁמְרֶךָ

יָאֵר ה' פָּנָיו אֵלֶיךָ וִיחֻנֶּךָּ

יִשָּׂא ה' פָּנָיו אֵלֶיךָ וְיָשֵׂם לְךָ שָׁלוֹם"

"בְּשֵׁם ה' אֱלֹקֵי יִשְׂרָאֵל: מִימִינִי מִיכָאֵל, מִשְּׂמֹאלִי גַּבְרִיאֵל, מִלְּפָנַי

אוּרִיאֵל, מֵאַחֲרַי רְפָאֵל, וְעַל רֹאשִׁי - שְׁכִינַת אֵל.

This blessing is addressed to the mother by all the grandmothers present:

May God bless you and protect you;

May He cause His face to shine upon you, and be gracious to you;

May God turn His face to you and grant you peace.

In the Name of the Lord God of Israel: on my right—Michael; on
my left—Gabriel; in front of me—Uriel; behind me—Raphael;
and above my head—God's Divine Presence.

The mother now recites aloud Psalm III:

Halleluyah

I shall praise God with all my heart, in the assembly of the upright
and the congregation.

Great are the acts of God, sought by all who seek them.

His work is glorious and magnificent, and His righteousness
endures forever.

He causes His wonders to be commemorated; God is gracious and
merciful.

He gives food to those who fear Him; He remembers His covenant
forever.

He has told His people of the power of His works, to give them
the heritage of the nations.

Truth and justice are the works of His hands; all of His
commandments are everlasting.

They stand forever and ever, made in truth and uprightness.

He sent redemption to His nation, commanding His covenant
forever; holy and awesome is His Name.

"הַלְלוּיָהּ

אוֹדֶה ה' בְּכָל לֵבָב בְּסוֹד יְשָׁרִים וְעֵדָה:

גְּדֹלִים מַעֲשֵׂי ה' דְּרוּשִׁים לְכָל חֶפְצֵיהֶם:

הוֹד וְהָדָר פָּעֳלוֹ וְצִדְקָתוֹ עֹמֶדֶת לָעַד:

זֵכֶר עָשָׂה לְנִפְלְאֹתָיו חַנּוּן וְרַחוּם ה':

טֶרֶף נָתַן לִירֵאָיו יִזְכֹּר לְעוֹלָם בְּרִיתוֹ:

כֹּחַ מַעֲשָׂיו הִגִּיד לְעַמּוֹ לָתֵת לָהֶם נַחֲלַת גּוֹיִם:

מַעֲשֵׂי יָדָיו אֱמֶת וּמִשְׁפָּט נֶאֱמָנִים כָּל פִּקּוּדָיו:

סְמוּכִים לָעַד לְעוֹלָם עֲשׂוּיִם בֶּאֱמֶת וְיָשָׁר:

פְּדוּת שָׁלַח לְעַמּוֹ צִוָּה לְעוֹלָם בְּרִיתוֹ קָדוֹשׁ

וְנוֹרָא שְׁמוֹ: רֵאשִׁית חָכְמָה יִרְאַת ה' שֵׂכֶל טוֹב

לְכָל עֹשֵׂיהֶם תְּהִלָּתוֹ עֹמֶדֶת לָעַד" [תהלים קי"א].

אֶת אֲשֶׁר יֶשְׁנוֹ פֹּה עִמָּנוּ הַיּוֹם... וְאֶת אֲשֶׁר אֵינֶנּוּ פֹּה עִמָּנוּ הַיּוֹם.

קריאת פרשיית הברית מספר דברים לכבודו של הילד החדש ולכבודם של כל הילדים
הגדולים והקטנים אשר עימנו, מתוך תפילה ובקשה על אלה אשר אינם עדיין פה:

"אַתֶּם נִצָּבִים הַיּוֹם כֻּלְּכֶם לִפְנֵי ה' אֱלֹקֵיכֶם רָאשֵׁיכֶם, שִׁבְטֵיכֶם, זִקְנֵיכֶם
וְשֹׁטְרֵיכֶם כֹּל אִישׁ יִשְׂרָאֵל. טַפְּכֶם נְשֵׁיכֶם וְגֵרְךָ אֲשֶׁר בְּקֶרֶב מַחֲנֶיךָ מֵחֹטֵב
עֵצֶיךָ עַד שֹׁאֵב מֵימֶיךָ. לְעָבְרְךָ בִּבְרִית ה' אֱלֹקֶיךָ וּבְאָלָתוֹ אֲשֶׁר ה' אֱלֹקֶיךָ
כֹּרֵת עִמְּךָ הַיּוֹם. לְמַעַן הָקִים אֹתְךָ הַיּוֹם לוֹ לְעָם, וְהוּא יִהְיֶה לְּךָ לֵאלֹקִים
כַּאֲשֶׁר דִּבֶּר לָךְ וְכַאֲשֶׁר נִשְׁבַּע לַאֲבֹתֶיךָ לְאַבְרָהָם לְיִצְחָק וּלְיַעֲקֹב. וְלֹא
אִתְּכֶם לְבַדְּכֶם אָנֹכִי כֹּרֵת אֶת הַבְּרִית הַזֹּאת וְאֶת הָאָלָה הַזֹּאת. כִּי אֶת

The beginning of wisdom is the fear of God; good sense to all who perform [His commandments]; His praise endures forever.

The following excerpt from the book of Deuteronomy, setting out the covenant between Israel and God, is read in honor of the new baby and for all children present with a prayer in memory of those who have passed away:

"You are standing here today, all of you, before the Lord your God—your leaders, your tribes, your elders, and your officers—every man of Israel, your children, your wives, and the stranger in the midst of your camp, from the hewers of wood to the drawers of water, that you may pass into the covenant of the Lord your God and into the oath that the Lord your God forges with you today, in order that He may establish you this day as His nation, and that He may be your God, as He has spoken to you and as He promised to your forefathers—to Abraham, to Isaac, and to Jacob. It is not with you alone that I forge this covenant and this oath: it is with those who are here with us, standing this day before the Lord our God, and with those who are not here with us today." (Deuteronomy 29:9–14)

Bless us, our Father, all of us as one
With the illumination of Your countenance.

"The angel who redeems me from all evil—may he bless the children, and may my name be declared upon them, and the names of my forefathers, Abraham and Isaac, and may they proliferate abundantly, like fish, in the midst of the land." (Genesis 48:16)

אֲשֶׁר יֶשְׁנוֹ פֹּה עִמָּנוּ עֹמֵד הַיּוֹם לִפְנֵי ה׳ אֱלֹקֵינוּ, וְאֵת אֲשֶׁר אֵינֶנּוּ פֹּה עִמָּנוּ הַיּוֹם" (דברים כט 9-14).

בָּרְכֵנוּ אָבִינוּ כֻּלָּנוּ כְּאֶחָד
בְּאוֹר פָּנֶיךָ.

"הַמַּלְאָךְ הַגֹּאֵל אֹתִי מִכָּל רָע יְבָרֵךְ אֶת הַנְּעָרִים וְיִקָּרֵא בָהֶם שְׁמִי וְשֵׁם אֲבֹתַי אַבְרָהָם וְיִצְחָק וְיִדְגּוּ לָרֹב בְּקֶרֶב הָאָרֶץ" (בְּרֵאשִׁית מח 16).

CELEBRATION FOR A DAUGHTER
Sephardic Communities

The following verse is recited:

*M*y dove, who is in the clefts of the rock, in the hidden places of the terrace: Show me your countenance, let me hear your voice, for your voice is sweet and your countenance is beautiful. (Song of Songs 2:14)

If the daughter is the firstborn, the father adds:

*O*ne is my dove, my perfect one; the only one of her mother, the choice one of the one who bore her. The daughters saw her and heralded her; queens and concubines praised her. (Song of Songs 6:9)

Recently, there has been a revival of the custom of holding a celebration in honor of the birth of a daughter. Traditionally, the celebration is known as *zeved ha-bat*, which literally means "the gift of a daughter." Unlike a circumcision, the celebration is not required to be performed at a specific time, so usually it is held at a time that is convenient for the mother. The content of the ceremony differs from one community to the next and from one family to another; the absence of a standardized, formal ceremony allows a diverse array of customs to flourish. The celebration may include the recitation of blessings, biblical verses, psalms,

זֶבֶד הַבַּת

נוסח עדות המזרח

אומרים את הפסוק:

"וְּנָתִי בְּחַגְוֵי הַסֶּלַע, בְּסֵתֶר הַמַּדְרֵגָה
הַרְאִינִי אֶת־מַרְאַיִךְ, הַשְׁמִיעִינִי אֶת־קוֹלֵךְ,
כִּי־קוֹלֵךְ עָרֵב וּמַרְאֵיךְ נָאוֶה": [שיר השירים ב 14].

בלידת בת בכורה אומר האב:

"אַחַת הִיא יוֹנָתִי תַמָּתִי, אַחַת הִיא לְאִמָּה,
בָּרָה הִיא לְיוֹלַדְתָּהּ,
רָאוּהָ בָנוֹת וַיְאַשְּׁרוּהָ מְלָכוֹת וּפִילַגְשִׁים וַיְהַלְלוּהָ": [שיר השירים ו 9].

---

excerpts from classical and contemporary Jewish sources, poetry, brief Torah insights, personal wishes by the participants, or a speech by the baby's mother about the significance of the ceremony. Some ancient traditions that may also be integrated include the planting of a sapling (a cedar for the birth of a boy and a pine for a girl, based on the Babylonian Talmud, Gittin 57a) or the smelling of fragrant spices.

This is the generally accepted formula for a *zeved ha-bat* among Sephardic communities, but it also can serve as the basis for personalized variations.

The *Mi Sheberakh* prayer is recited by the rabbi who is conducting the ceremony:

*H*e Who blessed our matriarchs Sarah, Rebecca, Rachel, and Leah; the prophetess Miriam; Abigail; and Queen Esther, daughter of Abihail—

May He bless this lovely girl—

And let her name be [insert name], daughter of [insert father's name] and [insert mother's name], with good fortune and at a blessed time.

May they raise her in good health, peace, and tranquillity; and may her father and mother merit to witness her joy and her marriage, the birth of sons, wealth, and honor;

And "May they continue to be fruitful in old age, healthy, and vigorous" [a blessing for the grandparents];

And so may it be His will—that they continue to be fruitful in old age, healthy, and vigorous;

And let us say: Amen.

The gathered participants recite Psalm 128:

A song of ascents:

Happy is everyone who fears God and walks in His ways.

For you shall eat the labor of your hands; happy shall you be, and it will be well with you.

Your wife will be like a fruitful vine in the recesses of your house;

Your children—like olive saplings around your table.

Behold, thus shall the man be blessed who fears God.

May God bless you from Zion and may you witness goodness for Jerusalem all the days of your life.

And may you see your children's children, and peace upon Israel.

תפילת "מי שברך" (תפילה מיוחדת שבמהלכה מוענק השם לנולדת) נאמרת על־ידי הרב

עורך הטקס:

מִי שֶׁבֵּרַךְ אִמּוֹתֵינוּ שָׂרָה רִבְקָה רָחֵל וְלֵאָה וּמִרְיָם הַנְּבִיאָה וַאֲבִיגַיִל
וְאֶסְתֵּר הַמַּלְכָּה בַּת אֲבִיחַיִל,

הוּא יְבָרֵךְ אֶת הַיַּלְדָּה הַנְּעִימָה הַזֹּאת,

וְיִקָּרֵא שְׁמָהּ [פְּלוֹנִית] בַּת [פְּלוֹנִי וּפְלוֹנִית] בְּמַזָּל טוֹב וּבִשְׁעַת בְּרָכָה,

וְיַגְדִּלוּהָ בִּבְרִיאוּת שָׁלוֹם, מְנוּחָה,

וְיִזְכּוּ אָבִיהָ וְאִמָּהּ לִרְאוֹת בְּשִׂמְחָתָהּ וּבְחֻפָּתָהּ
בְּבָנִים זְכָרִים עֹשֶׁר וְכָבוֹד

וְעוֹד יְנוּבוּן בְּשֵׂיבָה דְּשֵׁנִים וְרַעֲנַנִּים [לְחַיֵּי הַסָּבִים וְהַסַּבְתּוֹת] וְכֵן יְהִי
רָצוֹן וְעוֹד יְנוּבוּן בְּשֵׂיבָה דְּשֵׁנִים וְרַעֲנַנִּים יִהְיוּ
וְנֹאמַר אָמֵן :

קהל המשתתפים בטקס אומר מזמור קכח בספר תהלים:

שִׁיר הַמַּעֲלוֹת
אַשְׁרֵי כָּל יְרֵא יי הַהֹלֵךְ בִּדְרָכָיו:
יְגִיעַ כַּפֶּיךָ כִּי תֹאכֵל אַשְׁרֶיךָ וְטוֹב לָךְ:
אֶשְׁתְּךָ כְּגֶפֶן פֹּרִיָּה בְּיַרְכְּתֵי בֵיתֶךָ
בָּנֶיךָ כִּשְׁתִלֵי זֵיתִים סָבִיב לְשֻׁלְחָנֶךָ:
הִנֵּה כִּי כֵן יְבֹרַךְ גָּבֶר יְרֵא יי:
יְבָרֶכְךָ יי מִצִּיּוֹן וּרְאֵה בְּטוּב יְרוּשָׁלִָם כֹּל יְמֵי חַיֶּיךָ:
וּרְאֵה בָנִים לְבָנֶיךָ שָׁלוֹם עַל יִשְׂרָאֵל:

127

Some people also add blessings adapted from the seven nuptial blessings or blessings that are meant for special occasions. There is also a custom of quoting excerpts from the Bible and the Midrash describing feminine figures throughout Jewish history. Some families choose to wait for this occasion to announce the baby's name and recite verses from the Song of Songs or Psalms that are associated with the letters of her name.

MOTHER'S PRAYER PRIOR TO
HER SON'S CIRCUMCISION

Rabbi Eliyahu ha-Kohen of Izmir

May it be Your will, Lord my God and God of my forefathers, that just as this child is favored before You now, free of sin and iniquity, so may he always be before You, never blemishing his covenant. May You not lead him into temptation, nor to disgrace. May he be healthy and strong in Your service, and may he always be guided by fear of You. May his mind and his will never turn from studying Your Torah and from performing Your commandments, and may he be wholeheartedly with You to his dying day. Grant him a livelihood from Your hand, and do not make him dependent on mortals, for this would be a barrier for him: he would not be able to serve You while covered with shame and dishonor, reliant on the whim of a miserable, stingy mortal whose gifts are meager—a little here, a little there. And because he would be reliant on others, his mind would

---

According to halacha, circumcision of the infant is the father's responsibility (Babylonian Talmud, Kiddushin 29a). However, the Torah tells us that it was Moses's wife Zipporah who circumcised their son, Eliezer, and by doing so saved her

תְּפִילַת הָאִשָּׁה לִפְנֵי מִילַת בְּנָהּ

רַבִּי אֵלִיָּהוּ הַכֹּהֵן מֵאִזְמִיר

יְהִי רָצוֹן מִלְּפָנֶיךָ יְיָ אֱלֹקַי וֵאלֹקֵי אֲבוֹתַי שֶׁכְּשֵׁם שֶׁהוּא רָצוּי לְפָנֶיךָ
עַכְשָׁיו שֶׁאֵין בּוֹ לֹא חֵטְא וְלֹא עָוֹן כָּךְ יִהְיֶה תָּמִיד לְפָנֶיךָ שֶׁלֹּא יִפְגֹּם
בְּרִיתוֹ. וְאַל תְּבִיאֵהוּ לִידֵי נִסָּיוֹן וְלֹא לִידֵי בִזָּיוֹן. וִיהִי בָּרִיא אוּלָם לַעֲבוֹדָתֶךָ.
וְתָמִיד יִהְיֶה נֶגֶד פָּנָיו יִרְאָתֶךָ. וְלֹא יָסִיר דַּעְתּוֹ וּרְצוֹנוֹ מִלִּמּוּד תּוֹרָתֶךָ
וּמֵעֲשִׂיַּת מִצְוֹתֶיךָ וִיהִי כֵן עִמְּךָ עַד יוֹם מוֹתוֹ. וְתַזְמִין לוֹ פַּרְנַסָתוֹ מִיָּדֶךָ. וְאַל
תְּבִיאֵהוּ לִידֵי בָּשָׂר וָדָם שֶׁזֶּהוּ מָסַךְ מַבְדִּיל לוֹ שֶׁלֹּא יוּכַל לְעָבְדֶךָ בִּהְיוֹתוֹ
מְכֻסֶּה בּוֹשֶׁת וּכְלִימָה לְצָפוֹת לְצַפּוֹת מִיַּד בָּשָׂר וָדָם נָבָל וְקַפְדָן וּמַתְּנָתוֹ מוּעֶטָה
וְעֵיר שָׁם וְעֵיר שָׁם. וְכֵיוָן שֶׁמְּצַפֶּה לַאֲחֵרִים חָכְמָתוֹ נִסְרַחַת וְנַפְשׁוֹ עָלָיו
נֶעֱצֶבֶת וּבְשָׂרוֹ עָלָיו יִכְאָב. לֹא כֵן הַמְקַבֵּל מִיָּדְךָ הַטּוֹבָה הַפְּתוּחָה וְהָרְחָבָה
וְהַמְּלֵאָה. וְלֹא יִצְטָרֵךְ מִן הַבְּרִיּוֹת עַד יוֹם מוֹתוֹ. וּכְשֶׁיִּזְכֶּה לְזִקְנָה יְהִי רָצוֹן
שֶׁלֹּא יָבֹאוּ עָלָיו יִסּוּרִים לֹא כְבֵדִים וְלֹא קַלִּים וְלֹא יֶאֶרְעוּ לוֹ חֳלָאִים בְּחַיָּיו.

---

husband's life (Exodus 4:24–26). The book of the Maccabees similarly notes that
during the Hasmonean period, mothers would circumcise their sons in secret, in
defiance of Antiochus's decree against circumcision.

waste away, his spirit would become disheartened, and his flesh full of pain. Not so the one who receives from Your good, open, generous, and full hand, such that he is not dependent on others until his death. And when he merits old age, may it be Your will that he not be beset with suffering, whether heavy or light, and that no disease befall him during his lifetime. Deliver him from all injury and accidents, that he may always be ready to perform Your will. May he not stumble in any matter in the world; neither in matters of Torah nor in matters of his own need. May no blemish appear in him as a result of illness or injury, and may he reach old age with sons and daughters whom he will see married and occupied with Torah and the commandments. May his death not be the result of severe and unusual illness, and may he come to the Holy One, blessed be He, whole in all of his limbs. Amen. May the words of my mouth and the thoughts of my heart find favor before You, Lord, my Rock and Redeemer.

וְתַצִּילֵהוּ מִכָּל פְּגָעִים וּמִקְרִים רָעִים כְּדֵי שֶׁתָּמִיד יִהְיֶה מוּכָן לַעֲשׂוֹת רְצוֹנֶךָ.

וְאַל יָבֹא לִידֵי שׁוּם מִכְשׁוֹל דָּבָר שֶׁבָּעוֹלָם לֹא בְּדִבְרֵי תּוֹרָה וְלֹא בְּדִבְרֵי

צָרְכוֹ. וְלֹא יִפּוֹל בּוֹ מוּם מֵחֲמַת חֳלִי אוֹ מַכָּה וְהַגִּיעֵהוּ לְזִקְנָה בְּבָנִים וּבָנוֹת

שֶׁיִּרְאֶה בְחֶפְצָן עוֹסְקִים בְּתוֹרָה וּמִצְוֹת. וְלֹא תִהְיֶה מִיתָתוֹ מֵחֳלִי כָבֵד

וּמִשֻׁנֶּה. וְיָבֹא אֶל הַקָּדוֹשׁ בָּרוּךְ הוּא שָׁלֵם בְּכָל אֵבָרָיו אָמֵן: יִהְיוּ לְרָצוֹן

אִמְרֵי פִי וְהֶגְיוֹן לִבִּי לְפָנֶיךָ יְיָ צוּרִי וְגוֹאֲלִי:

III

PRAYERS

for

MOTHERS

UPON BRINGING HER CHILD TO THE *MELAMED* (TORAH TEACHER)

Yiddish

Master of the world: Our Sages, of blessed memory, taught in the holy Gemara—"By what merit do women attain life in the World to Come? By the merit of bringing their sons to ḥeder to learn Torah." Therefore, Lord my God Who is good and Who performs good, I am thankful to You for the gift that You have given me—my sweet child, whom I merit this day to bring for the first time to the heder, to study Your holy Torah.

I ask of You, Sovereign of the world, that You grant my beloved child a good and God-fearing heart to study Your holy Torah, and give him intelligence and insight to understand and comprehend all that he learns from his teachers. Strengthen and fortify all of his limbs for the study of Your holy Torah. Bless the work of our hands to make a comfortable livelihood, so that we shall be able to pay his teachers' fees honorably. May

While the importance of Torah study for girls and women in our times is self-evident, it was not always regarded as such. Halacha historically regarded the formal obligation to engage in Torah study as incumbent upon men, while a woman was required to know only that which pertained to her spheres of practical activity. Nevertheless, reverence for Torah and promoting its study were regarded as central Jewish values. The Talmud (Berakhot 17a) formulated the woman's role in this regard in its assertion that she is rewarded in the World to Come for encouraging her husband and sons to study Torah. More than a thousand years later, Rabbi Yona Girondi (thirteenth century, Spain) reiterates the same idea in his book, *Igeret ha-Teshuva*, addressing the responsibilities of women in his time. He writes: "At the end of her prayers, her principal supplications should be for her sons and

תְּחִנָּה לְאֵם בְּעֵת הֲבָאַת בְּנָהּ אֶל הַמְלַמֵּד

אידיש

רִ בּוֹנוֹ שֶׁל עוֹלָם, חֲכָמֵינוּ זִכְרוֹנָם לִבְרָכָה אָמְרוּ בַּגְּמָרָא הַקְּדוֹשָׁה: "הָנֵי נָשֵׁי בְּמַאי קָא זָכְיָן?"

בְּאֵיזוֹ זְכוּת יְכוֹלוֹת הַנָּשִׁים לִזְכּוֹת לָעוֹלָם הַבָּא? – "בִּזְכוּת שֶׁמּוֹלִיכוֹת אֶת בְּנֵיהֶן אֶל הַחֵדֶר לִלְמוֹד תּוֹרָה". עַל-כֵּן, יי אֱלֹהַי, הַטּוֹב וְהַמֵּטִיב, מוֹדָה אֲנִי לְפָנֶיךָ עַל הַמַּתָּנָה שֶׁנָּתַתָּ לִי, הוּא בְּנִי הַנֶּחְמָד, שֶׁזָּכִיתִי הַיּוֹם לַהֲבִיאוֹ בְּפַעַם רִאשׁוֹנָה אֶל הַחֵדֶר לִלְמוֹד תּוֹרָתְךָ הַקְּדוֹשָׁה:

אֲבַקֵּשׁ מִמְּךָ, רִבּוֹנוֹ שֶׁל עוֹלָם, תָּחֹן אֶת בְּנִי מַחֲמַדִּי בְּלֵב טוֹב וְיִרְאַ לִלְמוֹד תּוֹרָתְךָ הַקְּדוֹשָׁה, וְתֵן בּוֹ חָכְמָה וּבִינָה לְהָבִין וּלְהַשְׂכִּיל כָּל אֲשֶׁר יְלַמֵּד מְרַבּוֹתָיו. חַזֵּק וְאַמֵּץ רמ"ח אֵבָרָיו וּשְׁסָ"ה גִידָיו לִלְמוֹד תּוֹרָתְךָ הַקְּדוֹשָׁה. וּתְבָרֵךְ אֶת מַעֲשֵׂה יָדֵינוּ בְּפַרְנָסָה בְּרֶוַח, כְּדֵי שֶׁנּוּכַל לְשַׁלֵּם שְׂכָרָם שֶׁל הַמְלַמְּדִים בְּכָבוֹד. וְנִזְכֶּה אֲנִי וְאִישִׁי לְגַדֵּל וּלְחַנֵּךְ בְּנֵנוּ זֶה וִשְׁאָר

---

daughters—that they should be God-fearing, and that her sons should be successful in their Torah study."

At the same time, the world of Jewish scholarship has been enriched by many exceptional women. Some were fortunate in having been born into families in which (sometimes for lack of sons) fathers taught their own daughters. Others absorbed their knowledge exclusively within the female domain, with mothers transmitting their living Torah to the next generation.

The women's Torah-study revolution is a significant achievement in the Jewish world, reflecting the changing role of women in religious action, leadership, and education. The feminine voice of scholarship represents not only empowerment and progress, but also the illumination of a rich and vital dimension to the modern Jewish experience.

my husband and I merit to raise and educate this child of ours, and our other children, in comfort and dignity, and may we merit to bring him under the yoke of the commandments, when the time comes, and to watch him enter the wedding canopy, with the spouse worthy of him.

Lord my God, Who is good and Who performs good—just as You protected Joseph, the righteous one, when he ruled over all of the land of Egypt, and guarded him from the evil eye, and gave him favor and grace in the eyes of kings and princes, so may You guard and protect my child from the evil eye, that it should have no control over him, and grant him favor and grace in Your eyes and in the eyes of mortals. May the merit of his study of our holy Torah stand for all of our brethren, the children of Israel, as our Sages of blessed memory taught: "All the world exists only by the merit of the words emanating from the mouths of children in study." And in this merit may You soon bring us the righteous redeemer, speedily in our days. Amen.

יְלָדֵינוּ בְּעֹשֶׁר וּבְכָבוֹד, וְנִזְכֶּה לְהַכְנִיסוֹ בְּעֹל הַמִּצְוֹת בְּהַגִּיעַ זְמַנּוֹ, וְלִרְאוֹתוֹ נִכְנָס לַחֻפָּתוֹ עִם זִוּוּגוֹ הֶהָגוּן לוֹ:

יי אֱלֹהַי, הַטּוֹב וְהַמֵּטִיב, כְּשֵׁם שֶׁגּוֹנַנְתָּ עַל יוֹסֵף הַצַּדִּיק בְּעֵת מָלְכוֹ עַל כָּל אֶרֶץ מִצְרַיִם וְשָׁמַרְתָּ עָלָיו מֵעֵינָא בִּישָׁא, וּנְתַתּוֹ לְחֵן וּלְחֶסֶד בְּעֵינֵי מְלָכִים וְשָׂרִים, כֵּן תִּשְׁמֹר וְתָגֵן עַל בְּנִי מֵעֵינָא בִּישָׁא, שֶׁלֹּא יִשְׁלֹט בּוֹ עַיִן הָרָע, וְתִתְּנֵהוּ לְחֵן וּלְחֶסֶד בְּעֵינֶיךָ וּבְעֵינֵי בְּנֵי אָדָם. וְזִכּוּת לְמוּדוֹ אֶת תּוֹרָתֵנוּ הַקְּדוֹשָׁה יַעֲמֹד לְכָל אַחֵינוּ בְּנֵי יִשְׂרָאֵל, כְּמַאֲמָרָם שֶׁל חֲכָמֵינוּ זִכְרוֹנָם לִבְרָכָה: כָּל הָעוֹלָם אֵינוֹ מִתְקַיֵּם אֶלָּא בִּזְכוּת הֶבֶל פִּיהֶם שֶׁל תִּינוֹקוֹת שֶׁל בֵּית רַבָּן. וּבִזְכוּת זֶה תְּמַהֵר וְתָבִיא לָנוּ גּוֹאֵל צֶדֶק בִּמְהֵרָה בְיָמֵינוּ, אָמֵן:

A DAUGHTER'S FIRST PERIOD

Ruth Lazare

Blessed are You, Lord, for having made me a woman.

During the six days of Creation You formed woman

And every month I recall Your goodness and Your wisdom.

Blessed are You for having granted me my beloved daughter

Whose body You created in wisdom and perfection

And within whom You implanted the power of fertility and
childbirth.

You have joined her to our mothers and matriarchs

In timeless merging of

Pain and knowledge.

תפילת האם שבתה קיבלה מחזור

רות לור

בָּרוּךְ אַתָּה ה׳ שֶׁעֲשִׂיתַנִי אִשָּׁה
בְּשֵׁשֶׁת יְמֵי הַבְּרִיאָה יָצַרְתָּ אֶת הָאִשָּׁה
וּמִדֵּי חֹדֶשׁ אֲנִי זוֹכֶרֶת אֶת טוּבְךָ וְחָכְמָתֶךָ.
בָּרוּךְ אַתָּה שֶׁהֶעֱנַקְתָּ לִי אֶת בִּתִּי הָאֲהוּבָה
שֶׁבָּרָאתָ אֶת גּוּפָהּ בְּחָכְמָה וּבִשְׁלֵמוּת
שֶׁנָּטַעְתָּ בָּהּ אֶת כֹּחַ הַפִּרְיוֹן וְהַהוֹלָדָה.
צֵרַפְתָּ אוֹתָהּ לְאִמּוֹתֵינוּ וְאִמָּהוֹת אִמּוֹתֵינוּ
הַמּוֹסִיפוֹת מִנִּי אָז
גַּם מַכְאוֹב וְגַם דַּעַת.

AT HER SON'S BAR MITZVAH

Fanny Neuda

"It was for this boy that I prayed, and God granted me my
request that I asked of Him. Now I, too, dedicate him to
God; so long as he lives he is devoted to God ..."

[1 SAMUEL 1:27–28]

*T*hank You, my God, for allowing me to celebrate this day: a day
of thanksgiving to You; a day of festivity and joy for me.

My good God, You have granted me the honor of educating and
guiding this boy with maternal love, with gentleness and pleasantness;
to take care of all his needs and to prepare him for the important and
great day when he would enter Your congregation and the gathering of
Your followers, becoming a member of Your nation, a partner in Your
covenant, fulfilling Your commandments and laws. Praise and glory and
thanksgiving for Your kindness and Your goodness.

Do not withhold Your kindness and Your mercy from my child, and
may the joy of Your Torah—whose commandments he assumes upon
himself this day—always fill his entire being. May his soul be illuminated
with the light of truth; arouse his heart to everything that is lofty and
great. May his spirit be strong and courageous, ready to confront and to
triumph over the dangers and challenges that await him in life, and to do
battle against sin and the powers of desire and temptation. Owner of the
heavens and the earth—may Your Name forever guide him in his path,
may his soul be bound up with You, and may all that he acquires be for
Your sake.

תפילת אם בשעת טקס קבלת מצוות של בנה

פאני נוידא

"אֶל־הַנַּעַר הַזֶּה הִתְפַּלָּלְתִּי וַיִּתֵּן ה׳ לִי אֶת־שְׁאֵלָתִי אֲשֶׁר שָׁאַלְתִּי מֵעִמּוֹ:
וְגַם אָנֹכִי הִשְׁאִלְתִּהוּ לַה׳ כָּל־הַיָּמִים אֲשֶׁר הָיָה הוּא שָׁאוּל לַה׳..."

[שמואל א, א 27–28]

תּוֹדָה, אֱלֹהַי, שֶׁנָּתַתָּ לִי לָחֹג אֶת הַיּוֹם הַזֶּה! יוֹם הוֹדָיָה לְךָ, יוֹם חַג
וְשִׂמְחָה לִי!

אֵלִי הַטּוֹב, נָתַתָּ לִי אֶת הַכָּבוֹד לְחַנֵּךְ וּלְהַנְחוֹת אֶת הַנַּעַר הַזֶּה
בְּאַהֲבַת־אֵם, בְּרֹךְ וּבְעֶדְנָה; לִדְאֹג לְכָל מַחְסוֹרוֹ וּלְהָכִין אוֹתוֹ לַיּוֹם הֶחָשׁוּב
וְהַגָּדוֹל, יוֹם שֶׁבּוֹ יָבוֹא בִּקְהָלְךָ וּבִקְהַל מַאֲמִינֶיךָ, יִהְיֶה לְבֶן לְעַמְּךָ, לְבֶן
בְּרִיתְךָ הַמְקַיֵּם אֶת מִצְווֹתֶיךָ וְהִלְכוֹתֶיךָ. הַשֶּׁבַח וְהַהַלֵּל וְהַהוֹדָיָה עַל חַסְדְּךָ
וְטוּבְךָ.

אַל תַּחְסִיר מִיַּלְדִּי אֶת חַסְדְּךָ וְאֶת רַחֲמֶיךָ, וְתֵן שֶׁשִּׂמְחַת תּוֹרָתְךָ,
שֶׁבְּעַל מִצְווֹתֶיהָ הוּא בָּא הַיּוֹם, תְּמַלֵּא תָּמִיד אֶת כָּל יְשׁוּתוֹ. תֵּן שֶׁנַּפְשׁוֹ
תֹּאַר בְּאוֹר הָאֱמֶת, עוֹרֵר אֶת לִבּוֹ לִנְכֹחַ כָּל דָּבָר נַעֲלֶה וְאַדִּיר, וְתֵן שֶׁרוּחוֹ
תִּהְיֶה אֵיתָנָה וְאַמִּיצָה, נְכוֹנָה לְמַאֲבָק וּלְנִצָּחוֹן עַל הַסַּכָּנוֹת וְהַנִּסְיוֹנוֹת
שֶׁנָּכוֹנוּ לוֹ בְּחַיָּיו, וּלְמַאֲבָק בַּחֵטְא וּבְכֹחָם שֶׁל הַתַּאֲווֹת וְהַפִּתּוּיִים. קוֹנֵה
שָׁמַיִם וָאָרֶץ, תֵּן שֶׁלְּעוֹלָם וָעֶד יִהְיֶה שְׁמֶךָ נֵר לְרַגְלָיו וְנַפְשׁוֹ קְשׁוּרָה בְּנַפְשֶׁךָ
וְכָל קִנְיָנוֹ - לְךָ יִהְיֶה.

תֵּן שֶׁהַיֶּלֶד יִגְדַּל לְבִרְכַּת עַמּוֹ וְאַרְצוֹ, לְתִפְאֶרֶת אֱמוּנָתוֹ, לְמַעֲשִׂים
טוֹבִים וּלְטוֹבַת הַכְּלָל.

אֵלִי שֶׁבַּשָּׁמַיִם, הַאֲזִינָה לִתְפִלַּת לֵב אֵם.

143

May this child grow up to earn the blessing of his nation and his country, a credit to his faith, performing good deeds, and contributing to the well-being of society.

My God in heaven, give ear to the prayer of a mother's heart.

May it be Your will that his strength grow and multiply, that his understanding mature, that he develop fully both inwardly and outwardly. Watch over him, my Lord, and preserve his integrity, the clarity of his soul, the tranquillity of his heart and his nature, which at this time fill all of his young and tender being.

May he be a mouthpiece for You all the days of his life, may You withhold nothing from his mouth, and may You lead him by green pastures and by sources of living water.

And to me, my God, grant the joy of watching over my child for many more years, with blessed maternal love and satisfaction, that my son may be a source of joy to me. Amen.

יְהִי רָצוֹן שֶׁיִּגְדַּל וְיִתְעַצֵּם כֹּחוֹ, שֶׁתַּבְשִׁיל בִּינָתוֹ, שֶׁתּוֹכוֹ וּבָרוּ לָעַד
יִתְפַּתְּחוּ בִּמְלוֹאָם. שָׁמְרֵנוּ, אֱלֹהַי, וּנְצֹר אֶת טֹהַר מִדּוֹתָיו, אֶת נִקְיוֹן נַפְשׁוֹ,
אֶת שַׁלְוַת לִבּוֹ וְאֶת אָפְיוֹ שֶׁל יַלְדִּי, שֶׁבְּשָׁעָה זוֹ מְמַלְּאִים אֶת הַוָיָתוֹ הָרַכָּה
וְהַצְּעִירָה. מִי יִתֵּן שֶׁכָּל יְמֵי חַיָּיו יִהְיֶה לְךָ לְפֶה, שֶׁמִּפִּיו לֹא תִּמָּנַע דָּבָר,
שֶׁתּוֹלִיכֵנוּ עַל נְאוֹת דֶּשֶׁא וְעַל מְקוֹרוֹת מַיִם חַיִּים.
וְלִי, אֵלִי, תֵּן אֶת הָאֹשֶׁר לִשְׁמֹר עַל יַלְדִּי עוֹד שָׁנִים רַבּוֹת, בְּאַהֲבַת־אֵם
מְבֹרֶכֶת וּשְׂבֵעַת־רָצוֹן, שֶׁיִּהְיֶה לִי בְּנִי מָקוֹר שֶׁל שִׂמְחָה. אָמֵן.

FOR A SON SERVING IN THE ARMY
Fanny Neuda

"Gird your sword upon your thigh, mighty warrior, your glory and your splendor. In your majesty ride prosperously for the sake of truth and for the cause of righteousness, and may your right hand show you awesome things."
[PSALMS 45:4–5]

*M*y God in the heavens, Lord of Hosts, Who rules with a high hand over the heavens and the earth: I offer my prayer to you from the depths of a mother's heart. My God and God of my forefathers—hear my prayer in Your great mercy. The time has come for my son to join the ranks of those who fight for our country, to maintain its security and to erase the plotting and wickedness that threaten the homeland and its inhabitants. I am thankful to You, my God in heaven, for granting me a child whose limbs are strong, who is able to bear arms in the noble war for our country.

But my maternal heart is fearful and trembles at the thought of the dangers and temptations that surround him. He is young and lacking in experience, far from the teaching of his mother and the guidance of his father. His heart may easily be drawn after some forbidden thing, and come to sin. Therefore I pour out my supplication before You, Almighty God of heaven. Spread Your protection over him, shield him, and surround him, in Your great kindness. Nurture and strengthen within him every refined emotion, every positive intention, every remembrance of parental guidance that is imprinted on his soul, that he may always have in mind

תפילת אם שבנה משרת בצבא

פאני נידא

"חֲגוֹר־חַרְבְּךָ עַל־יָרֵךְ גִּבּוֹר, הוֹדְךָ וַהֲדָרֶךָ; וַהֲדָרְךָ צְלַח רְכַב עַל־דְּבַר־
אֱמֶת וְעַנְוָה־צֶדֶק וְתוֹרְךָ נוֹרָאוֹת יְמִינֶךָ"

[תהלים מה 4–5]

אֵלִי שֶׁבַּשָּׁמַיִם, אֵל צְבָאוֹת, הַמּוֹשֵׁל בְּיָד רָמָה בַּשָּׁמַיִם וּבָאָרֶץ, אֵלֶיךָ
אֶשָּׂא תְּפִלָּתִי מִמַּעֲמַקֵּי לֵב אֵם. אֱלֹהַי וֵאלֹהֵי אֲבוֹתַי, שְׁמַע תְּפִלָּתִי בְּרַחֲמֶיךָ
הָרַבִּים. מָלְאוּ יְמֵי בְּנִי לְהִצְטָרֵף לְשׁוּרוֹת הַלּוֹחֲמִים לְמַעַן אַרְצֵנוּ, לִשְׁמֹר עַל
בִּטְחוֹנָהּ וּלְהָסִיר מִרְמָה וְרֶשַׁע הַמְאַיְּמִים עַל הַמְּכוֹרָה וְיוֹשְׁבֶיהָ. מוֹדָה אֲנִי
לְפָנֶיךָ, אֵלִי שֶׁבַּשָּׁמַיִם, שֶׁנָּתַתָּ לִי יֶלֶד שֶׁאֵבָרָיו חֲסֻנִּים, שֶׁנָּכוֹן לָשֵׂאת נֶשֶׁק
בְּמִלְחֶמֶת מִצְוָה עַל אַרְצֵנוּ.

אַךְ לִבִּי, לֵב אֵם, חָרֵד וְרוֹטֵט בְּזָכְרִי אֶת הַסַּכָּנוֹת וְהַפִּתּוּיִּים הַסּוֹבְבִים
אוֹתוֹ. צָעִיר וַחֲסַר נִסָּיוֹן הוּא, רָחוֹק מִתּוֹרַת אִמּוֹ וּמִמּוּסַר אָבִיו. עַל־נְקַלָּה
עָשׂוּי לִבּוֹ הַצָּעִיר לִנְהוֹת אַחַר דְּבַר עֲבֵרָה וְלָבוֹא לִידֵי חֵטְא; עַל כֵּן אֶשְׁפֹּךְ
תְּחִנָּתִי לְפָנֶיךָ, אֵל שָׁמַיִם כֹּל־יָכוֹל. פְּרֹשׂ עָלָיו אֶת חָסוּתְךָ, הֱיֵה לוֹ לְמָגֵן
וַעֲטֹף אוֹתוֹ בְּרֹב חַסְדְּךָ. אַמֵּץ וְחַזֵּק בּוֹ כָּל הַרְגָּשָׁה נַעֲלָה, כָּל כַּוָּנָה טוֹבָה,
כָּל זִכָּרוֹן שֶׁל מוּסַר הוֹרִים הַטָּבוּעַ בְּנַפְשׁוֹ, שֶׁלְּעוֹלָם יַעַמְדוּ לְנֶגֶד עֵינָיו
תּוֹרַת הַמּוּסָר וְיִרְאַת הָאֵל, שֶׁלֹּא יִתְנַכֵּר לֶאֱמוּנַת אֲבוֹתָיו, שֶׁחַיֵּי הַצָּבָא
וְהַנֶּשֶׁק לֹא יְקַשּׁוּ אֶת לִבּוֹ, שֶׁקּוֹלוֹת הַפִּתּוּיֵי הַזְּדוֹנִיִּים שֶׁל הַחֵטְא לָעוֹלָם לֹא
יִשְׁלְטוּ בּוֹ.

proper ethics and fear of God, that he not alienate himself from the faith of his forefathers, that military life and arms not harden his heart, that the insidious temptations of sin never control him.

Bless him, my God, with the wisdom and strength to behave conscientiously, to fulfill his difficult tasks properly. Let him not come to betray, nor to transgress, nor fall into error or doubt. Cause him to obey his commanders, and be loyal and ready to sacrifice, dedicated to his flag.

And on the day that he is called out to the battlefield, where death reaps its harvest—there, my God in heaven, spread Your mercy over him. May Your kindness be his shield and armor. Give strength to his arms, imbue his heart with courage, and let the remembrance of the mighty warriors of Israel guide his heart, that he may go out to battle gladly and with purpose, and with courage and presence of mind defend the glory of his God and his loyalty to the ruler, to his nation, and to his country.

My God in heaven, listen to my prayer. Let his mother's blessing hover over him. May this blessing be a protective banner, and at the conclusion of his service may he return, whole in body and spirit, decorated for having carried out his obligations, bringing gladness to my heart and praise and glory to Your great Name. Amen.

בָּרְכֵנוּ, אֱלֹהַי, בְּחָכְמָה וּבְכֹחַ לִשְׁקֹד עַל מַעֲשָׂיו, לְמַלֵּא תַּפְקִידָיו הַקָּשִׁים כַּהֲלָכָה. שֶׁלֹּא יָבוֹא לִידֵי בְגִידָה אוֹ עֲבֵרָה, שֶׁלֹּא יָבוֹא לִידֵי טָעוּת אוֹ פִקְפּוּק. עֲשֵׂה שֶׁיִּשְׁמַע בְּקוֹל מְפַקְּדָיו, נֶאֱמָן וְנָכוֹן לְהַקְרִיב, מָסוּר לְדִגְלוֹ.

וּבַיּוֹם שֶׁיִּקָּרֵא לָצֵאת אֶל שְׂדֵה הַקְּרָב, שָׁם קוֹצֵר הַמָּוֶת אֶת יְבוּלוֹ, שָׁם, אֵלִי שֶׁבַּשָּׁמַיִם, פְּרֹשׂ עָלָיו אֶת רַחֲמֶיךָ. מִי יִתֵּן וְיִהְיֶה לוֹ חַסְדְּךָ מָגֵן וְשִׁרְיוֹן; שָׁם חַזֵּק אֶת זְרוֹעוֹ, צוּק אֹמֶץ בְּלִבּוֹ, וְתֵן לְזִכְרוֹן גִּבּוֹרֵי יִשְׂרָאֵל לְצַוּוֹת עַל חָזֵהוּ, שֶׁיֵּצֵא לַקְּרָב בְּשִׂמְחָה וּבְהִתְלַהֲבוּת וּבְאֹמֶץ־לֵב וּבְקֹר־רוּחַ יִשְׁמֹר עַל כְּבוֹד אֱלֹהָיו וְעַל נֶאֱמָנוּתוֹ לַשַּׁלִּיט, לְעַמּוֹ וּלְאַרְצוֹ.

אֵלִי שֶׁבַּשָּׁמַיִם הַאֲזִינָה לִתְפִלָּתִי, תֵּן לְבִרְכַּת הָאֵם לְרַחֵף מֵעָלָיו, תִּהְיֶה זֹאת הַבְּרָכָה לְנֵס מְגוֹנֵן, וּבְתֹם שֵׁרוּתוֹ יָשׁוּב, בָּרִיא בְּגוּפוֹ וּבְנַפְשׁוֹ, עָטוּר אוֹת הוֹקָרָה עַל מִלּוּי חוֹבוֹתָיו, לְשִׂמְחַת לִבִּי, לְשַׁבֵּחַ וּלְהַלֵּל לְשִׁמְךָ הַגָּדוֹל. אָמֵן.

PRAYER OF A MOTHER-IN-LAW
Shulamit Eisenbach

*H*ashem, Creator of the world: Nothing is hidden from You;

Search my innermost parts and imbue me with a good spirit.

Grant me favor in the eyes of my sons-in-law and my daughters,

and grace with my sons and daughters-in-law.

Let me see no flaws in them, nor hear any faults;

Let me feel no resentment toward them, nor act in a miserly way;

Let no hint of jealousy be aroused in me, nor any vice lurk within.

Let me always encounter them at a good time, and nourish them

    with warmth and love.

May they raise their children with joy and earn a comfortable living;

May they be blessed from the Source of blessing—from Your

    generous and blessed hand.

Let me be worthy of the greatest kindness, that I may give thanks

    and perform goodness.

I place my faith in You, my God, and spread my prayer before You;

Let my lips utter prayer to You in awe and praise.

This unique prayer addresses the complex relationship between a mother-in-law and her daughter-in-law. The Bible presents us with two strikingly different paradigms for this relationship. Ruth, Naomi's daughter-in-law, is described as being better to her "than seven sons." The prophet Micah, on the other hand, depicts a far more fraught example, in which "Daughter shall rise up against her mother; a daughter-in-law against her mother-in-law..."

תְּפִלַּת הֶחָמוֹת

שׁוּלַמִּית אַייזנבך

ה' בּוֹרֵא הָעוֹלָם, מִלְּפָנֶיךָ אֵין נֶעֱלָם.

בְּחַן כִּלְיוֹתַי וְלִבִּי, שִׂים רוּחַ טוֹבָה בְּקִרְבִּי.

תֵּן חִנִּי בְּעֵינֵי חֲתָנַי וּבְנוֹתַי, וְחֶסֶד לִפְנֵי בָּנַי וְכַלּוֹתַי.

שֶׁלֹּא אֶרְאֶה בָּם כָּל נְגָעִים, שֶׁלֹּא אֶשְׁמַע דְּבָרִים רָעִים.

שֶׁלֹּא תְהֵא עֵינִי בָּם צָרָה, שֶׁלֹּא תְהֵא יָדִי קְצָרָה.

שֶׁלֹּא יִתְעוֹרֵר בִּי שֶׁמֶץ קִנְאָה, שֶׁלֹּא תִּמָּצֵא בִּי כָּל רִשְׁעָה.

שֶׁאֶמְצָאֵם תָּמִיד בְּשָׁעָה טוֹבָה, שֶׁאַשְׁפִּיעַ עֲלֵיהֶם חֹם וְאַהֲבָה.

שֶׁיִּזְכּוּ לְגַדֵּל יַלְדֵיהֶם בְּשִׂמְחָה, שֶׁתְּהֵא פַּרְנָסָתָם מְצוּיָה בִּרְוָחָה.

שֶׁיִּזְכּוּ לְהִתְבָּרֵךְ מִמְּקוֹר הַבְּרָכָה, תַּחַת יָדְךָ הָרְחָבָה וְהַבְּרוּכָה.

שֶׁאֶהְיֶה רְאוּיָה לַחֶסֶד הַגָּדוֹל, שֶׁאוּכַל לְהוֹדוֹת וְטוֹבָה לִגְמֹל.

בְּךָ אֱלֹקַי אֶבְטַח, בַּקָּשָׁתִי לְפָנֶיךָ אֶשְׁטַח.

שְׂפָתַי תַּבַּעְנָה תְּפִלָּה, לְךָ נוֹרָא תְּהִלָּה.

This prayer was composed by Shulamit Eisenbach on the eve of the marriage of her elder son in 1984. "I felt a need to utter a prayer that I could find nowhere in all of the traditional sources," Shulamit explained. "As the mother of two sons, it was a significant moment, representing the gift of a daughter—or the relinquishing of a son. Only fourteen years after writing the prayer, having succeeded in building a friendly and loving bond with my daughter-in-law, did I dare to publish it."

IV

WOMEN'S
MITZVOT

Lighting Candles

On Friday evenings before sunset, candles are lit to signal the start of Shabbat. According to Maimonides, "Both men and women are obligated to have a lit candle in their homes on Shabbat … but women have a special obligation in this regard." Whereas the husband traditionally participates in the ritual by preparing the candles and the wicks for lighting, it is the woman of the house who is honored with lighting the candles at the proper time and reciting the blessing over them. The custom is to light at least two candles, one commemorating the commandment to "Remember the Shabbat day to sanctify it" and the other for the commandment to "Observe the Shabbat day to sanctify it." In some communities, a mother lights the customary two candles and an additional candle for each of her children.

Whereas men traditionally usher in the Shabbat through communal prayer by participating in the *Kabbalat Shabbat* ("welcoming the Shabbat") prayer service in the synagogue, women are given the privilege of welcoming Shabbat into the private domain—the home. Thus, the Talmud explains, Shabbat enters women's homes of its own will, as it were, whereas men must leave their houses in order to welcome it.

The book *Eshet Hayil* by Rabbi Yaakov Mildola lists several reasons for lighting Shabbat candles, drawing on Talmudic sources for each. According to these sources, their light brings domestic harmony (*shalom bayit*), enhances the enjoyment of Shabbat, and further honors the sanctity of the day.

In previous centuries, the blessing for Shabbat candles generally did not appear in the standard prayer book. It was more commonly found in collections of women's prayers and supplications.

The blessing is not recited aloud, but rather in a whisper. According to Rabbeinu Tam, this practice is based on Hannah's prayer, concerning which we are told: "Only her lips moved, but her voice could not be heard."

Blessed are You, Lord our God, King of the universe,
Who has sanctified us with His commandments
And commanded us to light Shabbat candles.

LIGHTING SHABBAT CANDLES
Yiddish

*F*or the honor of the blessed God, for the honor of the holy commandment, for the honor of the holy Shabbat that our Lord has given us, instructing us concerning this beloved commandment: May it be Your will that I be able to fulfill it properly and that I be considered as having fulfilled the 613 commandments among all of Israel. Amen.

In accordance with Ashkenazic custom, the candles
are lit, and then the blessing is recited.

*B*lessed are You, Lord our God, King of the universe, Who has sanctified us with His commandments and commanded us to light Shabbat candles.

After lighting the Shabbat candles and reciting the blessing, it is customary to offer a personal, private prayer for oneself, one's household, and all of the Jewish nation. Each woman elaborates with her own individual supplications.

תחינה לפני הדלקת הנרות

אידיש

לְכְבוֹד הַשֵּׁם יִתְבָּרָךְ, לִכְבוֹד הַמִּצְוָה הַקְּדוֹשָׁה, לִכְבוֹד שַׁבַּת קֹדֶשׁ שֶׁנָּתַן לָנוּ אֲדוֹנֵינוּ, וְצִוָּנוּ עַל הַמִּצְוָה הַחֲבִיבָה הַזֹּאת. יְהִי רָצוֹן שֶׁאוּכַל לְקַיְּמָהּ בָּאֱמֶת, וְיֵחָשֵׁב לִי כְּאִילוּ קִיַּמְתִּי תַּרְיַ״ג מִצְוֹת בְּתוֹךְ כָּל כְּלָל יִשְׂרָאֵל, אָמֵן:

בָּרוּךְ אַתָּה יְיָ אֱלֹהֵינוּ מֶלֶךְ הָעוֹלָם, אֲשֶׁר קִדְּשָׁנוּ בְּמִצְוֹתָיו וְצִוָּנוּ לְהַדְלִיק נֵר שֶׁל שַׁבָּת:

רִבּוֹנוֹ שֶׁל עוֹלָם, בִּזְכוּת שֶׁקִיַּמְתִּי שָׁלֹשׁ הַמִּצְוֹת שֶׁצִוִּיתָ לָנוּ הַנָּשִׁים –
נִדָּה, חַלָּה וְהַדְלָקַת הַנֵּר – תִּהְיֶינָה הַמִּצְוֹת הָאֵלֶּה מְלִיצֵי יֹשֶׁר לִפְנֵי כִּסֵּא כְבוֹדֶךָ, שֶׁאֶזְכֶּה לְבָנִים צַדִּיקִים וְטוֹבִים, וְיִהְיוּ תַלְמִידֵי חֲכָמִים וְיָבִינוּ סוֹדוֹת תּוֹרָתְךָ הַקְּדוֹשָׁה, וְתִתְּנֵם לְחֵן וּלְחֶסֶד וּלְרַחֲמִים בְּעֵינֶיךָ וּבְעֵינֵי כָל רוֹאֵיהֶם, וְנִזְכֶּה אֲנִי וּבַעֲלִי לְגַדְּלָם בְּעֹשֶׁר וּבְכָבוֹד:
יְהִי רָצוֹן מִלְּפָנֶיךָ יְיָ אֱלֹהֵינוּ וֵאלֹהֵי אֲבוֹתֵינוּ, שֶׁיִּבָּנֶה בֵּית הַמִּקְדָּשׁ בִּמְהֵרָה בְיָמֵינוּ וְתֵן חֶלְקֵנוּ בְּתוֹרָתֶךָ, וְשָׁם נַעֲבָדְךָ בְּיִרְאָה כִּימֵי עוֹלָם וּכְשָׁנִים קַדְמוֹנִיּוֹת:

$\mathcal{M}$aster of the universe: By the merit of my having performed the three commandments that You have commanded us women—family purity, separation of challah, and lighting candles—may these commandments be advocates on my behalf before Your throne of glory, so that I may merit children who are righteous and good, and who will be learned scholars and understand the secrets of Your holy Torah. May You grant them favor and grace and mercy in Your sight and in the sight of all who behold them, and may my husband and I merit to raise them in wealth and honor.

May it be Your will, Lord our God and God of our forefathers, that the Holy Temple be rebuilt soon, in our times. Grant us our share in Your Torah, and we shall serve You there in awe, as in days of old and in former years.

LIGHT OF JOY

Ladino

To fulfill the commandment

That You have commanded us,

To light candles

On holy days:

May it be Your will

Lord our God

And God of our forefathers

That You multiply in my home

The light of joy

And blessing and peace

And good, unclouded life,

And that You illuminate our souls

This prayer over Shabbat candles was conveyed by Allegra ben-Melekh of Netanya, who was born in Turkey in 1920. In keeping with Sephardic practice, the prayer, concluding with the blessing, is recited prior to lighting the candles.

תפילה לפני הדלקת נרות שבת

לדינו

כְּדֵי לְמַלֵּא אֶת הַמִּצְוָה   פור אפ׳ירמאר לה אינקומינדאנסה

שֶׁצִּוִּיתָנוּ   קי נוס אינקומאנדאסטיס

כְּדֵי לְהַדְלִיק נֵר   פור אינסינדיר קאנדילה

בְּיָמִים קְדוֹשִׁים   אין דיאס סאנטוס

יְהִי רָצוֹן מִלְּפָנֶיךָ   סיאה ב׳ילונטאד די טי

ה׳ אֱלֹהֵינוּ   ה׳ נואיסטרו דייו

וֵאלֹהֵי אֲבוֹתֵינוּ   אי דייו די נואיסרוס פאדריס

שֶׁתַּרְבֶּה בְּבֵיתִי   קי מוג׳יגואיס אין מי קאזה

אוֹר שֶׁל שִׂמְחָה   לוז די אליגריאה

וּבְרָכָה וְשָׁלוֹם   אי בינדיסיון אי פאז

וְחַיִּים טוֹבִים וּבְהִירִים   אי ב׳ידאס בואינאס אי קלאראס

וְתָאִיר אֶת נִשְׁמוֹתֵינוּ   אי ארילומבריס נואיסטראס אלמאס

בְּאוֹר פָּנֶיךָ   קון לוז די טוס פ׳אסיס

וְשִׂמְחָה [תִּתֵּן]   אי אליגריאה

בְּמִשְׁפַּחְתֵּנוּ   אין נואיסטרה פ׳אמיאה

בָּרוּךְ אַתָּה ה׳ אֱלֹהֵינוּ   ב׳ינדיג׳ו טו ה׳ נואיסטרו דייו

מֶלֶךְ הָעוֹלָם   ריי די איל מונדו

אֲשֶׁר קִדְּשָׁנוּ   קי נו סאנטיפ׳יקו

בְּמִצְוֹתָיו   אין סוס אינקומינדאנסאס

וְצִוָּנוּ לְהַדְלִיק   אי נוס אינקומינדו פור אינסינדיר

נֵר שֶׁל שַׁבָּת.   קאנדילה די שבת.

With the radiance of Your countenance

And [grant] joy

Within our family.

Blessed are You, Lord our God

King of the universe

Who has sanctified us

With His commandments

And commanded us to light

Shabbat candles.

YEMENITE PRAYER AFTER
CANDLE LIGHTING

O, my Master; save us and deliver us and have mercy upon us, and
have mercy upon my children and their father. Imbue them with wisdom,
elevate their path, and smooth their life's trails. Grant them favor and
acceptance, endow them with complete health, and fulfill their wishes.
Keep troubled times from them, and allow no tormentor or enemy
to prevail over them. Guide them in Your way, to observe the Torah.
Please, God, watch over them. (Some add: "Blessed is He Who sanctifies
Shabbat.")

Archaeological evidence indicates that a Jewish community has existed in Yemen from
as early as the Second Temple period or perhaps even earlier. The Yemenite Jewish
community was always relatively isolated: Although some connection was maintained
between the spiritual leaders of Yemenite Jewry and the other major Jewish communities of the world, the sheer distance between them left its mark on the Yemenite customs and prayer tradition, which remain quite distinctive even to this day.

Rabbi Yosef Kapah (1917–2000, a leader of Yemenite Jewry in Israel and a
foremost expert on the writings of Maimonides) devoted one of the six chapters
of his compilation of folklore, *Halikhot Teiman*, to Yemenite home life. Most of this
chapter focuses on rituals and customs pertaining to women, such as arranging
marriages, wedding customs, childbirth, and women's clothing. It is clear from his
writings that the Yemenite Jewish home was the matriarch's kingdom; the mother
was responsible for teaching her children, taking care of the household and the

הַדְלָקַת נֵר שַׁבָּת בָּעֵדָה הַתֵּימָנִית

עַל-פִּי הָרַב קָאפַח

דּוֹי רִבּוֹנִי, הַצִּילֵנִי וּמַלְּטֵנִי וְרַחֵם עָלֵינוּ, וְרַחֵם עַל בָּנַי וַאֲבִיהֶם. חָנוֹן אֶת דַּעְתָּם וְרוֹמֵם דַּרְכָּם וְהָקֵל מְסִלּוֹת חַיֵּיהֶם, וְתֵן לָהֶם חֵן וְקִבּוּל, וְתֵן לָהֶם בְּרִיאוּת הַשְּׁלֵמָה וּמַלֵּא מִשְׁאֲלוֹתֵיהֶם וּדְחֵה מִפְּנֵיהֶם הַשָּׁעוֹת הָרָעוֹת, וְאַל תַּגְבִּיר עֲלֵיהֶם צַר וְאוֹיֵב וְהַדְרִיכֵם בְּדַרְכְּךָ לִשְׁמוֹר אֶת הַתּוֹרָה. אָנָּא הָאֱלֹהִים, הַשְׁגִּיחַ (וְיֵשׁ הַמְסַיְּמוֹת: בָּרוּךְ מְקַדֵּשׁ הַשַּׁבָּת).

---

extended family, and overseeing all family ceremonies. Yemenite Jewish tradition accords the matriarch the ability to influence her children's success through her prayers: A person who enjoys great success is described as one "blessed by his mother." The Yemenite woman's status remained intact even if she was widowed; in accordance with biblical law, the *ketubbah* (marriage document), with its conditions for the wife's maintenance, had first lien on the husband's estate.

Most Yemenite synagogues did not feature a section built specifically for women, although women—who were generally illiterate—frequented the synagogue to listen to the prayer service and the reading from the Torah.

Rabbi Kapaḥ describes how, following candle lighting on Friday evenings, Yemenite women would "sit in the room where they had lit the candles and enjoy the fragrance of the herbs that they would hold." This custom is known as *shimmur ha-nerot*, which literally means "watching the candles."

"THAT WHICH I KNOW NOT HOW TO ASK"

Conversos of Portugal

Prayer while preparing the wicks for Shabbat candles:

*M*ay the pleasantness of the Lord [prevail]—an exceedingly holy pleasantness.

I pray You, Lord: I knew not how to observe Your holy Torah, but now that I know, comfort me well through my observance of Your holy Torah. So may You watch over me and protect me, and grant me that which I know not how to ask of You: salvation for my soul and graciousness, that I may serve and exalt the God of the heavens. Amen. [...]

Blessing for the candles:

*B*lessed is the Almighty, my God, my Master, Who has commanded us with His blessed and holy commandments, that we should

---

Women held a special status in converso communities. The political, cultural, and religious reality of the Iberian Peninsula during the late fifteenth century and the sixteenth century chased religious practice from the public sphere into the hidden recesses of the home. There, women became guardians of Jewish continuity and played a unique role in transmitting the tradition to younger generations.

The iron arm of the Inquisition turned a living tradition into shards of memories. The connection between the new conversos and the unbroken Jewish tradition weakened with the years. Eventually, observance of Shabbat was limited to lighting candles behind closed doors. The blessing and prayers recorded here, which could only be transmitted orally, came to include errors; nevertheless, their similarity to the formulations one would find in a contemporary prayer book is remarkable.

ברכת נרות שבת

לפי מנהג אנוסי פורטוגל

תפילה בעת הכנת פתילות לנר השבת:

הִי נֹעַם אֲדֹנָי, נֹעַם קָדוֹשׁ מְאֹד.
אָנָּא אָדוֹן, לֹא יָדַעְתִּי לִשְׁמֹר אֶת תּוֹרָתְךָ הַקְּדוֹשָׁה, אֲבָל עַכְשָׁו שֶׁאֲנִי
יוֹדַעַת, נַחֲמֵנִי הֵיטֵב עַל יְדֵי מַה שֶּׁאֶשְׁמֹר אֶת תּוֹרָתְךָ הַקְּדוֹשָׁה. וְכֵן
תִּשְׁמְרֵנִי וְתָגֵן עָלַי, וְתֶן לִי מַה שֶּׁאֵינֶנִּי יוֹדַעַת לְבַקֵּשׁ מִמְּךָ: יְשׁוּעָה לְנַפְשִׁי
וְחֶסֶד לְמַעַן אֶעֱבֹד וַאֲרוֹמֵם אֶת אֱלֹהֵי הַשָּׁמַיִם. אָמֵן וְכוּ'.

ברכת הנר:

רוּךְ הָאֵל, אֱלֹהַי, אֲדוֹנִי שֶׁלִּי, אֲשֶׁר צִוָּנוּ בְּמִצְווֹתָיו הַמְבֹרָכוֹת
וְהַמְקֻדָּשׁוֹת שֶׁנַּדְלִיק [וְהָיוּ שֶׁאָמְרוּ: שֶׁנַּעֲשֶׂה] אֶת הַנֵּר הַזֶּה כְּדֵי לְהָאִיר

The life story of the Portuguese converso Donna Gracia provides a fascinating
glimpse into the world of the conversos. Born into Lisbon's high society in the
sixteenth century, Donna Gracia was baptized following her family's forced
conversion to Christianity. She became one of the wealthiest women in the world,
wielding political influence and devoting her life to expansive acts of philanthropy,
especially toward crypto-Jews seeking to escape the Inquisition.

Donna Gracia became aware of her Jewish heritage at the time of her bat
mitzvah. It was then that she discovered that her original name had been Hannah
Nassi. At the age of eighteen, she married Francisco Mendes, a converso banker.
They were married in a traditional Jewish ceremony held in secret, and in a huge,
public ceremony in a church. Eight years later, Donna Gracia was widowed, left
alone to care for her daughter, her younger sister, and her two nephews. The

light [some say: "prepare"] this candle in order to illuminate and celebrate this holy Friday evening, ushering in the holy and sanctified Shabbat, with new [or "pure"] olive oil and a flaxen wick.

Blessed angels, prophets, forefathers, and kings: Minister the Lord, I pray you, and bring before Him this wick, for the Lord's honor and exaltation, for the sake of the sixth day leading up to the holy and sanctified Shabbat day.

May this wick be blessed with the blessings that the Lord gave to His holy servants and handmaids. May this be so from the Lord to Abraham, Isaac, and Jacob, and may God have mercy upon our souls.

---

terrors of the Inquisition forced her to flee with her family to Antwerp, where she assisted her brother-in-law Diogo in handling the family's affairs. Persecution by the Church led the extended family to move again, and they eventually settled in Venice, the commercial and cultural center of the Renaissance. There, in addition to managing her family's business, Donna Gracia operated a wide-ranging network of undercover agents who helped converso Jews from all over Europe to flee the Inquisition.

Eventually, Donna Gracia was imprisoned for practicing Judaism, but when she was released shortly thereafter, the duke of Ferrara vowed to protect her, signing a letter promising that she would suffer no further persecution on account

וְלָחֹג אֶת לֵיל הַיּוֹם הַשִּׁשִּׁי הַקָּדוֹשׁ, לִפְנֵי הַשַּׁבָּת הַקְּדוֹשָׁה וְ(הַ)מְקֻדֶּשֶׁת בְּשֶׁמֶן זַיִת חָדָשׁ [אוֹ זָךְ] וּבִפְתִיל שֶׁל פִּשְׁתָּן.

מַלְאָכִים בְּרוּכִים, נְבִיאִים, אָבוֹת, מְלָכִים, יְשַׁמְּשׁוּ נָא לִפְנֵי הָאָדוֹן לְהָבִיא לְפָנָיו אֶת פְּתִיל הַזֶּה לִכְבוֹד הָאָדוֹן וּלְשַׁבְּחוֹ לְשֵׁם יוֹם הַשִּׁשִּׁי עַד יוֹם הַשַּׁבָּת הַקָּדוֹשׁ וְהַמְקֻדָּשׁ.

תְּהֵא הַפְּתִילָה הַזֹּאת מְבֹרָכָה בַּבְּרָכוֹת שֶׁחָלַק הָאָדוֹן לַעֲבָדָיו וּלְשִׁפְחוֹתָיו הַקְּדוֹשִׁים. מֵאֵת הָאֲדֹנָי תִּהְיֶה זֹאת לְאַבְרָהָם, לְיִצְחָק וּלְיַעֲקֹב וְרַחֲמֵי הָאֱלֹהִים יִהְיוּ עַל נַפְשֵׁנוּ.

---

of her faith. It was only at that point that Donna Gracia removed her Christian mask and became known publicly by her Jewish name, Hannah Nassi.

In 1553, Nassi moved to Constantinople and was active on behalf of the various Jewish communities there, providing assistance to the needy and involving herself in Jewish education. She also was extremely dedicated to Israel and obtained permission from Sultan Suleiman to establish a Jewish settlement in Tiberias, which she envisioned as a refuge for Jews fleeing the Inquisition. The rebuilding of the city wall around Tiberias in 1565 and reports of the Jewish settlement there aroused great hopes among Jews throughout the world and even expectations of redemption. The momentum ended with Donna Gracia's untimely death from illness at the age of fifty-nine.

HANNAH'S PRAYER
1 Samuel 2:1–10

*H*annah prayed, and she said: My heart rejoices in the Lord, my horn is exalted in the Lord; my mouth is enlarged over my enemies, for I rejoice in Your salvation.

There is none as holy as the Lord, for there is none beside You; nor is there any rock like our God.

Do not multiply your exceedingly proud speech, do not spew arrogance; for the Lord is a God of knowledge, by Him actions are weighed.

The bows of the mighty ones are broken, while those who stumbled are girded with strength.

Those who were full have hired themselves out for bread, and they that were hungry have ceased, while the barren one has borne seven, and she who has many children has become wretched.

Rabbi Yishaya Horowitz (c. 1565–1630), known as the "Shelah" (an acronym for his monumental work, *Shenei Luḥot ha-Berit*), was the first to record the custom of reciting Hannah's prayer of thanksgiving (which she composed following the birth of her son, Samuel) after candle lighting (Levine, 5766). The "Shelah" was born in Prague, moved to Poland as a child, studied with the leading Jewish scholars of his generation, and served as a rabbi in Europe. Toward the end of his life,

וַ תִּתְפַּלֵּל חַנָּה וַתֹּאמַר עָלַץ לִבִּי בַּיהוה רָמָה קַרְנִי בַּיהוה רָחַב פִּי עַל־
אוֹיְבַי כִּי שָׂמַחְתִּי בִּישׁוּעָתֶךָ:

אֵין־קָדוֹשׁ כַּיהוה כִּי־אֵין בִּלְתֶּךָ וְאֵין צוּר כֵּאלֹהֵינוּ:

אַל־תַּרְבּוּ תְדַבְּרוּ גְּבֹהָה גְבֹהָה יֵצֵא עָתָק מִפִּיכֶם כִּי אֵל דֵּעוֹת יְהוה
וְלוֹ נִתְכְּנוּ עֲלִלוֹת:

קֶשֶׁת גִּבֹּרִים חַתִּים וְנִכְשָׁלִים אָזְרוּ חָיִל:

שְׂבֵעִים בַּלֶּחֶם נִשְׂכָּרוּ וּרְעֵבִים חָדֵלּוּ עַד־עֲקָרָה יָלְדָה שִׁבְעָה וְרַבַּת בָּנִים
אֻמְלָלָה:

יְהוה מֵמִית וּמְחַיֶּה מוֹרִיד שְׁאוֹל וַיָּעַל:

יְהוה מוֹרִישׁ וּמַעֲשִׁיר מַשְׁפִּיל אַף־מְרוֹמֵם:

מֵקִים מֵעָפָר דָּל מֵאַשְׁפֹּת יָרִים אֶבְיוֹן לְהוֹשִׁיב עִם־נְדִיבִים וְכִסֵּא כָבוֹד
יַנְחִלֵם כִּי לַיהוה מְצֻקֵי אֶרֶץ וַיָּשֶׁת עֲלֵיהֶם תֵּבֵל:

---

he moved to Jerusalem, and he died in Tiberias. His influence on Jewish law and
philosophy is felt to this day.

Reciting Hannah's prayer following the kindling of Shabbat candles is thought
to bestow a special blessing for sons who are learned in Torah. Some women
follow the custom of reciting it at candle lighting on Rosh Hashanah.

The Lord brings death and gives life; He carries down to Sheol, and brings up.

The Lord makes poor and He makes rich; He brings low and raises up.

He raises the poor from the dust and lifts the needy from the dung-hill, seating them with princes and causing them to inherit the throne of glory; for the pillars of the earth belong to the Lord, and he has set the world upon them.

He guards the feet of His pious ones, but the wicked will be put to silence in darkness, for it is not by might that man prevails.

The Lord's adversaries shall be broken in pieces; in heaven He shall thunder upon them, the Lord will judge the ends of the earth, and give strength to His king, and raise up the horn of His anointed one."

In manuscripts of women's prayers from Italy, the biblical excerpt is followed with the words:

He Who answered Hannah in prayer, may He answer me.

רַגְלֵי חֲסִידָו יִשְׁמֹר וּרְשָׁעִים בַּחֹשֶׁךְ יִדָּמּוּ כִּי־לֹא בְכֹחַ יִגְבַּר אִישׁ:
יְהוָה יֵחַתּוּ מְרִיבָו עָלָו בַּשָּׁמַיִם יַרְעֵם יְהוָה יָדִין אַפְסֵי־אָרֶץ וְיִתֶּן־עֹז
לְמַלְכּוֹ וְיָרֵם קֶרֶן מְשִׁיחוֹ.

בכתבי־יד של תפילות נשים מאיטליה, מצאנו שלאחר שירת חנה היו מוסיפים את
הפסוק הבא:

מִי שֶׁעָנָה לְחָנָה בִּתְפִלָּתָהּ הוּא יַעֲנֵנִי.

PRAYERS FOR THE HOUSEHOLD

*M*ay it be Your will, Lord my God and God of Israel, that You show graciousness to me (and to my husband and to the members of my household) and to all my relatives, and grant us—and all of Israel—good, long life, and remember us for goodness and blessing, and recall us for salvation and mercy, and cause Your Presence to dwell in our midst. May we be worthy of raising children and grandchildren who are wise and understanding, who love God and fear the Lord, people of truth, holy offspring who cleave to God and bring light to the world through Torah and good deeds and all manner of labor in service of the Creator. I pray You, hear my supplication, in the merit of Sarah, Rebecca, Rachel, and Leah, our matriarchs. Cause our light to illuminate and never be extinguished, and may Your countenance shine so that we may be saved. Amen.

The oldest source hinting to the custom of a woman offering personal prayers after lighting Shabbat candles is the early thirteenth-century work *Arugat ha-Bosem* by Rabbi Avraham son of Azriel. A more explicit reference appeared some fifty years later in Rabbeinu Behaye's commentary on the Torah portion of *Yitro*. The

תפילת אשה על בני-ביתה

יְהִי רָצוֹן מִלְּפָנֶיךָ יְהוָה אֱלֹהַי וֵאלֹהֵי יִשְׂרָאֵל,
שֶׁתְּחוֹנֵן אוֹתִי [וְאֶת בַּעֲלִי וְאֶת בְּנֵי בֵּיתִי] וְאֶת כָּל קְרוֹבַי וְתִתֵּן לָנוּ
וּלְכָל יִשְׂרָאֵל חַיִּים טוֹבִים וַאֲרוּכִים, וְתִזְכְּרֵנוּ בְּזִכְרוֹן טוֹבָה וּבְרָכָה, וְתִפְקְדֵנוּ
בִּפְקֻדַּת יְשׁוּעָה וְרַחֲמִים, וְתַשְׁכִּין שְׁכִינָתְךָ בֵּינֵינוּ, וְזַכֵּנוּ לְגַדֵּל בָּנִים וּבְנֵי
בָנִים חֲכָמִים וּנְבוֹנִים, אוֹהֲבֵי ה', יְרֵאֵי אֱלֹהִים, אַנְשֵׁי אֱמֶת, זֶרַע קֹדֶשׁ, בַּה'
דְּבֵקִים, וּמְאִירִים אֶת הָעוֹלָם בַּתּוֹרָה וּבְמַעֲשִׂים טוֹבִים וּבְכָל מְלֶאכֶת עֲבוֹדַת
הַבּוֹרֵא. אָנָּא, שְׁמַע אֶת תְּחִנָּתִי, בִּזְכוּת שָׂרָה וְרִבְקָה רָחֵל וְלֵאָה אִמּוֹתֵינוּ,
וְהָאֵר נֵרֵנוּ שֶׁלֹּא יִכְבֶּה לְעוֹלָם וָעֶד, וְהָאֵר פָּנֶיךָ וְנִוָּשֵׁעָה, אָמֵן:

---

prayers here are some examples, gathered from a variety of sources, including
prayer book manuscripts from the Gross family Judaica collection, the National
Library in Jerusalem, and the JTS library in New York.

May it be Your will, Lord God, God of Israel, that You graciously grant to me and my husband (and my children) and all of my relatives and all of Israel, good and long life, in complete health, with deliverance from all that is evil and success in all that is good. Remember us for goodness and blessing, and recall us for salvation and mercy; bless us with great blessings, make our homes complete with many and great favors, and cause Your Presence to dwell among us. Let there be among us no man or woman who is barren, or bereaved, or widowed, and let there be no evil occurrences among us at all. May we merit to bear children and grandchildren who are wise and understanding and recognized, loving the Lord, fearing God and cleaving to Him, who will illuminate all of existence with Torah and good deeds and all manner of divine service. Please hear my supplication at this time, in the merit of Sarah and Rebecca, Rachel and Leah, our matriarchs, and cause our light to shine that it never be dimmed nor extinguished. Cause Your countenance to shine [upon us] that we may be redeemed, and upon all of Your nation, Israel, speedily in our days, Amen Selah.

May it be Your will, Lord God, God of Israel, that You infuse the upper and lower worlds with light and joy, gladness and honor, and grace, kindness, mercy, favor and good life, and blessing and peace. Illuminate us, our life-force, our spirit and our souls with the illuminating radiance of Your countenance, for the light of the countenance of the King gives life [...]. Graciously grant us the light of life, the hidden light concerning which it is written: God said, Let there be light—and there was light; Amen Selah.

יְ הִי רָצוֹן מִלְּפָנֶיךָ ה' אֱלֹקִים אֱלֹקֵי יִשְׂרָאֵל שֶׁתְּחוֹנֵן לִי וּלְאִישִׁי [וּלְבָנַי]
וּלְכָל קְרוֹבַי וּלְכָל יִשְׂרָאֵל חַיִּים טוֹבִים וַאֲרֻכִּים בִּבְרִיאוּת שְׁלֵמָה בְּהַצָּלָה
מִכָּל רָע וּבְהַצְלָחָה בְּכָל טוֹב, וְזָכְרֵנוּ בְּזִכְרָה טוֹבָה וּבְרָכָה, וּפָקְדֵנוּ בִּפְקֻדַּת
יְשׁוּעָה וְרַחֲמִים, וְתָבָרְכֵנוּ בְּרָכוֹת גְּדוֹלוֹת, וְתַשְׁלִים בָּתֵּינוּ בְּטוֹבוֹת רַבּוֹת
עֲצוּמוֹת, וְשַׁכֵּן שְׁכִינָתְךָ בֵּינֵינוּ. וְלֹא יִהְיֶה בָּנוּ לֹא עָקָר וְלֹא עֲקָרָה לֹא שְׁכוֹל
וְלֹא שְׁכוּלָה לֹא אַלְמוֹן וְלֹא אַלְמָנָה וְלֹא יִהְיֶה בָּנוּ דְּבָרִים רָעִים כְּלָל, וְתְזַכֵּנִי
לְהוֹלִיד בָּנִים וּבְנֵי בָנִים חֲכָמִים וּנְבוֹנִים וִידוּעִים אֹהֲבֵי יְיָ יִרְאֵי אֱלֹקִים בַּיְיָ
דְּבֵקִים שֶׁיָּאִירוּ עוֹלָמִים בַּתּוֹרָה וּבְמַעֲשִׂים טוֹבִים וּבְכָל מְלֶאכֶת עֲבֹדַת
הַבּוֹרֵא, וּשְׁמַע נָא אֶת תְּחִינָתִי בָּעֵת וּבָעוֹנָה הַזֹּאת בִּזְכוּת שָׂרָה וְרִבְקָה
רָחֵל וְלֵאָה אִמּוֹתֵינוּ וְהָאֵר נֵרֵנוּ שֶׁלֹּא יִדְעַךְ וְלֹא יִכְבֶּה לְעוֹלָם וְהָאֵר פָּנֶיךָ
וְנִוָּשֵׁעָה וּבְכָל עַמְּךָ יִשְׂרָאֵל בִּמְהֵרָה בְּיָמֵינוּ אָמֵן סֶלָה וָעֶד.

יְ הִי רָצוֹן מִלְּפָנֶיךָ יְיָ אֱלֹהִים אֱלֹהֵי יִשְׂרָאֵל שֶׁתַּשְׁבִּיעַ אוֹרָה וְשִׂמְחָה
וְשָׂשׂוֹן וִיקָר וְחֵן וָחֶסֶד וְרַחֲמִים וְרָצוֹן וְחַיִּים טוֹבִים וּבְרָכָה וְשָׁלוֹם לָעֶלְיוֹנִים
וְלַתַּחְתּוֹנִים. וְתָאִיר לָנוּ וּלְנַפְשׁוֹתֵינוּ וּלְרוּחֵנוּ וּלְנִשְׁמוֹתֵנוּ בְּאוֹר פָּנֶיךָ
הַמְּאִירִים, כִּי בְּאוֹר פְּנֵי מֶלֶךְ חַיִּים, כִּי עִמְּךָ מְקוֹר חַיִּים בְּאוֹרְךָ נִרְאֶה אוֹר.
אוֹר זָרֻעַ לַצַּדִּיק. וִיחַנֵּנוּ לְאוֹר הַחַיִּים לָאוֹר הַגָּנוּז שֶׁעָלָיו נֶאֱמַר וַיֹּאמֶר
אֱלֹהִים יְהִי אוֹר וַיְהִי אוֹר, אָמֵן סֶלָה וָעֶד.

רִ בּוֹנוֹ שֶׁל עוֹלָם תַּעַזְרֵנִי עַל דְּבַר כְּבוֹד שְׁמֶךָ, לְהַחֲזִירֵנִי בִּתְשׁוּבָה
שְׁלֵמָה לְפָנֶיךָ, וְתָשִׂים בְּלִבִּי יְדִיעַת וּתְשׁוּקַת אֱמוּנָתְךָ וְאַהֲבָתְךָ, וּלְהִזָּהֵר
בִּשְׁמִירַת שַׁבַּת קָדְשְׁךָ בְּכָל פְּרָטָיו. וּלְהִזָּהֵר מִמַּאֲכָלוֹת אֲסוּרוֹת. וְלִשְׁמֹר

*M*aster of the world, help me for the sake of the glory of Your Name, to bring me back in complete repentance before You. Imbue my heart with the knowledge of and desire for Your faith and love, and meticulouslness in observing Your holy Shabbat in all its details, and caution concerning forbidden foods, and observance of family purity in all of its details, that no stumbling should come about on my account, heaven forbid. Allow me to grow in holiness, purity, and modesty, and may my attire always be in accordance with Your will. Merciful Father, grant me sons and daughters who observe the Torah and the commandments. Help me to find them teachers, guides, and educators who are God-fearing, who provide guidance in the way of Torah and our tradition, Amen.

*R*emember us for life, O King Who desires life, and inscribe us in the book of life, for Your sake, O living God. Merciful Father—send complete healing to all the sick of Your nation, Israel. Bless us with a good livelihood, and may we be worthy of dwelling upon the holy land, in Your service and with awe of You; Amen.

טָהֳרַת הַמִּשְׁפָּחָה בְּכָל דִּקְדּוּקֶיהָ. וְשֶׁלֹּא יָבֹא שׁוּם מִכְשׁוֹל עַל יָדִי חַס
וְשָׁלוֹם. וּתְזַכֶּה אוֹתִי לְהִתְקָרֵב לִקְדֻשָּׁה טָהֳרָה וּצְנִיעוּת. וְתָמִיד יִהְיוּ
מַלְבּוּשַׁי כְּפִי רְצוֹנֶךָ. זַכֵּנִי בְּבָנִים וּבָנוֹת שׁוֹמְרֵי תּוֹרָה וּמִצְוֹת.
וְעָזְרֵנִי לְהַמְצִיא לָהֶם מְלַמְּדִים, מַדְרִיכִים, וּמְחַנְּכִים יִרְאֵי הַשֵּׁם. הַנּוֹתְנִים
חִנּוּךְ בְּדֶרֶךְ הַתּוֹרָה וְהַמְּסוֹרָה. אָמֵן:

זָכְרֵנוּ לְחַיִּים מֶלֶךְ חָפֵץ בַּחַיִּים, וְכָתְבֵנוּ בְּסֵפֶר הַחַיִּים לְמַעַנְךָ אֱלֹהִים
חַיִּים. אָב הָרַחֲמָן שְׁלַח רְפוּאָה שְׁלֵמָה לְכָל חוֹלֵי עַמְּךָ יִשְׂרָאֵל. וּבָרְכֵנוּ
בְּפַרְנָסָה טוֹבָה וּתְזַכֵּנוּ לֵישֵׁב עַל אַדְמַת הַקֹּדֶשׁ בַּעֲבוֹדָתֶךָ וּבְיִרְאָתֶךָ. אָמֵן.

FRIDAY PRAYER
Yaakov Freund

*C*reator of heaven and earth: On the sixth day of the six days
of Creation You created man from the dust of the earth. You breathed
into him a living soul, and he became a living creature. You formed him
from dust, but created him in Your image and in Your likeness. Indeed,
in view of reality, how could I question the idea that You created him a
duality—body and soul, "for you are dust, and to dust you shall return,"
but a person's soul lives forever; it returns to its God, to its Creator. God
and God of our fathers, may it be Your will that I never deviate from the
path of life that is prescribed by knowledge of the eternal soul. May it be
Your will that I always bear in mind that my body is dust and ashes. The
covering is transient, like all earthly things; its days are numbered, and
it is easily brought to its end. You have implanted in my body a soul to
guard me from foolish acts on the part of my body. I shall obey its voice,

---

Yaakov Freund—a teacher at the Jewish school in Breslau—compiled the *Prayer
Book for Jewish Women and Girls* in German, in 1867. It was first translated into Hebrew
by Katya Manor.

תפילת יום השישי

יעקב פרוינד

בּוֹרֵא שָׁמַיִם וָאָרֶץ! בְּיוֹם הַשִּׁשִּׁי בְּשֵׁשֶׁת יְמֵי הַבְּרִיאָה, מֵעֲפַר הָאֲדָמָה בָּרֵאתָ אֶת הָאָדָם, נָפַחְתָּ בּוֹ נִשְׁמַת חַיִּים וְהוּא הָיָה לִיצוּר חַי. מֵעֲפָר יְצַרְתּוֹ, אַךְ בְּצַלְמְךָ וּבִדְמוּתְךָ בְּרָאתוֹ. וּלְמַרְאֵה הַדְּבָרִים, אֵיךְ יוּכַל לַעֲלוֹת מִלְפָנַי הַסָּפֵק שֶׁבִּשְׁנַיִם יְצַרְתָּ אוֹתוֹ, בַּגּוּף וּבַנֶּפֶשׁ. "כִּי עָפָר אַתָּה וְאֶל עָפָר תָּשׁוּב", אַךְ נֶפֶשׁ הָאָדָם לָעַד קַיֶּמֶת; הִיא שָׁבָה אֶל אֱלֹהֶיהָ, אֶל בּוֹרְאָהּ. אֱלֹהֵינוּ וֵאלֹהֵי אֲבוֹתֵינוּ, יְהִי רָצוֹן מִלְפָנֶיךָ שֶׁלֹּא אָסוּר מִדֶּרֶךְ הַחַיִּים שֶׁמְּצַוָּה הַיְדִיעָה עַל דְּבַר הַנֶּפֶשׁ הַנִּצְחִית. יְהִי רָצוֹן שֶׁלְּנֶגֶד רוּחִי תָּמִיד תַּעֲלֶה הַמַּחְשָׁבָה, שֶׁגּוּפִי עָפָר וָאֵפֶר. הַמַּעֲטֶה הוּא בֶּן־חֲלוֹף כְּכָל הַדְּבָרִים הָאַרְצִיִּים. יָמָיו סְפוּרִים וְעַל נְקַלָּה יָבוֹא אֶל קִצּוֹ. נָטַעְתָּ בְּגוּפִי אֶת הַנֶּפֶשׁ שֶׁתִּשְׁמֹר עָלַי מִמַּעֲשֶׂה אִוֶּלֶת בְּגוּפִי. לְקוֹלָהּ אֶשְׁמַע, כִּי קוֹלָהּ קוֹל הַתְּבוּנָה הוּא, הַמַּזְהִיר אוֹתִי מִפְּנֵי הָעַבְדוּת לַהֲנָאָה, מִפְּנֵי הַפַּח שֶׁטּוֹמְנוּת לִי הָעַצְלוּת וְהָרַעַבְתָּנוּת, הַקּוֹל הַשּׁוֹמֵר עָלַי מִפְּנֵי נֶזֶק וּפֶגַע רַע. לְמַעְלָה

for its voice is the voice of understanding, warning me against becoming enslaved to pleasure, against the trap set for me by sloth and avariciousness, the voice that guards me from harm and evil accidents. Beyond this there is nothing that I can do for my body; its health and resilience are dependent upon Your manifold kindnesses, my good God.

And may I always remember that my soul is immortal, that it shall not return to the ground. The soul is meant to strive toward You, to honor You and praise You—the Rock Who is perfect—and to resemble You. My body shall return to the dust, material for a new being in the world of Creation. But my soul will be liberated from the chains of the body, to the place that it will have acquired for itself while in this world through wisdom and kindness. Therefore, merciful One, may my soul not be subservient to my body. Let my bodily powers serve the pure desires of my soul, to acquire understanding and knowledge, acts of kindness and insight. Amen.

מֶה אֵין לְאֵל יָדִי לַעֲשׂוֹת לְמַעַן גּוּפִי; בְּרִיאוּתוֹ וַחֲסִינוּתוֹ תְּלוּיוֹת בַּחֲסָדֶיךָ הָרַבִּים, אֵלִי הַטּוֹב!

וְתָמִיד תַּעֲלֶה לְנֶגֶד רוּחִי הַמַּחְשָׁבָה, שֶׁנַּפְשִׁי בַּת אַל־מָוֶת הִיא, שֶׁלֹּא אֶל הָאֲדָמָה תָּשׁוּב; הַנֶּפֶשׁ נוֹעֲדָה לִשְׁאֹף אֵלֶיךָ, לְכַבֵּדְךָ וּלְהַלֵּלְךָ, הַצּוּר תָּמִים, לְהִדָּמוֹת לְךָ. גּוּפִי יָשׁוּב אֶל הֶעָפָר, חֹמֶר לִיצִירָה חֲדָשָׁה בְּעוֹלָם הַבְּרִיאָה. אַךְ הַנֶּפֶשׁ תִּשְׁתַּחְרֵר מִכַּבְלֵי הַגּוּף, אֶל הַמָּקוֹם שֶׁקָּנְתָה לְעַצְמָהּ עֲלֵי אֲדָמוֹת בְּאֶמְצָעוּת הַחָכְמָה וְהַחֲסָדִים. וְעַל כֵּן, בַּעַל הָרַחֲמִים, אַל תְּהִי נַפְשִׁי כְּפוּפָה לְגוּפִי. תֵּן שֶׁכֹּחוֹת גּוּפִי יְשַׁמְּשׁוּ אֶת מַאֲוַיֶּיהָ הַטְּהוֹרִים שֶׁל נַפְשִׁי, לִרְכֹּשׁ בִּינָה וָדַעַת, גְּמִילוּת חֲסָדִים וּתְבוּנָה, אָמֵן!

Separating Challah

When preparing a substantial quantity of bread or other flour-based goods (using at least 2 kg of flour ground from wheat, spelt, rye, barley, or oats), Jewish law dictates that a handful of dough be removed and that a special blessing should be recited before baking. The Torah designates this portion, called challah, as one of the gifts to the *kohanim*, the descendants of Aaron who performed the Temple service. After the destruction of the Holy Temple, the *kohanim* were no longer permitted to eat any of the gifts that were their due during the time of the Temple; nevertheless, these gifts remain forbidden for regular consumption. Therefore, the custom is to take the separated challah and burn or dispose of it to commemorate the original commandment.

According to biblical law (Numbers 15:18–20), the commandment of separating challah belongs to a category of laws that are obligatory only in the Land of Israel, and only in a situation where the majority of the Jewish people is living in the land. Rabbinical decree extended this requirement to include bread baked outside of Israel, and also throughout the years of exile, so that the commandment would not be forgotten.

The following blessing is recited after kneading the dough, before separating the special portion:

Blessed are You, Lord our God, King of the universe,
Who has sanctified us with His commandments
And commanded us to separate challah from the dough
[some say: "... and commanded us to separate challah as a gift"].

PRAYER UPON SEPARATING CHALLAH
Yiddish

One recites the blessing, separates challah, and then declares:

*T*his is challah.

Then the following is recited:

*M*ay it be Your will, Lord our God and God of our forefathers, that the commandment of separating challah be regarded as having been fulfilled in all its details and requirements, and that the challah, which I now hold, be considered like the sacrifice offered upon the altar, which was accepted with favor. And just as in former times, the challah was given to the *kohen* and that was an atonement for one's sins, so may it be an atonement for my sins, that I may be as one born anew, clean of transgression and sin, that I might fulfill the commandment of the holy Shabbat and these holy days, with my husband (and our children), to be nourished by the sanctity of these days. Through the commandment of challah may our children always be nourished from the hand of the Holy One, blessed be He, in His great mercy and kindness, and with great love, and may the commandment of challah be accepted as though I had given a tithe. And just as I hereby fulfill the commandment of challah with all my heart, so may the mercy of the Holy One, blessed be He, be aroused to protect me from sorrow and from suffering for all time. Amen.

תחינה להפרשת חלה

אידיש

ותפריש את החלה ותאמר:

הֲרֵי זוֹ חַלָּה:

יְהִי רָצוֹן מִלְּפָנֶיךָ, יְיָ אֱלֹהֵינוּ וֵאלֹהֵי אֲבוֹתֵינוּ, שֶׁהַמִּצְוָה שֶׁל הַפְרָשַׁת חַלָּה תֵּחָשֵׁב כְּאִלּוּ קִיַּמְתִּיהָ בְּכָל פְּרָטֶיהָ וְדִקְדּוּקֶיהָ, וְתֵחָשֵׁב הֲרָמַת הַחַלָּה שֶׁאֲנִי מְרִימָה כְּמוֹ הַקָּרְבָּן שֶׁהִקְרַב עַל הַמִּזְבֵּחַ שֶׁנִּתְקַבֵּל בְּרָצוֹן, וּכְמוֹ שֶׁלְּפָנִים הָיְתָה הַחַלָּה נְתוּנָה לַכֹּהֵן וְהָיְתָה זוֹ לְכַפָּרַת עֲווֹנוֹת, כָּךְ תִּהְיֶה לְכַפָּרָה לַעֲווֹנוֹתַי, וְאָז אֶהְיֶה כְּאִלּוּ נוֹלַדְתִּי מֵחָדָשׁ נְקִיָּה מֵחֵטְא וְעָווֹן, וְאוּכַל לְקַיֵּם מִצְוַת שַׁבַּת קֹדֶשׁ וְהַיָּמִים הַטּוֹבִים הָאֵלֶּה, עִם בַּעְלִי [וִילָדַי] לִהְיוֹת נִזּוֹנִים מִקְּדֻשַּׁת הַיָּמִים וּמֵהַשְׁפָּעָתָהּ שֶׁל מִצְוַת חַלָּה יִהְיוּ יְלָדֵינוּ נִזּוֹנִים תָּמִיד מִיָּדָיו שֶׁל הַקָּדוֹשׁ בָּרוּךְ הוּא בְּרֹב רַחֲמָיו וַחֲסָדָיו, וּבְרֹב אַהֲבָה, וְשֶׁתִּתְקַבֵּל מִצְוַת חַלָּה כְּאִלּוּ נָתַתִּי מַעֲשֵׂר, וּכְשֵׁם שֶׁהִנְנִי מְקַיֶּמֶת מִצְוַת חַלָּה בְּכָל לֵב, כָּךְ יִתְעוֹרְרוּ רַחֲמָיו שֶׁל הַקָּדוֹשׁ בָּרוּךְ הוּא לְשָׁמְרֵנִי מִצַּעַר וּמִמַּכְאוֹבִים כָּל הַיָּמִים אָמֵן.

OFFERINGS OF LOVE
Fanny Neuda

*O*ur Father in heaven: By Your holy command, I am separating a measure of challah. At the same time, I recall ancient times when, with a willing heart, our forefathers would offer the first of their produce upon Your altar. Today, too, our God, we offer up offerings of love—may they find favor before You. Whenever we satisfy the hunger of those in need, easing their distress and their deprivation and relieving their concerns for their sustenance, we are offering a sacrifice before You, Father of the poor and the destitute. Our Father in heaven—accept my gift with mercy and favor and grant me a strong and loyal heart; then even if You demand great and difficult sacrifices of me, I shall offer them up and rejoice in my faith.

Allow us to earn our daily bread with dignity and not in dread. May we eat of it and may it bring us an abundance of blessing and prosperity. With good health and vigor may we rejoice in life and its grace, and with joyful heart and a good spirit, we shall praise You Who are good and Who performs good, and may You send blessing and success to our endeavors.

*B*lessed are You, Lord our God, King of the universe, Who has sanctified us with His commandments and commanded us to separate challah.

תפילת הפרשת החלה

פאני נוידא

אָבִינוּ שֶׁבַּשָּׁמַיִם! בְּמִצְוָתְךָ הַקְּדוֹשָׁה אֲנִי מַפְרִישָׁה שִׁעוּר מִן הַחַלָּה. עוֹד אֶזְכְּרָה שָׁנִים קַדְמוֹנִיּוֹת שֶׁבָּהֶן, בְּלֵב חָפֵץ, הֶעֱלוּ אֲבוֹתֵינוּ עַל מִזְבַּחֲךָ אֶת בִּכּוּרֵיהֶם. גַּם הַיּוֹם, אֱלֹהֵינוּ, אָנוּ מַעֲלִים לְפָנֶיךָ קָרְבְּנוֹת אַהֲבָה שֶׁיֵּרְצוּ לְפָנֶיךָ. בְּשָׁעָה שֶׁאָנוּ מַשְׂבִּיעִים אֶת רְעָבוֹנוֹ שֶׁל הַנִּצְרָךְ, מְקִלִּים עַל מְצוּקָתוֹ וְחֶסְרוֹנוֹ, וּמְסַלְּקִים אֶת דַּאֲגוֹת פַּרְנָסָתוֹ, אָנוּ מַעֲלִים קָרְבָּן לְפָנֶיךָ, אֲבִי דַלִּים וַעֲנִיִּים. אָבִינוּ שֶׁבַּשָּׁמַיִם, קַבֵּל בְּרַחֲמִים וּבְרָצוֹן אֶת תְּרוּמָתִי וְתֵן לִי לֵב חָזָק וְנֶאֱמָן, וְגַם אִם תִּדְרֹשׁ מִמֶּנִּי קָרְבָּנוֹת גְּדוֹלִים וַעֲצוּמִים, אַעֲלֶה אוֹתָם וְאֶשְׂמַח בֶּאֱמוּנָתִי.

תֵּן לָנוּ לְהַרְוִיחַ אֶת לֶחֶם יוֹמֵנוּ בְּכָבוֹד וְלֹא בְמוֹרָא, וְתֵן שֶׁנֹּאכַל מִמֶּנּוּ וְשֶׁיַּשְׁפִּיעַ עָלֵינוּ בְּרָכָה וְשִׂגְשׂוּג. וּבְרֹב בְּרִיאוּת וְכֹחַ נִשְׂמַח בַּחַיִּים וּבְחַסְדָּם, וּבְלֵב שָׂמֵחַ וּבְרוּחַ טוֹבָה נְהַלֶּלְךָ, הַטּוֹב וְהַמֵּטִיב. וּשְׁלַח בְּרָכָה וְהַצְלָחָה בְּמַעֲשֵׂי יָדֵינוּ.

בָּרוּךְ אַתָּה ה׳ אֱלֹהֵינוּ מֶלֶךְ הָעוֹלָם אֲשֶׁר קִדְּשָׁנוּ בְּמִצְווֹתָיו וְצִוָּנוּ לְהַפְרִישׁ חַלָּה.

BLESSING OVER A TITHE
Conversos of Portugal

*B*lessed is the Lord my God, my Master, Who commanded us—with His blessed and holy commandments—to tithe this bread, to appease the lion, as our brethren used to do in the holy Promised Land. Amen.

Like beloved family recipes, the laws, prayers, and blessings that conversos remembered were passed down orally from mother to daughter. The blessing over challah recorded here originated among the conversos of Portugal in the sixteenth century. The reference to "the lion" is a euphemism for Satan.

ברכת החלה

על־פי מנהג אנוסי פורטוגל

בָּרוּךְ ה׳ אֱלֹהַי, אֲדֹנָי שֶׁלִּי, אֲשֶׁר צִוָּנוּ בְּמִצְוֹתָיו הַבְּרוּכוֹת וְהַמְקֻדָּשׁוֹת שֶׁנַּעֲשֶׂה אֶת הַלֶּחֶם הַזֶּה, בִּשְׁבִיל פִּי הָאַרְיֵה, כְּשֵׁם שֶׁהָיוּ עוֹשִׂים אַחֵינוּ בְּאֶרֶץ הַמֻּבְטַחַת הַקְּדוֹשָׁה. אָמֵן.

PERFECT UNITY

By Perl, wife of Rabbi Levi Yitzhak of Berditchev

*M*aster of the world: I ask of You—please help me, such
that when my Levi Yitzhak recites the blessing over these loaves on
Shabbat, he should have in his heart the same meditations that I have
at this time, as I knead and bake.

Perl's prayer is recorded in *The Hidden Light* by Martin Buber. Tradition has it
that Perl, wife of the famed Hassidic master Rabbi Levi Yitzhak of Berditchev
(1740–1810) who was known as "Israel's advocate," would recite this prayer as she
kneaded dough and baked bread for Shabbat.

תחינת פרל

אשת ר׳ לוי יצחק מברדיטשוב

רִבּוֹנוֹ שֶׁל עוֹלָם, מְבַקֶּשֶׁת אֲנִי מִלְּפָנֶיךָ, אָנָּא עֲזֹר לִי, שֶׁכְּשֶׁיְּהֵא לֵוִי
יִצְחָק שֶׁלִּי מְבָרֵךְ בַּשַּׁבָּת עַל הַחַלּוֹת הָאֵלֶּה, יְכַוֵּן בְּלִבּוֹ אוֹתָן הַכַּוָּנוֹת שֶׁאֲנִי
מְכַוֶּנֶת בְּשָׁעָה זוֹ שֶׁאֲנִי לָשָׁה וְאוֹפָה.

Immersion and Purification

"Therefore a man shall leave his father and his mother, and
shall cleave to his wife, and they shall become one flesh."
[GENESIS 2:24]

Judaism perceives the physical bond between husband and wife as representing the ultimate opportunity for spiritual, physical, and emotional fulfillment. Sexual union adds sanctity to the world and bonds the couple together.

Renewing and nurturing the conjugal bond is the basis for the laws of family purity, which dictate that married couples refrain from physical contact during the wife's period of menstruation and the seven days following it. Prior to a husband and wife's reunion after the two weeks of physical separation, the wife immerses her entire body in a *mikveh* (ritual bath).

The *mikveh* is supremely important in Jewish society. Jewish law stipulates that if a community lacks both a *mikveh* and a synagogue, building a *mikveh* should be the first priority. Though modern, man-made *mikva'ot* offer convenience and privacy, in recent years a growing number of women are choosing to immerse in natural bodies of rainwater instead.

The blessing that a woman recites at the time of immersion is itself a prayer that God sanctify and bless her marriage and the bond between her and her husband:

> *Blessed are You, Lord, King of the universe,*
> *Who has sanctified us with His commandments*
> *And commanded us concerning immersion.*

PRAYER FOR THE FINAL DAY OF THE SEVEN CLEAN DAYS

Ben Ish Hai

*M*aster of the universe: It is clear and known to You that I have fulfilled Your commandments in observing the days of menstrual impurity and counting the seven clean days. Behold, now I am ready and prepared to fulfill the commandment of immersion in purifying water by Your command, which You have commanded me. I hereby fulfill this commandment for the sake of unifying the Holy One, blessed be He, and the divine presence in perfect unity, in the name of all of Israel, so as to repair the root of this commandment in the upper world. May it ascend before You as though I had maintained every appropriate thought and intention.

And just as I am cleansing my body of spiritual impurity in this water, so in Your great mercy and abundant kindness may You cleanse my soul of all impurity and dross, so that we might experience the fulfillment of

The prohibition against sexual relations with a menstrual woman appears in the Torah immediately after the prohibition against relations between a brother and sister. Rabbi Samson Raphael Hirsch (1808–1888) notes the possibility that this juxtaposition is intended "to teach us that there are times, in a Jewish marriage, when relations between husband and wife are just like relations between a brother and sister.

תפילה ליום מלאת שבעה ימים נקיים

ה"בן איש חי"

רִבּוֹנוֹ שֶׁל עוֹלָם, גָּלוּי וְיָדוּעַ לְפָנֶיךָ שֶׁקִּיַּמְתִּי מִצְוֹתֶיךָ בִּשְׁמִירַת יְמֵי
נִדּוּת וְסָפַרְתִּי שִׁבְעָה נְקִיִּים. וְהִנֵּה עַתָּה אָנֹכִי מוּכֶנֶת וּמְזֻמֶּנֶת לְקַיֵּם מִצְוַת
הַטְּבִילָה בְּמַיִם הַכְּשֵׁרִים בְּמִצְוָתְךָ אֲשֶׁר צִוִּיתָנִי. וְהִנֵּה אָנֹכִי מְקַיֶּמֶת מִצְוָה
זוֹ לְשֵׁם יִחוּד קוּדְשָׁא בְּרִיךְ הוּא וּשְׁכִינְתֵּיהּ בִּיחוּדָא שְׁלִים בְּשֵׁם כָּל
יִשְׂרָאֵל, לְתַקֵּן שֹׁרֶשׁ מִצְוָה זוֹ בְּמָקוֹם עֶלְיוֹן, וְיַעֲלֶה לְפָנֶיךָ כְּאִלּוּ כִּוַּנְתִּי בְּכָל
הַכַּוָּנוֹת הָרְאוּיוֹת לְכַוֵּן:

וּכְשֵׁם שֶׁאָנֹכִי מְטַהֶרֶת גּוּפִי מִן הַטֻּמְאָה בַּמַּיִם, כֵּן בְּרֹב רַחֲמֶיךָ וּבְרֹב
חֲסָדֶיךָ תְּטַהֵר נַפְשִׁי מִכָּל טֻמְאָה וְזֻהֲמָא, וְקַיֵּם בָּנוּ מִקְרָא שֶׁכָּתוּב:
וְזָרַקְתִּי עֲלֵיכֶם מַיִם טְהוֹרִים וּטְהַרְתֶּם, וְנֶאֱמַר: מִקְוֵה יִשְׂרָאֵל יְהֹוָה:

This [prohibition] in no way impairs the intimacy of marriage; on the contrary, it serves to deepen that intimacy and to elevate it, spiritually and morally."

Maimonides emphasizes that the customs and beliefs prevalent among other cultures, suggesting that a menstrual woman bears some mystical mark of disgrace, are to be rejected outright.

197

the verse: I shall sprinkle upon you water of purification, and you shall be purified, for as it is written, God is the Hope [*mikveh*] of Israel.

May it be Your will, Lord my God and God of my forefathers, that the commandment of observing the laws of menstrual bleeding and the law of counting seven clean days, and the commandment of purification and immersion in purifying waters, be accounted and accepted and find favor before You, so as to repair all of our spiritual shortcomings and the deficiencies of Adam and Eve, so that all dross might be separated from holiness, and that its glow be like a radiant light shining toward the place of holiness.

May it be Your will, Lord my God and God of my forefathers, that You grant my husband and me vigor, strength, support, and help in our union, and that we be worthy of children who are wise and understanding in Torah. I pray You, Lord, please save us; I pray You, Lord, please grant us success. I pray You, Lord, please save us; I pray You, Lord, please grant us success.

יְהִי רָצוֹן מִלְּפָנֶיךָ יְהוָה אֱלֹהַי וֵאלֹהֵי אֲבוֹתַי, שֶׁתִּהְיֶה חֲשׁוּבָה וּמְקֻבֶּלֶת וּרְצוּיָה לְפָנֶיךָ מִצְוַת שְׁמִירַת נִדּוּת וּמִצְוַת סְפִירַת שִׁבְעָה יָמִים נְקִיִּים וּמִצְוַת הַטָּהֳרָה וְהַטְּבִילָה בַּמַּיִם הַכְּשֵׁרִים, לְתַקֵּן אֶת כָּל פְּגָמֵינוּ וּפִגְמֵי אָדָם וְחַוָּה, וְיִתְפָּרְדוּ כָּל הַסִּיגִים מִן הַקְּדֻשָּׁה וְנֹגַהּ כְּאוֹר תִּהְיֶה אֶל מְקוֹם הַקֹּדֶשׁ.

וִיהִי רָצוֹן מִלְּפָנֶיךָ יְהוָה אֱלֹהַי וֵאלֹהֵי אֲבוֹתַי, שֶׁתִּתֵּן לִי וּלְאִישִׁי כֹּחַ וְיָכֹלֶת וְעֵזֶר וְסִיּוּעַ לַזִּוּוּג שֶׁלָּנוּ וְנִזְכֶּה לְבָנִים חֲכָמִים וּנְבוֹנִים בַּתּוֹרָה: אָנָּא ה' הוֹשִׁיעָה נָּא, אָנָּא ה' הַצְלִיחָה נָּא: אָנָּא ה' הוֹשִׁיעָה נָּא, אָנָּא ה' הַצְלִיחָה נָּא.

BLESSING UPON IMMERSING IN A *MIKVEH*
Book of Blessings, Vienna

I am hereby ready and prepared to fulfill the commandment of immersing and restoring my status of purity [to render me permissible] to my husband, as commanded us by the Holy One, blessed be He and blessed be His great Name. Blessed are You, Lord our God, King of the universe, Who has sanctified us with His commandments and commanded us concerning the commandment of immersion.

During the eighteenth century—a time when Jewish calligraphy began to flourish—miniature illuminated books featuring blessings for various occasions and illustrations by leading Jewish artists of the time were popular in central Europe. This blessing, meant to be recited by a woman before immersing in a *mikveh*,

ברכת האשה הטובלת במקווה

ספר סדר ברכות – וינה

הֲרֵינִי מוּכָן וּמְזוּמָן לְקַיֵּם הַמִּצְוָה לְטַהֵר אוֹתִי לְבַעֲלִי כְּמוֹ שֶׁצִוָּה לָנוּ הַבּוֹרֵא יִתְבָּרַךְ בָּרוּךְ הוּא וּבָרוּךְ שְׁמוֹ הַגָּדוֹל. בָּרוּךְ אַתָּה יְיָ אֱלוֹהֵינוּ מֶלֶךְ הָעוֹלָם אֲשֶׁר קִדְּשָׁנוּ בְּמִצְוֹתָיו וְצִוָּנוּ עַל מִצְוַת טְבִילָה.

---

appears in one such book, currently housed in the Budapest Jewish Museum. The traditional introduction to the blessing ("I am hereby ready and prepared ..."), which in this case is unquestionably meant to be recited by women, appears in this particular book in masculine form.

LIKE THE RADIANCE OF THE MOON
Ruth Lazare

My God, Creator of beauty and purity

Molder of body and soul,

I am the woman now standing before You in prayer.

Purify me at brooks of water

Anoint me with myrrh and incense

Renew light within me like the radiance of the moon.

My Lord,

My womb which You have given me

Is pure;

Place a soul in my midst.

Then may my home be whole before You,

And my insides be lined with love.

Jewish sources—especially mystical works—discuss the multilayered symbolic association between woman and the moon. Like the moon, which waxes and wanes, women possess unique powers of physical and spiritual renewal. Ruth Lazare's prayer draws on this analogy.

Some view immersion in a *mikveh* as symbolic of the world prior to creation: Just as the world emerged from primordial water, so the woman is reborn through water untouched by human hands.

תפילה לאשה הטובלת במקווה

רות לזר

אֱלֹהַי, בּוֹרֵא הַיֹּפִי וְהַצַּחוּת
יוֹצֵר הַגּוּף וְהַנֶּפֶשׁ,
אֲנִי הָאִשָּׁה הַנִּצֶּבֶת עִמְּךָ בָּזֶה לְהִתְפַּלֵּל
טַהֲרֵנִי עַל אֲפִיקֵי מַיִם
מְשָׁחֵנִי מֹר וּלְבוֹנָה
חַדֵּשׁ בִּי אוֹר כְּזִיו הַלְּבָנָה.
אֱלֹהַי,
רַחֲמֶי שֶׁנָּתַתָּ בִּי
טָהוֹר הוּא,
תֵּן בְּקִרְבִּי נְשָׁמָה.
וִיהִי בֵּיתִי שָׁלֵם לְפָנֶיךָ,
וִיהִי תוֹכִי רָצוּף אַהֲבָה.

A BLESSED UNION
Rabbi Dr. Rafael Mildola

*M*ay it be Your will that You cause Your divine presence to dwell with me and my husband, and unite over us Your holy Name of *yod heh*. Place in our hearts a pure and holy spirit, and distance us from all evil thoughts. Bestow a pure and unsullied soul-bond between my husband and me, such that neither of us will be drawn to any person in the world, only me to my husband, and he to me. Let it appear to me that there is no man in the world as good, handsome, and charming as my husband [...] And likewise may it seem to my husband that there is no woman in the world so beautiful and graceful and worthy as I, and may all his thoughts be of me, and not of anyone else in the world [...]. As it is written, "Therefore a man shall leave his father and his mother and cleave to his wife."

And may it be Your will, Lord God, that our union prosper: a worthy union with love and fraternity, peace and friendship; a proper union according to the teachings of the Torah and Jewish tradition; a worthy union with fear of heaven and fear of sin; a union producing children who are worthy, righteous,

This prayer is taken from *Huppat Hatanim* by Rabbi Rafael Mildola.

תפילה לאשה קודם ייחוד

הרב ד״ר רפאל מילדולה

יְהִי רָצוֹן מִלְפָנֶיךָ שֶׁתַּשְׁרָה שְׁכִינָתְךָ בֵּינִי וּבֵין בַּעֲלִי, וּתְיַחֵד עָלֵינוּ שִׁמְךָ הַקָּדוֹשׁ יו״ד ה״א. וְתַכְנִיס בְּלִבֵּנוּ רוּחַ טָהֳרָה וּקְדוּשָׁה וְתַרְחִיק מִמֶּנוּ כָּל מַחְשָׁבוֹת וְהִרְהוּרִים רָעִים. וְתִתֶּן לִי נֶפֶשׁ זַכָּה וּבָרָה בֵּינִי וּבֵין בַּעֲלִי וְלֹא נִתֵּן אֲנַחְנוּ שְׁנֵינוּ אֶת עֵינֵינוּ בְּשׁוּם אָדָם בָּעוֹלָם כִּי אִם עֵינֵי בְּבַעֲלִי וְעֵינֵי בַעֲלִי בִּי. וְיִהְיֶה בְּעֵינֵי כְּאִילוּ אֵין אָדָם טוֹב וְיָפֶה וּבַעַל חֵן בָּעוֹלָם כְּמוֹ בַּעֲלִי. כַּדָּבָר שֶׁנֶּאֱמַר שִׁמְעִי בַת וּרְאִי וְהַטִּי אָזְנֵךְ וְשִׁכְחִי עַמֵּךְ וּבֵית אָבִיךְ, וְנֶאֱמַר כִּי הוּא אֲדוֹנַיִךְ וְהִשְׁתַּחֲוִי לוֹ. וְכֵן יִהְיֶה בְּעֵינֵי בַּעֲלִי כְּאִילוּ אֵין אִשָּׁה יָפָה וּבַעֲלַת חֵן וַהֲגוּנָה בָּעוֹלָם כְּמוֹתִי. וְיִהְיוּ כָּל מַחְשְׁבוֹתָיו בִּי וְלֹא בְּשׁוּם בְּרִיָּה אַחֶרֶת בָּעוֹלָם. כַּדָּבָר שֶׁנֶּאֱמַר יָפְיָפִיתָ מִבְּנֵי אָדָם הוּצַק חֵן שְׂפְתוֹתֶיךָ. וְנֶאֱמַר וְיִתְאָו הַמֶּלֶךְ יָפְיֵךְ וְנֶאֱמַר עַל כֵּן יַעֲזָב אִישׁ אֶת אָבִיו וְאִמּוֹ וְדָבַק בְּאִשְׁתּוֹ.

וִיהִי רָצוֹן מִלְפָנֶיךָ יְיָ הָאֱלֹהִים שֶׁיִּהְיֶה וִזּוּגֵינוּ עוֹלֶה יָפֶה. וִזּוּג הָגוּן שֶׁל אַהֲבָה וְאַחֲוָה שָׁלוֹם וְרֵעוּת. זִוּוּג כָּשֵׁר כְּדָת מֹשֶׁה וִיהוּדִית. זִוּוּג הָגוּן שֶׁל יִרְאַת שָׁמַיִם וְיִרְאַת חֵטְא. זִוּוּג שֶׁל בָּנִים הֲגוּנִים צַדִּיקִים וּתְמִימִים וְיְשָׁרִים.

whole, and upright; a union of healthy progeny; a union of blessing, as it is written, "The Lord has remembered us, He shall bless; He shall bless the house of Israel"; a union in which I may embody the verse, "Your wife is like a fertile vine in the inner chambers of your home; your children—like olive saplings around your table"; a union in which my husband shall rejoice in me more than in all the good things that he has in the world, as it is written, "A house and riches are an inheritance from one's ancestors, but a prudent wife is from the Lord"; a union such that there shall never be, between myself and my husband, either anger or resentment, jealousy or competition, but rather love and fraternity, peace and friendship, and humility and meekness and patience; a union of love, fairness and kindness, and doing good for others; a union that will produce live, healthy, good offspring who will not suffer—either in themselves or in any of their limbs—any harm or deficiency, nor damage nor plague, nor illness, nor sickness, nor pain, nor sorrow, nor weakness, nor faltering, and may they lack nothing that is good all the days of their lives; a union in which You will draw sanctity and purity into our souls, our spirits, our life-force and our bodies, in our thoughts, speech, and actions [. . .] a union that is proper in accordance with the law of the holy nation of Israel. A union of success and blessing—blessings of the heavens above, blessings of the deep crouching below, blessings of the breast and of the womb. A union of holy, pure seed, good and beautiful, fine and acceptable. And therefore, for the sake of unifying the Holy One, blessed be He, and the divine presence, with awe and reverence, to unite the Name *yod heh* with the Name *vav heh*; I am hereby ready and prepared to immerse, in accordance with the law of Moses and Israel. May it be Your will, Lord God, that You purify us and sanctify us and shower us with a pure and holy spirit emanating from You and that You view us and our actions with favor. May we always be worthy of performing Your will, all the days of our lives, and may You bless us from Your blessings, for You are the Source of blessings. Blessed is the Lord forever. Amen.

זוּג שֶׁל זֶרַע קַיָּמָא. זוּג שֶׁל בְּרָכָה כַּדָּבָר שֶׁנֶּאֱמַר זִכְרֵנוּ יְבָרֵךְ יְבָרֵךְ אֶת בֵּית יִשְׂרָאֵל. זוּג שֶׁיִּקִים בִּי הַדָּבָר שֶׁנֶּאֱמַר אֶשְׁתְּךָ כְּגֶפֶן פּוֹרִיָּה בְּיַרְכְּתֵי בֵיתֶךָ בָּנֶיךָ כִּשְׁתִלֵי זֵיתִים סָבִיב לְשֻׁלְחָנֶךָ. זוּג שֶׁיִּהְיֶה שָׂמֵחַ בִּי בַּעֲלִי יוֹתֵר מִכָּל הַטּוֹבוֹת שֶׁיֵּשׁ לוֹ בָּעוֹלָם. כַּדָּבָר שֶׁנֶּאֱמַר בַּיִת וָהוֹן נַחֲלַת אָבוֹת וּמֵיְיָ אִשָּׁה מַשְׂכָּלֶת. זוּג שֶׁלֹּא יִהְיֶה בֵּינִי וּבֵין בַּעֲלִי לְעוֹלָם לֹא כַּעַס. וְלֹא רֹגֶן וְלֹא קִנְאָה. וְלֹא תַחֲרוּת. אֶלָּא אַהֲבָה וְאַחֲוָה שָׁלוֹם וְרֵעוּת וַעֲנָוָה וְרוּחַ נְמוּכָה וְסַבְלָנוּת. זוּג שֶׁל אַהֲבָה צְדָקָה וּגְמִילוּת חֲסָדִים וַעֲשִׂיַּת טוֹבָה לַבְּרִיּוֹת. זוּג שֶׁל זֶרַע שֶׁל קַיָּמָא בָּרִיא וְטוֹב שֶׁלֹּא יִהְיֶה בּוֹ וְלֹא בְּשׁוּם אֶחָד מֵאֵבָרָיו שׁוּם נֶזֶק וְלֹא חִסָּרוֹן. לֹא פֶּגַע וְלֹא נֶגַע וְלֹא מַחֲלָה וְלֹא מַדְוֶה וְלֹא כְּאֵב. וְלֹא צַעַר וְלֹא רִפְיוֹן וְלֹא כִשָּׁלוֹן. וְלֹא יַחְסַר כָּל טוֹב כָּל יְמֵי חַיָּיו. זוּג שֶׁתַּמְשִׁיךְ עָלֵינוּ בִּנְשָׁמָתֵנוּ. וְרוּחֵנוּ וְנַפְשֵׁנוּ וְגוּפֵינוּ קְדוּשָׁה וְטָהֳרָה, בְּמַחֲשָׁבָה בְּדִבּוּר וּבְמַעֲשֶׂה, כִּיהוּדִים כְּשֵׁרִים. זוּג כָּשֵׁר כְּדִין יִשְׂרָאֵל קְדוֹשִׁים. זוּג שֶׁל הַצְלָחָה וּבְרָכָה. בִּרְכוֹת שָׁמַיִם מֵעַל. בִּרְכוֹת תְּהוֹם רוֹבֶצֶת תַּחַת. בִּרְכוֹת שָׁדַיִם וָרָחַם. זוּג שֶׁל זֶרַע קָדוֹשׁ וְטָהוֹר. טוֹב וְיָפֶה מְתֻקָּן וּמְקֻבָּל. וְכֵן לְשֵׁם יִחוּד קוּדְשָׁא בְּרִיךְ הוּא וּשְׁכִינְתֵּיהּ בִּדְחִילוּ וּרְחִימוּ לְיַחֲדָא שֵׁם יוֹ"ד הֵ"א בְּשֵׁם וָא"ו הֵ"א הֲרֵינִי מוּכֶנֶת וּמְזוּמֶנֶת לַעֲשׂוֹת טְבִילָה כְּדָת מֹשֶׁה וְיִשְׂרָאֵל. יְהִי רָצוֹן מִלְּפָנֶיךָ יְיָ אֱלֹהִים שֶׁתְּטַהֲרֵנוּ וּתְקַדְּשֵׁנוּ וְתַשְׁפִּיעַ עָלֵינוּ רוּחַ טָהֳרָה וְקִדֻשָּׁה מֵאִתְּךָ וְתִתְרַצֶּה בָּנוּ וּבְמַעֲשֵׂינוּ וּתְזַכֵּנוּ לַעֲשׂוֹת רְצוֹנֶךָ תָּמִיד כָּל יְמֵי חַיֵּינוּ וּתְבָרֵךְ אוֹתָנוּ מִבִּרְכוֹתֶיךָ כִּי אַתָּה הוּא מְקוֹר הַבְּרָכוֹת. בָּרוּךְ יְיָ לְעוֹלָם אָמֵן וְאָמֵן.

PRAYERS FOR CONCEPTION
Italy

$\mathcal{M}$ay it be Your will, Lord my God and God of my forefathers, that You grant me this day a good gift and a good livelihood, and recall me for a good remembrance before You, and grant me salvation and mercy, for the sake of Your great Name, and grant me a worthy, upright, righteous child who is God-fearing both inwardly and outwardly. And grant me a good portion and a good reward and good luck, that I may merit life in the World to Come. Let me hear of good things; bring me good tidings. Grant me length of days and years of life in tranquillity, contentment and security, wisdom, knowledge and understanding, favor and grace and mercy before You and before Your Throne of Glory and before all those who have dealings with me. Direct my heart to love and fear Your Name, incline my heart to perform Your will wholeheartedly, and let my portion be with the righteous. Satiate me with Your goodness and show me mercy with Your salvation, for the sake of Your great Name. Blessed are You, Lord, Who hears prayer.

May it be Your will, Rock of all the worlds, that You grant me pure and holy descendants, to serve You and to fear You and to study Your Torah. Let no harm come to me, nor let the Other Side control me. Deliver me from the hand of a foreign god and from any evil adversary on the way,

---

In 1786, Dr. Yosef (Giuseppe) Coen of Italy gave his fiancée of two years a very special gift: a book of prayers for the married Jewish woman. Written in Hebrew and beautifully illuminated by hand in shades of green and gold, this magnificent collection included private prayers based on a woman's needs and the events comprising her biological and spiritual life cycle. A comparison with earlier manuscripts located in libraries and private collections shows that Dr. Coen did not

תפילות האשה למתנה טובה
איטליה

יְהִי רָצוֹן מִלְּפָנֶיךָ יְיָ אֱלֹהַי וֵאלֹהֵי אֲבוֹתַי שֶׁתִּתֶּן לִי הַיּוֹם מַתָּנָה טוֹבָה
וּפַרְנָסָה טוֹבָה, וְזָכְרֵנִי בְּזִכְרוֹן טוֹב לְפָנֶיךָ וּפָקְדֵנִי בִּפְקֻדַּת יְשׁוּעָה וְרַחֲמִים
לְמַעַן שִׁמְךָ הַגָּדוֹל, וְתִתֶּן לִי בֵּן הָגוּן זָכָר צַדִּיק יָשָׁר צַדִּיק וִירֵא שָׁמַיִם בַּסֵּתֶר
וּבַגָּלוּי, וְתִתֶּן לִי חֵלֶק טוֹב וְשָׂכָר טוֹב וּמַזָּל טוֹב כְּדֵי שֶׁאֶזְכֶּה לְחַיֵּי הָעוֹלָם
הַבָּא, וְתַשְׁמִיעֵנִי שְׁמַע טוֹב וּתְבַשְּׂרֵנִי בְּשׂוֹרוֹת טוֹבוֹת, וְתִתֶּן לִי אֹרֶךְ יָמִים
וּשְׁנוֹת חַיִּים וְשַׁלְוָה וְהַשְׁקֵט וָבֶטַח וְחָכְמָה וְדַעַת וּבִינָה וְחֵן וְחֶסֶד וְרַחֲמִים
לְפָנֶיךָ וְלִפְנֵי כִסֵּא כְבוֹדֶךָ וְלִפְנֵי כָל הַבְּרִיּוֹת שֶׁרוֹאִין אֶת פָּנַי, וְיַחֵד לְבָבִי
לְאַהֲבָה וּלְיִרְאָה אֶת־שְׁמֶךָ וְהַט לִבִּי לַעֲשׂוֹת רְצוֹנְךָ בְּלֵבָב שָׁלֵם, וְתֵן חֶלְקִי
עִם הַצַּדִּיקִים וְשַׂבְּעֵנִי מִטּוּבֶךָ וְרַחֵם עָלַי בִּישׁוּעָתְךָ לְמַעַן שִׁמְךָ הַגָּדוֹל.
בָּרוּךְ אַתָּה יְיָ שׁוֹמֵעַ תְּפִלָּה:

יְהִי רָצוֹן מִלְּפָנֶיךָ צוּר הָעוֹלָמִים שֶׁתְּזַמֵּן לִי זֶרַע טָהוֹר וְקָדוֹשׁ לַעֲבוֹדָתְךָ
וּלְיִרְאָתְךָ וּלְתַלְמוּד תּוֹרָתֶךָ, וְלֹא יִפְגַּע־בִּי שׁוּם פֶּגַע רַע וְלֹא שִׁלְטוֹן מִסִּטְרָא
אַחֲרָא וְתַצִּילֵנִי מִיַּד אֵל נֵכָר וּמִכָּל־אוֹיֵב רָע בַּדֶּרֶךְ וּמִכַּף מְעַוֵּל וְחוֹמֵץ,
כִּי אַתָּה תִּקְוָתִי וְאַתָּה אֱלֹהִים מִבְטַחִי עָלֶיךָ, וְאִם בְּאוּלַי תַּעֲלֶה הֵרָיוֹנִי
בְּהִתְלַוּוֹת אִישִׁי אֵלַי הַלַּיְלָה הַזֶּה כִּי לַעֲשׂוֹת מִצְוֹתֶיךָ חָפַצְתִּי וְתָגֵל לִבִּי

---

create these prayers as his own original works, but rather gathered existing, familiar
texts. Handed down from generation to generation, the book has been preserved
remarkably well; it was donated by Harry G. Friedman to the Rare Book Room of
the Jewish Theological Seminary in New York. In 1995, Rabbi Nina Beth Cardin
published a book called *Out of the Depths I Call to You*, which includes an English
translation of the prayers in Dr. Coen's book and her own commentary on them.

and from the grasp of the unjust and the wicked, for You are my hope and You are God; my trust is in You. And if perchance I should conceive as I am united with my husband tonight—for I desire to fulfill Your commandments, and my soul shall rejoice in Your salvation; I shall sing to the Lord for He has been kind to me—then, Lord my God, show me kindness; sustain me that I may merit to raise the child created for Your service and Your reverence, in truth and with a perfect heart, according to his good and upright desire. May the Holy One, blessed be He, forge this wish into reality. Amen.

May it be Your will, Lord my God and God of my forefathers, God of Abraham, God of Isaac, and God of Jacob, that You show me kindness such that I may conceive, on this night that approaches for peace, through my husband. Let the child who will be formed from this immersion be a Torah scholar who is God-fearing [even] in private and Who observes Your commandments, statutes, and judgments for their own sake. Master of the world, please accept my prayer and imbue within me a pure and unblemished soul, that I not be defiled, heaven forefend, with children who are not worthy. Remove from me any foreign thought, and deliver me from the evil inclination, lest it divert me and surround me with evil thoughts. And as for my husband—grant good thoughts in his heart, when he is ready to unite with me, so that we may merit to bear a child who is pure, untainted, and good-hearted. May all of my thoughts and intentions be for the good, that I may be worthy of having my wishes granted. For You are God Who is the One King, upright and faithful, accepting the prayers of Your creatures. And so may it be Your will. Amen. Act for Your Name's sake, act for the sake of Your right hand, act for the sake of Your Torah, act for the sake of Your holiness. May the words of my mouth and the thoughts of my heart find favor before You, Lord, my Rock and my Redeemer.

בִּישׁוּעָתֶךָ אָשִׁירָה לַיְיָ כִּי גָמַל עָלַי כִּי אַתָּה יְיָ אֱלֹקַי חָנֵּנִי וַהֲקִימֵנִי עַד שֶׁאֶזְכֶּה לְגַדֵּל הַיֶּלֶד הַנּוֹצַר לַעֲבוֹדָתְךָ וְיִרְאָתֶךָ בֶּאֱמֶת וּבְלֵב שָׁלֵם כִּרְצוֹנוֹ הַטּוֹב וְהַיָּשָׁר, וְכַוָּנָה טוֹבָה הַקָּדוֹשׁ בָּרוּךְ הוּא יְצָרְפֶנָה לְמַעֲשֶׂה, אָמֵן.

יְהִי רָצוֹן מִלְּפָנֶיךָ יְיָ אֱלֹקַי וֵאלֹקֵי אֲבוֹתַי אֱלֹקֵי אַבְרָהָם אֱלֹקֵי יִצְחָק וֵאלֹקֵי יַעֲקֹב שֶׁתְּחָנֵּנִי שֶׁאֶתְעַבֵּר הַלַּיְלָה הַבָּאָה לִקְרָאתֵנוּ לְשָׁלוֹם מִבַּעֲלִי וְהַיֶּלֶד הַנּוֹצַר מִטְּבִילָה הַזֹּאת יִהְיֶה תַּלְמִיד חָכָם וִירֵא שָׁמַיִם בַּסֵּתֶר וּמְקַיֵּם מִצְוֹתֶיךָ חֻקֶּיךָ וּמִשְׁפָּטֶיךָ לִשְׁמָם, רִבּוֹנוֹ שֶׁל עוֹלָם קַבֵּל נָא אֶת תְּפִלָּתִי וְתַשְׁפִּיעַ בְּמֵעַי נְשָׁמָה זַכָּה וּטְהוֹרָה וְלֹא אֶתְחַלֵּל חַס וְשָׁלוֹם בְּבָנִים שֶׁאֵינָם הֲגוּנִים וְהָסֵר מִמֶּנִּי כָּל מַחֲשָׁבָה זָרָה וְתַצִּילֵנִי מִיֵּצֶר הָרָע לְבַל יְסִיתֵנִי לְבַלְּעֵנִי בְּמַחֲשָׁבוֹת רָעוֹת, וּלְבַעֲלִי תֵּן בְּלִבּוֹ מַחֲשָׁבָה טוֹבָה כִּשְׁרוֹצָה לְהִזְדַּוֵּג עִמִּי כְּדֵי שֶׁנִּזְכֶּה לְהוֹלִיד בֵּן זָךְ וְטָהוֹר וְטוֹב לֵב וְיִהְיוּ כָּל עֶשְׁתּוֹנוֹתַי וּמַחְשְׁבוֹתַי לְטוֹבָה כְּדֵי שֶׁאֶזְכֶּה שֶׁיְּמַלְּאוּ מִשְׁאֲלוֹתַי, כִּי אֵל מֶלֶךְ יָחִיד וְנֶאֱמָן אַתָּה וּמְקַבֵּל תְּפִלּוֹת יְצוּרֶיךָ, וְכֵן יְהִי רָצוֹן אָמֵן, עֲשֵׂה לְמַעַן שְׁמֶךָ, עֲשֵׂה לְמַעַן יְמִינֶךָ, עֲשֵׂה לְמַעַן תּוֹרָתֶךָ, עֲשֵׂה לְמַעַן קְדֻשָּׁתֶךָ: יִהְיוּ לְרָצוֹן אִמְרֵי פִי וְהֶגְיוֹן לִבִּי לְפָנֶיךָ יְיָ צוּרִי וְגוֹאֲלִי.

PRAYER AT MENOPAUSE

Ruth Lazare

You created my body with wisdom

You have taught me the secret of filling and of absence;

The powers of growth and giving.

And now I am prepared and ready for a new life.

Ruth Lazare has ventured to add to the compendium of women's prayers some meditations for moments that others have generally avoided addressing. Menopause, she declares, is not only an end, but also a new beginning in a woman's life.

תפילה לאשה בגיל המעבר

רות לור

רָאִיתָ אֶת גּוּפִי בְּחָכְמָה
לִמַּדְתָּ אוֹתִי אֶת סוֹד הַהִתְמַלְּאוּת וְהֶהָעֵדֶר
אֶת כֹּחוֹת הַצְּמִיחָה וְהַהֲעֵנָקָה.
וְעַתָּה אֲנִי מוּכָנָה וּמְזֻמֶּנֶת לְחַיִּים חֲדָשִׁים.

V

FESTIVALS
and
HOLY DAYS

Shabbat

Shabbat, the fourth of the Ten Commandments, is the Jewish nation's day of rest. In formalizing what seems to be a basic human need for a day of rest, Shabbat also recalls the creation of the world, when God ceased His creative work on the seventh day.

The sanctity of Shabbat is inherent and objective; it is independent of both the solar and the lunar cycle. Its status is not established by the Jewish people—unlike the festivals, whose sanctity is dependent on the acknowledgment of the new moon. It falls every seventh day, starting from the first Shabbat, at the time of Creation, and continuing to this day.

Shabbat is celebrated with special prayers and ceremonies. It is officially welcomed just before sunset on Friday afternoon with the lighting of candles. Kiddush (sanctification of the day) is recited over a cup of wine, with two loaves of bread at each meal, and songs are sung in tribute to the day. Shabbat concludes with the *Havdala* (separation) ceremony at nightfall on Saturday, which marks the beginning of a new week with wine, a special braided candle, and fragrant spices meant to refresh and revive the spirit as one bids Shabbat farewell.

WELCOMING THE ANGELS
Italy

I give thanks before You, my God, for all the kindness which You have shown to me, and which You will show me and all of Your creations in the future. Blessed are Your angels, who perform Your will wholeheartedly. Lord of peace—bless us and remember us for a good life and for peace, and let me and my descendants be worthy of finding favor and grace in the eyes of all those who behold us. Erase my sins and forgive my iniquities and transgressions. Permit me to welcome Sabbaths with great joy, with wealth and dignity, and with few sins. Remove from me—and from all of Your nation Israel—every sort of evil disease and every type of suffering, and all forms of poverty and wretchedness. Grant me a positive inclination and life in the World to Come, and much wealth and dignity, to serve You with awe and love. Blessed are You, King of Glory. Peace to you, angels of mercy. Come in peace, angels of peace. Angels of mercy, ministering angels—come in peace, as our Lord, the Holy King of Glory, has commanded you. Lord of peace, merciful Father—imbue me with a positive inclination, [that] with love and awe [I may be] dignified in Your eyes and in the eyes of all those who behold me, for You are the true and affirmed King. Amen, Selah.

This prayer was found in a handwritten collection of women's prayers that was dedicated to "The honorable Lady Sara, wife of K. Ḥizkiyah Levi—may the Almighty watch over him and protect him—a cherished member of the community of Chieri, may God protect it, in the year 5574."

מוֹדִית אֲנִי לְפָנֶיךָ

מוֹדִית אֲנִי לְפָנֶיךָ אֱלֹקַי עַל כָּל הַחֶסֶד אֲשֶׁר עָשִׂיתָ עִמָּדִי וַאֲשֶׁר
אַתָּה עָתִיד לַעֲשׂוֹת עִמִּי וְעִם כָּל בְּרִיּוֹתֶיךָ וּבְרוּכִים מַלְאָכֶיךָ שֶׁעוֹשִׂים
רְצוֹנְךָ בְּלֵבָב שָׁלֵם. אֲדוֹן הַשָּׁלוֹם תְּבָרְכֵנוּ וְתִפְקְדֵנוּ לְחַיִּים טוֹבִים וּלְשָׁלוֹם
וּתְזַכֶּה אוֹתִי וְאֶת זַרְעִי לִמְצֹא חֵן וְחֶסֶד בְּעֵינֵי כָּל רוֹאַי וְתַעֲבִיר עֲווֹנִי וְתִמְחַל
פְּשָׁעַי וְחַטֹּאתַי וּתְזַכֵּנִי לְקַבֵּל שַׁבָּתוֹת מִתּוֹךְ רֹב שִׂמְחָה וּמִתּוֹךְ עֹשֶׁר וְכָבוֹד
וּמִתּוֹךְ מִעוּט עֲווֹנוֹת וְתַעֲבִיר מִמֶּנִּי וּמִכָּל עַמְּךָ יִשְׂרָאֵל כָּל מִינֵי חֳלָאִים
רָעִים וְכָל מִינֵי מַדְוֶה וְכָל מִינֵי דַלּוּת וַעֲנִיּוּת וְתַנְחִילֵנִי יֵצֶר טוֹב וְחַיֵּי עוֹלָם
הַבָּא וְרֹב עֹשֶׁר וְכָבוֹד לְעָבְדְךָ בְּיִרְאָה וּבְאַהֲבָה. בָּרוּךְ אַתָּה הַמֶּלֶךְ הַכָּבוֹד.
שָׁלוֹם לָכֶם מַלְאֲכֵי רַחֲמִים. בּוֹאֲכֶם לְשָׁלוֹם מַלְאֲכֵי הַשָּׁלוֹם. מַלְאֲכֵי רַחֲמִים,
מַלְאֲכֵי הַשָּׁרֵת, בּוֹאֲכֶם לְשָׁלוֹם כַּאֲשֶׁר צִוָּה אֶתְכֶם אֲדוֹנֵנוּ הַמֶּלֶךְ הַכָּבוֹד
וְהַקָּדוֹשׁ. אֲדוֹן הַשָּׁלוֹם אַב הָרַחֲמָן תֶּן בִּי יֵצֶר טוֹב בְּאַהֲבָה וּבְיִרְאָה מְכֻבֶּדֶת
בְּעֵינֶיךָ וּבְעֵינֵי כָּל רוֹאַי כִּי אַתָּה הַמֶּלֶךְ אֱמֶת וְנָכוֹן אָמֵן סֶלָה.

The reference to angels is based on a Talmudic legend describing two angels
that visit every Jewish home on Shabbat, bestowing a blessing that the ambiance
of light and peace be re-created the following week.

BLESSING THE CHILDREN

The parent giving the blessing places his or her hands upon the child's head and says:

[For daughters:]

*M*ay God make you like Sarah, Rebecca, Rachel, and Leah.

[For sons:]

*M*ay God make you like Ephraim and Menasheh.

Blessing for a daughter according to Rabbi Aharon Berakhia:

*M*ay God make you like Sarah, Rebecca, Rachel, and Leah. May the Name of the Holy One, blessed be He, be blessed; in His mercy

---

It is customary on the eve of Shabbat or a festival, upon returning home from the synagogue (or, as among Bukharan Jews, before leaving for the synagogue), to bless one's children. In many families the custom continues even after the children are married.

The late-sixteenth- and early-seventeenth-century author Rabbi Aharon Berakhia of Modena, one of the greatest kabbalists of the time, wrote: "... The custom of blessing [one's children] on the holy Shabbat—and particularly on Shabbat eve—

ברכת הבנות והבנים

המברך מניח ידיו על המתברך, ואומר:

לבנות:

יְשִׂמֵךְ אֱלֹהִים כְּשָׂרָה רִבְקָה רָחֵל וְלֵאָה.

לבנים:

יְשִׂמְךָ אֱלֹהִים כְּאֶפְרַיִם וְכִמְנַשֶּׁה.

הברכה לבת:

יְשִׂמֵךְ אֱלֹקִים כְּשָׂרָה רִבְקָה רָחֵל וְלֵאָה: יִתְבָּרֵךְ שְׁמוֹ שֶׁל הַקָּדוֹשׁ
בָּרוּךְ הוּא וְהוּא בְּרַחֲמָיו יִשְׁמְרֵךְ מִכָּל רַע, יִשְׁמֹר אֶת נַפְשֵׁךְ וִיתַקְנֵךְ בְּעֵצָה
טוֹבָה מִלְּפָנָיו וְתִהְיִי אֵשֶׁת חַיִל יְרֵאַת ה׳ [וְאִם הִיא רוֹקָה: וּבְחַיִּק יְרֵא

---

is of the essence of the Shabbat Queen ... and the essence of the 'extra soul,' for
the blessings fall upon the one giving the blessing as well as the one receiving it.
Furthermore, there is no [influence of] Satan or any evil force on Shabbat, to stand
as an accuser against the blessing ..."

may He protect you from all evil, guard your soul, and grant you good guidance from before Him. May you be a God-fearing woman of valor [if she is not yet married, insert: and may you be among those who fear the Lord, for the life of your father and your mother]. May you not miscarry or be barren, nor widowed, but rather a joyful mother of children for the length of [your] days and years of life. May you be whole in your traits and beliefs and in all manner of perfection. May you find favor and good understanding in the eyes of God and in the eyes of your husband, and may you rejoice in your offspring. Amen.

Rabbi Yehuda Henkin, author of the four volumes of responsa known as *Benei Vanim*, blesses his daughters with the following words:

*M*ay God make you like Rachel and Leah, who jointly built the house of Israel.

In his book Rabbi Henkin writes that his wife, too, blesses their sons and daughters, but she uses the traditional formula (above).

אֱלֹקִים תְּנָתֵנִי לְחַיֵּי אָבִיךְ וְאִמֵּךְ] לֹא תִהְיִי מְשֻׁכֶּלֶה וַעֲקָרָה וְלֹא אַלְמָנָה אֶלָּא אֵם הַבָּנִים שְׂמֵחָה לְאֹרֶךְ יָמִים וּשְׁנוֹת חַיִּים וְתִהְיִי שְׁלֵמָה בַּמִּדּוֹת וּבַדֵּעוֹת וּבְכָל מִינֵי שְׁלֵמוּת וְתִמְצְאִי חֵן וְשֵׂכֶל טוֹב בְּעֵינֵי אֱלֹקִים וּבְעֵינֵי בַּעֲלֵךְ וְתִשְׂמְחִי בְּצֶאֱצָאֵי מֵעַיִךְ. אָמֵן:

יִתֵּן אוֹתָךְ [אוֹ יְשִׂימֵךְ] אֱלֹקִים כְּרָחֵל וּכְלֵאָה אֲשֶׁר בָּנוּ שְׁתֵּיהֶן אֶת בֵּית יִשְׂרָאֵל.

FOR BEAUTIFYING THE SYNAGOGUE

Prayer book of the Jewish community of Rome

*H*e Who blessed Sarah, Rebecca, Rachel, and Leah—may He bless every daughter of Israel who fashions a coat or covering with which to adorn the Torah, or who prepares a candle in honor of the Torah. May the Holy One, blessed be He, pay her reward and grant her the good that she deserves, and let us say: Amen.

Synagogues in Italy were magnificently adorned with works of embroidery interwoven with silver thread that were used as belts for the rolled Torah scroll, cloths for covering the Torah while the blessings over it were recited, and coats to clothe the scroll while not in use.

The women of the community were responsible for decorating the synagogue. The Torah cloths and coats that have been preserved reveal fascinating biographical details: the name of the embroiderer, the name of the woman donating it as a gift to the congregation, and the date of the work. In many cases, a woman added further personal details, such as her date of birth, a dedication in memory of a family member, or a prayer for long life. Fortunately, these items have been preserved over time, thanks to the care with which ritual objects always have been treated.

"מי שברך" לנשים – שבת בבוקר

מחזור התפילה של בני רומא

מִי שֶׁבֵּרֵךְ שָׂרָה רִבְקָה רָחֵל וְלֵאָה הוּא יְבָרֵךְ אֶת כָּל בַּת יִשְׂרָאֵל
שֶׁעוֹשָׂה מְעִיל אוֹ מִטְפַּחַת לִכְבוֹד הַתּוֹרָה וְהַמַתְקֶנֶת נֵר לִכְבוֹד הַתּוֹרָה.
הַקָבַּ"ה יְשַׁלֵּם שְׂכָרָה וְיִתֵּן לָה גְמוּלָה הַטּוֹב וְנֹאמַר אָמֵן.

* * *

This *Mi Sheberakh* prayer, unique to the Italian Jewish prayer book and a variation on the familiar formula that is routinely recited during Shabbat morning prayers, refers to these embroiderers. Perhaps it was because of their involvement in the beautification of the community's most sacred objects that the Jewish women of Italy were generally held in such high esteem.

The Roman siddur appears to be the first prayer tradition to have been consolidated outside of the Land of Israel and Babylon; its source dates back prior to the redaction of the Babylonian Talmud.

OPENING THE GATES
Yiddish

*M*aster of the universe. Just as the Holy Ark is opened here, so may a window be opened in heaven: the gates of a time of favor, the gates of a time of asking, the gates of prayer, and the gates of mercy. May my prayer be accepted among the other pure prayers that are surely accepted before You, and may it be a crown for Your head. May it be Your will that You deliver me, along with my husband and my children and close ones, and may my prayer be as praiseworthy and sweet for You as though I had offered a sacrifice in the Holy Temple. Almighty Lord of Hosts, open Your gates before me—gates of favor, gates of mercy, the gates of heaven, and the gates of prayer and supplication. May the merit of Shabbat endure for me so that all of my prayers come before You, and that no barrier stand before our prayers, in either the physical or the spiritual realm, such that we may become one with Your supreme holiness. Remember me, my

In some synagogues in Europe, the women's section was not located within the main synagogue building, but was rather housed in a separate structure joined to the synagogue. The prayer service in the women's synagogue was different from that of the men; it was adapted to the needs and concerns of the women. Women prayer leaders would recite the prayers aloud, while the other women worshippers repeated and responded.

Various sources attest to the degree to which the Hebrew language was in-

תחינה לאומרה בשעת "אנעים זמירות"

רִבּוֹנוֹ שֶׁל עוֹלָם, כְּמוֹ שֶׁנִּפְתַּח כָּאן אֲרוֹן הַקֹּדֶשׁ, כֵּן יִפָּתַח חַלּוֹן בָּרָקִיעַ, שַׁעֲרֵי עֵת רָצוֹן. שַׁעֲרֵי עֵת בַּקָּשָׁה, שַׁעֲרֵי תְּפִלָּה וְשַׁעֲרֵי רַחֲמִים. תִּתְקַבֵּל תְּפִלָּתִי בֵּין שְׁאָר הַתְּפִלּוֹת הַטְּהוֹרוֹת שֶׁבְּוַדַּאי מִתְקַבְּלוֹת לְפָנֶיךָ, וְתִהְיֶה כֶּתֶר לְרֹאשֶׁךָ. יְהִי רָצוֹן שֶׁתּוֹשִׁיעֵנִי עִם בַּעֲלִי וּבָנַי וִידִידַי, וּתְפִלָּתִי תִּהְיֶה מְשֻׁבַּחַת וּמְתוּקָה וּמְתוּקָה לְפָנֶיךָ כְּאִילּוּ הִקְרַבְתִּי קָרְבָּן בְּבֵית הַמִּקְדָּשׁ. אֵל שַׁדַּי צְבָאוֹת פְּתַח לְפָנַי שְׁעָרֶיךָ, שַׁעֲרֵי רָצוֹן, שַׁעֲרֵי רַחֲמִים, שַׁעֲרֵי שָׁמַיִם וְשַׁעֲרֵי תְּפִילוֹת וּבַקָּשׁוֹת, זְכוּת הַשַּׁבָּת תַּעֲמֹד לִי שֶׁכָּל תְּפִלּוֹתַי יָבוֹאוּ לְפָנֶיךָ, שׁוּם מְחִיצָה לֹא תַּפְסִיק בִּפְנֵי תְּפִילוֹתֵינוּ בֵּין בְּגַשְׁמִיוּת בֵּין בְּרוּחָנִיּוּת, וְנִתְחַבֵּר לַקְּדֻשָּׁה הָעֶלְיוֹנָה. תִּפְקֹד אוֹתִי וְאֶת בַּעֲלִי וּבָנַי הָאֲהוּבִים וִידִידַי הָאֲהוּבִים, בְּשָׁעָה שֶׁשָּׁמָּה עֵת רָצוֹן וְעֵת הַצְלָחָה, שֶׁחַיֵּינוּ יִקָּרְאוּ חַיִּים שֶׁל שִׂמְחָה, חַיִּים שֶׁל פַּרְנָסָה, חַיִּים שֶׁל בְּרָכָה, חַיִּים שֶׁל

---

accessible to the general Jewish public. As a result, many prayers were recited in Yiddish rather than in Hebrew.

This prayer is meant to be recited prior to *An'im Zemirot* (known as the "Song of Glory" and recited with the Holy Ark open and the Torah scrolls displayed), or as an alternative to it. *An'im Zemirot* is one of the most complex of the liturgical poems, in terms of both language and substance. It was perhaps the difficulties encountered by many—including women—in understanding and reciting *An'im Zemirot* that prompted the creation of alternative prayers and supplications.

husband, my beloved children, and dear ones, at the time that is called a time of favor and a time of success, so that our lives may be called lives of joy, lives of sustenance, lives of blessing, lives of peace, lives of mercy, and of Your good teachings. Bless us with the three keys that have never been handed over to any emissary, but come about only through Your own blessing. With this I conclude; hurry to my aid, God of my deliverance.

Master of the universe: I pray You, may the merit of Shabbat protect us, that we may merit to have children who are Torah scholars and upright, who are pious, bearers of the mystical tradition, and knowing the secrets of the Torah. Let nothing unworthy emerge from me or from my children, heaven forfend, and may I embody the words, "'Happy are you'—in this world, 'and it shall be good for you'—in the World to Come." May we be worthy of observing the Shabbat as is proper, and may You deliver me and all who are mine from sin and from worry. Protect us all from that which my heart fears, and spare me, my husband, and my children from mortal charity. Hear my prayer, [insert name of worshipper], daughter of [insert name of worshipper's mother], as You heard the righteous Hannah and the other righteous women. Amen, Selah.

שָׁלוֹם, חַיִּים שֶׁל רַחֲמִים וְשֶׁל לֶקַח טוֹב. תְּבָרְכֵנוּ בִּשְׁלֹשֶׁת הַמִּפְתָּחוֹת שֶׁלֹּא נִמְסְרוּ עַל יְדֵי שָׁלִיחַ רַק מִבִּרְכָתֶךָ. וּבְזֶה אֲסַיֵּם, חוּשָׁה לְעֶזְרָתִי ה' תְּשׁוּעָתִי.

רִבּוֹנוֹ שֶׁל עוֹלָם, אָנָּא תָּגֵן עָלֵינוּ זְכוּת הַשַּׁבָּת שֶׁנִּזְכֶּה לְבָנִים זְכָרִים תַּלְמִידֵי חֲכָמִים וַהֲגוּנִים, שֶׁיִּהְיוּ חֲסִידִים וּבַעֲלֵי קַבָּלָה בַּעֲלֵי סוֹדוֹת הַתּוֹרָה. אַל יֵצֵא חַס וְשָׁלוֹם מִמֶּנִּי אוֹ מִבָּנַי שׁוּם פְּסוּל, וְיִתְקַיֵּם בִּי מַה שֶּׁכָּתוּב אַשְׁרֶיךָ בָּעוֹלָם הַזֶּה וְטוֹב לְךָ לָעוֹלָם הַבָּא. נִזְכֶּה לִשְׁמֹר אֶת הַשַּׁבָּת כָּרָאוּי, וְתַצִּיל מֵחֲטָאִים וּמִדְּאָגוֹת אוֹתִי וְאֶת כָּל אֲשֶׁר לִי. שְׁמֹר אֶת כֻּלָּנוּ מִמַּה שֶּׁלִּבִּי מְפַחֵד מִפָּנָיו, וְתַצִּיל אוֹתִי וְאֶת בַּעֲלִי וּבָנַי מִמַּתְּנַת בָּשָׂר וָדָם. תִּשְׁמַע תְּפִלָּתִי [פ״ב] כְּמוֹ שֶׁשָּׁמַעְתָּ לַצַּדֶּקֶת חַנָּה וְלִשְׁאָר נָשִׁים צַדְקָנִיּוֹת, אָמֵן סֶלָה.

AT THE CONCLUSION OF SHABBAT

Ladino

I shall drink this water
From the well of Miriam, the prophetess
Who heals from all affliction
And from all evil that may befall us
And who gives us sustenance without sorrow.

According to both Ashkenazic and Sephardic traditions, at the conclusion of each Shabbat, the well that provided water for the Israelites in the desert in the merit of the righteous Miriam flows to all the rivers and wells in the world. Anyone who drinks from those waters is healed of all illness. Hence the custom exists, in many communities, of drawing water immediately after Shabbat.

Ladino-speaking women would traditionally utter these words before drinking water after Shabbat.

תפילה לאשה במוצאי־שבת

לדינו

באר של מרים

אֶשְׁתֶּה מַיִם אֵלֶּה   יו ביב׳ו איסטה אגואה

מִבְּאֵרָה שֶׁל   דיל פוזו די לה סיניורה

מִרְיָם הַנְּבִיאָה   די מרים לה נביאה

הַמְרַפְּאָה מִכָּל צָרָה   קי סאנה מי מיליזינה

וּמִכָּל רָעָה שֶׁתִּפְקְדֵנוּ   אי טודוס לוס מאליס לוס קורה

וְהַנּוֹתֶנֶת לָנוּ פַּרְנָסָה לְלֹא צַעַר.   אי מוס דה פרנסה סין סאר.

The New Moon

According to the Midrash, Rosh Hodesh (the new moon) is
considered a women's holiday. Indeed, Jewish women throughout
the ages have observed Rosh Hodesh as a day of celebration
and rest. In some communities they abstained only from
housework, whereas in other places, where women worked as
professional seamstresses and embroiderers, they abstained from
their professional occupations, too. I remember how my own
grandmother, Hannah Mashiah, of blessed memory—a member
of the Bukharan community in Jerusalem who was born at the
beginning of the twentieth century—would light a candle on the
eve of the new moon and refrain from all housework during that
night and the following day. Malka Pietrokowsky, director of the
beit midrash at Midreshet Lindenbaum (the first seminary for higher
Torah education for women, established in Jerusalem in the late
1980s), has called for a revival of this custom and the declaration
of Rosh Hodesh as a day of rest for women.

PRAYER FOR THE EVE
OF THE NEW MOON
Sarah Bat-Tovim

Our Father, merciful Father, show us Your power and might; help us and lead us to the chosen land, as You promised us, for You are faithful and Your words are faithful. But we ask of You, kind and merciful God, that You bring our redemption speedily, that we may see it with our own eyes. Our Father, our King: When we sinned in the desert, Moses, our teacher, of blessed memory, offered a prayer on our behalf: Our Father, our King, please forgive this nation in which You took pride and which You called, My firstborn son, Israel. I know that You are full of the attribute of mercy. Hear my voice as You heard the prayers of our earliest righteous forefathers when they cried out to You; hear me this day, O Searcher

---

Sarah Bat-Tovim was one of the most famous composers of *tekhines* in Yiddish. Her supplications are characterized by heartfelt emotion and honesty. Sarah's charismatic personality and her awareness of those precious moments in a woman's life—sometimes greatly moving, sometimes paralyzing, when she experiences, with full force, the essence of life—led to her broad popularity throughout the Ashkenazic Diaspora.

Sarah Bat-Tovim called for simplicity, asking women not to visit the synagogue wearing fancy clothing, and spoke of the communal and Jewish obligation borne by each and every individual. Her ability to express herself in the language of the people, to admit to her personal weaknesses, and to interject a dash of humor served to establish her status as the "queen of *tekhines*." Her works have acquired

תְּחִנָּה לְעֶרֶב רֹאשׁ-חֹדֶשׁ

שָׂרָה בַּת טוֹבִים

אָבִינוּ אָב הָרַחֲמָן הַרְאֵה לָנוּ אֶת כֹּחֲךָ וּגְבוּרָתֶךָ וְעָזְרֵנוּ וְהוֹלִיכֵנוּ לְאֶרֶץ הַבְּחִירָה כְּפִי שֶׁהִבְטַחְתָּנוּ כִּי אַתָּה נֶאֱמָן וְנֶאֱמָנִים דְּבָרֶיךָ, אַךְ מְבַקְשִׁים אָנוּ מִמְּךָ אֵל רַחוּם וְחַנּוּן שֶׁתָּחִישׁ גְּאֻלָּתֵנוּ וְנִרְאֶה זֹאת בְּמוֹ עֵינֵינוּ. אָבִינוּ מַלְכֵּנוּ, כַּאֲשֶׁר חָטָאנוּ בַּמִּדְבָּר נָשָׂא מֹשֶׁה רַבֵּנוּ ע"ה תְּפִלָּה עֲבוּרֵנוּ: אָבִינוּ מַלְכֵּנוּ, סְלַח נָא לְעָם הַזֶּה אֲשֶׁר בּוֹ הִתְפָּאַרְתָּ וְקָרֵאתָ לוֹ בְּנֵי בְּכוֹרִי יִשְׂרָאֵל. יוֹדֵעַ אֲנִי שֶׁמִּדָּתְךָ מְלֵאַת רַחֲמִים הִיא. שְׁמַע לְקוֹלִי כְּשֵׁם שֶׁשָּׁמַעְתָּ לִתְפִלַּת אֲבוֹתֵינוּ קַדְמוֹנֵינוּ הַצַּדִּיקִים בְּעֵת שַׁוְּעָם אֵלֶיךָ, שְׁמָעֵנִי הַיּוֹם בּוֹחֵן לְבָבוֹת, אַל תַּשְׁלִיכֵנִי לְעֵת זִקְנָה וְאוֹכַל לְעָבְדְּךָ בְּלֵבָב שָׁלֵם, וּמַה שֶּׁחָטָאתִי מְחַל נָא לִי וְשֶׁלֹּא אֶחֱטָא יוֹתֵר, שֶׁלֹּא יִשְׂמְחוּ שׂוֹנְאַי

─── ✦ ───

a permanent place in the compendium of Jewish prayer. For many years after her death, new *tekhines* continued to be attributed to her.

At the beginning of her book, she writes: "I composed this book, *Sheker ha-Hen*, as a remedy for the soul in this world and in the World to Come. Do not skimp, if you are able to acquire this book; as a reward we shall merit the World to Come …" In several places in her book she rebukes women for their character traits and moral standards. She adopted strict standards for her own behavior: At the beginning of her book of *tekhines*, *Shelosha She'arim*, she seeks forgiveness: "May the blessed God forgive me for chatting, in my youth, in the women's section of the synagogue during the prayer service and the reading of our beloved Torah."

of hearts; do not cast me out in my old age, so that I might serve You wholeheartedly. That which I have sinned—please forgive me, and may I not sin anymore, so that my enemies should not rejoice over my failure, nor be able to harm me. Let the angels of mercy carry up my prayer before You; treat me with kindness and mercy and not with anger, heaven forfend. I pray You, Knower of thoughts—look upon my wretchedness and take up my grievance, for You are righteous and upright; it is my sins alone that have caused me to need to work hard to make a living and to preserve my health.

בְּכִשְׁלוֹנִי וְלֹא יוּכְלוּ לַעֲשׂוֹת עִמִּי רַע. יִשְׂאוּ מַלְאֲכֵי הָרַחֲמִים אֶת תְּפִלָּתִי לְפָנֶיךָ וּנְהַג בִּי בְּחֶסֶד וּבְרַחֲמִים וְלֹא בְרֹגֶז חָלִילָה. אָנָּא יוֹדֵעַ מַחֲשָׁבוֹת, רְאֵה בְעָנְיִי וְרִיבָה רִיבִי, כִּי צַדִּיק וְיָשָׁר אַתָּה וְרַק עֲווֹנוֹתַי הֵם שֶׁגָּרְמוּ לִי שֶׁאֶצְטָרֵךְ לַעֲמֹל בְּפֶרֶךְ לְכַלְכָּלָתִי וּלְבְרִיאוּת גּוּפִי.

MATRIARCHS' SUPPLICATION

Rabbanit Sheril (Sarah Rivkah Rachel Leah) Horowitz

*M*aster of the universe, great and awesome God: In Your great mercy You created the heaven and the earth and all of Creation, in six days and with ten utterances. On the seventh day, the holy Shabbat, You rested from Your work and commanded Your nation Israel—in which You are glorified, as it is written: "Israel, in whom I shall be glorified"—likewise to rest on Shabbat from all their labor and from speaking of mundane things; rather, all of their speech should concern Torah, each person in accordance with his level and ability. And those who are unable to study—including we, the women of Your nation, Israel—should read books of instruction as to how to serve God and fulfill the commandments that God gave us.

You also have given us new moons, the times when the holy High Court would declare the beginning of the months. But since the day when we were exiled from our land, nothing remains for us of the commandment to sanctify the new moon but our declaration and blessing of the new month

Rabbanit Sheril (Sarah Rivkah Rachel Leah) Horowitz was born in 1715. She composed *tekhines* in Aramaic, in rabbinical style, which were translated into Yiddish in later collections of *tekhines*. This particular *tekhineh*, meant to be recited on the Shabbat preceding Rosh Ḥodesh, is interwoven with descriptions of events from the Torah, biblical exegesis, and moral teachings.

תחינת אמהות לברכת החודש

הרבנית שריל [שרה רבקה רחל לאה] הורוביץ

בּוֹן הָעוֹלָמִים, אֵל גָּדוֹל וְנוֹרָא! אַתָּה בָּרָאתָ בְּרַחֲמֶיךָ הָרַבִּים אֶת הַשָּׁמַיִם וְאֶת הָאָרֶץ וְאֶת כָּל הַבְּרוּאִים, בְּשִׁשָּׁה יָמִים וּבַעֲשָׂרָה מַאֲמָרוֹת; וּבַיּוֹם הַשְּׁבִיעִי, שֶׁהוּא שַׁבַּת קֹדֶשׁ, נַחְתָּ מִמְּלַאכְתֶּךָ, וְצִוִּיתָ לְעַמְּךָ יִשְׂרָאֵל, אֲשֶׁר אַתָּה מִתְפָּאֵר בָּהֶם, כְּמוֹ שֶׁכָּתוּב: "יִשְׂרָאֵל אֲשֶׁר בְּךָ אֶתְפָּאָר", שֶׁיָּנוּחוּ גַם הֵם בְּיוֹם הַשַּׁבָּת מִכָּל מְלַאכְתָּם, וּמִלְּדַבֵּר דִּבְרֵי חֹל; אֶלָּא יִהְיֶה כָּל דִּבּוּרָם בְּעֵסֶק הַתּוֹרָה, אִישׁ אִישׁ כְּכֹחוֹ וִיכָלְתּוֹ. וְאֵלּוּ שֶׁאֵין בְּכֹחָם לִלְמֹד – וּבִכְלָלָם אָנוּ נְשֵׁי עַמְּךָ יִשְׂרָאֵל – יִקְרְאוּ בַּסְּפָרִים הַמְלַמְּדִים כֵּיצַד לַעֲבוֹד אֶת הַשֵּׁם וּלְקַיֵּם הַמִּצְוֹת שֶׁצִּוָּנוּ הַשֵּׁם:

כֵּן נָתַתָּה לָנוּ רָאשֵׁי חֳדָשִׁים, בְּעֵת שֶׁהָיוּ מְקַדְּשִׁים סַנְהֶדְרִין הַקְּדוֹשִׁים אֶת הֶחֳדָשִׁים. אֲבָל מִיּוֹם שֶׁגָּלִינוּ מֵאַרְצֵנוּ, לֹא נוֹתַר לָנוּ מִמִּצְוֹת הֶחֳדָשִׁים אֶלָּא מַה שֶׁאָנוּ מַכְרִיזִים וּמְבָרְכִים הַחֹדֶשׁ בְּשַׁבָּת שֶׁלִּפְנֵי רֹאשׁ הַחֹדֶשׁ, וְזוֹהִי הָעֵת וְהָעוֹנָה לְהִתְחַנֵּן לְפָנֶיךָ, יְיָ אֱלֹהֵינוּ. לָכֵן אָנוּ שׁוֹפְכוֹת לְבָבֵנוּ

on the Shabbat preceding the new moon, and this is the time and the moment to plead before You, Lord our God. Therefore, we pour out our heart in prayer and make our voices heard before You. We pray that You return us to Jerusalem, Your city of holiness, and renew our days as of old. For Your nation today is like a young, weak flock with no shepherd, and fear of our enemies disturbs the joy of our *Shabbatot*, our festivals, and our new months. [...] In the merit of our matriarch Sarah—whom You did not allow the gentile Abimelech to harm, along with Your righteous one, Abraham, so may no destroyer have the power to harm her descendants.

And likewise in the merit of our matriarch Rebecca, through whom our forefather Jacob received the blessings from Isaac, his father—so may we be worthy of having those blessings fulfilled speedily among the nation of Israel, her descendants.

And likewise in the merit of our faithful matriarch Rachel—to whom You, God, promised that in the merit of her prayers, her descendants would be redeemed from all their enemies. For when Israel went into exile, they passed by the burial place of our matriarch Rachel, and asked their captors to allow them to pray at her grave. So the exiles came to her grave and cried out before You, and wept: Our mother; our mother—how can you bear to see our distress and our departure from our land into exile! Then Rachel ascended to the blessed God and cried out with a bitter cry:

Master of the world—Your mercy is greater than mortal mercy. Nevertheless, I had mercy upon my sister, Leah, when my father exchanged me and gave my sister to my husband, Jacob, in my stead. This caused me great anguish, but I overcame my pain and had pity upon my sister, so that she would not be shamed. How much more should You, merciful and kind One, have pity and show favor toward Your nation. And You, good God, answered her: Your words are true! Return to your rest, and the children shall return to their borders.

בִּתְפִלָּה וּמַשְׁמִיעוֹת קוֹלֵנוּ לְפָנֶיךָ, וּמִתְפַּלְלוֹת שֶׁתַּחֲזִירֵנוּ לִירוּשָׁלַיִם עִיר קָדְשֶׁךָ, וּתְחַדֵּשׁ יָמֵינוּ כְּקֶדֶם. שֶׁהֲרֵי עַמְּךָ הַיּוֹם דּוֹמֶה לְצֹאן צָעִיר וְחַלָּשׁ אֲשֶׁר אֵין לוֹ רוֹעֶה, וּמִפַּחַד הַצּוֹרְרִים לָנוּ, מוּפֶרֶת שִׂמְחַת שַׁבְּתוֹתֵינוּ, חַגֵּינוּ וַחֲדָשֵׁינוּ... בִּזְכוּת אִמֵּנוּ שָׂרָה, שֶׁלֹּא הִנַּחְתָּ לַגּוֹי אֲבִימֶלֶךְ לָגַעַת בָּהּ וּבְצַדִּיקְךָ אַבְרָהָם, כֵּן לֹא יִהְיֶה בְּכֹחוֹ שֶׁל שׁוּם מַכְלִים לָגַעַת בְּבָנֶיהָ לְרָעָה.

וּבִזְכוּת אִמֵּנוּ רִבְקָה, שֶׁעַל יָדָהּ קִבֵּל אָבִינוּ יַעֲקֹב אֶת הַבְּרָכוֹת מִיִּצְחָק אָבִיו, כֵּן נִזְכֶּה שֶׁיְּקֻיְּמוּ הַבְּרָכוֹת בִּמְהֵרָה בְּעַם יִשְׂרָאֵל, בָּנֶיהָ.

וּבִזְכוּת אִמֵּנוּ הַנֶּאֱמָנָה רָחֵל, שֶׁאַתָּה הַשֵּׁם הִבְטַחְתָּהּ שֶׁבִּזְכוּת תְּפִלּוֹתֶיהָ יִגָּאֲלוּ בָּנֶיהָ מִכָּל צָרוֹתֵיהֶם. כִּי כְּשֶׁיָּצְאוּ יִשְׂרָאֵל לַגָּלוּת, עָבְרוּ דֶּרֶךְ קְבוּרַת רָחֵל אִמֵּנוּ, וּבִקְשׁוּ מְשׁוֹבֵיהֶם שֶׁיָּנִיחוּם לְהִשְׁתַּטֵּחַ עַל קִבְרָהּ. וּבָאוּ הַגּוֹלִים אֶל קִבְרָהּ וְצָעֲקוּ לְפָנֶיךָ וּבָכוּ: אִמֵּנוּ, אִמֵּנוּ, כֵּיצַד תּוּכְלִי לִרְאוֹת בְּצָרוֹתֵינוּ וּבִיצִיאָתֵנוּ מֵאַרְצֵנוּ לַגָּלוּת! אָז עָלְתָה רָחֵל אֶל הַשֵּׁם יִתְבָּרֵךְ וְזָעֲקָה בִּזְעָקָה מָרָה:

"רִבּוֹנוֹ שֶׁל עוֹלָם, רַחֲמֶיךָ הֲרֵי גְדוֹלִים הֵם מֵרַחֲמֵי בָּשָׂר וָדָם; לַמְרוֹת זֹאת נִכְמְרוּ רַחֲמַי עַל אֲחוֹתִי לֵאָה כַּאֲשֶׁר הֶחֱלִיפַנִי אָבִי וְנָתַן אֶת אֲחוֹתִי לְבַעֲלִי יַעֲקֹב בִּמְקוֹמִי. הַדָּבָר הֵצַר לִי מְאֹד, אַךְ כָּבַשְׁתִּי צַעֲרִי וְרִחַמְתִּי עַל אֲחוֹתִי לְמַעַן לֹא תֵבוֹשׁ" – מִכָּל שֶׁכֵּן אַתָּה, רָחוּם וְחַנּוּן, צָרִיךְ אַתָּה לְרַחֵם וְלַחֲנֹן אֶת בְּנֵי עַמְּךָ. וְאַתָּה, הַשֵּׁם הַטּוֹב, עֲנִיתָהּ: "הַצֶּדֶק בְּדִבְרַיִךְ! שׁוּבִי לִמְנוּחָתֵךְ, וְשָׁבוּ בָנִים לִגְבוּלָם." קַיֵּם נָא בִּמְהֵרָה בְּיָמֵינוּ הַבְטָחָה זוֹ שֶׁהִבְטַחְתָּהּ:

וּבִזְכוּת אִמֵּנוּ לֵאָה, שֶׁהִזִּילָה דְּמָעוֹת יוֹמָם וָלֵיל כְּדֵי שֶׁלֹּא תִּפֹּל בְּגוֹרָלוֹ שֶׁל עֵשָׂו הָרָשָׁע, עַד שֶׁנַּעֲשׂוּ עֵינֶיהָ רַכּוֹת, בִּזְכוּתָהּ הָאֵר עֵינֵינוּ מִצָּרוֹתֵינוּ, אָנוּ בְּנֵי אַבְרָהָם. הָרַב כַּבְּסֵנוּ מֵעֲוֺנֵינוּ וּמֵחַטֹּאתֵינוּ טַהֲרֵנוּ, כִּי כָל גָּלוּתֵנוּ הִיא בַּעֲוֺנוֹתֵינוּ וּבַחֲטָאֵינוּ, לָכֵן חַדֵּשׁ עָלֵינוּ אֶת הַחֹדֶשׁ הַזֶּה לְטוֹבָה, וְהָבֵא לָנוּ בְּחֹדֶשׁ זֶה שָׂשׂוֹן וְשִׂמְחָה, וַהֲפֹךְ לָנוּ, גְּאוֹן עֻזֵּנוּ, אֶת כָּל רָעוֹתֵינוּ לְטוֹבָה, בִּזְכוּת אֲבוֹתֵינוּ הַצַּדִּיקִים, אַבְרָהָם יִצְחָק וְיַעֲקֹב:

Please fulfill, speedily in our days, this promise that You made to her.

And in the merit of our matriarch Leah, who wept day and night [pleading] that she not be destined to marry the evil Esau, until her eyes became soft: In her merit, illuminate our eyes from our afflictions—we, the descendants of Abraham. Cleanse us soon of our sins and purify us of our transgressions, for all of our exile is the result of our sins and transgressions. Therefore, may You renew this month for us for goodness and bring us, in this month, gladness and joy, and overturn—O Pride of our strength—all of our afflictions for good, in the merit of our righteous forefathers, Abraham, Isaac, and Jacob.

Master of the universe, You have called us Your chosen ones and Your beloved ones; therefore we call to You, good God, and plead before You, that You grant to us and to all who engage in Your holy Torah, and to all who arrive at proper insights from it, and to all who offer prayers and supplications before You, the gift of worthy, live, and healthy seed; may they all be learned scholars who serve You with love and with a perfect heart, as the early pious ones used to do. Amen; so may it be His will.

רִבּוֹן הָעוֹלָמִים, אַתָּה קְרָאתָנוּ ״סְגֻלָּתְךָ וַאֲהוּבֶיךָ״ לָכֵן קוֹרְאוֹת אָנוּ
לְךָ, הַשֵּׁם הַטּוֹב, וּמִתְחַנְּנוֹת לְפָנֶיךָ, שֶׁתִּתֵּן לָנוּ וּלְכָל הָעוֹסְקִים בְּתוֹרָתְךָ
הַקְּדוֹשָׁה, וּלְכָל הַמְחַדְּשִׁים בָּהּ חִדּוּשִׁים נְכוֹנִים, וּלְכָל הַמִּתְפַּלְּלִים לְפָנֶיךָ
תְּפִלּוֹת וְתַחֲנוּנִים, שֶׁתִּזְכֶּה לָנוּ וְלָהֶם בְּזֶרַע כָּשֵׁר, חַי וְקַיָּם, שֶׁיִּהְיוּ כֻלָּם
תַּלְמִידֵי חֲכָמִים וְיַעַבְדוּךָ בְּאַהֲבָה וּבְלֵב תָּמִים, כַּאֲשֶׁר עֲבָדוּךָ הַחֲסִידִים
הָרִאשׁוֹנִים, אָמֵן כֵּן יְהִי רָצוֹן.

Pesach

According to the Torah, the Jewish calendar starts at the beginning of the month of Nissan, making Pesach (Passover, the festival of freedom) the first festival of the Jewish year. The first night of Pesach—the Seder night—is celebrated with great splendor. (Outside of Israel, a Seder is held on both the first and second nights.) During the time of the Holy Temple, Jews would celebrate by sacrificing the paschal lamb; today, we read the Haggadah—perhaps the world's earliest multimedia, interactive learning manual—which recounts the story of the exodus from Egypt and commemorates the sacrifice in various symbolic ways.

Women played a central role in the exodus from Egypt, as many commentators on the biblical narrative have pointed out. One example is Pharaoh's daughter Bitya, who drew Moses out of the water, adopted him, and gave him his name. The Midrash credits Bitya with saving Moses's life and thereby filling a critical role in Israel's redemption from Egypt. More generally, midrashic literature attributes the redemption from Egypt to the merit of the women of Israel. During the many years of cruel slavery, the Midrash explains, Jewish women offered moral support to their husbands, kept themselves far from improper sexual relations, and encouraged their husbands to continue to procreate, despite their dire reality.

However, the woman who without a doubt was most directly responsible for the redemption was the prophetess Miriam, Moses's elder sister.

PASCHAL PRAYER

Rachel Luzzatto Morpurgo

*H*e Who blessed our ancestors—Abraham, Isaac, and Jacob; Sarah, Rebecca, Rachel, and Leah—may He bless the entire congregation of Israel; and may we be worthy of living to ascend [to Jerusalem] to offer paschal sacrifices upon the altar, joyful and glad in the rebuilding of our Holy Temple, speedily in our days. Amen.

The erudite Italian Jewish poet Rachel Morpurgo (1790–1871) composed this *Mi Sheberakh* prayer in 1850 and included it in a letter she sent to her cousin, the well-known scholar of Judaism Shemuel David Luzzatto. The prayer was printed in a collection of her poems and writings, *Oneg Rachel*, which was published posthumously in 1890 to commemorate the one-hundred-year anniversary of her birth. In this prayer, Morpurgo expresses her wish for the Holy Temple to be rebuilt and for the nation of Israel to ascend to Jerusalem and offer the paschal sacrifice. During the nineteenth century there was some halakhic debate as to the possibility of reintroducing the paschal sacrifice ceremony, even without the Temple being rebuilt. Morpurgo's prayer seems to reflect this influence.

מִי שֶׁבֵּרַךְ אֲבוֹתֵינוּ אַבְרָהָם יִצְחָק וְיַעֲקֹב שָׂרָה רִבְקָה רָחֵל וְלֵאָה
יְבָרֵךְ אֶת כָּל קְהַל עֲדַת יִשְׂרָאֵל וְנִזְכֶּה וְנִחְיֶה וְנַעֲלֶה לְהַקְרִיב פְּסָחִים עַל
גַּבֵּי הַמִּזְבֵּחַ, שְׂמֵחִים וְשָׂשִׂים בְּבִנְיַן בֵּית מִקְדָּשֵׁנוּ בִּמְהֵרָה בְּיָמֵינוּ אָמֵן.

As far as we are aware, this is the first *Mi Sheberakh* prayer to be composed by a woman. At the beginning of the prayer, the matriarchs are mentioned along with the traditional invocation of the forefathers.

Dr. Yael Levine has proposed a modern revival of this prayer, to be recited by the entire congregation around Pesach—either on the Shabbat preceding Rosh Hodesh Nissan, on Rosh Hodesh Nissan itself, on *Shabbat ha-Gadol* (the Shabbat preceding Pesach), on the eve of Pesach, or on the Seder night, just after eating the matzah, and expressing the hope for the reinstatement of the Pesach sacrifice: "... There we shall eat of the offerings and the Pesach sacrifices ..."

247

MIRIAM'S SONG

In Persian siddurim, the blessing of redemption in the evening
and morning prayers on Shabbat is formulated as follows:

*M*oses and Aaron and Miriam, and all of the children of Israel,
when they emerged from the sea, answered You with song, in joy and
singing and happiness and great rejoicing; they all answered and said, Who
is like You.

And Miriam the prophetess, sister of Aaron, took up the tambourine in
her hand, and all the women went out after her with tambourines and with
dancing.

And Miriam answered them: Sing to the Lord for He has dealt proudly;
He has vanquished both horse and rider in the sea. [Exodus 15:20–21]

After the parting of the Reed Sea during the Israelites' exodus from Egypt, the
men of Israel sang "The Song of the Sea," which is recorded in the Torah and
is recited daily as part of the morning prayer service. The Torah tells us that
the women sang out in praise, too, led in song and dance by the prophetess
Miriam. In some congregations (among Yemenite Jews, for example), the verses

שֶׁה וְאַהֲרֹן וּמִרְיָם וְכָל בְּנֵי יִשְׂרָאֵל כְּשֶׁעָלוּ מִן הַיָּם לְךָ עָנוּ שִׁירָה
בְּגִילָה בְּרִנָּה בְּשִׂמְחָה וְצָהֲלָה רַבָּא עָנוּ וְאָמְרוּ כֻּלָּם מִי כָמְכָה.
וַתִּקַּח מִרְיָם הַנְּבִיאָה אֲחוֹת אַהֲרֹן אֶת הַתֹּף בְּיָדָהּ וַתֵּצֶאןָ כָל הַנָּשִׁים
אַחֲרֶיהָ בְּתֻפִּים וּבִמְחֹלֹת:
וַתַּעַן לָהֶם מִרְיָם שִׁירוּ לַיהוה כִּי גָאֹה גָּאָה סוּס וְרֹכְבוֹ רָמָה בַיָּם: (שמות
טו, 20-21).

of Miriam's song are recited daily, whereas other communities, such as Persian
Jews, recite them on Shabbat. Bukharan, Moroccan, and Georgian communities
recite Miriam's song on the Shabbat when *Beshalah*, the weekly Torah portion that
includes Miriam's song, is read, as well as on the seventh day of Pesach, which
commemorates the crossing of the Reed Sea.

"I SHALL SING LIKE THE SONG OF MOSES AND MIRIAM"

Liturgical Poem for the Seventh Day of Pesach

I shall sing like the song of Moses—a song that will not be forgotten:
"Then sang Moses" the words of the song.

I shall sing like the song of Miriam at the seashore:
"And Miriam answered them" with the words of the song.

I shall sing like the song of Joshua upon Mount Gilboa:
"Then sang Joshua" the words of the song.

I shall sing like the song of Solomon, wearing the crown with
    which his mother crowned him:
"The Song of Songs unto Solomon."

I shall sing like the song of Deborah, at Mount Tabor:

On the eve of the seventh day of Pesach it is customary to recite a *tikkun* that includes the ten biblical songs (referred to in midrashic literature and the Aramaic
translation of the Song of Songs). This custom is reflected in this poem, which
was recited in some oriental communities on the eighth day of Pesach. (The last
day of Pesach, like the other festivals listed in the Torah, is celebrated over two
days outside of Israel.) Neither the author of the poem nor its date of com-

אשירה כשירת משה ומרים

פיוט לשביעי של פסח

אָ‏שִׁירָה כְּשִׁירַת מֹשֶׁה שִׁיר לֹא יִנָּשֶׁה.

אָז יָשִׁיר מֹשֶׁה אֶת דִּבְרֵי הַשִּׁירָה:

אָשִׁירָה כְּשִׁירַת מִרְיָם עַל שְׂפַת הַיָּם.

וַתַּעַן לָהֶם מִרְיָם אֶת דִּבְרֵי הַשִּׁירָה:

אָשִׁירָה כְּשִׁירַת יְהוֹשֻׁעַ בְּהַר הַגִּלְבֹּעַ.

אָז יָשִׁיר יְהוֹשֻׁעַ אֶת דִּבְרֵי הַשִּׁירָה:

אָשִׁירָה כְּשִׁירַת שְׁלֹמֹה בַּעֲטָרָה שֶׁעִטְּרָה לוֹ אִמּוֹ,

שִׁיר הַשִּׁירִים אֲשֶׁר לִשְׁלֹמֹה:

אָשִׁירָה כְּשִׁירַת דְּבוֹרָה בְּהַר תָּבוֹרָה.

---

position is known to us. It is made up of eight stanzas identical in form, each of which refers to one of the biblical "songs" (three of which are attributed to women): the song of Moses, the song of Miriam, the song of Joshua, the song of Solomon, the song of Deborah, the song of Hannah, the song of David, and the song that Israel will sing in the time to come, with the arrival of the Messiah.

"And Deborah sang" the words of the song.

I shall sing like the song of Hannah with her husband, Elkanah:

"And Hannah prayed" [sang] the words of the song.

I shall sing like the song of David, weaver of psalms:

David spoke the words of the song.

I shall sing like the song of Israel with the coming of the
    Redeemer:

Then shall Israel sing the words of the Torah—the song.

וַתָּשַׁר דְּבוֹרָה אֶת דִּבְרֵי הַשִּׁירָה:

אָשִׁירָה כְּשִׁירַת חַנָּה עִם בַּעְלָהּ אֶלְקָנָה.

וַתִּתְפַּלֵּל [וַתָּשַׁר] חַנָּה אֶת דִּבְרֵי הַשִּׁירָה:

אָשִׁירָה כְּשִׁירַת דָּוִד מִזְמוֹרִים יַצְמִיד.

וַיְדַבֵּר דָּוִד אֶת דִּבְרֵי הַשִּׁירָה:

אָשִׁירָה כְּשִׁירַת יִשְׂרָאֵל בְּבִיאַת הַגּוֹאֵל. אָז יָשִׁיר יִשְׂרָאֵל אֶת דִּבְרֵי הַתּוֹרָה [הַשִּׁירָה]:

"IT WAS IN THE MIDDLE OF THE NIGHT"

Yael Levine

You have promised a covenant to the head of the Matriarchs   at night.

She who has been taken to Pharaoh and Avimelekh
    you have saved   at night.

She who has been likened to a rose suggested to
    exchange the blessings   at night.

It was in the middle of the night.

The woman who gave birth cried out and
    you smote the firstborn   at night.

You saved a firstborn, her candle did not extinguish   at night.

Hadassah was busy with the feast of Haman   at night.

It was in the middle of the night.

The liturgical poem (*piyyut*) "It Was in the Middle of the Night" is one of many composed by the poet Yannai, who lived in Israel during the sixth or seventh century C.E. Up until the discovery of the Cairo Geniza, Yannai's identity was cloaked in mystery. It was only then that the wealth of his oeuvre was revealed: Research in the Cairo Geniza showed that Yannai composed about two thousand poems in total, most of them sets of prayer-poems known as *kerovot*. A very small portion of his work was integrated into the standard liturgy; the best-known example is the poem "It Was in the Middle of the Night," which was widely known in Europe from the Middle Ages onward. It is traditionally recited at the end of the Passover Seder, though it was originally composed for recitation on *Shabbat ha-Gadol*, the Shabbat preceding Passover.

ויהי בחצי הלילה

יעל לוין

לַיְלָה   בְּרִית הִבְטַחְתָּ אֶת רֹאשׁ הָאִמָּהוֹת

לַיְלָה   מוּבֶלֶת לְבֵית־פַּרְעֹה וְלַאֲבִימֶלֶךְ הִצַּלְתָּ

בַּלַּיְלָה   מְשׁוּלַת שׁוֹשַׁנָּה יָעֲצָה לְהַחְלִיף הַבְּרָכוֹת

וַיְהִי בַּחֲצִי הַלַּיְלָה

בַּלַּיְלָה   צַעֲקָה הַיּוֹלֶדֶת וְהִכִּיתָ רֵאשִׁית אוֹנִים

בַּלַּיְלָה   בְּכוֹרָה מְלַטְתָּ לֹא יִכְבֶּה נֵרָהּ

בַּלַּיְלָה   הֲדַסָּה עֲסוּקָה הָיְתָה בִּסְעוּדָתוֹ שֶׁל הָמָן

וַיְהִי בַּחֲצִי הַלַּיְלָה.

The poem lists biblical events that took place on the night of the fifteenth of Nissan—the same date as the night of the exodus from Egypt. It is written in acrostic form, and each line ends with the word *layla* (night). Though there is one indirect reference to Sarah, who was taken to Abimelech on the eve of the fifteenth of Nissan, the vast majority of the events referred to in the poem involved male personalities. Based on midrashic references to events on the Eve of Passover involving female figures, in 2002 Yael Levine, who holds a doctorate in Talmud from Bar-Ilan University, composed two additional stanzas for this *piyyut* that call attention to instances of miraculous divine intervention that women have experienced on this night. These two stanzas are meant to be recited at the end of the poem—not only by women, but by all gathered at the Seder table. (English translation also by Dr. Yael Levine.)

AUSCHWITZ HAGGADAH OF FREEDOM

Toby Trackeltaub

Pesach 5705

We wish to celebrate but we are unable to, we desire

to believe and that is the only thing that we have that they are
unable to take
from us; in it is memory, that alone can give us hope for a better
and more beautiful future that we wish to think about and not
to lower our heads.

And if God redeemed our forefathers from Egypt, He will also
save
us from our bitter enslavement, and restore us to the land of our
forefathers.

Toby Trackeltaub, from the city of Munkacs in Hungary, prepared a unique
Haggadah for Pesach of 1945 while imprisoned in the concentration camp at
Auschwitz. A moment before she collapsed and died on the death march in January
of that year, she handed it over for safekeeping to her friend, Aliza Klein. Aliza
lived to see the liberation and kept her friend's gift for many years; eventually
she transferred the Haggadah for safekeeping to the Hedva Eibeschitz Institute
of Holocaust Studies in Haifa.

Toby's Haggadah, written on scraps of toilet paper, is organized into the form
of a tiny book. On the binding there is a framed map of the Land of Israel and
the word "Zion," all embroidered with threads that she had unraveled from her
prisoner's garments.

This is not a Haggadah reproduced from memory—although several such

הגדת החירות

טובי טרקלטאוב ממונקאטש

פסח תש"ה

אֲנַחְנוּ רוֹצִים לַחֲגֹג אֲבָל אֵינֶנּוּ יְכוֹלִים, אֲנוּ חֲפֵצִים
לְהַאֲמִין וְכְּבָר הַיְחִידִי מָה שֶׁיֵּשׁ לָנוּ וּמָה שֶׁאֵינָם יְחוֹלִים לָקַחַת
מֵאִתָּנוּ בּוֹ הַזִּכָּרוֹן רַק זֶה יָכוֹל לָתֵת לָנוּ תִּקְוָה לֶעָתִיד טוֹב וְיָפָה יוֹתֵר
עָלָיו אֲנוּ רוֹצִים לַחְשֹׁב וְלֹא לְהוֹרִיד אֶת רֹאשֵׁנוּ.

וְאִם ה' גָּאַל אֶת אֲבוֹתֵינוּ מִמִּצְרַיִם יַצִּיל גַּם
אוֹתָנוּ מֵעַבְדוּתֵנוּ הַמָּרָה. וְיָשִׁיבֵנוּ לְאֶרֶץ אֲבוֹתֵינוּ.

---

documents exist from a number of ghettos and concentration camps. Rather, it is a rewriting of the Haggadah in Auschwitz, in keeping with the commandment, "In every generation one is obligated to see himself as though he had left Egypt." In each generation, the Exodus story must be retold in the language and imagery of that generation. Toby's vision of freedom and declaration of faith ring out in defiance of the wretchedness of her imprisonment and seeming abandonment by God.

Hungary was one of the last countries to be occupied by the Nazis during World War II. On Adolf Eichmann's instructions, the "Jewish Council" was formed in March 1944, including eight representatives of different streams within the Hungarian Jewish community. Between March 1944 and January 1945, 618,000 Hungarian Jews lost their lives, some 450,000 of them at Auschwitz.

Tish'ah be-Av

The ninth day of the month of Av, known in Hebrew as *Tish'ah be-Av*, is a day of fasting that commemorates the destruction of the Holy Temple and Jerusalem. At the same time, the date also recalls several other catastrophes that have taken place throughout Jewish history. The Babylonian Talmud enumerates five major catastrophes that the Jewish people experienced on the ninth of Av: It was on that day that God decreed that the generation that left Egypt would not enter the Promised Land; both the First Temple (586 B.C.E.) and the Second Temple (70 C.E.) were destroyed; the city of Beitar was captured during the Bar Kokhba Revolt (135 C.E.); and following the siege of Jerusalem in 70 C.E., the city was razed by the servants of Hadrian, who wanted to destroy the city to its very foundations and to rebuild it and dedicate it to the Roman gods. Many centuries later, the same fateful day was set as the final date for the expulsion of Jews from Spain (1492).

Tish'ah be-Av is both a day of mourning over the tragedies that occurred in the past and also a time for crying out to God for reconciliation and repair. The laws pertaining to *Tish'ah be-Av* reflect both aspects: There are laws of mourning, with prohibitions against bathing, anointing oneself, wearing leather shoes, engaging in marital intimacy, studying Torah, and greeting one another; and there is the fast, which is meant to arouse one to repentance.

In many communities, women hold their own special, separate mourning ceremonies on *Tish'ah be-Av*, in addition to the prayer service and the reading of the book of Lamentations in the synagogue.

THE SUPPLICATION OF THE MOTHERS FOR THE REBUILDING OF THE TEMPLE

Yael Levine

When the Second Temple was destroyed

the souls of our fathers and mothers

descended to the Temple Mount

and composed lamentations.

At that time, the Holy One, blessed be He,

turned to them from the heavens on high and said:

Why are my beloved people reciting dirges in my home?

Thereupon the fathers said:

We are ashamed,

that strangers could enter Your Sanctuary.

Our holy and glorious Temple has been consumed by fire,

all that was dear to us has been laid waste,

and Your people are dispersed amongst the nations.

The Supplication of the Mothers for the Rebuilding of the Temple, excerpts of which are presented here, is a literary work written in the style of the aggadic midrashim. It depicts biblical and postbiblical female figures who beseech God, on the basis of their merits, to rebuild the Temple. The work portrays the deep connection between women and the Temple throughout the ages. Its thematic components are

תחינת הנשים לבניין המקדש

יעל לוין

שָׁנוּ רַבּוֹתֵינוּ:

כְּשֶׁחָרַב הַבַּיִת בַּשְּׁנִיָּה

נִתְכַּנְּסוּ אֲבוֹת הָעוֹלָם עִם הָאִמָּהוֹת

וּבָאוּ לִמְקוֹם הַמִּקְדָּשׁ וְקָשְׁרוּ שָׁם מִסְפֵּד גָּדוֹל.

אוֹתָהּ שָׁעָה נִזְקַק לָהֶם הַקָּדוֹשׁ־בָּרוּךְ־הוּא

מִשְּׁמֵי מָרוֹם וְאָמַר לָהֶם:

מַה לְאוֹהֲבַי בְּבֵיתִי עוֹשִׂים מִסְפֵּד?

פָּתְחוּ הָאָבוֹת וְאָמְרוּ:

כִּסְּתָה כְלִמָּה פָנֵינוּ כִּי בָאוּ זָרִים עַל מִקְדְּשֵׁי בֵית ה'.

בֵּית קָדְשֵׁנוּ וְתִפְאַרְתֵּנוּ הָיָה לִשְׂרֵפַת אֵשׁ

וְכָל מַחֲמַדֵּינוּ הָיָה לְחָרְבָּה

וְהָעָם הָיָה לִכְלִי נִדָּח בֵּין אֻמּוֹת הָעוֹלָם...

---

based on Talmudic, midrashic, and aggadic literature, and on the Zohar. Since its publication in 1996, this supplication has been recited every year in various communities and by individuals on either the eve or the day of *Tish'ah be-Av* as an extra-liturgical text. The English translation was prepared by Dr. Yael Levine.

Then the soul of Hannah spoke:

On the pilgrimage festivals

I would ascend to the Temple in Shiloh

and behold all of Israel spread out before me. I said to You:

Master of the Universe, Your multitudes serve You

and I have not even one of them?

And You have now scattered Your people

amongst the nations of the world,

and they cannot go up and appear in worship before You

to perform their obligations in the House of Your choice,

in the great and holy House

upon which Your Name was proclaimed,

because of the hand that struck Your Sanctuary.

And because I often went to pray in the Temple

and supplicate before You,

my lips moving silently,

You heard my prayer and remembered me.

Will You not remember the people of Israel

who endure trouble and distress,

whose hearts are as broken as your glorious house?

As You have heard my voice,

"Close not Your ears to my groan, to my cry"!

The soul of Jonah's wife,

the daughter-in-law of Yo'am, came forth to plead:

Without being commanded,

I would ascend to the Temple for the festivals,

my heart bursting with joy,

my soul full of song,

בָּאָה נִשְׁמַת חַנָּה, סָחָה וְשָׁאֲלָה:
בְּפַעֲמֵי רְגָלִים הָיִיתִי עוֹלָה לְבֵית הַמִּקְדָּשׁ שֶׁבְּשִׁילֹה,
וְרָאִיתִי אֶת כָּל יִשְׂרָאֵל שָׁם. אָמַרְתִּי לְפָנֶיךָ:
רִבּוֹנוֹ שֶׁל עוֹלָם, כָּל הַצְּבָאוֹת הָאֵלּוּ יֵשׁ לְךָ
וְלִי אֵין אֶחָד מֵהֶם?
וְעַתָּה, פֻּזַּרְתָּם לְבֵין אֻמּוֹת הָעוֹלָם
וְאֵין הֵם יְכוֹלִים לַעֲלוֹת וְלֵרָאוֹת וּלְהִשְׁתַּחֲווֹת לְפָנֶיךָ
וְלַעֲשׂוֹת חוֹבוֹתֵיהֶם בְּבֵית בְּחִירָתֶךָ, בַּבַּיִת הַגָּדוֹל וְהַקָּדוֹשׁ
שֶׁנִּקְרָא שִׁמְךָ עָלָיו, מִפְּנֵי הַיָּד שֶׁנִּשְׁתַּלְּחָה בְּמִקְדָּשֶׁךָ.
עַל שֶׁהָיִיתִי תְּדִירָה עוֹלָה וּמִתְפַּלֶּלֶת בְּבֵית הַמִּקְדָּשׁ
וּמִתְחַנֶּנֶת לְפָנֶיךָ, עַל כֵּן שָׁמַעְתָּ תְּפִלָּתִי וַתִּפְקְדֵנִי,
וְלֹא תִּפְקֹד אֶת עַמְּךָ יִשְׂרָאֵל הַנְּתוּנִים בְּצָרָה וּבְצוּקָה?
קוֹלִי שָׁמַעְתָּ, אַל תַּעְלֵם אָזְנְךָ לְרַוְחָתִי לְשַׁוְעָתִי!

יָצְאָה נִשְׁמַת אֵשֶׁת יוֹנָה, כַּלַּת יוֹעָם, וּבִקְשָׁה:
אַף עַל פִּי שֶׁלֹּא הָיִיתִי מְצֻוָּה,
עוֹלָה הָיִיתִי בָּרְגָלִים לַמִּקְדָּשׁ
וְלֹא מִחוּ בִּי חֲכָמִים.
וְאַתָּה, שֶׁצִּוִּיתָ לְעַמְּךָ יִשְׂרָאֵל הַזְּכָרִים
לַעֲלוֹת לָרֶגֶל
שָׁלֹשׁ פְּעָמִים בַּשָּׁנָה,
הֵיאַךְ יוּכְלוּ לְקַיֵּם מַאֲמָרְךָ
כְּשֶׁאֵין הַמִּקְדָּשׁ עוֹמֵד עַל תִּלּוֹ,
כְּשֶׁעָרְבָה כָּל שִׂמְחָה
וּכְשֶׁנִּשְׁכַּח בְּצִיּוֹן מוֹעֵד וְשַׁבָּת?

and the Sages did not object.

And You, who have commanded all males of Your people Israel

to ascend for the pilgrimage festivals

three times a year—

how can Your word now be observed

when the Temple no longer stands?

Reduced to rubble and a pile of stones,

only the voice of the wind is heard there now,

when all joy has waned,

and festival and Sabbath are forgotten in Zion?

The souls of a group of women gathered together,

their words heavy upon their tongues:

Oh, what has befallen us!

When Nehemiah ben Hacaliah came up from the exile

to the Land of Israel,

we and our families accompanied him,

our faces blackened by the sun,

and from the cold of the hard journey,

and from sorrow and worry.

Our husbands left us for heathen women.

Many times we ascended the altar on the right side—

we together with the maidens of Israel,

a large congregation of women—

and surrounded it seven times,

as on the seventh day of *aravah,*

which is the seventh day of Sukkot,

the day when the final judgment

is meted for the coming year.

נִקְהֲלוּ וְנֶאֶסְפוּ נִשְׁמוֹת נָשִׁים וּמִלְּתָן בִּלְשׁוֹנָן:
אוֹי מֶה הָיָה לָנוּ!
בְּשָׁעָה שֶׁעָלָה נְחֶמְיָה בֶּן חֲכַלְיָה מִן הַגּוֹלָה
עָלֵינוּ אָנוּ וּמִשְׁפְּחוֹתֵינוּ עִמּוֹ
וְנִתְפַּחֲמוּ פָּנֵינוּ מִפְּנֵי הַחַמָּה
הַצִּנָּה הַיָּגוֹן וְהַדְּאָגָה.
הִנִּיחוּנוּ אִישֵׁינוּ
וְהָלְכוּ וְנָשְׂאוּ לָהֶם נָשִׁים נָכְרִיּוֹת.
עוֹלוֹת הָיִינוּ לַמִּזְבֵּחַ דֶּרֶךְ יָמִין
וּמַקִּיפוֹת אוֹתוֹ
אָנוּ וּבְנוֹת יִשְׂרָאֵל אִתָּנוּ
עַם רַב מְאֹד
לֹא פַּעַם אַחַת בִּלְבַד, כִּי אִם שֶׁבַע פְּעָמִים,
כְּבַשְּׁבִיעִי שֶׁל עֲרָבָה, הוּא שְׁבִיעִי שֶׁל חַג,
יוֹם סִיּוּם הַדִּין,
וְיוֹרְדוֹת הָיִינוּ דֶּרֶךְ שְׂמֹאל,
כְּדֶרֶךְ הָעוֹלִים לַמִּזְבֵּחַ וְהַיּוֹרְדִים מִמֶּנּוּ.
הָאִשָּׁה דְּמָעֲתָהּ מְצוּיָה –
בְּאִשָּׁה סְתָם דִּבְּרוּ וְכָל שֶׁכֵּן בָּנוּ –
וְנוֹשְׂאוֹת הָיִינוּ נְהִי בְּכִי תַמְרוּרִים מֵאֵין הֲפוּגוֹת
וְהָיָה הַמִּזְבֵּחַ מוֹרִיד עִמָּנוּ דְּמָעוֹת.
נִתְעַטְּפָה עָלֶיהָ כָּל אִשָּׁה רְוָחָהּ וּפִלְלָהּ:
'אַל־תִּרְאַנִי שֶׁאֲנִי שְׁחַרְחֹרֶת שֶׁשְּׁזָפַתְנִי הַשָּׁמֶשׁ',
שֶׁהֲרֵי בְּנוֹת יִשְׂרָאֵל מֵעִקָּרָן נָאוֹת הֵן
וְאֵינוֹ דוֹמֶה אָדָם הַיּוֹצֵא מִמְּעֵי אִמּוֹ כָּעוּר
לְמִי שֶׁהוּא נָאֶה וְנִתְנַוֵּל, שֶׁסּוֹפוֹ לַחֲזוֹר לִהְיוֹת נָאֶה.

We descended the altar on the left side,

in the prescribed manner.

A women's tears are frequent—

this refers to an ordinary woman, how much more so ourselves—

and we wailed and wept bitterly without respite,

and even the altar shed tears with us.

Our spirits failed us, and each one of us entreated:

"Do not look at me because I am swarthy,

For the sun has gazed upon me."

For the daughters of Israel are by nature beautiful

and one may not liken a person who was born ugly

to one who was born beautiful, but later turned ugly,

for in the end he will again be beautiful.

Our countenances have dimmed, but will yet become beautiful.

Nehemiah, Your servant, came and sent away the foreign women,

and our husbands returned.

And at that hour, our faces shone once again as of old.

Will You not put our tears in Your flask

to redeem Your people whose eyes are spent,

having poured out our hearts before You?

Even if the gates of prayer are closed,

the gates of tears have not been sealed.

The souls of three sisters came down and poured out their hearts:

Our father set a condition

with his sons and daughters:

"I shall slaughter the Passover offering on behalf of

whichever of you goes up first to Jerusalem."

שְׁחוֹרוֹת אָנוּ, אַךְ סוֹפֵנוּ לָשׁוּב לִהְיוֹת נָאוֹת.

בָּא נְחֶמְיָה עַבְדְּךָ וְרִחֵק הַנָּשִׁים הַזָּרוֹת

וְשָׁבוּ בְּעָלֵינוּ לְחֵיקֵינוּ

וּבָה בַּשָּׁעָה חָזַר זִיו פָּנֵינוּ לְהַבְהִיק כְּבָרִאשׁוֹנָה.

וְכִי לֹא תָשִׂים כְּהַיּוֹם הַזֶּה דִּמְעוֹתֵינוּ אֵלֶּה בְּנֹאדֶךָ

לִפְדּוֹת עַמְּךָ הַמֻּכְלִים בַּדְּמָעוֹת עֵינֵיהֶם בְּשָׁפְכָם לִבָּם נִכְחֲךָ כַּמָּיִם?

וְאַף גַּם זֹאת, אִם נִנְעֲלוּ שַׁעֲרֵי תְפִלָּה, שַׁעֲרֵי דְמָעוֹת הֲרֵי לֹא נִנְעֲלוּ.

יָרְדוּ נִשְׁמוֹתֵיהֶן שֶׁל שָׁלֹשׁ אֲחָיוֹת וְשָׁפְכוּ אֶת שִׂיחָן:

מַעֲשֶׂה וְאָבִינוּ הִתְנָה עִם בָּנָיו וְעִם בְּנוֹתָיו

'הֲרֵינִי שׁוֹחֵט אֶת הַפֶּסַח עַל מִי שֶׁיַּעֲלֶה מִכֶּם רִאשׁוֹן לִירוּשָׁלַיִם.'

קָדַמְנוּ אָנוּ הַבָּנוֹת לִפְנֵי אַחֵינוּ,

וְהִכְנַסְנוּ אֶת רָאשֵׁינוּ וְאֶת רַבֵּינוּ לְתוֹךְ יְרוּשָׁלַיִם

וְזָכִינוּ אֶת אַחֵינוּ עִמָּנוּ

וְנִמְצֵאנוּ זְרִיזוֹת לְקַיֵּם מִצְוַת הַקְרָבַת קָרְבַּן פֶּסַח,

שֶׁהִיא זֵכֶר לִיצִיאַת מִצְרַיִם.

וְאַתָּה שֶׁהוֹצֵאתָנוּ מִמִּצְרַיִם, מֵעַבְדוּת לְחֵרוּת וּמִיָּגוֹן לְשִׂמְחָה,

הֶחֱזַרְתָּנוּ לְשִׁעְבּוּד וְלַאֲפֵלָה

וְשַׂמְתָּנוּ לִסְחִי וּלְמָאוֹס בְּקֶרֶב הָעַמִּים,

לֹא תָשִׁיב אֶת הָעֲבוֹדָה לִדְבִיר בֵּיתֶךָ וְסֵדֶר הָעֲבוֹדָה לִירוּשָׁלַיִם?

יָצְאָה בַת־קוֹל וְאָמְרָה:

נִצְּחוּנִי בְּנוֹתַי! נִצְּחוּנִי בְּנוֹתַי!

לְמַעַנְכֶן לְמַעַנְכֶן אֲנִי עוֹשָׂה!

בְּרֶגַע קָטֹן עֲזַבְתִּיכֶם וּבְרַחֲמִים גְּדוֹלִים אֲקַבְּצְכֶם.

בְּשֶׁצֶף קֶצֶף הִסְתַּרְתִּי פָנַי רֶגַע מִכֶּם

Swift as gazelles, we, the daughters, outstripped our brothers

and entered the city before our brethren,

thus acquiring our portions on their behalf.

We were, then, quick, to fulfill

the commandment of offering the paschal sacrifice

in memory of the Exodus from Egypt.

And You, who have taken us out of Egypt,

from slavery to freedom and from anguish to joy,

have now returned us to enslavement and darkness,

making us a filth and refuse in the midst of the nations.

Will You not restore the service to Your Temple

and the order of the offerings in Your Sanctuary?

A heavenly voice came forth and cried:

My daughters have won me over! My daughters have won me over!

Their tears have compelled me.

For your sake, for your sake I will act!

For a short while I have forsaken you,

but with great mercy I will gather you in.

For a moment, in great anger I hid my face from you.

But with everlasting kindness I will have compassion upon you.

From the day the Temple and Jerusalem were destroyed,

there is no joy for me

until I rebuild Jerusalem and return Israel to its midst.

And I shall rejoice in the city and delight in My people.

And the voice of weeping and wailing shall be heard no more.

For I shall return to Zion and dwell in Jerusalem.

Jerusalem will be called the City of Truth,

and the mountain of the Lord of Hosts the Holy Mountain.

וּבְחֶסֶד עוֹלָם אֲרַחֲמְכֶם.

מִיּוֹם שֶׁחָרַב בֵּית הַמִּקְדָּשׁ וְחָרְבָה יְרוּשָׁלַיִם

אֵין שִׂמְחָה לְפָנַי

עַד שֶׁאֶבְנֶה אֶת יְרוּשָׁלַיִם וְאַחֲזִיר אֶת יִשְׂרָאֵל לְתוֹכָהּ.

וְגָלִיתִי בִּירוּשָׁלַיִם וְשַׂשְׂתִּי בְּעַמִּי

וְלֹא יִשָּׁמַע בָּהּ עוֹד קוֹל בְּכִי וְקוֹל זְעָקָה.

כִּי שָׁב ה׳ אֶל צִיּוֹן וְשָׁכַן בְּתוֹךְ יְרוּשָׁלַיִם

וְנִקְרְאָה יְרוּשָׁלַיִם עִיר הָאֱמֶת וְהַר ה׳ צְבָאוֹת הַר הַקֹּדֶשׁ.

WOMEN'S LAMENTATIONS
FOR *TISH'AH BE-AV*
Kurdistan

Eulogy over Hannah and Her Seven Sons

Where is the blood-filled pit;

Where is the place of their slaughter?

Woe, poor Serah,

For they were slaughtered all seven.

Where is the blood-filled pit;

Where is the place of their slaughter?

Woe, poor Hannah

For they were slaughtered all seven.

Kurdistan produced a remarkable seventeenth-century Jewish woman scholar and poetess, Osnat Mizrahi. Her father, Shemuel Barazani, established a yeshiva in Mosul. Osnat married Rabbi Yaakov Mizrahi, the rabbi of the community of Amadia, and she taught at the yeshiva that her husband headed. When Osnat's father died, her husband replaced him as the head of his yeshiva. When Rabbi Yaakov himself died, Osnat headed the yeshiva in Kurdistan. Revered by the Jews of Kurdistan to the same degree as her father had been, she earned the title *tanna'it*, which literally means a female Talmudic Sage.

Many legends surround this remarkable figure, whose name was even used as a talisman. According to her own testimony in a letter that she wrote in Hebrew, she engaged in no occupation or labor in her father's house except for divine service, and she made her husband swear that he would allow her to continue this custom.

270

הספד על חנה ושבעת בניה

אַיֵּה בּוֹר הַדָּם
וְאַיֵּה מָקוֹם שְׁחִיטָתָם
הוֹי מִסְכֵּנָה סָרַח
וְנִשְׁחֲטוּ שִׁבְעָתָם

אַיֵּה בּוֹר הַדָּם
וְאַיֵּה מָקוֹם שְׁחִיטָתָם
הוֹי מִסְכֵּנָה חַנָּה
וְנִשְׁחֲטוּ שִׁבְעָתָם

Osnat wrote a commentary on the book of Proverbs—although some opinions attribute the commentary to her husband.

On *Tish'ah be-Av* in Iraq and Kurdistan, lamentations were traditionally recited for Hannah and her seven sons. Women and girls from the Kurdish community would hold a mourning ceremony near the Euphrates River. They would form graves using the sand on the banks of the river, and place sticks over them as gravestones. Then they would walk around the graves and offer eulogies.

The eulogies that appear here were conveyed by Gorgia Avraham-Avishur, from the town of Aana. The first mourns Hannah and her seven sons, along with a character who is unfamiliar to us, named Serah (spelled here with a *samekh*). The "Eulogy for the Slaughterhouse" likewise originated in the town of Aana, on the

*A*haron shall eulogize, he shall eulogize
The slaughterhouse is in mourning.

Why are you not grieving
For the learned scholars who were slaughtered?

Why are you not grieving
For the young men who were slaughtered?

---

banks of the Euphrates. It personifies the slaughterhouse as being in mourning because Jewish law forbids eating meat during the nine days preceding *Tish'ah be-Av.*

אַ הָרֹן יְסֹפֵד יְסֹפֵד
הַמִּשְׁחָטָה [בֵּית הַמִּטְבָּחַיִם] אֲבֵלָה.

לָמָּה לֹא הָיִית אֲבֵלָה?
עַל הַחֲכָמִים שֶׁשְּׁחָטוּם

לָמָּה לֹא הָיִית אֲבֵלָה?
עַל הַבַּחוּרִים שֶׁשְּׁחָטוּם.

The Month of Elul, Rosh Hashanah, and Yom Kippur

The month of Elul is a time of repentance and forgiveness: a month of preparation for the Day of Judgment. According to Sephardic custom, special penitential prayers—*selihot*—are recited throughout the month before morning prayers; in Ashkenazic communities the shofar is sounded at the end of the morning prayers, and Psalm 27 is recited ("By David: God is my light and my salvation …").

Rosh Hashanah, the Jewish New Year, is celebrated on the first two days of the month of Tishrei. It is the Day of Judgment for every living thing—the day on which God, as King of the world, assesses every individual for their actions of the past year. The central commandment on Rosh Hashanah is the sounding of the shofar. In fact, the Torah never refers to the holiday as Rosh Hashanah, which means "the beginning of the year" but rather calls it the "day of sounding [the shofar]" or a "day of remembrance of sounding [the shofar]." Maimonides explains that although the Torah does not explicitly state a reason for the commandment, the sounding of the shofar "conveys a veiled message, as if to say:

Awaken, sleeping ones, from your sleep, and slumbering ones—wake up from your deep slumber; examine your deeds and engage in repentance, and remember your Creator ..."

Yom Kippur, the Day of Atonement, is observed on the tenth day of Tishrei. On Yom Kippur God seals every individual's fate for the coming year. It is the holiest day of the Jewish calendar, and the climax of the month of Elul and the "Ten Days of Penitence" that begin on Rosh Hashanah. It was on this day that Moses descended from Mount Sinai, bearing the second set of Tablets, following the nation's penitential prayer and fasting over the sin of the golden calf. On that day, God told Moses, "I have forgiven as you have spoken," and the day was established as a day of forgiveness for all generations.

Five afflictions are observed on Yom Kippur: a prohibition against eating and drinking, a prohibition against bathing, a prohibition against anointing the body with oil or fragrance, a prohibition against wearing leather shoes, and a prohibition against engaging in marital relations.

MATRIARCHS' PRAYER FOR ELUL AND ROSH HASHANAH

Rabbanit Sheril (Sarah Rivkah Rachel Leah) Horowitz

*M*aster of all the world: Before I begin confessing before You as I should, I cast myself down and ask that Your mercy overcome Your anger, and that You open my mouth in the proper way so that I may confess in a worthy manner before You.

Act toward me with Your great mercy. I ask of You that You treat me with kindness and righteousness, in Your manifold mercies, and accept my prayer, for I have no one to appeal to on my behalf before Your holy attribute of kindness and mercy.

Please accept my confession and open the gates of repentance of the seven heavens, as You opened them at the time when Israel received the beloved Torah at Mount Sinai. I ask of You that You accept my bitter tears, as You accepted the tears of the weeping angels when Abraham, our forefather, sought to bind his beloved son as a sacrifice. Their tears

---

The special prayer for the month of Elul that appears here in abbreviated form was composed by Rabbanit Sheril Horowitz, who lived in the city of Lemberg (Lvov) in the mid-nineteenth century. The title of the prayer alludes to her full Hebrew name: Sarah Rivkah Rachel Leah (the names of the four biblical matriarchs). The prayer testifies to the composer's extensive background in Torah scholarship, including Gemara and Midrash.

תחינת אמהות לראש-חדש אלול

הרבנית שריל [שרה רבקה רחל לאה] הורוביץ

אָדון כָּל הָעוֹלָם, לִפְנֵי שֶׁאֲנִי מַתְחִילָה לְהִתְוַדּוֹת לְפָנֶיךָ כָּרָאוּי, הֲרֵינִי נוֹפֶלֶת עַל פָּנַי, וּמְבַקֶּשֶׁת שֶׁרַחֲמֶיךָ יִגְבְּרוּ עַל כַּעַסְךָ, וְתִפְתַּח אֶת פִּי כָּרָאוּי שֶׁאוּכַל לְהִתְוַדּוֹת לְפָנֶיךָ כַּהֹגֶן.

עֲשֵׂה עִמָּדִי בְּחַסְדְּךָ הַגָּדוֹל. אֲבַקֵּשׁ מִמְּךָ שֶׁתַּעֲשֶׂה עִמִּי חֶסֶד וּמִשְׁפָּט בְּרַחֲמֶיךָ הָרַבִּים וּתְקַבֵּל אֶת תְּפִלָּתִי, כִּי אֵין לִי מֵלִיץ יֹשֶׁר לִפְנֵי מִדָּתְךָ הַקְּדוֹשָׁה חֶסֶד וְרַחֲמִים. אָנָּא קַבֵּל אֶת וִדּוּיִי, וּפְתַח אֶת שַׁעֲרֵי הַתְּשׁוּבָה מִשִּׁבְעַת הָרְקִיעִים, כַּאֲשֶׁר פָּתַחְתָּ בְּשָׁעָה שֶׁיִּשְׂרָאֵל קִבְּלוּ אֶת הַתּוֹרָה הָאֲהוּבָה עַל הַר סִינַי. אֲבַקֵּשׁ מִמְּךָ שֶׁתְּקַבֵּל אֶת דִּמְעוֹתַי הַמָּרוֹת, כַּאֲשֶׁר קִבַּלְתָּ אֶת דִּמְעוֹת בְּכִי הַמַּלְאָכִים בְּשָׁעָה שֶׁאַבְרָהָם אָבִינוּ רָצָה לְהָבִיא אֶת בְּנוֹ הָאָהוּב לַעֲקֵדָה. דִּמְעוֹתֵיהֶם נָשְׁרוּ עַל הַסַּכִּין שֶׁל אַבְרָהָם וּמָנְעוּ מִמֶּנּוּ לִשְׁוֹחֲטוֹ, כֵּן יִזְלְגוּ דִמְעוֹתֵינוּ עַל סַכִּינוֹ שֶׁל מַלְאַךְ הַמָּוֶת, וְיִמְנְעוּ מִמֶּנּוּ שֶׁחָלִילָה לֹא יִשְׁלֹט בָּנוּ אוֹ חָלִילָה בִּילָדַי הַקְּטַנִּים וְכָל יְדִידַי. אֲבַקֵּשׁ מִמְּךָ

The supplication is meant to be uttered every day during the month of Elul and on Rosh Hashanah during the recital of the thirteen attributes of mercy and during the sounding of the shofar.

fell upon Abraham's knife and held him back from slaughtering him; so may our tears fall upon the knife of the Angel of Death and prevent him, heaven forfend, from prevailing over us or, heaven forfend, my small children, or any of my acquaintances. I ask of You that You have mercy upon us and that You Yourself plead our case in judgment. Accept my supplication and grant atonement for my sins. Amen.

[...] How shall I start to plead before You, that You may forgive my grave transgressions? I know that I have no advocates, only my bitter tears. As it is written: All the gates are locked; only the gates of tears are not locked. Merciful Father: Take my tears that I have poured out before You and place them in Your depository. Cleanse my sins with them, abandon the attribute of strict judgment and take up the attribute of mercy. In Your kindness and truth, let my supplication come before You, so that evil, accusing angels not be able to come between my prayer and Your Throne of Glory. Stretch out Your hand to my prayer, that it need not pass by the angels, for I am fearful.

I ask of You that You return Your sword to its scabbard, and place Your hand upon us, Your holy children. Amen.

[...] See our distress and save us, and accept our prayer. I know that I am not worthy of opening my mouth to make requests of You, for I have committed grave transgressions through my mouth—foolishness and vulgar language. But You are the Lord Who is merciful [...].

[...] How shall I not be afraid and tremble when I shall have to stand in judgment before the heavenly court and answer for my sins, if You, Lord, are to act in the manner of a mortal king? When one stands in judgment before a mortal king, it is he who acquits, or punishes severely, and there is no mercy in his judgment. But You, Lord, perform wonders, and at the time of judgment You show Your mercy. Have mercy upon me and be

שֶׁתְּרַחֵם עָלֵינוּ, וְתִהְיֶה בְּעַצְמְךָ הַמֵּלִיץ יֹשֶׁר בַּמִּשְׁפָּט. קַבֵּל אֶת בַּקָּשָׁתִי וְכַפֵּר עַל חֲטָאַי, אָמֵן.

רַחֲמֶיךָ הַגְּדוֹלִים יָגֵנּוּ עָלַי, כִּי יָרֵאָה אֲנִי מְאֹד מִגֹּדֶל עֲוֹנוֹתַי, וּמַעֲשַׂי הַטּוֹבִים אֵינָם רְאוּיִים לְשָׂכָר, אֵינֶנִּי יוֹדַעַת אֵיךְ לְהַתְחִיל לְבַקֵּשׁ מִלְּפָנֶיךָ. תִּתְקַבֵּל לְפָנֶיךָ זְכוּת אֲבוֹתַי, כַּכָּתוּב בְּתוֹרָתְךָ הַקְּדוֹשָׁה: וְאֶעֱשֶׂה חֶסֶד וְזָכַרְתִּי זְכוּת אָבוֹת עַל בָּנִים וְעַל בְּנֵי בָנִים, וְאַתָּה אֱלֹקֵינוּ וֵאלֹקֵי אֲבוֹתֵינוּ וּמְנַחֲמֵנוּ רַחֵם עָלֵינוּ וּתְנַחֲמֵנוּ, אָמֵן.

יְהִי נָא חַסְדְּךָ לְנַחֲמֵנִי, וְנַחֵם אוֹתִי בְּצַעֲרִי הַגָּדוֹל, יְהִי רָצוֹן שֶׁיִּתְקַיֵּם בָּנוּ מַה שֶּׁכָּתוּב: עֲשֵׂה עִמָּנוּ אוֹת לְטוֹבָה, וְיִרְאוּ שׂוֹנְאֵינוּ וְיֵבוֹשׁוּ כִּי אַתָּה ה' עֲזַרְתָּנוּ וְנִחַמְתָּנוּ, כִּי אַתָּה עוֹזֵר וּמְנַחֵם לְכָל קוֹרְאֶיךָ בְּלֵב נִשְׁבָּר, כַּכָּתוּב בְּתוֹרָתְךָ: וְהָשִׁיב לֵב נִשְׁבָּר וְנִדְכֶּה, אָמֵן.

לְמִשְׁפָּטֶיךָ יַעֲמְדוּ כֻּלָּנוּ, וְנִזְעַק לְשִׁמְךָ הַקָּדוֹשׁ שֶׁתִּתְקַבְּלֵנוּ בְּחֶסֶד וּבְרַחֲמִים, תֵּשֵׁב בְּעַצְמְךָ לְמִשְׁפָּטֵנוּ, וְאַל תַּעֲנִישֵׁנוּ בִּגְזֵרוֹת אַכְזָרִיּוֹת. נִזְכֶּה לְגַדֵּל אֶת בָּנֵינוּ לְטוֹבָה, וְהֵם יִזְכּוּ לְגַדֵּל אֶת בְּנֵיהֶם, כִּי אַתָּה מְרַחֵם עַל עוֹלְלִים.

בַּמֶּה אֲקַדֵּם לְחַנְּנֶךָ, שֶׁתִּמְחַל עַל חֲטָאַי הַחֲמוּרִים. יוֹדַעַת אֲנִי שֶׁאֵין לִי כְּלָל מְלִיצִים רַק דִּמְעוֹתַי הַמָּרוֹת, כְּמוֹ שֶׁנֶּאֱמַר כָּל הַשְּׁעָרִים נִנְעֲלוּ, וְרַק שַׁעֲרֵי דִמְעוֹת אֵינָם נִנְעָלִים. אָב הָרַחֲמָן, קַח אֶת דִּמְעוֹתַי שֶׁשָּׁפַכְתִּי לְפָנֶיךָ, וְשִׂים אוֹתָם בְּנֹאדֶךָ. כַּבֵּס בָּהֶם אֶת עֲוֹנוֹתַי, וְתַעֲבֹר מִמִּדַּת הַדִּין לְמִדַּת הָרַחֲמִים. בְּחֶסֶד וֶאֱמֶת תִּקְרַב תְּחִנָּתִי לְפָנֶיךָ, וְלֹא יוּכְלוּ מַלְאָכִים רָעִים וּמְקַטְרְגִים לְהַפְסִיק בֵּין תְּפִלָּתִי לְכִסֵּא הַכָּבוֹד. הוֹשֵׁט אַתָּה אֶת יָדְךָ לִתְפִלָּתִי שֶׁלֹּא תִצְטָרֵךְ לַעֲבֹר דֶּרֶךְ מַלְאָכִים, כִּי יָרֵאָה אֲנִי.

אֲנִי מְבַקֶּשֶׁת מִמְּךָ שֶׁתָּשִׁיב חַרְבְּךָ לְנַדְנָהּ, וְשִׂים יָדְךָ עָלֵינוּ בָּנֶיךָ הַקְּדוֹשִׁים, אָמֵן.

הַטֵּה אָזְנְךָ לְרִנָּתִי ה' הָאָדוֹן הָאָהוּב, שָׁמְרֵנִי מִכָּל רַע, חֶרְפָּה וּבִזָּיוֹן, וּמִמַּתְנַת בָּשָׂר וָדָם, וְיִתְקַיֵּם בִּי מַה שֶּׁכָּתוּב בַּתּוֹרָה הַקְּדוֹשָׁה: פּוֹתֵחַ אֶת

gracious unto me; grant life to me, to my husband, to my children, and to grandchildren. Amen.

Remove Your anger from upon me, and let the sound of the shofar silence Satan, who continually accuses us. Grant atonement for our sins through the sound of the shofar, for just as the shofar is curved, so we bend our hearts to repent for our sins. May the sound of the shofar cleanse the stains that we have brought upon our souls, and may the breath that emerges from the shofar weigh upon the scales of good deeds, so as to tip them away from the side of transgressions. May it be Your will that during this year we shall merit to hear the shofar of the Messiah.

[...] I begin my request with great trepidation, in fear and trembling. Woe is me for not having feared the two witnesses—the angels who testify to my bitter sins; for when I am made to stand in judgment they will show me my own stamp, that I myself inscribed my own sins. How did I not have mercy upon my small children—may they not be taken from me, heaven forfend, for my sins? Therefore I ask of You that in Your mercy You have pity upon me. Amen.

[...] How shall I make appeasement before You, that You might grant atonement for my sins? If it be through confession and repentance, behold—I am returning to You and confessing my sins before You. If it be through weeping and crying out that You may be appeased, behold—I come weeping before You, that I may be granted atonement for all my sins. Amen.

[...] Have mercy upon Your children as a father has mercy upon his children. And if we be viewed as servants—have mercy upon us as a master has mercy upon his servants. With the passing years we grow few; our blood is spilled; You, Lord, will arise to help us. Amen.

I know that I have turned from Your commandments, but I place my trust in Your holy Name, that You will not be exacting with me,

יָדֶךָ וּמַשְׂבִּיעַ לְכָל חַי רָצוֹן, דְּהַיְנוּ שֶׁאַתָּה בְּעַצְמְךָ תְּפַרְנֵס לֹא עַל יְדֵי בְּנֵי אָדָם, אָמֵן.

רְאֵה עָנְיֵנוּ וְהוֹשִׁיעֵנוּ, וְקַבֵּל תְּפִלָּתֵנוּ. יוֹדַעַת אֲנִי שֶׁאֵינִי רְאוּיָה לִפְתּוֹחַ פִּי לְבַקֵּשׁ מִלְּפָנֶיךָ, כִּי עֲבֵרוֹת גְּדוֹלוֹת עָבַרְתִּי בְּפִי, לֵיצָנוּת וְנִבּוּל פֶּה, אֲבָל אַתָּה ה' רַחוּם, רַחֵם עָלַי וְקַבֵּל בַּקָּשָׁתִי. כְּמוֹ שֶׁקִּבַּלְתָּ אֶת תְּפִלַּת חַנָּה אִמֵּנוּ, כֵּן תְּקַבֵּל אֶת תְּפִלָּתִי וּתְכַפֵּר לַעֲווֹנוֹתַי, אָמֵן.

בְּכָל לִבִּי אֶקְרָאֶךָ, שֶׁתַּעַזְרֵנִי כַּאֲשֶׁר עֲזַרְתָּנִי עַד עַתָּה. מַפִּילָה אֲנִי אֶת תְּחִנָּתִי לְפָנֶיךָ כְּבֵן לְאָב, שֶׁתַּעֲנֵנִי וּתְרַחֵם עָלַי כְּאָב עַל בָּנִים, כְּמוֹ שֶׁכָּתוּב בַּתּוֹרָה: כְּרַחֵם אָב עַל בָּנִים כֵּן תְּרַחֵם ה' עָלֵינוּ בְּנֵי יִשְׂרָאֵל, אָמֵן.

הַעֲבֵר מִמֶּנִּי אַפְּךָ וַחֲרוֹנְךָ ה' אֱלֹקַי וֵאלֹקֵי אֲבוֹתַי, וְקַבֵּל בַּקָּשָׁתִי, כַּפֵּר לַחֲטָאַי כִּי לֹא אָשׁוּב עוֹד לַעֲשׂוֹתָם, וּרְצוֹנִי לַעֲשׂוֹת מִצְווֹתֶיךָ שֶׁצִּוִּיתָ לְחַנָּה אִמֵּנוּ. חַזֵּק אֶת יָדַי לָתֵת צְדָקָה וּלְהַדְלִיק נֵרוֹת, וְחַזֵּק אֶת רַגְלַי לָלֶכֶת לְבֵית הַכְּנֶסֶת לְשַׁבְּחֶךָ, אָמֵן.

מַה נֹּאמַר וּמַה נְּבַקֵּשׁ, יוֹדַעַת אֲנִי מְעוּט מַעֲשַׂי, אֲבָל אֲנִי נִשְׁעֶנֶת עַל זְכוּת יְלָדַי הַקְּטַנִּים, שֶׁלֹּא יִהְיוּ אֶצְלִי לְעוֹלָם צוּחָה וְיָגוֹן, רַק אֹשֶׁר וְשִׂמְחָה, אָמֵן.

אוֹדְךָ בְּכָל לְבָבִי, כִּי אַתָּה מְפֹאָר בְּפִי כֹל, מְרַחֵם עַל כֹּל, וְנִסְתָּר מִכֹּל. שׁוֹמֵעַ כָּל הַתְּפִלּוֹת, מְכַפֵּר עַל כָּל הַחֲטָאִים שֶׁעָשִׂינוּ, וְאַתָּה קָדוֹשׁ וְנוֹרָא. אֲבַקֵּשׁ בְּשִׁמְךָ הָאָהוּב, שֶׁתַּכְנִיס לְמִדַּת הַדִּין מִמִּדַּת הָרַחֲמִים וּכְמוֹ שֶׁמַּכְנִיסִים לְדָבָר מַר קְצָת מְתִיקוּת, כֵּן תַּמְתִּיק דִּינֵנוּ, אָמֵן.

אַל תּוֹכִיחֵנִי בַּחֲמָתֶךָ, כִּי שִׁמְךָ נִקְרָא שׁוֹפֵט אֱמֶת, דָּן מִשְׁפַּט אֱמֶת, וְעוֹשֶׂה חֶסֶד וֶאֱמֶת. בָּזֶה אָגִיל, כִּי אֲקַוֶּה שֶׁתְּכַפֵּר עַל חֲטָאַי שֶׁאֲנִי מִתְחָרֶטֶת עֲלֵיהֶם, וּרְצוֹנִי לְשַׁבְּחֶךָ וּלְעָבְדְךָ בְּכָל לְבָבִי, אָמֵן.

...הָקֵם לַאֲמָתְךָ חַסְדֶּךָ, כִּי נִכְנַעַת אֲנִי לְפָנֶיךָ וּמְבַקֶּשֶׁת חַסְדֶּךָ. אֵיךְ לֹא אִירָא בְּפַחַד וּרְעָדָה כְּשֶׁאֶצְטָרֵךְ לַעֲמֹד לְמִשְׁפָּט לִפְנֵי בֵּית דִּין שֶׁל מַעְלָה וְלַעֲנוֹת עַל עֲווֹנוֹתַי, כִּי אַתָּה ה' אֱלֹקַי נוֹהֵג כְּמִנְהַג מֶלֶךְ בָּשָׂר וָדָם.

and that You will act toward me as it is written in the Torah—passing over transgressions one by one, such that the merits will prevail over the transgressions, Amen.

[...] In Your righteousness wash away the stains that I have made upon the garments of my soul, through grave sins. What profit is it for You if we die, or—heaven forfend—if our children die? What have we done to Your holy Name by our sins? We have brought harm only upon ourselves, for Your Name is always holy, forever. Have mercy upon us, and may we witness the fulfillment of the verse: You are close to those who call upon You. Have mercy upon those who coronate You, for we are Your flock. Have mercy upon us, restore Your divine presence to Zion, and may the redeemer come to Zion. Amen Selah.

כְּשֶׁעוֹמְדִים לְמִשְׁפָּט לִפְנֵי מֶלֶךְ בָּשָׂר וָדָם, הֲרֵי הוּא שֶׁמְזֻכֶּה, אוֹ שֶׁמַּעֲנִישׁ בְּחֶמְלָה וְאֵין לְפָנָיו רַחֲמִים בַּדִּין, אֲבָל אַתָּה ה' עוֹשֶׂה נִפְלָאוֹת וּבְעֵת הַמִּשְׁפָּט אַתָּה מַרְאֶה רַחֲמֶיךָ, רַחֵם עָלַי וְחָנֵּנִי, וְתֶן חַיִּים לִי, לְבַעֲלִי, לְבָנַי וְלִבְנֵי בָנַי, אָמֵן.

גַּל מֵעָלַי חֶרְוֹנְךָ, וּבְקוֹל הַשּׁוֹפָר חֲסֹם אֶת הַשָּׂטָן הַמְקַטְרֵג עָלֵינוּ תָּמִיד. כַּפֵּר לַחֲטָאֵינוּ בְּקוֹל הַשּׁוֹפָר, כִּי כְּמוֹ שֶׁהַשּׁוֹפָר כָּפוּף, כֵּן נָכוּף לִבֵּנוּ לָשׁוּב בִּתְשׁוּבָה עַל עֲוֹנוֹתֵינוּ. בְּקוֹל הַשּׁוֹפָר תְּנַקֶּה אֶת הַכְּתָמִים שֶׁהִכְתַּמְנוּ בָּהֶם אֶת נִשְׁמוֹתֵינוּ, וּבָרוּחַ הַיּוֹצֵא מֵהַשּׁוֹפָר תִּנְשֹׁף עַל כַּף מֹאזְנֵי הַמִּצְוֹת שֶׁיַּכְרִיעוּ אֶת כַּף הָעֲבֵרוֹת. יְהִי רָצוֹן שֶׁבְּזוֹ הַשָּׁנָה נִזְכֶּה לִשְׁמֹעַ שׁוֹפָרוֹ שֶׁל מָשִׁיחַ.

...וְאֶשָּׂא שְׂפָתַי לְבַקֵּשׁ חָסֶד. הִנְנִי מַתְחִילָה לְבַקֵּשׁ בְּיִרְאָה גְדוֹלָה, בְּחִיל וּבִרְעָדָה. אוֹי לִי שֶׁלֹּא יָרֵאתִי מִשְּׁנֵי הָעֵדִים, הַמַּלְאָכִים הַמְּעִידִים עַל חֲטָאַי הַמָּרִים, וּכְשֶׁיַּעֲמִידוּנִי לְמִשְׁפָּט יַרְאוּנִי אֶת חֲתִימַת יָדִי, שֶׁכָּתַבְתִּי בְּעַצְמִי אֶת עֲווֹנוֹתַי. אֵיךְ לֹא רִחַמְתִּי עַל בָּנַי הַקְּטַנִּים, שֶׁחָלִילָה לֹא יִלָּקְחוּ מִמֶּנִּי בַּעֲווֹנוֹתַי, לָכֵן אֲבַקֵּשׁ מִמְּךָ שֶׁבְּחַסְדְּךָ תְּרַחֵם עָלַי, אָמֵן.

לוּלֵי חֲסָדֶיךָ עַל מַה אֶסְמֹךְ בַּיָּמִים הָאֵלֶּה. הֵם חֲמוּרִים מְאוֹד שֶׁבָּהֶם קוֹרְאִים אֶת מַעֲשַׂי כֻּלָּם, וְעַל מַה אֶסְמֹךְ. אֵין לִי לְהִשָּׁעֵן אֶלָּא עַל הַתְּשׁוּבָה, כִּי בָּרָאתָ אֶת הַתְּשׁוּבָה לִפְנֵי הָעֲבֵרוֹת, עַל כֵּן אֲנִי מְקַבֶּלֶת עָלַי לַחֲזֹר בִּתְשׁוּבָה וְלָשׁוּב אֵלֶיךָ, אָמֵן וְאָמֵן.

בְּחַסְדְּךָ תְּדִינֵנִי, תְּכַפֵּר עַל חֲטָאַי וּתְקַבֵּל תְּשׁוּבָתִי. הִתְעוֹרְרוּ אֲבוֹתַי שֶׁבִּמְעָרַת הַמַּכְפֵּלָה לְעֻזְרֵנִי, כִּי אֵין בִּי מַעֲשִׂים טוֹבִים. ה' אֱלֹקֵי הֲשִׁיבֵנוּ אֵלֶיךָ שֶׁנִּקָּרֵא שׁוּב עַם קְדוֹשֶׁיךָ, וְרַחֵם עָלֵינוּ בְּחֶסֶד בִּזְכוּת אֲבוֹתֵינוּ.

צַר לִי מֵהַמַּעֲשִׂים הָרָעִים שֶׁעָשִׂיתִי, וּבַמֶּה אֶתְרַצֶּה לְפָנֶיךָ שֶׁתְּכַפֵּר עַל חֲטָאַי. אִם בְּוִדּוּי וּתְשׁוּבָה, הֲרֵינִי שָׁבָה אֵלֶיךָ וּמִתְוַדָּה חֲטָאתִי לְפָנֶיךָ, וְאִם בִּבְכִי וּזְעָקָה תִּתְרַצֶּה, הֲרֵינִי בָּאָה בִּבְכִיָּה לְפָנֶיךָ שֶׁתְּכַפֵּר עַל כָּל עֲווֹנוֹתַי, אָמֵן.

הֵן רַחֲמֶיךָ חָפַצְתִּי. אַל תָּבוֹא בְּמִשְׁפָּט עִמָּנוּ, כִּי מִי יַעֲמוֹד לְפָנֶיךָ,
חֶסֶד וֶאֱמֶת יְקַדְּמוּ פָּנֶיךָ, מִלְּפָנֶיךָ מִשְׁפָּטֵינוּ יֵצֵא, עֵינֶיךָ תֶּחֱזֶינָה מֵישָׁרִים.
בְּמִשְׁפָּטֶיךָ חָיֵינוּ כִּי אַתָּה אָבִינוּ וַאֲנוּ בָנֶיךָ, וְאֵיךְ תִּשְׁמַע לִבְכִיֵנוּ. רַחֵם עָלֵינוּ
וְהַקְשֵׁב לְתַחֲנוּנֵנוּ, אָמֵן.

וְעַל בָּנֶיךָ תְּרַחֵם כְּרַחֵם אָב עַל בָּנִים. וְאִם כַּעֲבָדִים, רַחֵם עָלֵינוּ כְּרַחֵם
אָדוֹן עַל עֲבָדָיו. בְּרֹבוֹת הַיָּמִים אָנוּ נִמְעָטִים, אֶת דָּמֵנוּ שׁוֹפְכִים, וְאַתָּה ה'
הִתְעוֹרֵר לְעֶזְרֵנוּ, אָמֵן.

רַעַשׁ יוֹם יִקְרַב מִשְׁפָּט. תְּנַהֲגֵנוּ בְּחֶסֶד בְּרַעַשׁ יוֹם הַדִּין, וְעַד מָתַי
תִּשְׁכָּחֵנוּ. בִּזְכוּת אַהֲבַת אֲבוֹתֵינוּ עֹזְרֵנוּ בְּיָמֵינוּ וְרַחֵם עָלֵינוּ, אָמֵן.

רַחֲמֶיךָ יָלִיצוּ בְּעַד רְשׁוּמִים בַּכִּסֵּא, כִּי הַשֵּׁם יִשְׂרָאֵל חָקוּק בְּכִסֵּא
הַכָּבוֹד. בִּזְכוּת יוֹסֵף הַצַּדִּיק שֶׁעָשָׂה כָּבוֹד לִשְׁמֶךָ, תִּזְכְּרֵנוּ לְכָבוֹד וְלֹא
חָלִילָה לִשְׁפְלוּת וָעֹנִי, אָמֵן.

יָדַעְתִּי כִּי סַרְתִּי מִמִּצְוֹתֶיךָ, אַךְ שַׂמְתִּי מִבְטַחִי בְּשִׁמְךָ הַקָּדוֹשׁ שֶׁלֹּא
תְדַקְדֵּק עִמִּי, וִיקֻיַּם בִּי מַה שֶּׁכָּתוּב בַּתּוֹרָה מַעֲבִיר רִאשׁוֹן רִאשׁוֹן וְהַזְּכוּיּוֹת
יַכְרִיעוּ אֶת הָעֲבֵרוֹת, אָמֵן.

עֵת תָּקוּם לְמִשְׁפָּטֶיךָ, אֲבַקֵּשׁ מִמְּךָ שֶׁתָּקוּם מִכִּסֵּא דִין וְתֵשֵׁב עַל כִּסֵּא
רַחֲמִים. אַל תְּיַסְּרֵנִי כְּחַטָּאתִי, כִּי אֶגְדֹּר פְּרָצִי וְאָצוּם לְבַל אָשׁוּב לְכִסְלָה.

קוֹל שַׁוְעָתֵנוּ תִּשְׁמַע וְתַאֲזִין, כִּי אֲנִי עוֹשֶׂה תְשׁוּבָה עַל חֲטָאַי. יְהִי רָצוֹן
שֶׁיִּתְקַיֵּם בִּי הַפָּסוּק וְתַעֲשֶׂה זְדוֹנוֹת כִּזְכוּיּוֹת, אָמֵן.

בְּצִדְקָתְךָ תָּדִיחַ כְּתָמִים שֶׁהִכְתַּמְתִּי בִּגְדֵי נִשְׁמָתִי בַּעֲבֵרוֹת גְּדוֹלוֹת.
מַה בֶּצַע לְךָ בְּמִיתָתֵנוּ אוֹ חָלִילָה בְּמִיתַת בָּנֵינוּ. מֶה עָשִׂינוּ לְשִׁמְךָ הַקָּדוֹשׁ
בְּחֶטְאָתֵינוּ, רַק לְעַצְמֵנוּ הָרֵיעוֹנוּ, כִּי שִׁמְךָ קָדוֹשׁ תָּמִיד לָנֶצַח. רַחֵם עָלֵינוּ,
וְיִתְקַיֵּם בָּנוּ מַה שֶּׁכָּתוּב קָרוֹב אַתָּה לְקוֹרְאֶיךָ. רַחֵם עַל מַמְלִיכֶךָ, כִּי אֲנַחְנוּ
צֹאן מַרְעִיתֶךָ. רַחֵם עָלֵינוּ, הָשֵׁב שְׁכִינָתְךָ לְצִיּוֹן, וּבָא לְצִיּוֹן גּוֹאֵל, אָמֵן סֶלָה.

AS THE TORAH SCROLL IS
CARRIED FROM THE HOLY ARK
ON ROSH HASHANAH

Yiddish

*M*aster of the universe, I place my trust in Your thirteen attributes
of mercy and in Your Holy Name. Just as the doors of the Holy Ark
are opened in order to bring out Your holy Torah, so may You open
the gates of mercy; have mercy upon us in Your great mercy and forgive
our sins. Just as we have clothed the Torah scrolls in white, so may You
whiten the stains that we have brought upon the garments of our souls
through our transgressions, as it is written in the Torah: Even though
your transgressions are red as scarlet, they shall become white as wool.

Master of the universe, as we now take out the Torah scroll, inscribe
us in the scroll of life, the book of blessing. And as we read in the Torah
that You answered the prayer of Sarah on Rosh Hashanah, so answer our
prayer on Rosh Hashanah. As we read in the additional reading [from the
books of the prophets] that You answered the prayer of Hannah, so answer
our prayer this day. As You caused Your servant Joseph to emerge from
his imprisonment, so help us emerge from the Day of Judgment. You write

---

God revealed the thirteen attributes of mercy to Moses following the sin of the
golden calf (Exodus 32–34). Moses, faced with the enormity of the sin and
the responsibility for pleading for forgiveness on behalf of the nation, is shown the
order of prayer by God. He is told, "Whenever Israel sin, let them perform this

תְּחִינָה לְאוֹמְרָהּ בִּשְׁעַת הוֹצָאַת
סֵפֶר־תּוֹרָה בְּרֹאשׁ הַשָּׁנָה

אידיש

רִבּוֹנוֹ שֶׁל עוֹלָם, סָמַכְתִּי עַל שְׁלֹשׁ עֶשְׂרֵה מִדּוֹת שֶׁל רַחֲמִים, וְעַל שִׁמְךָ הַקָּדוֹשׁ. כְּשֵׁם שֶׁנִּפְתָּחִים שַׁעֲרֵי אֲרוֹן הַקֹּדֶשׁ לְהוֹצִיא אֶת תּוֹרָתְךָ הַקְּדוֹשָׁה, כֵּן תִּפְתַּח שַׁעֲרֵי רַחֲמִים, תְּרַחֵם עָלֵינוּ בְּרַחֲמִים גְּדוֹלִים וְתִמְחַל לַעֲווֹנוֹתֵינוּ, וּכְמוֹ שֶׁהִלְבַּשְׁנוּ מְעִילִים לְבָנִים לְסִפְרֵי הַתּוֹרָה, כֵּן תַּלְבִּין כְּתָמִים שֶׁהִכְתַּמְנוּ בִּגְדֵי נִשְׁמָתֵנוּ בְּגֹדֶל חֲטָאֵינוּ, כְּמוֹ שֶׁכָּתוּב בַּתּוֹרָה אִם יַאְדִּימוּ חֲטָאֵיכֶם כַּתּוֹלָע כַּצֶּמֶר יִלְבִּינוּ.

רִבּוֹנוֹ שֶׁל עוֹלָם, כְּמוֹ שֶׁאָנוּ מוֹצִיאִים עַתָּה אֶת סֵפֶר הַתּוֹרָה, כֵּן תִּכְתְּבֵנוּ בְּסֵפֶר הַחַיִּים סֵפֶר בְּרָכָה, וּכְשֵׁם שֶׁנִּקְרָא בְּסֵפֶר הַתּוֹרָה שֶׁעָנִית לִתְפִלַּת שָׂרָה בְּרֹאשׁ הַשָּׁנָה, כֵּן תַּעֲנֶה לִתְפִלָּתֵנוּ בְּרֹאשׁ הַשָּׁנָה. וּכְמוֹ שֶׁנִּקְרָא בַּהַפְטָרָה שֶׁעָנִית לִתְפִלַּת חַנָּה, כֵּן תַּעֲנֶה לִתְפִלָּתֵנוּ הַיּוֹם הַזֶּה. וּכְשֵׁם שֶׁהוֹצֵאתָ אֶת עַבְדְּךָ יוֹסֵף הַצַּדִּיק מִבֵּית הָאֲסוּרִים, כֵּן תּוֹצִיאֵנוּ מִיּוֹם הַדִּין. כָּתַבְתָּ בְּתוֹרָתְךָ כָּל הַשְּׁעָרִים נִנְעָלִים חוּץ מִשַּׁעֲרֵי דְמָעוֹת, עַל כֵּן נִזְעַק וְנִבְכֶּה:

---

service before Me and I will forgive them" (Babylonian Talmud, Rosh Hashanah 17b). For this reason, the recitation of the thirteen attributes is a central feature of the prayer service at this time of year.

in Your Torah that all the gates are locked except for the gates of tears; therefore we cry out and weep.

Hear our supplication and inscribe us for a year of good health. Do not take us from this world, heaven forfend, before we have lived a full seventy years, so that we not—heaven forfend—leave our children as young orphans, and so that we may raise them to Your holy Torah, for the sake of Your Holy Name. Do not take our children from us in our lifetime, so that they may be able to fulfill the commandment of honoring parents when we grow old. Merciful God, I prostrate myself and ask of You that You not take our husbands, as it is written: I shall mourn as a widow for her husband. And do not, heaven forfend, take our fathers or mothers, sisters or brothers. Let our tears plow a path beneath Your Throne of Glory, so that our prayers may come close to You. We ask also that the Torah scrolls that are now being brought out should stand in our defense, so that Satan will not be able to accuse us. And may the attribute of mercy protect us from our deeds (for you—the holy scrolls of the Torah—have no reason to plead on our behalf, since we have performed the opposite of what is written in you; that which is forbidden, we have committed). But we place our trust in that which is written in the Torah—that You forgive sins, one by one. Therefore we ask that this be a time of forgiveness, as it is written in Your holy Torah—that there is nothing that stands in the way of repentance.

Merciful Father; we have broken our heart into thirteen pieces, corresponding to Your thirteen attributes of mercy. We shall not sin again; grant atonement for our transgressions. Your holy prophets told Israel that the time would come when the righteous Messiah would redeem us; therefore we ask of You that You fulfill Your word and send Your help, that the righteous Redeemer come speedily in our days. Amen.

שְׁמַע בַּקָּשָׁתֵנוּ וְכָתְבֵנוּ לִשְׁנַת בְּרִיאוּת. אַל תִּקָּחֵנוּ מִזֶּה הָעוֹלָם חָלִילָה לִפְנֵי מְלֹאת יָמֵינוּ שִׁבְעִים שָׁנָה, כְּדֵי שֶׁלֹּא נַשְׁאִיר חָלִילָה יְתוֹמִים קְטַנִּים, וְנוּכַל לְגַדְּלָם לְתוֹרָתְךָ הַקְּדוֹשָׁה לְמַעַן שִׁמְךָ הַקָּדוֹשׁ. אַל תִּקַּח אֶת בָּנֵינוּ בְּחַיֵּינוּ, כְּדֵי שֶׁיּוּכְלוּ לְקַיֵּם מִצְוַת כִּבּוּד אָב וְאֵם לְעֵת זִקְנָתֵנוּ. ה' הָרַחוּם, אֶפֹּל עַל פָּנַי, וַאֲבַקֵּשׁ מִמְּךָ שֶׁלֹּא תִּקַּח אֶת בַּעֲלֵינוּ, כְּמוֹ שֶׁכָּתוּב וַאֲקוֹנֵן כְּאַלְמָנָה עַל בַּעֲלָהּ, וְאַל תִּקַּח חָלִילָה אֶת אָבִינוּ וְאִמֵּנוּ וְאַחֵינוּ וְאַחְיוֹתֵינוּ, וְדִמְעוֹתֵינוּ יֵחָתְרוּ חֲתִירָה תַּחַת כִּסֵּא כְּבוֹדְךָ שֶׁתְּפִלּוֹתֵינוּ יָבוֹאוּ לְיָדְךָ. כְּמוֹ כֵן אָנוּ מְבַקְּשִׁים, שֶׁסִּפְרֵי הַתּוֹרָה שֶׁמּוֹצִיאִים עַתָּה יִהְיוּ מְלִיצֵי יֹשֶׁר שֶׁהַשָּׂטָן לֹא יְקַטְרֵג עָלֵינוּ, וּמִדַּת הָרַחֲמִים תָּגֵן עַל מַעֲשֵׂינוּ. וַהֲרֵי אַתֶּם סִפְרֵי הַתּוֹרָה הַקְּדוֹשִׁים אֵין לָכֶם סִבָּה לְבַקֵּשׁ בַּעֲדֵנוּ, כִּי עָשִׂינוּ הַהֵפֶךְ מִמַּה שֶּׁכָּתוּב בָּכֶם, וּמַה שֶּׁאָסוּר עָשִׂינוּ, אֲבָל סָמַכְנוּ עַל מַה שֶּׁכָּתוּב בַּתּוֹרָה מוֹחֵל עֲוֹנוֹת רִאשׁוֹנִים, לָכֵן נְבַקֵּשׁ שֶׁיִּהְיֶה כָּעֵת זְמַן הַמְּחִילָה, כְּמוֹ שֶׁכָּתוּב בְּתוֹרָתְךָ הַקְּדוֹשָׁה אֵין לְךָ דָּבָר הָעוֹמֵד בִּפְנֵי הַתְּשׁוּבָה.

אָב רַחוּם, שַׁבְּרֵנוּ לְבַבֵנוּ עַתָּה לִשְׁלֹשָׁה-עָשָׂר חֲלָקִים כְּנֶגֶד שְׁלֹשׁ-עֶשְׂרֵה הַמִּדּוֹת. שׁוּב לֹא נֶחֱטָא, וְכַפֵּר לַחֲטָאֵינוּ. נְבִיאֶיךָ הַקְּדוֹשִׁים אָמְרוּ לְיִשְׂרָאֵל שֶׁיַּגִּיעַ זְמַן וּמָשִׁיחַ הַצַּדִּיק יִגְאָלֵנוּ, עַל כֵּן נְבַקֵּשׁ מִלְּפָנֶיךָ שֶׁתְּקַיֵּם דְּבָרֶיךָ, וְתִשְׁלַח לָנוּ אֶת עֶזְרָתְךָ שֶׁיָּבוֹא גּוֹאֵל צֶדֶק בִּמְהֵרָה בְיָמֵינוּ, אָמֵן.

YOM KIPPUR IN SICILY

"*T*he women come, family by family, to prostrate themselves and to kiss the Torah scrolls. They enter by one entrance and leave by the opposite one. Throughout the night, one enters as the other leaves."

Rabbi Ovadia of Bartenura is known primarily for his commentary on the Mishnah, but he also left a legacy of fascinating anthropological details about Jewish life in fifteenth-century Europe. After a lengthy journey from Italy to Israel, during the course of which he visited many different Jewish communities, he finally reached Jerusalem, where he was immediately appointed as a religious leader. A few months later, around Pesach in 1488, Rabbi Ovadia sent a letter to his father

ליל יום הכיפורים

בְּאוֹת הנשים משפחות משפחות להשתחוות ולנשק הספרי־תורה.
ובפתח האחד תכנסנה ונכחו תצאנה. וכל הלילה זו נכנסת וזו יוצאת.

---

in Italy, describing his journey to Israel, his experiences along the way, and the
different customs of the Jews whom he met while traveling to Jerusalem. In Sicily, he wrote, it was customary for the entire family to take part in the ceremony
of kissing the Torah scroll in the synagogue on the night of Yom Kippur and on
Hoshana Rabbah. The excerpt here is his description of the unique custom that
he witnessed.

Sukkot

Sukkot, the holiday that immediately follows the solemnity of
Rosh Hashanah and Yom Kippur, is a time for rejoicing and
gaiety. In the Torah, Sukkot has two names: the "festival of
sukkot" (tabernacles), in commemoration of the ancient Israelites'
wanderings in the desert and of the temporary structures in which
they dwelled; and the "festival of the ingathering," referring to
the season of the agricultural year. The festival lasts for one week,
starting on the fifteenth of Tishrei. The special commandments
that the Torah prescribes for this festival include rejoicing ("You
shall rejoice in your festival … you shall be only joyful"), dwelling
in a sukkah (a structure covered with a roof of branches or reeds),
and waving the "four species," which include a palm branch, a
citron (*etrog*), myrtle twigs, and willow branches.

FOLLOWING CANDLE LIGHTING ON SUKKOT
Yiddish

To be recited with intense devotion on the first two nights of Sukkot and on the Shabbat that falls during the week of the festival, after lighting candles.

*A*ccept with favor the words of my mouth and the thoughts of my heart.

May my discourse be sweet before You; may You hear my pleas.

Arouse Your manifold mercies toward me, Your maidservant;

Let Your kindness not abandon me; let Your right hand support me,

Shade me with Your might; let me take shelter under Your wings.

In the merit of the commandment of the sukkah, save us from exile;

Protect us lest our enemies rule over us.

Gather our scatterings from the four corners of the earth

The rebuilding of the Temple, a recurring theme in many *tekhines* and in Jewish prayer in general, has special significance on Sukkot. The prophet Amos, describing the final redemption, conveys God's promise: "On that day I will raise up the fallen sukkah of David"—a reference to the Davidic monarchy and the Temple.

תחינה לסוכות לאחר הדלקת הנרות

אידיש

קַבֵּל נָא בְּרָצוֹן אִמְרֵי פִי וְהֶגְיוֹן לִבִּי,

שִׂיחָתִי יֶעֱרַב לְפָנֶיךָ וְתַאֲזִין תַּחֲנוּנִי,

עוֹרְרָה רַחֲמֶיךָ הַמְרֻבִּים עֲלֵי אֲמָתֶךָ,

אַל יַעַזְבוּנִי חֲסָדֶיךָ וִימִינְךָ תִּסְעָדֵנִי,

בְּאֶבְרָתְךָ תָּסֶךְ עָלַי וְתַחַת כְּנָפֶיךָ אֶחֱסֶה,

וּבִזְכוּת מִצְוַת סֻכָּה תַּצִּילֵנוּ מִגָּלוּת,

וְתָגֵן עָלֵינוּ לְבַל יִשְׁלְטוּ בָנוּ שׂוֹנְאֵינוּ,

וּתְקַבֵּץ נְפוּצוֹתֵינוּ מֵאַרְבַּע כַּנְפוֹת הָאָרֶץ,

וְתַצִּילֵנוּ מִשִּׁבְיָה וּמִמַּאֲסָר עַל יְדֵי עֲלִילָה,

וְאַל יִשְׁלוֹט בָּנוּ עַיִן הָרָע לְעוֹלָם,

And redeem us from captivity and imprisonment through conspiracy,

And let the evil eye never control us.

Rebuild Your Holy Temple and restore Your divine presence to Jerusalem.

May the blessing that I recite over the candles rise up and find favor before You,

And may You guard all the houses of Israel from fire and destruction,

And let there not be excessive rain throughout the seven days of the festival

And let the winds not extinguish the candles that we have lit.

Illuminate our fortune for livelihood and sustenance

And illuminate the eyes of my husband and children with Your holy Torah.

Turn Your anger away from upon Israel, Your nation.

Act for the sake of those who have perished by fire for the holiness of Your Name;

Act for the sake of Abraham, Isaac, and Jacob.

Master of the universe—in the merit of lighting the festival candles

And in the merit of our illuminating the sukkah with the light of Your sanctity

May it be Your will to arouse the merits of Abraham, our patriarch,

Who was cast into the fiery furnace; And the merit of Isaac, our patriarch, who was bound upon an altar of wood and fire; and the merit of Jacob, our forefather,

Who fought with an angel of fire. Remember their merits this day in our favor.

Amen; so may it be His will.

בְּנֵה בֵית מִקְדָּשְׁךָ וְהָשֵׁב שְׁכִינָתְךָ לִירוּשָׁלַיִם,
וְתַעֲלֶה לְפָנֶיךָ בְּרָצוֹן בִּרְכָתִי עַל הַנֵּרוֹת,
וְתִשְׁמֹר אֶת כָּל בָּתֵּי יִשְׂרָאֵל מִשְּׂרֵפָה וְתַבְעֵרָה,
וְלֹא יִרְבּוּ הַגְּשָׁמִים בְּכָל שִׁבְעַת יְמֵי הֶחָג,
וְאַל יְכַבּוּ הָרוּחוֹת אֶת הַנֵּרוֹת אֲשֶׁר הִדְלַקְנוּ,
וְתָאִיר אֶת מַזָּלֵנוּ לְפַרְנָסָה וּלְכַלְכָּלָה,
וְתָאִיר אֶת עֵינֵי בַּעֲלִי וּבָנַי בְּתוֹרָתְךָ הַקְּדוֹשָׁה,
וְתָסִיר אֶת כַּעַסְךָ מֵעַל יִשְׂרָאֵל עַמֶּךָ,
עֲשֵׂה לְמַעַן בָּאֵי בָאֵשׁ עַל קְדֻשַּׁת שְׁמֶךָ,
עֲשֵׂה לְמַעַן אַבְרָהָם יִצְחָק וְיַעֲקֹב,
רִבּוֹנוֹ שֶׁל עוֹלָם, בִּזְכוּת הַדְלָקַת הַנֵּרוֹת שֶׁל חַג
וּבִזְכוּת שֶׁאָנוּ מְאִירִים אֶת הַסֻּכָּה בְּאוֹרוֹת קָדְשֶׁךָ,
יְהִי רָצוֹן שֶׁיִּתְעוֹרְרוּ זְכִיּוֹתָיו שֶׁל אַבְרָהָם אָבִינוּ
שֶׁהֻשְׁלַךְ לְכִבְשַׁן הָאֵשׁ: וּבִזְכוּת יִצְחָק אָבִינוּ שֶׁנֶּעֱקַד
עַל מִזְבַּח הָעֵצִים וְהָאֵשׁ: וּבִזְכוּת יַעֲקֹב אָבִינוּ
שֶׁנֶּאֱבַק עִם מַלְאַךְ הָאֵשׁ. זְכֹר לָנוּ כַּיּוֹם אֶת זְכִיּוֹתֵיהֶם.
אָמֵן כֵּן יְהִי רָצוֹן.

UPON TAKING UP THE FOUR SPECIES
Yiddish

*M*ay it be Your will, Lord, Supreme God and Supreme Master, that You accept with love and favor Your commandment, which I fulfill today in the blessing and taking up of the four species, as though I had performed it with all the proper mystical intentions, and may the light of this commandment illuminate the heavens.

May it be Your will, Lord my God and God of my forefathers, that in the merit of having taken up the citron, referred to in the Torah as the "fruit of the beautiful tree," You will remember in our favor our patriarch Abraham and our matriarch Sarah, whom You adorned with old age and veneration, as it is written: "Abraham and Sarah were old, full of days."

May it be Your will, Lord my God and God of my forefathers, that in the merit of having held in my hand the citron, which resembles a person's heart, You will forgive me for the evil thoughts of my heart.

The four species, also referred to as *lulav* and *etrog*, are held together and waved on each day of the festival, except for Shabbat. This commandment may be fulfilled any time during the day, from sunrise until sunset. The palm branch, willows, and myrtles are held in the right hand, the citron in the left, and one recites the blessing, "Blessed are You, Lord our God, King of the universe, Who has sanctified us with His commandments and commanded us concerning taking up the *lulav*." Then the citron is brought close to touch the *lulav*, and the four species are gently waved together in all four directions, and also upward and downward. On the first day, the *Sheheheyanu* blessing also is recited.

תחינה לאחר נטילת ארבעת המינים

אידיש

יְהִי רָצוֹן מִלְּפָנֶיךָ יְיָ אֱלֹהֵי הָאֱלֹהִים וַאֲדוֹנֵי הָאֲדוֹנִים, שֶׁתִּתְקַבֵּל בְּאַהֲבָה וּבְרָצוֹן מִצְוָתְךָ שֶׁקִּיַּמְתִּי הַיּוֹם בְּבִרְכַּת וּנְטִילַת אַרְבַּעַת הַמִּינִים, כְּאִלּוּ כִּוַּנְתִּי בְּכָל הַכַּוָּנוֹת הָרְאוּיוֹת לְכֵן בְּמִצְוָה זוֹ, וְאוֹר הַמִּצְוָה יָאִיר בִּשְׁמֵי הַשָּׁמָיִם:

יְהִי רָצוֹן מִלְּפָנֶיךָ יְיָ אֱלֹהַי וֵאלֹהֵי אֲבוֹתַי, שֶׁבִּזְכוּת שֶׁנָּטַלְתִּי בְּיָדִי הָאֶתְרוֹג הַנִּקְרָא "פְּרִי עֵץ הָדָר", תִּזְכֹּר לָנוּ זְכוּת אָבִינוּ אַבְרָהָם וְאִמֵּנוּ שָׂרָה, שֶׁהִדַּרְתָּ אוֹתָם בְּזִקְנָה וְשֵׂיבָה, כַּכָּתוּב: "וְאַבְרָהָם וְשָׂרָה זְקֵנִים בָּאִים בַּיָּמִים".

וִיהִי רָצוֹן מִלְּפָנֶיךָ יְיָ אֱלֹהַי וֵאלֹהֵי אֲבוֹתַי, שֶׁבִּזְכוּת שֶׁנָּטַלְתִּי בְּיָדִי הָאֶתְרוֹג הַדּוֹמֶה לְלִבּוֹ שֶׁל אָדָם, תִּסְלַח לִי עַל מַחְשְׁבוֹת לִבִּי הָרָעוֹת:

יְהִי רָצוֹן מִלְּפָנֶיךָ יְיָ אֱלֹהַי וֵאלֹהֵי אֲבוֹתַי, שֶׁבִּזְכוּת שֶׁנָּטַלְתִּי בְּיָדִי אֶת הַלּוּלָב הָאָגוּד, תִּתְעוֹרֵר עָלַי זְכוּת יִצְחָק אָבִינוּ, שֶׁנֶּעֱקַד עַל גַּבֵּי הַמִּזְבֵּחַ,

---

Although the Torah provides no explanation for this commandment, several symbolic significances have been proposed. According to one view, the different species represent the different types of people who comprise the nation of Israel; the gathering and waving of all of them together in an act of divine worship carries a message of national unity in the service of God. A different interpretation, as reflected in this prayer, views the different species as symbolizing various parts of the human body: The upright, still tightly closed palm branch represents the spine; the shape of the myrtle leaves is reminiscent of the eye; the elongated willow leaves are like lips, and the citron is the heart. The bringing together of the four species serves to internalize one's personal consciousness of holistic dedication to the service of God.

May it be Your will, Lord my God and God of my forefathers, that in the merit of having held in my hand the bound *lulav*, the merit of our patriarch Isaac, who was bound upon the altar, will be recalled to memory in my favor, and the merit of our matriarch Rebecca, who was like a *lulav*: Just as the *lulav* bears good fruit but also has thorns, so both Jacob, our forefather, and Esau, his brother, emerged from her.

May it be Your will, Lord my God and God of my forefathers, that in the merit of having taken in my hand the *lulav* that is compared to a person's spine, You will grant me atonement for all that I have sinned through my spine which was not properly straightened and devoted to Your service.

May it be Your will, Lord my God and God of my forefathers, that in the merit of having held in my hand the three myrtle twigs, the merit of our forefather Jacob—the third of the three holy patriarchs—will be recalled in my favor, for he was like a myrtle: Just as the myrtle sprouts abundant leaves, so our patriarch, Jacob, had many children.

May it be Your will, Lord my God and God of my forefathers, that in the merit of my having held in my hand this day the holy myrtle twigs, whose leaves resemble a person's eyes, You will grant me atonement for the transgressions that I have committed through the sight of my eyes.

May it be Your will, Lord my God and God of my forefathers, that in the merit of having held in my hand this day the branches of the willow, which withers earlier than other species, the merit of the righteous Joseph will be recalled in my favor, for he was like a willow: He died before his brothers, the fathers of the holy tribes of Israel. And may the merit of our matriarch Rachel, who died before our matriarch Leah, also be recalled to memory in my favor.

וּזְכוּת רִבְקָה אִמֵּנוּ, שֶׁנִּמְשְׁלָה אֶל הַלּוּלָב: מָה הַלּוּלָב יֵשׁ בּוֹ פְּרִי טוֹב וְגַם קוֹץ וָחוֹחַ, כֵּן יָצְאוּ מִמֶּנָּה יַעֲקֹב אָבִינוּ וְעֵשָׂו אָחִיו:

יְהִי רָצוֹן מִלְּפָנֶיךָ יְיָ אֱלֹהַי וֵאלֹהֵי אֲבוֹתַי, שֶׁבִּזְכוּת שֶׁנָּטַלְתִּי בְּיָדִי אֶת הַלּוּלָב הַדּוֹמֶה לְשִׁדְרָתוֹ שֶׁל אָדָם, תְּכַפֵּר לִי עַל כָּל מַה שֶּׁחָטָאתִי בְּשִׁדְרָתִי וְלֹא יִשַּׁרְתִּיהָ לַעֲבוֹדָתְךָ כָּרָאוּי:

יְהִי רָצוֹן מִלְּפָנֶיךָ יְיָ אֱלֹהַי וֵאלֹהֵי אֲבוֹתַי, שֶׁבִּזְכוּת נְטִילָתִי בְּיָדִי שְׁלֹשֶׁת בַּדֵּי הַהֲדַס, תִּתְעוֹרֵר עָלַי זְכוּתוֹ שֶׁל יַעֲקֹב אָבִינוּ, הַמְשֻׁלָּשׁ בָּאָבוֹת הַקְּדוֹשִׁים, וְנִמְשָׁל לַהֲדַס: מָה הַהֲדַס מְרֻבֶּה בְּעָלִים, כֵּן יַעֲקֹב אָבִינוּ מְרֻבֶּה בְּבָנִים:

יְהִי רָצוֹן מִלְּפָנֶיךָ יְיָ אֱלֹהַי וֵאלֹהֵי אֲבוֹתַי, שֶׁבִּזְכוּת שֶׁנָּטַלְתִּי בְּיָדִי הַיּוֹם הַהֲדַסִּים הַקְּדוֹשִׁים, הַדּוֹמִים בַּעֲלֵיהֶם לְעֵינָיו שֶׁל אָדָם, תְּכַפֵּר לִי עַל עֲוֹנוֹתַי שֶׁחָטָאתִי בִּרְאִיַּת עֵינָי:

יְהִי רָצוֹן מִלְּפָנֶיךָ יְיָ אֱלֹהַי וֵאלֹהֵי אֲבוֹתַי, שֶׁבִּזְכוּת שֶׁנָּטַלְתִּי בְּיָדִי הַיּוֹם אֶת בַּדֵּי הָעֲרָבָה, שֶׁדַּרְכָּהּ לִבֹּל וְלִכְמֹשׁ קֹדֶם שְׁאָר הַמִּינִים, כֵּן תִּתְעוֹרֵר עָלַי זְכוּתוֹ שֶׁל יוֹסֵף הַצַּדִּיק, שֶׁנִּמְשַׁל לָעֲרָבָה, וּמֵת קֹדֶם לְאֶחָיו, הַשְּׁבָטִים הַקְּדוֹשִׁים. וְכֵן תַּעֲמֹד לִי זְכוּתָהּ שֶׁל אִמֵּנוּ רָחֵל, שֶׁנִּפְטְרָה מִן הָעוֹלָם קֹדֶם לְאִמֵּנוּ לֵאָה:

יְהִי רָצוֹן מִלְּפָנֶיךָ יְיָ אֱלֹהַי וֵאלֹהֵי אֲבוֹתַי, שֶׁבִּזְכוּת שֶׁנָּטַלְתִּי בְּיָדִי בַּדֵּי הָעֲרָבָה, שֶׁהִיא דוֹמָה בְּעָלֶיהָ לִשְׂפָתוֹתָיו שֶׁל אָדָם, תִּמְחַל לִי עַל כָּל מַה שֶּׁחָטָאתִי לְפָנֶיךָ בִּשְׂפָתַי:

רִבּוֹנוֹ שֶׁל עוֹלָם, אֵל רַחוּם וְחַנּוּן לְכָל בְּרִיּוֹתָיו, זְכֹר נָא עַמְּךָ יִשְׂרָאֵל אֲהוּבֶיךָ, הַשּׁוֹמְרִים פִּקּוּדֶיךָ וּמְהַלְלִים אוֹתְךָ עִם אַרְבַּעַת הַמִּינִים – אֶתְרוֹג, לוּלָב, הֲדַס וַעֲרָבָה. וּבִזְכוּת שֶׁאָנוּ מוֹנְעִים עַצְמֵנוּ מֵאֲכִילָתָם וַהֲנָאָתָם שֶׁל

May it be Your will, Lord my God and God of my forefathers, that in the merit of having held in my hand the branches of the willow, whose leaves resemble a person's lips, You will forgive me for all that I have transgressed before You through my lips.

Master of the universe, God Who is merciful and gracious toward all of His creations—I pray You—remember Your nation Israel, Your beloved ones, who observe Your commandments and give praise to You with the four species: the citron, the palm branch, the myrtle, and the willow. In the merit of our refraining from consuming and using these holy articles for our benefit throughout the seven days of the festival, may You help us and guard us from all evil that comes from the four directions of the world. Please erase the sin of Adam and Eve, who ate from the Tree of Knowledge before You permitted them to partake of it, thereby bringing death to all generations. Bless us, good God, with a beneficent fate with the approach of the new year. May we be sealed for a long and good life, and may we be worthy of the coming of our righteous Messiah speedily in our days. Amen.

הַמִּינִים הַקְּדוֹשִׁים בְּכָל שִׁבְעַת יְמֵי הֶחָג, כֵּן תִּהְיֶה בְּעֶזְרֵנוּ וְתִשְׁמְרֵנוּ מִכָּל
רַע הַבָּא מֵאַרְבַּע רוּחוֹת הָעוֹלָם. וּמְחַק נָא חֶטְאָם שֶׁל אָדָם וְחַוָּה, שֶׁאָכְלוּ
מֵעֵץ הַדַּעַת טֶרֶם שֶׁהִתְּרְתָ לָהֶם לֶאֱכוֹל מִמֶּנּוּ וְגָרְמוּ מִיתָה לְכָל הַדּוֹרוֹת,
בָּרְכֵנוּ, הָאֵל הַטּוֹב, בְּפִתְקָא טָבָא בְּבוֹא הַשָּׁנָה הַחֲדָשָׁה, וְנֵחָתֵם לְחַיִּים
אֲרֻכִּים וְטוֹבִים, וְנִזְכֶּה לְבִיאַת מְשִׁיחַ צִדְקֵנוּ בִּמְהֵרָה בְּיָמֵינוּ, אָמֵן.

UPON REMOVING THE
PITTAM OF THE *ETROG*
Yiddish

*M*aster of the universe: On account of the sin of Eve, who ate of
the Tree of Knowledge, death came to the world. Had I lived at that time
I would not have eaten it and would not have savored it, just as I did not
wish to disqualify this *etrog* during the past seven days of the festival. Today,
as I disqualify it, it no longer represents a commandment. Just as I savor
this *pittam*, so I would have savored the mere sight of the Tree of Knowledge,
concerning which the Holy One told Adam and Eve, "You shall not eat of
it," and I would not have transgressed His command. Accept with favor my
supplication and prayer that I not die in this childbirth; help me to give
birth easily and without distress, and may there be no harm to me or to
my infant, for You are the God of salvation.

During the seven days of Sukkot, the *etrog*—and especially the *pittam*, the protru-
sion at the opposite end from the stem—is guarded with care so that it remains
fit for ritual use. After the festival, the *etrog* may be eaten. The *pittam* represents the
remnants of the female part of the flower, the stigma. Unlike other types of fruit,

תְּפִלָּה לְאִשָּׁה בְּעֵת נְטִילַת פִּטָּם הָאֶתְרוֹג

אידיש

רִבּוֹנוֹ שֶׁל עוֹלָם, בִּשְׁבִיל חַוָּה שֶׁהָיְתָה אוֹכֶלֶת מֵעֵץ הַדַּעַת, גָּרַם אוֹתוֹ חֵטְא מִיתָה בָּעוֹלָם, וְאִם הָיִיתִי בְּאוֹתוֹ זְמַן לֹא הָיִיתִי אוֹכַלְתּוֹ וְלֹא הָיִיתִי נֶהֱנֵית מִמֶּנּוּ, כְּמוֹ שֶׁלֹּא רָצִיתִי לִפְסֹל אֶתְרוֹג זֶה בְּשִׁבְעַת יְמֵי הֶחָג שֶׁעָבְרוּ, וְהַיּוֹם שֶׁפְּסַלְתִּי אֵין בּוֹ מִצְוָה. וּכְשֵׁם שֶׁיֵּשׁ לִי הֲנָאָה בְּפִטָּם זֶה כָּךְ הָיִיתִי נֶהֱנֵית לִרְאוֹת עֵץ הַדַּעַת, שֶׁאָמַר הַקָּדוֹשׁ־בָּרוּךְ־הוּא לְאָדָם וְחַוָּה "לֹא תֹּאכַל", וְלֹא הָיִיתִי עוֹבֶרֶת אֶת צִוּוּיוֹ, וּתְקַבְּלֵנִי בְּרָצוֹן אֶת תְּפִלָּתִי וְאֶת תְּחִנָּתִי, שֶׁלֹּא אָמוּת מִלֵּדָה זוֹ, וְתוֹשִׁיעֵנִי לֵילֵד בְּנַחַת וּבְלִי צַעַר, וְלֹא יִהְיֶה לִי וְלֹא לְוַלְדִּי שׁוּם נֶזֶק, כִּי אַתָּה הָאֵל הַמּוֹשִׁיעַ.

---

the *etrog* retains this remnant of the flower even after the fruit ripens. Owing to this quality, along with the fact that the *etrog* tree produces fruit all year long, the *etrog* is viewed as a symbol of fertility. This special prayer is meant for a woman who eats the *pittam* in the hope of conceiving or experiencing an early birth, or for a pregnant woman who craves the fruit.

Shemini Atzeret and Simhat Torah

The holiday of Shemini Atzeret falls on the day after the festival of Sukkot ends. Outside of Israel, it is celebrated over two days; the second day is referred to as Simhat Torah, which means "rejoicing over the Torah." On Shemini Atzeret, a special prayer for rain is recited in the synagogue, signifying the start of Israel's rainy season. In Israel, the prayer for rain and the celebration of the Torah take place on the same day.

PRAYER FOR RAIN
Leah Shakdiel

The prayer is recited standing, with the Holy Ark open.

(All sing)

> Pour out your heart like water, standing in the presence of God
>
> (Lamentations 2:19)

(Leader)

> Our God, and God of our Fathers and Mothers:

(All sing each stanza, then the leader calls out the final line, which is repeated by all)

> Remember the Mother who drew—for the servant and his
>
> camels—water
>
> And was drawn after him to his master in Canaan, tranquil as water
>
> She loved her son, Jacob, for her prophecy was clear as water

Leah Shakdiel, who lives in the Israeli town of Yeruham, composed a prayer for rain for her synagogue's women's prayer group. "The prayer for rain," Shakdiel explained, "makes reference to a string of characters who are all male; all patriarchs of the Jewish nation. So I sat down to write a poem based upon the traditional format of the prayer for rain, but relying entirely upon feminine figures, and only

תפילת הגשם

לאה שקדיאל

התפילה נאמרת בעמידה, כאשר ארון־הקודש פתוח:

(כולן שרות):

שִׁפְכִי כַמַּיִם לִיבֵּךְ נֹכַח פְּנֵי ה׳:

(חזנית):

אֱלוֹהֵינוּ וֵאלוֹהֵי אֲבוֹתֵינוּ וְאִמּוֹתֵינוּ:

(בכל בית, כולן שרות עם החזנית):

זְכוֹר אֵם אֲשֶׁר בְּכַדָּהּ שָׁאֲבָה לָעֶבֶד וְלַגְּמַלִּים מַיִם
וְאַחֲרָיו לִכְנַעַן אֶל אֲדוֹנוֹ נִמְשְׁכָה בְּנַחַת כַּמַּיִם
אֶת יַעֲקֹב בְּנָהּ אָהֲבָה כִּי נְבוּאָתָהּ זַכָּה כַּמַּיִם
וּלְאָחִיהָ שְׁלָחַתּוּ לְהַצִּילוֹ מִנִּקְמַת עֵשָׂו פָּחֲזָה כַּמַּיִם –

---

those who were really connected to water, one way or another ... Thus, while the men in the synagogue offer the prayer for rain, reminding the Holy One of the merit of our forefathers, we—the women—mention in our prayers before God the merit of our matriarchs. Our aim is identical: that there should be rain."

And sent him to her brother, to save him from the revenge of Esau,
fickle as water—

(Congregation and leader)

For the sake of Rebecca, do not withhold water!

(Leader)

Remember the Mother who met her beloved, as she was grazing
sheep, at the well of water

She helped her sister, and when her womb closed up she poured
tears like water

Therefore You promised her son, Joseph, to deliver Israel from the
land of the Nile water.

She cried when they were led into exile, and her reward—that You
would be their redeeming water—

(Congregation and leader)

For the sake of Rachel's righteousness, grant abundant water!

(Leader)

Remember the king's daughter who went down to bathe at the river
of water

Who, pitying the boy crying in the basket, drew him from the water

And raised him as a Hebrew, redeemer of his brothers, to lead them
through water;

In the Garden of Eden, she teaches proselytes the Torah, which is
compared to water—

(קהל וחזנית):

בַּעֲבוּר רִבְקָה אַל תִּמְנַע מָיִם!

(חזנית):

זְכוֹר אֵם רוֹעָה צֹאן פָּגְשָׁה אֲהוּבָהּ עַל בְּאֵר מַיִם
לַאֲחוֹתָהּ עָזְרָה, אַךְ בִּסְגוֹר רַחֲמָהּ שָׁפְכָה דְּמָעוֹת כַּמַּיִם
לָכֵן הִבְטַחְתָּ לִבְנָהּ יוֹסֵף לִפְקֹד יִשְׂרָאֵל מֵאֶרֶץ יְאוֹר מַיִם
וּבְגָלוּתָם בָּכְתָה, וּשְׂכַר פְּעוּלָתָהּ – שֶׁתִּהְיֶה לָהֶם אַתָּה מִקְוֵה
מָיִם –

(קהל וחזנית):

בְּצִדְקַת רָחֵל חוֹן חַשְׂרַת מָיִם!

(חזנית):

זְכוֹר בַּת מֶלֶךְ אֲשֶׁר יָרְדָה לִרְחֹוץ עַל הַיְאוֹר מַיִם
חָמְלָה עַל נַעַר בּוֹכֶה בַּתֵּבָה וּמְשִׁתְהוּ מִן הַמַּיִם
גִּדְּלַתְהוּ כְּעִבְרִי גוֹאֵל אֶחָיו וּמַעֲבִירָם בַּמַּיִם
בְּגַן עֵדֶן מְלַמֶּדֶת לְגִיּוֹרוֹת תּוֹרָה נִמְשְׁלָה לְמָיִם –

(קהל וחזנית):

בַּעֲבוּר בִּתְיָה אַל תִּמְנַע מָיִם!

(חזנית):

זְכוֹר מְיַלֶּדֶת יְרְאַת אֱלֹקִים לֹא הִשְׁלִיכָה בָּנִים לַמַּיִם
נִבְּאָה כִּי אָחִיהָ יִגְאַל יִשְׂרָאֵל וְהִתְיַצְּבָה לִשְׁמְרוֹ בַּמַּיִם
בְּתֹף וּבְמָחוֹל הוֹצִיאָה הַנָּשִׁים לָשִׁיר לַה' עַל נֵס הַמַּיִם
בִּזְכוּתָהּ הָלְכָה בַּמִּדְבָּר עִם הָעָם אַרְבָּעִים שָׁנָה בְּאֵר מָיִם –

(Congregation and leader)

> For the sake of Bitya, do not withhold water!

(Leader)

> Remember the God-fearing midwife who did not cast boys into
>> water
> Who, prophesizing that her brother would redeem Israel, stood to
>> watch over him in water
> And led the women out with tambourines and dancing to sing to
>> God over the miracle of the water
> In her merit for forty years in the desert with the nation there went
>> a well of water—

(Congregation and leader)

> For the sake of Miriam's righteousness, grant abundant water!

(Leader)

> Remember the righteous one like a tree planted at pools of water
> Who went up with her husband to pray, when the world needed
>> water
> The cloud came up from her corner, for she gave to the poor
>> bread and water
> And pleaded for mercy for the wicked, so they made their
>> repentance pure as water—

(Congregation and leader)

> For the sake of the wife of Abba Ḥilkiya, do not withhold water!

בְּצִדְקַת מִרְיָם חוֹן חֲשֶׁרֶת מָיִם!

(חזנית):

זְכוֹר צַדִּיקָה כְּעֵץ שָׁתוּל עַל פַּלְגֵי מַיִם

עָלְתָה עִם אִישָׁה לְהִתְפַּלֵּל כְּשֶׁנִּצְרַךְ הָעוֹלָם לְמַיִם

עָלָה הֶעָנָן מִזְּוִית שֶׁלָּהּ כִּי לֶעָנִי נָתְנָה לֶחֶם וּמַיִם

וְעַל רְשָׁעִים בִּקְשָׁה רַחֲמִים וְעָשׂוּ תְּשׁוּבָה טְהוֹרָה כַּמַּיִם –

(קהל וחזנית):

בַּעֲבוּר אֵשֶׁת אַבָּא חִלְקִיָּה אַל תִּמְנַע מָיִם!

(חזנית):

זְכוֹר שְׁבָטִים אֲחֵי־דִּינָה שֶׁהֶעֱבַרְתָּ בִּגְזֵרַת מַיִם

שֶׁהִמְתַּקְתָּ לָמוֹ מְרִירוּת מַיִם

תּוֹלְדוֹתָם נִשְׁפַּךְ דָּמָם עָלֶיךָ כַּמַּיִם

תֵּפֶן, כִּי נַפְשֵׁנוּ אָפְפוּ מָיִם –

(קהל וחזנית):

בְּצִדְקָם וּבְצִדְקָן חוֹן חֲשֶׁרֶת מָיִם!

(החזנית):

שָׁאַתָּה הוּא ה׳ אֱלֹהֵינוּ, מַשִּׁיב הָרוּחַ וּמוֹרִיד הַגֶּשֶׁם!

(קהל וחזנית):

לִבְרָכָה וְלֹא לִקְלָלָה!

313

(Leader)

Remember the tribes, brothers of Dinah, whom You led through
the parting of water

And for whom You sweetened the bitterness of water

The blood of their descendants has been poured for Your sake
like water

Turn to us, for our souls swirl like water—

(Congregation and leader)

For the sake of their righteousness, grant abundant water!

(Leader)

For You are the Lord our God, Who causes the wind to blow and
Who brings rain.

(Congregation)

For a blessing and not for a curse!

(Leader)

For a blessing and not for a curse!

(Congregation)

Amen.

(Congregation)

For life and not for death!

(Leader)

For life and not for death!

314

(החזנית):

לִבְרָכָה וְלֹא לִקְלָלָה!

(המתפללות):

אָמֵן!

(המתפללות):

לְחַיִּים וְלֹא לְמָוֶת!

(החזנית):

לְחַיִּים וְלֹא לְמָוֶת!

(המתפללות):

אָמֵן!

(המתפללות):

לְשֹׂבַע וְלֹא לְרָזוֹן!

(החזנית):

לְשֹׂבַע וְלֹא לְרָזוֹן!

(המתפללות):

אָמֵן!

סוגרים את הארון.

(Congregation)

> Amen.

(Congregation)

> For abundance and not for lack!

(Leader)

> For abundance and not for lack!

(Congregation)

> Amen.

The Holy Ark is closed.

SONG FOR SIMḤAT TORAH

Rivka bat Meir Tiktiner

One is our God; You are my Lord	Praise God
Who created my soul and body for me	Praise God
You created heaven and earth	Praise God
Therefore Your praise will last forever	Praise God
You have always been and will always be	Praise God
[...]	
Jewish children—set yourselves upon the straight path	Praise God
Then I shall lengthen your days	Praise God
I shall replace brass with gold	Praise God
And iron with silver	Praise God
I shall gather for you from dawn until dusk	Praise God

At the heart of the Simḥat Torah celebration are the *hakkafot* in the synagogue during both the evening and morning prayers: All of the Torah scrolls are removed from the Holy Ark, and the congregation sings and dances with them around the podium of the synagogue. In recent years it has also become acceptable in many communities for women to dance with the Torah scrolls in the women's section of the synagogue.

Afterward, the last portion of Deuteronomy is read, immediately followed by a reading of the first portion in Genesis, demonstrating that Torah study is a cyclical, ongoing endeavor.

Rivka bat Meir Tiktiner, a sixteenth-century composer of *tekhines*, Yiddish writer, translator, and poet, wrote this women's song of praise to be recited on Simḥat

שיר לשמחת תורה

רבקה בת מאיר טיקטינר

הַלְלוּיָה	אֶחָד אֱלֹהֵינוּ אַתָּה אֵלִי
הַלְלוּיָה	אֲשֶׁר בָּרָא אֶת נַפְשִׁי וְגוּפִי לִי
הַלְלוּיָה	בָּרָאתָ אֶת הַשָּׁמַיִם וְהָאָרֶץ
הַלְלוּיָה	לָכֵן תְּהִלָּתְךָ לָנֶצַח תִּהְיֶה
הַלְלוּיָה	הָיִיתָ וְתִהְיֶה לָנֶצַח
	[...]
הַלְלוּיָה	יְלָדִים יְהוּדִים, פְּנוּ לָכֶם לְדֶרֶךְ הַיָּשָׁר
הַלְלוּיָה	וְאָז אַאֲרִיךְ לָכֶם אֶת יְמֵיכֶם
הַלְלוּיָה	תַּחַת הַנְּחֹשֶׁת אָבִיא זָהָב
הַלְלוּיָה	וְתַחַת הַבַּרְזֶל אָבִיא כֶסֶף

Torah. Tiktiner had a broad religious education and translated several religious works, including *Duties of the Hearts*, an early-twelfth-century work of Jewish philosophy by Rabbeinu Behaye. She also published a book called *Meineket Rivka*, which discusses a woman's obligation to educate her children and includes moral teachings, chapters from the Gemara, excerpts from the Midrash, quotes from *musar* literature from the Middle Ages, and original Torah insights. It was first published in Prague in 1609, four years after her death. Her grave remains to this day in the city's ancient Jewish cemetery.

This song—the first, as far as we are able to ascertain, to be written in Yiddish by a woman—was meant to be sung while the women were busy decorating the Torah scrolls in preparation for Simhat Torah. It is presented here in abbreviated form.

Good food that cannot be kept for long.	Praise God
Like a single person	Praise God
In Your light we shall walk	Praise God
We give praise to the Only God	Praise God
Who created all of us	Praise God

אֶאֱסֹף לָכֶם מִשַּׁחַר הַשֶּׁמֶשׁ עַד הַשְּׁקִיעָה   הַלְלוּיָהּ
אֹכֶל טוֹב שֶׁלֹּא נִתַּן לְשָׁמְרוֹ זְמַן רַב   הַלְלוּיָהּ
כְּאִישׁ אֶחָד   הַלְלוּיָהּ
בְּאוֹרְכֶם אָנוּ נֵלֵךְ   הַלְלוּיָהּ
אָנוּ נְהַלֵּל אֶת הָאֵל הַיָּחִיד   הַלְלוּיָהּ
אֲשֶׁר אֶת כֻּלָּנוּ בָּרָא   הַלְלוּיָהּ

Hanukkah

Hanukkah commemorates two historical events: the military victory of the small, rebel Hasmonean forces over the Syrian-Greek rulers of the Land of Israel and the subsequent liberation, purification, and rededication of the Temple on the twenty-fifth of Kislev in 164 B.C.E.; and the miracle that the small amount of ritually pure oil that was found in the Holy Temple after it was liberated—containing sufficient oil to light the holy menorah for only one day—lasted for eight days, enough time to produce more oil.

The significance of the victory of the Hasmoneans extended far beyond the military or the political realm. Their rebellion had arisen against the background of a cultural war: The Syrian-Greek rulers used their power to promote their culture and ideology, outlawing Judaism on punishment of death and ordering all Jews to serve their pagan gods. The liberation and purification of the Temple, therefore, symbolized the triumph of the Jewish spirit and culture despite the odds—a victory that remains relevant and meaningful today.

Hanukkah lasts for eight days. One candle is lit on the first night, and then an additional candle is lit on each subsequent night until the final night, when eight candles are lit. The *hanukkiyah* (candelabrum) is placed either at a window or outside the entrance to the home, so as to publicize the miracle of Hanukkah.

JUDITH'S PLEA
The book of Judith

Judith fell upon her face and put ashes upon her head, and tore her garment and uncovered the sackcloth that she wore. And at the time when, in the House of God in Jerusalem, they were offering the evening incense, she cried out to God with a loud voice and said: Lord God of my ancestor, Simeon, to whom You gave a sword with which to take revenge on strangers who allowed a virgin to be defiled and who uncovered the thigh for shame and violated her womb to her reproach, for You declared, "Such thing shall not be done"—but they had done it. For that reason You put their princes to death by the sword, and their bed—ashamed at the deceit that they practiced—was dyed with blood, and You slew servants with their lords, and the lords upon their thrones. And you gave their wives as prey, and their daughters into captivity, and all their spoils to be divided among Your beloved children, who were zealous for You and despised the defilement of their blood, and called upon You for help. My God, my God—hear also me, a widow. For You performed things that preceded that, and those things, and that which came after; You have thought about that which is, and that

---

The apocryphal book of Judith—one of the historical chronicles that was not included in the Bible—was originally written in Hebrew, but only its translations into Greek and Latin remain. It is from these translations that the contemporary Hebrew version was created. The book describes how Holofernes, the military commander of the armies of Nebuchadnezzar, king of Assyria, was sent on a mission of conquest, during the course of which he brought to submission the entire region stretching from Persia to Tyre and Sidon. On his way to Jerusalem, he laid siege to the fortified town of Bethulia, home to a beautiful and noble young widow named Judith. Judith sought to save her town and the honor of Jerusalem. She devised a plan whereby she succeeded in leaving the town and entering the camp of Holofernes, who was captivated by her great charm and beauty and set up

יהודית

ספר יהודית

וְיהוּדִית נָפְלָה עַל פָּנֶיהָ וַתָּשֶׂם אֵפֶר עַל רֹאשָׁהּ, וַתִּקְרַע אֶת מְעִילָהּ,
וַתְּגַל אֶת הַשַּׂק אֲשֶׁר לָבָשָׁה. וּבָעֵת הַהִיא הִקְרִיבוּ בִּירוּשָׁלַם בְּבֵית
הָאֱלוֹהִים אֶת קְטֹרֶת הָעֶרֶב הַהוּא. וַתִּזְעַק בְּקוֹל גָּדוֹל אֶל יְיָ וַתֹּאמֶר: [ב]
יְיָ אֱלֹהֵי אָבִי שִׁמְעוֹן, אֲשֶׁר נָתַתָּ לוֹ חֶרֶב בְּיָד לְנָקָם מִנָּכְרִים אֲשֶׁר הִתִּירוּ
פְאֵר בְּתוּלָה לְטֻמְאָה וַיְגַלּוּ יָרֵךְ לְבֹשֶׁת וַיְחַלְּלוּ רֶחֶם לְחֶרְפָּה, כִּי אָמַרְתָּ
"לֹא יֵעָשֶׂה כֵן", וַיַּעֲשׂוּ: [ג] יַעַן זֹאת נָתַתָּ נְשִׂיאֵיהֶם לְחֶרֶב וְיצוּעָם אֲשֶׁר
הוֹבִישׁ הַמִּפְתָּה לְדָם, וַתַּךְ עֲבָדִים עַל מוֹשְׁלִים וּמוֹשְׁלִים עַל כִּסְאוֹתָם:
[ד] וַתִּתֵּן נְשֵׁיהֶם לָבַז וּבְנוֹתָם בַּשְּׁבִית וְכָל שְׁלָלָם חֵלֶק לִבְנֵי אֹהֲבֶיךָ, אֲשֶׁר
קִנְאוּ אֶת קִנְאָתְךָ וַיִּתְעֲבוּ טֻמְאַת דָּמָם וַיִּקְרָאוּךָ לְעֶזְרָה. אֵלִי אֵלִי שְׁמַע גַּם
אֵלַי הָאַלְמָנָה: [ה] הֵן אַתָּה עָשִׂיתָ הָרִאשׁוֹנוֹת מֵהֶם וְהַדְּבָרִים הָהֵם וַאֲשֶׁר
אַחֲרֵיהֶם, גַּם הַהֹוִיּוֹת וְהַנִּהְיוֹת חָשַׁבְתָּ וַיִּהְיוּ אֲשֶׁר בִּינוֹת: [ו] גַּם יִתְיַצְּבוּ
אֲשֶׁר יָעַצְתָּ וְאָמְרוּ הִנֶּנּוּ, כִּי כָל דְּרָכֶיךָ נָכוֹנוּ וּמִשְׁפָּטֶיךָ לְעוֹלָם: [ז] כִּי הִנֵּה
עָצְמוּ הָאַשּׁוּרִים בְּחֵילָם, רָמוּ בְסוּס וְרֹכֵב עָלְצוּ בְּשׁוֹק רַגְלַיִם, בָּטְחוּ בְמָגֵן
וּבְכִידוֹן וּבְקֶשֶׁת וָקֶלַע, וְלֹא יָדְעוּ כִּי אַתָּה יְיָ אִישׁ מִלְחָמָה יְיָ שְׁמֶךָ: [ח] מַגֵּר

---

an intimate banquet in her honor. Judith plied Holofernes with strong wine and cheese, waited until he was completely inebriated and then cut off his head.

As early as the Middle Ages, the book of Judith was linked to the period and battle of the Hasmoneans. Although the text states explicitly that Judith was a descendant of the tribe of Simeon, midrashic sources maintain that she was the daughter of Johanan, the High Priest, and sister of the Hasmonean brothers. Despite the fairly clear indications that Holofernes—if indeed such a historical character actually existed—would have been active during the Persian period, tradition holds that Judith's act of valor took place during the Hasmonean revolt.

The book of Judith, which is written as prose, includes two poem-prayers: One is Judith's prayer to God before going out to the camp of Holofernes, and which has come to be, and understand that which is to come. The things that You decided have come to pass, they declare, "Here we are"—for all of Your ways are prepared, and Your judgments last forever. For behold, the power of the Assyrians has become stronger: They are exalted with horses and men, they glory in their army of foot-soldiers; they trust in shield and spear and bow and sling, they do not know that You, Lord, are a valiant warrior; the Lord is Your Name. Throw down their strength in Your might; bring down their force in Your wrath, for they intend to desecrate Your holy place, to defile the Sanctuary where Your glorious Name rests, and to cut down with iron sword the horn of Your altar. Look upon their pride; send Your anger upon their heads, give into my widow's hand the strength that I plot. Smite with the deceit of my lips the servant with the prince, and the prince with the servant; let their stature be broken down at the hand of a woman. For Your power is not in numbers, nor Your might in strong men. For You are the God of the destitute, helper of the oppressed, upholder of the weak, protector of the forlorn, savior of the unfortunate. So then, God of my father, God of the inheritance of Israel, Master of the heaven and the earth, Creator of water, King of every creature—hear my prayer. Let my words and temptation be their wound and injury, for they have planned evil against Your covenant and Your holy Temple and the head of Zion and the house of Your children's possession. Bring knowledge to every nation and every tribe, that they may know that You are the God of all valor and might and there is none other than You, Protector of the seed of Israel.

---

the other is her psalm of praise following her victory: "Then Judith took olive branches and distributed them among the women who were with her, and they made wreaths for their heads ... and she led the women in dancing, and all the men of Israel, with their swords at their sides and adorned with wreaths, followed them, in a festive procession with songs and praises."

Judith's prayer prior to going out to Holofernes's camp recalls the revenge wrought by Simeon and Levi in Shekhem following the rape of their sister, Dinah. This

כֹּחָם בִּגְבוּרָתֶךָ, הוֹרֵד עֻזָּם בְּאַפֶּךָ, כִּי נוֹעֲצוּ לְחַלֵּל קָדְשֶׁיךָ לְטַמֵּא מִשְׁכַּן מְנוּחַת שֵׁם כְּבוֹדֶךָ, לְגַדֵּעַ בְּבַרְזֶל קֶרֶן מִזְבְּחֶךָ: [ט] הַבֵּט עַל גַּאֲוָתָם, שְׁלַח חֲרוֹנְךָ בְּרָאשֵׁיהֶם, תֵּן בְּיָדִי הָאַלְמָנָה אֶת הָעוֹז אֲשֶׁר זַמֹּתִי: [י] הַךְ מִשְׁפְּתֵי פְתוּיֵּי עֶבֶד עַל שַׂר וְשַׂר עַל מְשָׁרְתוֹ, רְעַץ קוֹמָתָם בְּיַד נְקֵבָה: [יא] כִּי לֹא בְּרַבִּים עֻזֶּךָ, וְלֹא בַעֲצוּמִים גְּבוּרָתֶךָ, כִּי אַתָּה אֱלֹהֵי עֲנִיִּים, עֹזֵר דַּלִּים, מִשְׂגָּב לַכְּשָׁלִים, סִתְרָה לְאוֹבְדִים, מוֹשִׁיעַ אֶבְיוֹנִים: [יב] אָכֵן, אָכֵן אֱלֹהֵי אָבִי אֱלֹהֵי נַחֲלַת יִשְׂרָאֵל, אֲדוֹן שָׁמַיִם וָאָרֶץ, יוֹצֵר הַמַּיִם, מֶלֶךְ כָּל קִנְיָנֶךָ, אַתָּה תִשְׁמַע תְּפִלָּתִי: [יג] וְנָתַתָּ דְּבָרַי וּפִתּוּיַי לְפִצְעָם וְחַבּוּרָתָם, כִּי יָעֲצוּ קָשָׁה עַל בְּרִיתֶךָ וּבֵית קָדְשֶׁךָ וְרֹאשׁ צִיּוֹן וּבֵית אַחֲזַת בָּנֶיךָ: [יד] וְעָשִׂיתָ דַעַת בְּכָל גּוֹי וְכָל מִשְׁפָּחָה, וְיָדְעוּ כִּי אַתָּה אֱלֹהֵי כָל חַיִל וָעֹז וְאֵין אַחֵר מִבַּלְעָדֶיךָ, מָגֵן לְזֶרַע יִשְׂרָאֵל.

---

reflects Judith's perception of the battle at hand: She alludes to the decree under Greek reign stating that a Jewish bride must allow the king the "right of the first night" on the eve before her marriage. The Midrawsh *Ma'aseh Hannukah* describes the initiative of the daughter of Mattathias (Judith) to cancel this decree, culminating in the scene where "Judah and his comrades, together with his sister, went in to the general, and they chopped off his head and looted all that he had, and slaughtered his officers and servants, and trod upon the Greeks until they were gone."

Tu bi-Shevat

According to the Mishnah, the fifteenth day of the month of Shevat, also known as *Tu bi-Shevat*, is the New Year for trees—the day from which the age of a tree would be calculated for the purposes of tithes. Today, it is customary to celebrate *Tu bi-Shevat* by planting trees and eating fruits and nuts.

SEDER FOR *TU BI-SHEVAT*

The husband recites the blessing over wheat.

Following the Grace after Meals he says:

"*M*ay He satiate you with the fat of wheat"

in order that he be provided with abundant sustenance.

The wife recites the blessing over the vine, as it is written:

"*Y*our wife is like a fertile vine."

The son recites the blessing over olives, as it is written:

"*Y*our sons are like olive saplings around your table."

The origin of the custom of eating fruit on *Tu bi-Shevat* is unknown. During the early eighteenth century, an anonymous author wrote a kabbalistic work called *Hemdat ha-Yamim*. Though the book became the subject of considerable controversy because it was suspected of being inspired by Sabbateanism, the chapter that was devoted to customs for *Tu bi-Shevat* was later printed separately, as a work called *Peri Etz Hadar*.

During the early days of Zionism, *Tu bi-Shevat* came to symbolize the connection between the Jewish nation and its land. The *Tu bi-Shevat* Seder, a celebratory meal in

סדר טו בשבט

האיש, בעל הבית, מברך את החיטה, ולאחר ברכת המזון אומר:

"חֵלֶב חִטִּים יַשְׂבִּיעֵךְ",

כדי שיהיו לו מזונות ברווח.

האשה מברכת על הגפן – ככתוב:

"אֶשְׁתְּךָ כְּגֶפֶן פֹּרִיָּה".

הבן מברך על הזית – ככתוב:

"בָּנֶיךָ כִּשְׁתִלֵי זֵיתִים סָבִיב לְשֻׁלְחָנֶךָ".

---

honor of the holiday featuring various symbolic fruits, has since become popular even outside of Israel, with a range of fruits and texts adopted by different communities. (In Israel, the celebration centers mainly around the "seven species" mentioned in the Torah in connection with the Land of Israel: wheat, barley, grapes, figs, pomegranates, olives, and dates.)

Rabbi Ḥayim Falaji of Izmir (1788–1869) proposed this fascinating gender-based approach to the ceremony and its symbols.

The daughters recite the blessing over pomegranate and nuts, hinting to the verse:

"*A*ll the glory of the king's daughter is inward," since in the case of the pomegranate and nuts one is obliged to exert effort in order to reach that which is inside, and to reveal their beauty and their fine flavor. Likewise much effort must be exerted to reveal a daughter's heart, in her great modesty and bashfulness.

An infant is given apple and honey, hinting to the verses:

"*U*nder the apple tree I aroused you" and "Honey and milk are under your tongue."

הבנות מברכות על רימון ואגוז – על שם:

"בְּ לִ־כְבוּדָּה בַת־מֶלֶךְ פְּנִימָה".

כפי שבפרי הרימון ובאגוז יש לטרוח כדי להגיע אל התוך ולגלות יופים וטעמם הטוב, כך יש לטרוח רבות כדי לגלות ליבה של הבת, בצניעותה ובבישנותה כי רבות.

לתינוקות יינתנו תפוח ודבש – על שם:

"תַּ חַת הַתַּפּוּחַ עוֹרַרְתִּיךָ" וּ"דְבַשׁ וְחָלָב תַּחַת לְשׁוֹנֵךְ".

Purim

The festival of Purim centers on the great miracle that took place during the reign of Ahasuerus: the salvation of the Jews from Haman's evil decree. At the apogee of the Persian Empire in the fifth century B.C.E., when Ahasuerus ruled over the greater part of the world and the entire Jewish nation lived under his reign, the evil Haman, the most senior of the king's ministers, plotted to annihilate the Jewish people, "from children to old people, infants and women, on one day." Queen Esther, Ahasuerus's Jewish wife who had been keeping her religion secret from him, together with her uncle Mordecai, foiled Haman's plans and risked their lives to bring about the salvation of the Jews.

According to Maimonides, "When the Messiah comes, the Books of the Prophets and the other holy Writings will fall away. What will remain? The Torah (Pentateuch) and the Oral Law, and the Scroll of Esther, as it is written: 'These days of Purim will not pass over from amongst the Jews, and their memory will not be lost from their descendants' (Esther 9:28)."

QUEEN ESTHER'S PLEA

*T*hereafter she raised her voice in prayer and said:

You are the great Lord, the God of Abraham, Isaac, and Jacob, and the God of Benjamin, my ancestor. It is not because I am worthy before You that I come before this king, but rather for the sake of Your nation, the house of Israel, in order that they not cease to exist. For it was on account of Israel that You created the entire world, and if Israel is lost to the world, who will utter before You, "Holy, holy, holy" three times every day? Just as You saved Hananiah, Mishael, and Azariah from the fiery furnace, and Daniel from the lions' den, so save me from the hand of this foolish king, and grant me the kindness of finding favor in his eyes.

*W*ith tears Esther said this, and with pleading she set out her prayer:

I ask of You, Who hears prayer: Hear my prayer at this time. We

---

During King Ahasuerus's reign, entering the king's inner courtyard without a royal invitation was punishable by death. Despite the danger, Queen Esther agreed to Mordecai's suggestion that she approach King Ahasuerus to plead on behalf of the Jewish people. Before going in, she asked all the Jews of Persia to gather together and support her with prayer and a three-day fast. According to *Pirkei de-Rabbi Eliezer*,

תפילת אסתר המלכה

א אַחֲרֵי כֵן הֵרִימָה קוֹלָהּ בִּתְפִלָּה וַתֹּאמַר:
אַתָּה הוּא הָאֵל הַגָּדוֹל, אֱלֹהֵי אַבְרָהָם יִצְחָק וְיַעֲקֹב, וֵאלֹהֵי בִּנְיָמִין אָבִי,
לֹא מִפְּנֵי שֶׁטּוֹבָה אֲנִי לְפָנֶיךָ בָּאָה אֲנִי לִפְנֵי הַמֶּלֶךְ הַזֶּה, כִּי אִם עַל עַמְּךָ בֵּית
יִשְׂרָאֵל שֶׁלֹּא יֹאבְדוּ מִן הָעוֹלָם, כִּי בַּעֲבוּר יִשְׂרָאֵל בָּרָאתָ אֶת הָעוֹלָם כֻּלּוֹ,
וְאִם יִשְׂרָאֵל יֹאבְדוּ מִן הָעוֹלָם מִי יֹאמַר לְפָנֶיךָ קָדוֹשׁ קָדוֹשׁ קָדוֹשׁ בְּכָל יוֹם
וָיוֹם שָׁלֹשׁ פְּעָמִים. כַּאֲשֶׁר הִצַּלְתָּ אֶת חֲנַנְיָה מִישָׁאֵל וַעֲזַרְיָה מִתּוֹךְ כִּבְשַׁן
הָאֵשׁ, וְאֶת דָּנִיֵּאל מִבּוֹר הָאֲרָיוֹת, כֵּן תַּצִּילֵנִי מִיַּד הַמֶּלֶךְ הַטִּפֵּשׁ הַזֶּה, וּגְמָל
נָא חֵן וָחֶסֶד עִמָּדִי בְּעֵינָיו.

ב דְּמָעוֹת אָמְרָה אֶסְתֵּר הַדָּבָר, וּבְתַחֲנוּנִים סִדְּרָה תְּפִלָּתָהּ:
בְּבַקָּשָׁה מִמְּךָ שׁוֹמֵעַ תְּפִלּוֹת, שְׁמַע תְּפִלָּתִי בָּעֵת הַזֹּאת, גָּלִינוּ
וְנִתְרַחַקְנוּ מֵאַרְצֵנוּ, וּבַעֲוֹונוֹתֵינוּ מְכַרְתָּנוּ, לְמַעַן יִתְקַיֵּם בָּנוּ מִקְרָא שֶׁכָּתוּב

---

because the fast coincided with Pesach and violated the obligation to eat matzah
on the Seder night, Mordecai initially opposed it. In response, Esther argued: "If
there is no Israel, who will care about Pesach?" After three days of fasting, according to *Targum Shani* (an ancient collection of midrashic teachings on the Scroll of
Esther, written in Aramaic), Esther offered this prayer.

337

have been exiled and distanced from our land. For our sins You have sold us, to fulfill that which was written, "You shall be sold there to your enemies as slaves and maidservants, and there shall be none to buy you" (Deuteronomy 28:68). The decree has been issued that we be killed; we have all been abandoned as one to the sword, slaughter, death, and complete annihilation. The descendants of Abraham are wearing sackcloth and have placed ashes upon their heads. If the ancestors have sinned—what fault is it of the children? If we are lost, who will give thanks before You? If even the young have sinned and angered You, what fault is it of the infants who suckle at the breast? Those at rest in Jerusalem will turn in their graves for Your giving their children to be slaughtered; You cause us to pass on like the clouds of the heavens. How few are the days of our joyousness; You have given us to the wicked Haman, and into the hands of our enemies, to kill us.

I recall to You the deed of Your beloved one; of Abraham I say: You tried him with every trial; You tested him and found his heart to be faithful to You. Be a helper and support for the children of Your beloved one, and bring them into the sign of the covenant. Fight our battle against Haman and exact our revenge against the son of Hammedatha through Your nation, Israel. The one who distresses and provokes Your nation seeks to annihilate us like a lone lamb; he has become their enemy in all of their places. You have made an eternal oath of covenant with us; may the binding of Isaac be recalled in our favor. Haman cast silver before the king, to buy us for ten thousand silver talents. Hear our voice; answer us and bring us from affliction to relief. He Who breaks enemies—break Haman, and let him not rise up again.

[דברים כח 68] וְהִתְמַכַּרְתֶּם שָׁם לְאוֹיְבֶיךָ לַעֲבָדִים וְלִשְׁפָחוֹת וְאֵין קֹנֶה. וְהַדָּת נִתְּנָה לְהָרְגֵנוּ, וְכֻלָּנוּ נִמְסַרְנוּ לַחֶרֶב וְהָרֶג וְאַבְדָן וְלִכְלָיָה גְמוּרָה כְּאֶחָד. זַרְעוֹ שֶׁל אַבְרָהָם לוֹבְשִׁים שַׂקִּים וְיַשְׁלִיכוּ אֵפֶר עַל רָאשֵׁיהֶם. אִם חָטְאוּ הָאָבוֹת מֶה חָטְאוּ הַבָּנִים, אִם נֹאבַד מִי יִהְיֶה מוֹדֶה לְפָנֶיךָ, הַטַּף אִם חָטְאוּ וְהִכְעִיסוּ, מֶה עָשׂוּ יוֹנְקֵי שָׁדַיִם. יוֹשְׁבֵי יְרוּשָׁלַיִם יָנוּעוּ מִקִּבְרָם עַל כִּי מָסַרְתָּ בְּנֵיהֶם לַטֶּבַח, כְּעַנְנֵי שָׁמַיִם אַתָּה מַעֲבִיר אוֹתָנוּ. כַּמָּה מְעַטִּים יְמֵי שִׂמְחָתֵנוּ, לְהָמָן הָרָשָׁע נָתַתָּ אוֹתָנוּ וּבְיַד אוֹיְבֵינוּ לְהָרְגֵנוּ.

מ זְכֹרֶת אֲנִי לְפָנֶיךָ מַעֲשֵׂה אֲהוּבֶךָ, מֵאַבְרָהָם אָחֵל לֵאמֹר, נִסִּיתָ אוֹתוֹ בְּכָל הַנִּסְיוֹנוֹת, בָּחַנְתָּ אוֹתוֹ וּמָצָאתָ לְבָבוֹ נֶאֱמָן לְפָנֶיךָ, סוֹעֵד וְסוֹמֵךְ הָיָה לִבְנֵי אֲהוּבֶךָ וְהִכְנֵס אוֹתָם בְּאוֹת בְּרִית, רִיבָה רִיבֵנוּ אֶת הָמָן וּנְקֹם נִקְמָתֵנוּ בְּבֶן-הַמְּדָתָא עַל יְדֵי עַמְּךָ יִשְׂרָאֵל. הַצַּר וְהַמֵּצִיק לְעַמְּךָ בִּקֵּשׁ לְכַלּוֹתֵנוּ כְּשֶׁה אֶחָד, וַיְהִי לְאוֹיֵב לָהֶם בְּכָל מְקוֹמוֹתֵיהֶם, שְׁבוּעַת בְּרִית עוֹלָם נִשְׁבַּעְתָּ עִמָּנוּ, עֲקֵדַת יִצְחָק תָּרוּם אוֹתָנוּ, זָרַק הָמָן אֶת הַכֶּסֶף לִפְנֵי הַמֶּלֶךְ לִקְנוֹת אוֹתָנוּ בַּעֲשֶׂרֶת אֲלָפִים כִּכְּרֵי כֶסֶף, שְׁמַע קוֹלֵנוּ עֲנֵנוּ וְהוֹצִיאֵנוּ מִצָּרָה לִרְוָחָה, שׁוֹבֵר אוֹיְבִים שָׁבַר אֶת הָמָן וְלֹא תִהְיֶה תְּקוּמָה לְמַפַּלְתּוֹ.

VI

TIMES

of

CRISIS

Illness

"*When is prayer heard? When the soul is not resigned.*"

[RABBI YEHUDAH AL<u>H</u>ARIZI, 1165–1225]

MOTHER'S PRAYER FOR THE RECOVERY OF HER SICK CHILD

Fanny Neuda

"I pray You, Lord, please grant salvation; I pray You, Lord, please grant success."
[PSALMS 118:25]

*M*y God! Fear and pain tear at my heart, and in unbearable suffering I lift my hands to You. You—Who created man's heart, Who hears its keening sobs; You know a mother's heart and its anguish. How great and overwhelming is the pain; my child is ill, my child may die.

To Your bosom I flee, merciful Father, at this time of trouble. Our Father in heaven, in the shade of Your cover I seek refuge from the agony and fear. In Your great mercy, shine Your countenance toward me; show me Your love and Your kindness. Do not abandon my soul to fear, and my heart to anguish. Spread Your wings over my child; allow him to recover and to grow. My soul is bound up with his; he is my blood, he is my flesh, he is my life. With love and pain I carried him beneath my heart; with love and pain I bore him and have taught him, cared for him and nurtured him; with concern and love I have guarded every moment of his life, and with fear and love my searing tears flow this day, my heart cries out to You. Have mercy, my God, have mercy; restore my child to me—this delicate flower that has almost not been touched by the light of day. Allow me once more to see his warm smile, to watch his childish, happy play, and every day of my life I shall give thanks to You. I shall gather all of my

תפילת אם לשלום ילדה החולה

פאני נוידא

"אָנָּא ה' הוֹשִׁיעָה נָּא, אָנָּא ה' הַצְלִיחָה נָּא"

[תהלים קיח 25]

אֲלֶלַי! פַּחַד וּכְאֵב קוֹרְעִים אֶת לִבִּי וּבְסֵבֶל כָּבֵד מְנֻשָּׂא אֲנִי נוֹשֵׂאת אֵלֶיךָ אֶת כַּפַּי! אַתָּה, שֶׁיָּצַרְתָּ לֵב אָדָם, הַשּׁוֹמֵעַ נְהִי בִּכְיוֹ, אַתָּה יוֹדֵעַ לֵב אֵם וּמְצוּקָתוֹ. מָה עָצוּם וְרַב הַכְּאֵב: יַלְדִּי חוֹלֶה, יַלְדִּי נוֹטֶה לָמוּת.

לְחֵיקְךָ, אַב הָרַחֲמִים, אֲנִי נִמְלְטָת בְּעֵת צָרָה. אָבִינוּ שֶׁבַּשָּׁמַיִם, בְּצֵל כְּנָפֶיךָ אֲבַקֵּשׁ מִסְתּוֹר מִן הַיָּגוֹן וְהַפַּחַד. בְּרַחֲמֶיךָ הָרַבִּים, הָאֵר אֵלַי פָּנֶיךָ, הַרְאֵה לִי אֶת אַהֲבָתְךָ וַחֲסָדֶיךָ, אַל תַּפְקִיר אֶת נַפְשִׁי לְפַחַד וְאֶת לִבִּי לְיָגוֹן. פְּרֹשׂ כְּנָפֶיךָ עַל יַלְדִּי, תֵּן שֶׁיַּבְרִיא וְיִגְדַּל. נַפְשִׁי קְשׁוּרָה בְּנַפְשׁוֹ בַּעֲבֹתוֹת, הוּא דָּמִי, הוּא בְּשָׂרִי הוּא חַיַּי. בְּאַהֲבָה וּבִכְאֵב נְשָׂאתִי אוֹתוֹ מִתַּחַת לְלִבִּי, בְּאַהֲבָה וּבִכְאֵב יְלַדְתִּי וְחָנַכְתִּי אוֹתוֹ, טִפַּלְתִּי וְטִפַּחְתִּי, בְּפַחַד וּבְאַהֲבָה שָׁמַרְתִּי כָּל שָׁעָה מִשְׁעוֹת חַיָּיו, וּבְפַחַד וּבְאַהֲבָה יוֹקְדוֹת זוֹלְגוֹת הַיּוֹם דִּמְעוֹתַי, זוֹעֵק לִבִּי אֵלֶיךָ. רַחֵם, אֵלִי, רַחֵם, הָשֵׁב לִי אֶת יַלְדִּי, אֶת הַפֶּרַח הֶעָנֹג שֶׁאוֹר הַיּוֹם כִּמְעַט שֶׁלֹּא נָגַע בּוֹ; תֵּן לִי לָשׁוּב וְלִרְאוֹת אֶת חִיּוּכוֹ הַחַם, לָשׁוּב וְלִרְאוֹת בְּמִשְׂחָקוֹ הַיַּלְדוּתִי וְהָעַלִּיז, וְכָל יוֹם מִימוֹת חַיָּי אוֹדֶה לְךָ; אֶת כָּל כֹּחוֹתַי אֶאֱזֹר כְּדֵי לְחַנֵּךְ אֶת יַלְדִּי כְּבָבַת־עֵינְךָ, שֶׁחַיָּיו יִהְיוּ קֹדֶשׁ לְךָ, שֶׁשִּׁמְךָ הַקָּדוֹשׁ יִהְיֶה חָרוּט לָעַד עַל לוּחַ־לִבּוֹ וְהוּא יִלְמַד לְכַבֵּד וְלַעֲבֹד אוֹתְךָ לְאֹרֶךְ יָמִים! אֵלִי שֶׁבַּשָּׁמַיִם אַל תְּדַחֵנִי, אַל תַּעֲנִישֵׁנִי עַל

strength to teach my child like the spark of Your eye, that his life may be devoted to You, that Your holy Name may be forever inscribed upon his heart, and that he may learn to honor and serve You for all of his years. My God in heaven—do not turn me away; do not punish me for my sins, do not cause me to suffer Your anger. In Your great mercy forgive my sins, for the sake of my innocent child; preserve his beautiful life for me—this pure life, clear of any stain, so that with his clear light he may sanctify and purify my heart and my home, and fill them with joy and happiness. Hear, my God, the supplication that burns in my bones. God of abundant kindness—send me Your aid; all my hope and trust is in You. Amen.

חֲטָאַי, אַל תְּיַסְּרֵנִי בַּחֲרוֹנְךָ. בְּרַחֲמֶיךָ הָרַבִּים, מְחַל לִי עַל חֲטָאַי, בַּעֲבוּר
תֹּם בְּנִי, נְצֹר לִי אֶת חַיָּיו הַיָּפִים, הַחַיִּים הַזַּכִּים הַנְּקִיִּים מִכָּל רְבָב, שֶׁבְּאוֹרוֹ
הַבָּהִיר יְקַדֵּשׁ וִיזַכֵּךְ אֶת לִבִּי וּבֵיתִי וִימַלֵּא אוֹתָם בִּשְׂמָחוֹת־אֲשֶׁר. שְׁמַע אֵלַי
לִתְחִנָּתִי הַבּוֹעֶרֶת בְּעַצְמוֹתַי. אֵל רַב חֶסֶד, שְׁלַח לִי אֶת עֶזְרָתְךָ, כָּל תִּקְוָתִי
וֶאֱמוּנָתִי בָּךְ. אָמֵן.

PRAYER FOR A HUSBAND WHO IS ILL
Fanny Neuda

"May the Lord strengthen him upon his sickbed;
whenever he lies ill You overturn his illness."

[PSALMS 41:4]

*M*y God in heaven: In Your great mercy I seek refuge at this time
of pain. Grant me consolation, my Deliverer and Savior; deliver me at this
time of anguish.

You, my God in heaven, have brought illness and pain upon my husband,
the father of my children, the crowning glory of my life. Danger threatens his
precious life. With fear and trembling I lift my eyes, "from whence my aid
comes." Man will not save me: Mortal aid is weak and feeble, like a fragile
reed it shatters into thousands of splinters in the face of Your Almighty will.
Man's understanding is blind, unless You illuminate it from above with a ray
of light. Only Your hand holds power and might; in Your right hand is the
cup of healing. Only You are a faithful Healer, true and merciful. Therefore,
Eternal One, I pray for Your help; my eyes look to You with hope and
longing; to You my lips whisper; my heart calls out with silent groaning, and
all of my being is dissolved before You in burning prayer and supplication.
God of kindness and mercy, save my husband; let him drink from the cup
of good health; restore him the strength he needs for his home, his labor, his
obligation to live and to act. Protect him for the sake of our poor children
who have done no wrong, for You appointed him to see to their sustenance,
education, and protection. My God, watch over my husband, my most
faithful friend in all the world. He is the sun and the light that illuminate
my day; if that be extinguished, night and darkness shall be my fate. He is

תפילה לשלום הבעל החולה

פאני נוידא

"ה' יִסְעָדֶנּוּ עַל עֶרֶשׂ דְּוָי כָּל מִשְׁכָּבוֹ הָפַכְתָּ בְחָלְיוֹ"

[תהלים מא 4]

אֵלִי שֶׁבַּשָּׁמַיִם, בְּרַחֲמֶיךָ הָרַבִּים אֲנִי מְבַקֶּשֶׁת מִפְלָט בְּשָׁעָה זוֹ שֶׁל כְּאֵב. תֶּן לִי נֶחָמָה, מַצִּילִי וּמוֹשִׁיעִי, וְהַצִּילֵנִי בִּשְׁעַת מְצוּקָה.

אַתָּה, אֵלִי שֶׁבַּשָּׁמַיִם, הֵבֵאתָ חֲלִי וּכְאֵב עַל בַּעֲלִי, אֲבִי יַלְדִּי, נֵר חַיַּי. סַכָּנָה מְאַיֶּמֶת עַל חַיָּיו הַיְקָרִים. בְּחִיל וּרְעָדָה אֲנִי נוֹשֵׂאת אֶת עֵינַי, "מֵאַיִן יָבוֹא עֶזְרִי". לֹא הָאָדָם יוֹשִׁיעֶנּוּ. עֶזְרַת הָאָדָם לֵאָה וְחַסְרַת אוֹנִים, כְּקָנֶה רָצוּץ הִיא נִתֶּצֶת לְאַלְפֵי רְסִיסִים לְנֹכַח רְצוֹנְךָ הַכֹּל-יָכוֹל; תְּבוּנַת הָאָדָם עִוֶּרֶת, אִם לֹא מִמַּעַל תָּאִיר עָלֶיהָ קֶרֶן אוֹר. רַק בְּיָדְךָ הַכֹּחַ וְהַגְּבוּרָה, בִּימִינְךָ גְּבִיעַ הַמַּרְפֵּא. רַק אַתָּה רוֹפֵא נֶאֱמָן, כֵּן וְרַחוּם. עַל כֵּן, חֵי הָעוֹלָמִים, אֲנִי מְיַחֶלֶת לְעֶזְרָתְךָ, אֵלֶיךָ מַבִּיטוֹת עֵינַי בְּתִקְוָה וּבִכְמִיהָה, אֵלֶיךָ מְדַבְּרוֹת שִׂפְתוֹתַי הָרוֹחֲשׁוֹת, קוֹרֵא לִבִּי בְּאַנְקַת לֵב אַלְמוּת, וְכָל כֻּלִּי נִמְסָה לְפָנֶיךָ בְּמִשְׁאָלוֹת וּבִתְפִלּוֹת לוֹהֲטוֹת. אֵל הַחֶסֶד וְהָרַחֲמִים, הַצֵּל אֶת בַּעֲלִי, הַשְׁקֵה אוֹתוֹ כּוֹס שֶׁל בְּרִיאוּת, הָשֵׁב לוֹ אֶת הַכֹּחַ הַנִּדְרָשׁ לוֹ לְבֵיתוֹ, לַעֲמָלוֹ, לְחוֹבָתוֹ לִחְיוֹת וְלִפְעֹל. שְׁמֹר עָלָיו לְמַעַן יְלָדֵינוּ הָאֻמְלָלִים שֶׁאֵין עֹל בְּכַפָּם, שֶׁאַתָּה מֵנִית אוֹתוֹ לִדְאֹג לִמְזוֹנָם, לְחִנּוּכָם וְלַהֲגַנָּתָם. שְׁמֹר אֵלִי עַל אִישִׁי, יְדִידִי הַנֶּאֱמָן בְּיוֹתֵר עֲלֵי אֲדָמוֹת. הוּא הַשֶּׁמֶשׁ וְהָאוֹר הַמְּאִירִים אֶת יוֹמִי, וְאִם יִכְבֶּה נֵרוֹ - לַיְלָה וַחֲשֵׁכָה יִהְיוּ גוֹרָלִי. הוּא עַמּוּד הַתָּוֶךְ שֶׁל בֵּיתִי וְאִם יִתְמוֹטֵט - יִזְדַּעֲזַע וְיִקְרֹס עָלַי עוֹלָמִי. לְצִדּוֹ - אֶצְעַד בְּלֹא פַחַד בַּשְּׁבִילִים הָאֲפֵלִים שֶׁל כָּל רָעָה וְצָרָה, אֶשָּׂא בְּאֹמֶץ וּבִגְבוּרָה כָּל אֲשֶׁר תָּשִׁית לְפָנַי.

349

the pillar that supports my home; if he falls, my world will be shaken and collapse over me. At his side I step fearlessly through the gloomy pathways of any trouble or distress; I bear courageously and valiantly whatever You set before me. Without him I am a twig with no support, a boat with no mast or rudder in the open, stormy sea.

My God, have mercy upon me; do not recall my transgressions and wrongdoings. "Lord, do not punish me in Your fury, do not cause me suffering in Your anger." Remember me in Your great mercy and accept with love and conciliation my intentions, the vows that I have made—my honest decision and desire to help the unfortunate and the oppressed, to walk in the paths of justice and faith, and to flee from the temptations of sin. Accept all of these as a sacrifice of atonement, as an offering of good favor. May they draw Your kindness and Your mercy upon me and upon my husband. Send me Your mercy, my God, my Father; grant me Your aid. Amen.

You are God Who is good and Who performs good, Helper and Friend of all of Your children. You count every tear that is shed; You are close to everyone whose heart is bent over and pining, and You stand with love and mercy over every patient.

Lord in heaven—Who is close to me, Who stands at my side and at the side of my husband: The knowledge of Your closeness is a comforting, healing balm for my suffering. For I do not sit alone, abandoned in my anguish. You, my God, are witness to my tears; You behold my pain, You see my torment. You are the source of kindness and mercy; You bestow Your kindness upon me, too, allowing the sun of Your mercy to shine upon me and not withholding Your help from me. May I, with my hope and my faith, not become an object of scorn and shame. May Your love never leave me; may Your comfort uplift my heart. In Your great mercy may You remove this distress and torment, that my pain may become joy. You are my aid and my trust. Amen.

בִּלְעָדֶיו – אֲנִי זַלְזַל נְטוּל מִשְׁעֶנֶת, סְפִינָה לְלֹא תֹּרֶן וְהֶגֶה בַּיָּם הַפָּתוּחַ וְהַסּוֹעֵר.

אֵלִי, רַחֵם עָלַי, אַל תִּזְכֹּר לִי אֶת חֲטָאַי וּמְשׁוּגוֹתַי. "ה' אַל בְּקֶצְפְּךָ תוֹכִיחֵנִי וּבַחֲמָתְךָ תְיַסְּרֵנִי." זָכְרֵנִי בְּרֹב רַחֲמֶיךָ וְקַבֵּל בְּחִבָּה וּבְפִיּוּס אֶת כַּוָּנוֹתַי, וְאֶת הַנְּדָרִים שֶׁנָּדַרְתִּי, אֶת הַחְלָטוֹתַי וּרְצוֹנוֹתַי הַכֵּנִים לְסַיֵּעַ לָאֻמְלָלִים וְלַנִּדְכָּאִים; לָלֶכֶת בְּדַרְכֵי צֶדֶק וֶאֱמוּנָה וְלָנוּס מִפְּנֵי נִסְיוֹנוֹת הַחֵטְא. קַבֵּל אֶת כָּל אֵלֶּה כְּקָרְבָּן כַּפָּרָה, כְּמִנְחַת רָצוֹן. מִי יִתֵּן וְאֵלֶּה יָבִיאוּ עָלַי וְעַל בַּעֲלִי אֶת חֲסָדֶיךָ וְרַחֲמֶיךָ. שְׁלַח לִי אֶת רַחֲמֶיךָ, אֵלִי, אָבִי, חֹן אוֹתִי בְּעֶזְרָתְךָ. אָמֵן.

אַתָּה הָאֵל הַטּוֹב וְהַמֵּטִיב, עוֹזֵר וְרֵעַ לְכָל יְלָדֶיךָ. אַתָּה הַמּוֹנֶה כָּל דִּמְעָה הַזּוֹלֶגֶת מֵעַיִן. אַתָּה הַקָּרוֹב לְכָל מִי שֶׁלִּבּוֹ כָּפוּף וְדוֹאֵב וְעוֹמֵד בְּאַהֲבָה וּבְרַחֲמִים לִמְרַאֲשׁוֹתָיו שֶׁל כָּל חוֹלֶה.

אֱלֹהֵינוּ שֶׁבַּשָּׁמַיִם, הַקָּרוֹב לִי, הָעוֹמֵד לְצִדִּי וּלְצַד בַּעֲלִי, הַהֲכָרָה בְּקִרְבָתְךָ הִיא נֶחָמָה מוֹשִׁיעָה צְרִי לְיִסּוּרַי. כִּי לֹא בָּדָד אֵשֵׁב, נְטוּשָׁה בִּמְצוּקָתִי. אַתָּה, אֵלִי, עֵד לְדִמְעוֹתַי, אַתָּה רוֹאֶה לִכְאֵבִי, מַבִּיט אֶל יְגוֹנִי, אַתָּה מְקוֹר הַחֶסֶד וְהָרַחֲמִים, אַתָּה תַּשְׁפִּיעַ גַּם עָלַי מֵחַסְדְּךָ, תִּתֵּן לְשֶׁמֶשׁ רַחֲמֶיךָ לִזְרֹחַ מֵעָלַי וְלֹא תִּמְנַע מִמֶּנִּי אֶת עֶזְרָתְךָ. מִי יִתֵּן וּבְתִקְוָתִי וּבֶאֱמוּנָתִי לֹא אֶהְיֶה לְחֶרְפָּה וּלְקָלוֹן, מִי יִתֵּן וְאַהֲבָתְךָ לְעוֹלָם לֹא תָסוּר מִמֶּנִּי, נֶחָמָתְךָ תְּרוֹמֵם אֶת לִבִּי. מִי יִתֵּן וּבְרֹב רַחֲמֶיךָ תָּסִיר מִמֶּנִּי אֶת הַצָּרָה וְהַצּוּקָה, וְהָיָה מַכְאוֹבִי לְמָשׁוֹשׂ. אַתָּה מִסְעָדִי וּמִבְטַחִי, אָמֵן.

351

CHANGE OF NAME FOR
A WOMAN WHO IS ILL
Rabbi Avraham Abuḫbut

*A*nd her name shall be called in Israel [insert name], as it is written: "Sarai your wife shall not be called Sarai, for Sarah is her name." May it be Your will, Lord our God and God of our forefathers, that this change of her name serve to cancel all harsh and evil decrees from upon us and to nullify any evil verdict from upon her. And if death was decreed for [insert previous name], it was not decreed for [insert new name]; she is as though a different woman, a new creation, like a baby girl born to a good life and length of years and fulfillment of days. And it is written: "I have heard your prayer; I have seen your tears; behold, I shall heal you; on the third day you shall go up to the house of the Lord" (2 Kings 20:5), and it is written (Hosea 6:2): "After two days He will revive us; on the third day He will raise us up and we shall live in His Presence."

This prayer appears in the personal prayer book of the kabbalist Rabbi Avraham Abuḫbut of Morocco (1872).

תפילה לחולה – שינוי השם לאשה

המקובל הרב אברהם אבוחבוט

וְ‏יִקָּרֵא שְׁמָהּ בְּיִשְׂרָאֵל [פְּלוֹנִית] כְּמוֹ שֶׁכָּתוּב שָׂרַי אִשְׁתְּךָ לֹא־תִקְרָא אֶת־שְׁמָהּ שָׂרָי כִּי שָׂרָה שְׁמָהּ. יְהִי רָצוֹן מִלְּפָנֶיךָ ה' אֱלֹהֵינוּ וֵאלֹהֵי אֲבוֹתֵינוּ שֶׁיְּהֵא שִׁנּוּי שְׁמָהּ זֶה לְבַטֵּל מֵעָלֵינוּ כָּל גְּזֵרוֹת קָשׁוֹת וְרָעוֹת וְלִקְרֹעַ מֵעָלֶיהָ כָּל רוֹעַ גְּזַר דִּין. וְאִם נִקְנְסָה מִיתָה עַל [פְּלוֹנִית], עַל [פְּלוֹנִית] זוֹ לֹא נִגְזְרָה וַהֲרֵי הִיא כְּאִשָּׁה אַחֶרֶת וּכְבִרְיָה חֲדָשָׁה וּכְקַטַנָּה שֶׁנּוֹלְדָה לְחַיִּים טוֹבִים וְלַאֲרִיכוּת שָׁנִים וְלִמְלוֹאֵי יָמִים וְנֹאמַר שָׁמַעְתִּי אֶת תְּפִלָּתֶךָ רָאִיתִי אֶת דִּמְעָתֶךָ הִנְנִי רוֹפֵא לָךְ, בַּיּוֹם הַשְּׁלִישִׁי תַּעֲלֶה בֵּית יהוה יְחַיֵּנוּ מִיֹּמָיִם בַּיּוֹם הַשְּׁלִישִׁי יְקִמֵנוּ וְנִחְיֶה לְפָנָיו.

PRAYER OF A SICKLY WOMAN

Fanny Neuda

"You know no God but Me, and there is no savior besides Me."

[HOSEA 13:4]

*M*y Maker and Creator: Bent over and weak from the suffering that has tormented me now for many days, I stand before You, seeking to find in Your bosom protection, strength, and aid. The pain that does not leave me robs me of air to breathe, it removes my joy for life. It happens even that my weak and fragile body has a bitter effect on my soul. Often I am short-tempered and tend to anger; I am bitter toward those around me, and I am not tolerant of the decrees that You have decreed upon me, my Maker. I tend to forget that everything that happens to us—even that which is painful and causes us to suffer—is decreed out of Your great love and wisdom, and is meant to help us and save us.

My Father, merciful and kind Father, could You possibly cause me to suffer in vain? Perhaps You bring this suffering upon me as a punishment for a sin that I committed and obligations that I have accumulated, imposing them on me in order that I may improve my ways; You rebuke me and remind me that I must return to the straight path, to turn away from the inebriating pleasures of the senses, to remove myself from the vanities of the world and from seeking to impress, and to open my heart to fear of heaven and good deeds. Or perhaps You afflict me in order to test my devotion and my faith in You, allowing me to examine myself and come to know my feelings and my heart's principles.

תפילת האשה החולה

פאני ניידא

"וֵאלֹהִים זוּלָתִי לֹא תֵדָע וּמוֹשִׁיעַ אַיִן בִּלְתִּי"

[הושע יג 4]

וֹצְרִי וּבוֹרְאִי, כְּפוּפָה וּרְצוּצָה מִיִּסּוּרִים הַפּוֹקְדִים אוֹתִי זֶה יָמִים רַבִּים, אֲנִי עוֹמֶדֶת לְפָנֶיךָ מְבַקֶּשֶׁת לִמְצֹא בְּחֵיקְךָ מָגֵן, כֹּחַ וְעֹז. הַכְּאֵב שֶׁאֵינוֹ מַרְפֶּה מִמֶּנִּי, גּוֹזֵל מִמֶּנִּי אֶת הָאֲוִיר לִנְשִׁימָה, נוֹטֵל מִמֶּנִּי אֶת שִׂמְחַת הַקִּיּוּם. וְלֹא פַּעַם יְקָרָה שֶׁלְּגוּפִי הַחַלָּשׁ וְהַשַּׁבְרִירִי תִּהְיֶה הַשְׁפָּעָה מָרָה עַל נִשְׁמָתִי! תָּדִיר אֲנִי קְצָרַת רוּחַ וְנוֹטָה לְכַעַס, מְרִירָה לַסּוֹבְבִים אוֹתִי, אֵינִי מְגַלָּה סַבְלָנוּת לַגְּזֵרוֹת שֶׁגָּזַרְתָּ עָלַי יוֹצְרִי. אֲנִי נוֹטָה לִשְׁכֹּחַ שֶׁכָּל שֶׁהוּא מְנָת חֶלְקֵנוּ, גַּם הַכְּאֵב וְהַמִּיַּסֵּר, נִגְזָר מֵאַהֲבָתְךָ וְחָכְמָתְךָ כִּי רַבָּה, וְנוֹעָד לַעֲזֹר לָנוּ וּלְהוֹשִׁיעַ.

אָבִי, אָב הָרַחֲמָן וְרַב הַחֶסֶד, אַתָּה תִּתֵּן לִי לִסְבֹּל לַשָּׁוְא?! אֶפְשָׁר שֶׁאַתָּה מֵבִיא עָלַי אֶת הַיִּסּוּרִים כְּעֹנֶשׁ עַל חֵטְא שֶׁחָטָאתִי וְחוֹבוֹת שֶׁצָּבַרְתִּי, מֵשִׂית אוֹתָם עָלַי כְּדֵי שֶׁאֵיטִיב דְּרָכַי, אַתָּה מוֹכִיחַ אוֹתִי וּמַזְכִּיר לִי שֶׁעָלַי לָשׁוּב אֶל דֶּרֶךְ הַיָּשָׁר, לָסוּר מֵהֲנָאוֹת הַחוּשִׁים הַמְשַׁכְּרוֹת, לְהִסְתַּלֵּק מֵהַבְלֵי הָעוֹלָם וּגְנֵבַת דַּעַת וְלִפְתֹּחַ אֶת לִבִּי לְיִרְאַת שָׁמַיִם וּלְמַעֲשִׂים טוֹבִים. אוֹ שֶׁמָּא אַתָּה מְיַסֵּר אוֹתִי כְּדֵי לִבְחֹן אֶת מְסִירוּתִי וֶאֱמוּנִי בָּךְ, עַל מְנָת לָתֵת לִי הִזְדַּמְּנוּת לִבְחֹן אֶת עַצְמִי, וּלְהַכִּיר לָדַעַת אֶת רִגְשׁוֹתַי וְעֶקְרוֹנוֹת לִבִּי.

אִם עֹנֶשׁ גָּזַרְתָּ עָלַי, עָלַי לָשֵׂאת אוֹתוֹ בְּסַבְלָנוּת שֶׁל יֶלֶד, לָסוּר לְמָרוּתוֹ, בַּאֲדִיקוּת וּבְאַהֲבָה לְקַבֵּל אֶת הַתְּבוּנָה הָאֱלֹהִית, וְלֹא לָשֵׂאת אוֹתוֹ מִתּוֹךְ עֶלְבּוֹן וְשִׁפְלוּת רוּחַ.

If it is a punishment that You have decreed upon me, I must bear it with the patience of a child, obey its authority, accept divine wisdom with faith and love, and not bear it with resentment and a downcast spirit.

And if You seek to test me in some matter, should I not gather all of my faculties, bring together courage and fortitude, in order to show You, my God, my integrity and my faith? From this test, which will be considered an honor for me, I shall emerge strengthened and clean.

My God—stand at my side; strengthen and reinforce my heart with Your faith, so that when I turn my face to You I may hope for Your kindness, that I might await Your mercy, and that I might be able to bear, in tranquillity and self-sacrifice, the pain and the suffering that my illness brings me. May Your mercy toward me be my hope and my consolation. No, my hands shall not grow feeble, and I shall not submit to grief and anguish. You are my Father, and Your love and kindness surround all of Your children; You carry me, too, close to your warm and loving heart. You—Who, after night and mist, send the earth the sun's rays—You will send also into my bleak life, my life of illness and suffering, the ray that will bring me healing, the pure and heartening ray of light. You—Who, at the end of winter, cause the warm and pleasant breeze of spring to blow, in order to restore life, to arouse the frozen ground—You, with Your healing breath, will restore youth to my depleted strength and my frozen vitality. You will endow them with new life, and arouse them to a life of productive activity among my beloved ones who are so dear to me.

My God—may the life-restoring dew of Your kindness drip upon my body, may You spread Your mercy over me, and in Your love hear my voice and save me. Amen.

וְאִם בִּקַּשְׁתָּ לְנַסּוֹת אוֹתִי דָּבָר, הַאֵין עָלַי לְאֱסוֹר אֶת כָּל תַּעֲצוּמוֹת הַנֶּפֶשׁ, לֶאֱגֹד בִּכְפִיפָה אַחַת אֹמֶץ וְעַזּוּת לֵב, כְּדֵי לְהוֹכִיחַ לְךָ, אֵלִי, אֶת יָשְׁרִי וְאֶת אֱמוּנָתִי; וּמִן הַנִּסָּיוֹן, שֶׁלִּכְבוֹד יֵחָשֵׁב לִי, אֵצֵא מְחֻזֶּקֶת וּלְלֹא רְבָב.

הוֹ אֵלִי, עֲמֹד לִימִינִי, חַזֵּק וְחַשֵּׁל אֶת לִבִּי בֶּאֱמוּנָתְךָ; וּבְשָׁעָה שֶׁאֶשָּׂא פָנַי אֵלֶיךָ אֲיַחֵל לְחַסְדְּךָ, אֲצַפֶּה לְרַחֲמֶיךָ, אוּכַל לָשֵׂאת בְּשַׁלְוָה וּבִמְסִירוּת נֶפֶשׁ אֶת הַכְּאֵב וְהַיִּסּוּרִים שֶׁמְּבִיאָה עָלַי מַחֲלָתִי.

רַחֲמֶיךָ, אֵלִי, יִהְיוּ לִי תִּקְוָה וְנֶחָמָה. לֹא, יָדַי לֹא יִרְפּוּ, וַאֲנִי לֹא אֶכָּנַע לְיָגוֹן וּלְעַגְמַת הַנֶּפֶשׁ! אַתָּה, שֶׁאַהֲבָתְךָ וַחֲסָדֶיךָ אוֹפְפִים אֶת כָּל יְלָדֶיךָ, נוֹשֵׂא גַּם אוֹתִי עַל לוּחַ לִבְּךָ הַחַם וְהָאוֹהֵב. אַתָּה, שֶׁבְּעֵת לַיִל וַעֲרָפֶל שׁוֹלֵחַ לַיְקוּם אֶת קַרְנֵי הַשֶּׁמֶשׁ, אַתָּה תִּשְׁלַח גַּם לְחַיַּי הַקּוֹדְרִים, חַיֵּי מַחֲלָה וְיִסּוּרִים, אֶת הַקֶּרֶן שֶׁתַּמְצִיא לִי רְפוּאָה, קֶרֶן הָאוֹר הַזַּכָּה וְהַמְשַׂמַּחַת.

אַתָּה, שֶׁבְּעֵת הַחֹרֶף מֵשִׁיב אֶת רוּחַ הָאָבִיב הַחֲמִימָה וְהָעֲנֻגָּה, כְּדֵי לְשׁוּב וּלְהַחֲיוֹת, לְעוֹרֵר אֶת הָאֲדָמָה הַקְּפוּאָה – אַתָּה בְּהֶבֶל פִּיךָ הַמְרַפֵּא תָּשִׁיב לְכֹחוֹתַי הַמִּדַּלְדָּלִים, לְמִיצֵי הַחַיִּים הַקּוֹפְאִים שֶׁלִּי אֶת עֲלוּמֵיהֶם, תִּסֹּךְ בָּהֶם חַיִּים חֲדָשִׁים, תְּעוֹרֵר אוֹתָם לְחַיֵּי עֲשִׂיָּה וִיצִירָה בְּקֶרֶב אֲהוּבֵי נַפְשִׁי הַיְקָרִים לִי.

אֵלִי, מִי יִתֵּן שֶׁטַּל חֲסָדֶיךָ מְחַיֵּה הַנֶּפֶשׁ יִזַּל עַל גּוּפִי, שֶׁתִּפְרֹשׂ עָלַי אֶת רַחֲמֶיךָ וּבְאַהֲבָתְךָ תִּשְׁמַע אֶל קוֹלִי וְתַצִּילֵנִי! אָמֵן.

Loss and Bereavement

We learn from Abraham's example, following the death of his wife, Sarah, that it is praiseworthy to eulogize the dead: "Sarah died ... and Abraham came to eulogize Sarah and to mourn for her" (Genesis 23:2).

It is customary to speak of the positive qualities of the deceased, though care is taken not to exaggerate his or her praise.

MOTHER'S PRAYER AT
HER CHILD'S GRAVE
Fanny Neuda

"Therefore I say, Look away from me; I shall weep bitterly."

[ISAIAH 22:4]

*L*ord: How overwhelming and great is Your power; how terrible
Your judgment. You stretch forth Your hand, and the burning sun is
extinguished. At Your word the pillars of the earth tremble. As Your
wind blows, the greatest of cedars falls; the green pasture that has just
blossomed becomes a desolate, parched wasteland. You have granted man
an abundance of youthful vitality; You have imbued him with hopes for a
life of happiness. Now, You send the bitterness of death, and behold—a
human flower has withered and dried out, and become like dust and ashes.

Beneath this mound rests my love's flower; flesh of my flesh, the joy of
my soul, my child. I cannot hope to hold back my pain; my tears flow.

Bruriah, the wife of the Talmudic Sage Rabbi Meir, found two of her children
dead in her home one Shabbat while her husband was teaching in the *beit midrash*.
Bruriah laid the two corpses on the bed and covered them with a sheet. When
Shabbat was over, Rabbi Meir came home and asked about his sons. Bruria handed
him a goblet over which to recite the *Havdala* blessing, marking the end of Shabbat.
After he had eaten and recited the Grace after Meals, she said to him: "Yesterday,

תְּפִלַת הָאֵם לְיַד קֶבֶר יַלְדָּה

פֶאני נוידא

"עַל כֵּן אָמַרְתִּי שְׁעוּ מִנִּי אֲמָרֵר בַּבֶּכִי"

[ישעיה כב 4]

ה' מָה עָצוּם וְרַב כֹּחֶךָ, מַה נּוֹרָא מִשְׁפָּטֶךָ. זַרְעֲךָ תּוֹשִׁיט, וְלַהַט
הַחַמָּה יִכְבֶּה. לְדִבְרֵךָ יֶרְעֲדוּ סִפֵּי אֶרֶץ. לְמַשָּׁב רוּחֲךָ הָעֵנָק בָּאֲרָזִים יִקְרֹס
תַּחְתָּיו, הַשָּׂדֶה הַמּוֹרִיק שְׁזֶה עַתָּה עָלָה וּפָרַח יִהְיֶה לְצִיָּה חֲרֵבָה וְשׁוֹמֵמָה.
נָתַתָּ לָאָדָם שֶׁפַע נְעוּרִים, נָטַעְתָּ בּוֹ תִּקְווֹת חוֹבְקוֹת לְחַיֵּי אֹשֶׁר – וְעַתָּה
אֶת מַר הַמָּוֶת אַתָּה שׁוֹלֵחַ, וְרָאֹה, פָּרַח הָאָדָם נָבֵל, יָבֵשׁ וְהָיָה לְעָפָר וָאֵפֶר!
מִתַּחַת לַתְּלוּלִית זוֹ נָח פֶּרַח אַהֲבָתִי, בְּשַׂר מִבְּשָׂרִי, מְשׁוֹשׁ נַפְשִׁי, יַלְדִּי.
לַשָּׁוְא אֲנַסֶּה לַעֲצֹר בְּעַד כְּאֵבִי, דִּמְעוֹתַי זוֹלְגוֹת.
אֵלֹהַי, שֶׁבָּרָאתָ וְיָצַרְתָּ אֶת לֵב הָאָדָם וְנַפְשׁוֹ, אַתָּה יוֹדֵעַ מַה יָּקָר יֶלֶד
לְאִמּוֹ, אַתָּה יוֹדֵעַ אֶת הַנִּימִים וְהָעֲבֻתּוֹת שֶׁבָּהֶם אוֹסֵר לֵב אֵם אֶת יַלְדָּהּ

---

someone came and gave me something for safekeeping. Now he has come to take
it—shall we return it to him?" Rabbi Meir did not hesitate: "An object deposited for safekeeping must be returned!" She led him to the room where the dead
children lay and removed the sheet from over them. Rabbi Meir wept. Bruria said
to him: "Rabbi! You yourself taught me that an object deposited for safekeeping
must be returned; and thus it is written: 'The Lord has given and the Lord has
taken; blessed be the Name of the Lord'" (Midrash Mishlei 31: 10).

My God, Who created and formed man's heart and his soul: You know how precious a child is to his mother; You know the cords and ties with which a mother's heart binds her child and embraces him. And when death rests its cold hand upon the child and tears him away from her, it tears her heart, too, and leaves it bleeding.

I pray You, my God, do not be angry at me over my pain; have mercy upon me in my suffering, fill my heart with Your divine consolation, and grant me strength to bear the loss and to pardon. You have given and You have taken; may Your Name be blessed.

All of Your actions are good and worthy; how can man—with his feeble understanding—delve into Your hidden ways? Your reign in opacity is sealed to us, but all that You decree upon us is meant for our healing and our salvation. You are our Father and we are Your children; You are our King and we are Your people; You are our Shepherd and we are Your flock. Could You decree for us anything that is not for our benefit?

In my love and faith in You I shall find comfort and relief. Let the uplifting and refined words of Your holy Torah be my daily bread. Strengthen me with the faith that You have gathered my pure child to Your dwelling place with love and affection, so as to distance his pure soul from all transgression and all iniquity, to protect him from earthly pain and suffering.

Our Father in heaven, Who is good and Who performs good, let my child—like a shining angel—look down to me; let his pure image never leave me. When I am about to transgress before You, let his voice warn me of the danger. Let his eyes shine upon me when I perform Your will. And when I am recalled to the heavenly court, let it be he who receives me. Amen.

וּבָהֶם חוֹבֵק אוֹתוֹ. וּבְשָׁעָה שֶׁהַמָּוֶת מַנִּיחַ אֶת יָדוֹ הַקָּרָה עַל הַיֶּלֶד וְקוֹרֵעַ
אוֹתוֹ מֵעָלֶיהָ, גַּם אֶת לִבָּהּ הוּא קוֹרֵעַ וּמוֹתִיר אוֹתוֹ שׁוֹתֶת דָּם.

אָנָּא, אֵלִי, אַל יִהְיֶה בְּלִבְּךָ עָלַי, עַל כְּאֵבִי, רַחֵם עָלַי בְּיִסּוּרַי, צוּק לְלִבִּי
אֶת נֶחָמָתְךָ הָאֱלֹהִית, וְתֵן לִי כֹּחַ לָשֵׂאת אֶת הָאָבְדָן וְלִמְחֹל. "אַתָּה נָתַתָּ,
וְאַתָּה לָקַחְתָּ, יְהִי שִׁמְךָ מְבֹרָךְ".

כָּל מַעֲשֶׂיךָ טוֹבִים וּרְצוּיִים; אֵיכָה יוּכַל הָאָדָם, בְּבִינָתוֹ הַדַּלָּה, לַחְקֹר
אֶת דְּרָכֶיךָ הַנִּסְתָּרוֹת! מְמַשְׁלוֹת לֵילְךָ חֲתוּמוֹת בְּפָנֵינוּ, אַךְ כָּל שֶׁתִּגְזֹר
עָלֵינוּ, לְמַרְפֵּא הוּא וְלִישׁוּעָה לָנוּ. אַתָּה אָבִינוּ וַאֲנַחְנוּ בָּנֶיךָ, אַתָּה מַלְכֵּנוּ
וַאֲנַחְנוּ עַמֶּךָ, אַתָּה רוֹעֵנוּ וַאֲנַחְנוּ עֶדְרֶךָ. הֲתוּכַל לִגְזֹר עָלֵינוּ בִּלְתִּי אִם
מַרְפֵּא?!

בְּאַהֲבָתִי וּבְנֶאֱמָנוּתִי אֵלֶיךָ, אֶמְצָא לִי נֶחָמָה וָצֳרִי. תֵּן שֶׁהַמִּלִּים
הַמְרוֹמְמוֹת וְהַמְעֻדָּנוֹת שֶׁל תּוֹרָתְךָ הַקְּדוֹשָׁה יִהְיוּ לֶחֶם חֻקִּי. חַזְּקֵנִי
בֶּאֱמוּנָה שֶׁאֶת יַלְדִי הַזֶּךְ אָסַפְתָּ אֶל מִשְׁכְּנוֹתֶיךָ בְּאַהֲבָה וּבְחִבָּה, כְּדֵי
לְהַרְחִיק אֶת נִשְׁמָתוֹ הַטְּהוֹרָה מִכָּל חֵטְא וּמִכָּל עָווֹן, לִשְׁמֹר עָלָיו מִמַּכְאוֹבֵי
אֶרֶץ וְיִסּוּרִים.

אָבִינוּ שֶׁבַּשָּׁמַיִם, הַטּוֹב וְהַמֵּטִיב, תֵּן שֶׁיַּלְדִּי, תֵּן שֶׁמַּלְאָךְ צָחוֹר, יַשְׁפִּיל מַבָּטוֹ
אֵלַי, שֶׁדְּמוּתוֹ הַזַּכָּה לְעוֹלָם לֹא תָּמוּשׁ מִלְּפָנַי. בְּשָׁעָה שֶׁאֲנִי עוֹמֶדֶת לַחֲטֹא
לְפָנֶיךָ, תֵּן לְקוֹלוֹ לְהַזְהִיר אוֹתִי מִפְּנֵי הַסַּכָּנָה, שֶׁעֵינָיו תָּאִיר אֵלַי בִּשְׁעַת
מִצְוָה, וּבְשָׁעָה שֶׁאֶתְבַּקֵּשׁ לִישִׁיבָה שֶׁל מַעֲלָה, תֵּן שֶׁיְּקַבֵּל הוּא אֶת פָּנַי.
אָמֵן!

YIZKOR PRAYER FOR A SON
Dalia Wertheim-Yohanan

*M*ay God remember the soul of my deceased son, Matanya.

My God—You, Who created and formed man's heart and his soul—You know how precious a child is to his father and mother.

You know that Matanya is my firstborn son, flesh of my flesh, the joy of my soul.

I shall not try to hold back my pain. My tears flow for my son, who gave up his life for the sanctification of God, the nation, and our land.

I ask of You, my God, that You grant me strength to bear the loss and the longing.

All the days of my life, let his pure image never leave me, and when I am called to the heavenly tribunal, let it be he who receives me.

You are the Master of mercy; shelter him in the shade of Your wings forever; may his soul be bound up in the cluster of life, and may he rest in peace, And let us say: Amen.

Dalia Wertheim-Yohanan lives on Kibbutz Tirat Tzvi and is a teacher of literature and history. She composed this prayer after a dear friend of hers, Reena Robinson, lost her eldest son, Staff Sergeant Matanya Robinson, during Israel's Operation Protective Shield, on April 8, 2002. During the memorial service for the departed in the synagogue, Reena had wanted to recite a *Yizkor* prayer for her son—but no such option appears in the prayer book. Dalia wanted to preserve the model of a brief text, like the *Yizkor* recited in memory of parents or sib-

תפילת יזכור לבן

דליה ורטהיים־יוחנן

יִזְכֹּר אֱלֹקִים אֶת נִשְׁמַת בְּנִי מַתָּנָה שֶׁהָלַךְ לְעוֹלָמוֹ.

אֱלֹקַי, אַתָּה שֶׁבָּרָאתָ וְיָצַרְתָּ אֶת לֵב הָאָדָם וְנַפְשׁוֹ, אַתָּה יוֹדֵעַ מַה יָּקָר יֶלֶד לְאָבִיו וּלְאִמּוֹ.

אַתָּה הַיּוֹדֵעַ שֶׁמַּתָּנָה הוּא בְּנִי בְּכוֹרִי, בָּשָׂר מִבְּשָׂרִי, מְשׂוֹשׂ נַפְשִׁי.

לֹא אֲנַסֶּה לַעֲצֹר בְּעַד כְּאֵבִי. דִּמְעוֹתַי זוֹלְגוֹת עַל בְּנִי שֶׁמָּסַר אֶת נַפְשׁוֹ עַל קְדֻשַּׁת ה׳, הָעָם וְהָאָרֶץ.

אֲנִי מְבַקֶּשֶׁת מִמְּךָ, אֱלֹקַי, שֶׁתִּתֵּן לִי כֹּחַ לָשֵׂאת אֶת הָאָבְדָן וְאֶת הַגַּעְגּוּעִים.

בְּכָל יְמֵי חַיַּי, עֲשֵׂה שֶׁדְּמוּתוֹ הַזַּכָּה לֹא תָּמוּשׁ מִלְּפָנַי, וּבְשָׁעָה שֶׁאֶתְבַּקֵּשׁ לִישִׁיבָה שֶׁל מַעְלָה, תֵּן שֶׁיְּקַבֵּל הוּא אֶת פָּנַי. אַתָּה הוּא בַּעַל הָרַחֲמִים, הַסְתֵּר אוֹתוֹ בְּצֵל כְּנָפֶיךָ לְעוֹלָמִים וְתִצְרֹר בִּצְרוֹר הַחַיִּים אֶת נִשְׁמָתוֹ וְיָנוּחַ בְּשָׁלוֹם עַל מִשְׁכָּבוֹ וְנֹאמַר אָמֵן.

---

lings, so that it could be integrated easily into the rest of the prayer service. The prayer that she composed was inspired by Fanny Neuda's "Mother's Prayer at Her Child's Grave," and also includes elements drawn from the *Yizkor* prayer for fallen Israel Defense Forces (IDF) soldiers.

This prayer is indicative of how the discovery and restoration of women's prayers from previous centuries has inspired a creative awakening within modern Israeli society.

YAHRZEIT PRAYER

Hanna Mikhae Friedman

On the anniversary of the death, it is proper for a woman to go to the study hall to pray, and to recite this supplication prior to *Ashrei* and *U-Va le-Tzion*. Beforehand she should give charity in accordance with her means, or at least put money aside to give to charity. Thereafter she recites the following:

Sovereign of the world, Master of the world: Behold, I come before You with a broken heart and lowly spirit. This day is for me, every year, a day of mourning and weeping, a dark, bitter, and sad day on which I lost my crowning glory. On this day my [insert relationship to loved one], [insert name of loved one], son/daughter of [insert loved one's mother's name] died, and therefore this day every year is a day of agony and sorrow. When this day comes, each year, I am reminded of my catastrophe and I weep anew, inconsolable. I do not protest Your actions, heaven forfend; I accept them with love. You, Lord, are kind and merciful; that which You

Several halakhic rulings published over the past two hundred years suggest that it is permissible for a woman to recite the Mourners' Kaddish for her parents, and today many women follow this practice. This prayer was written as "A supplication for the *yahrzeit* [anniversary of the death of a loved one] and for the days of mourning, following the prayer service."

תחינת צרור החיים

חנה מיכאע פרידמאן

ביום השנה מן הנכון שתלך האשה לבית המדרש להתפלל, ותאמר תחנה זו לפני אשרי ובא לציון. לפני כן ראוי שתתן צדקה לפי אפשרותה, ולפחות תניח כסף מיחד ליתנו לצדקה. אחר כך תאמר זאת:

בּוֹנוֹ שֶׁל עוֹלָם אֲדוֹן הָעוֹלָם, הִנְנִי בָּאָה לְפָנֶיךָ בְּלֵב שָׁבוּר וְרוּחַ נְמוּכָה. יוֹם זֶה הוּא בִּשְׁבִילִי כָּל שָׁנָה יוֹם קִינָה וִילָלָה, יוֹם חֹשֶׁךְ מַר וְעָצוּב, בּוֹ נָפַל כֶּתֶר רֹאשִׁי. בְּיוֹם זֶה נִפְטַר/ה [הֻקְרְבָה] הַנִּקְרָא/ת (פב״פ), וְלָכֵן הוּא אֶצְלִי כָּל שָׁנָה יוֹם שֶׁבֶר וְצַעַר. כְּשֶׁמַּגִּיעַ יוֹם זֶה כָּל שָׁנָה אֲנִי נִזְכֶּרֶת בַּאֲסוֹנִי, וּמִיַּבֶּבֶת מֵחָדָשׁ מִבְּלִי לְהִנָּחֵם, אֵינֶנִּי מִתְרַעֶמֶת חָלִילָה עַל מַעֲשֶׂיךָ, וַאֲנִי מְקַבֶּלֶת אוֹתָם בְּאַהֲבָה. אַתָּה ה׳ בַּעַל חֶסֶד וְרַחֲמִים, וּמַה שֶׁעָשִׂיתָ מִסְתָּמָא כָּךְ הָיָה צָרִיךְ לִהְיוֹת וְכָךְ טוֹב, וַאֲנִי מַאֲמִינָה בַּקָּדוֹשׁ בָּרוּךְ הוּא שֶׁכָּל מַה שֶׁעוֹשֶׂה הוּא לְטוֹבָה, אֶלָּא שֶׁבְּיוֹם זֶה אֲנִי נִזְכֶּרֶת בְּמַעֲשִׂים הָרָעִים שֶׁהִכְעַסְתִּי וְחָטָאתִי לְפָנֶיךָ, וְלֹא הָיִיתִי רְאוּיָה שֶׁ[הֻקְרְבָה] יְ/תִחְיֶה] יְ/תִחְיֶה. בְּיוֹם זֶה

do must be what needs to be done, and so it is good, and I trust in the Holy One, blessed be He, that all that He does is for the good. But on this day I am reminded of my evil deeds in angering and sinning before You, such that I was not worthy of having my [insert relationship to loved one] live. I remember that on this day my fortune was darkened, and my heart is anxious that the day not continue to be an omen of evil. Therefore tears pour from my eyes, asking of You, blessed God, to arouse some of Your mercifulness within me this day, to enhance and elevate my fortune, so that I will know no more sorrow and weeping, death will visit my home no more, no one will be torn away from me, and no more tragedy will visit my family. Do not remove Your beneficent vigilance from me, that I may not know another day that is bitter, dark, and pitiful, nor any sorrow or anguish.

Hear the sound of my weeping, Master of the universe; see my tears and my broken heart, and fulfill my request. You inflict and You heal; You have broken me on this day, and You are able to comfort me. Therefore I look to You and to Your great mercy, that You may hear the sound of my prayer, and arouse the merit of the holy soul of my [insert relationship] who passed away on this day, in my favor, and may the merit of his/her good deeds stand in my favor on this day and on every day. Amen.

I pray with an outpouring of my heart before You, blessed God, that You arouse Your mercy to remember the soul of my [insert name of loved one] who passed away on this day; to elevate it to a lofty place, that it may stand at the foot of Your throne of glory, shining and radiant like the brilliance of the firmament. May it have a place among the holy souls of

אֲנִי נִזְכֶּרֶת שֶׁבּוֹ מַזָּלִי חָשַׁךְ, וְלִבִּי דוֹאֵג שֶׁלֹּא יַמְשִׁיךְ לִהְיוֹת לְרָעָה. עַל כֵּן זוֹלְגוֹת מֵעֵינַי דְּמָעוֹת לְבַקֵּשׁ מִמְּךָ הַשֵּׁם בָּרוּךְ הוּא, שֶׁתִּתְעוֹרֵר בְּקִרְבִּי הַיּוֹם מֵרַחֲמָנוּתְךָ לְהֵיטִיב וּלְרוֹמֵם אֶת מַזָּלִי שֶׁלֹּא אֵדַע יוֹתֵר שֶׁבֶר וָיִלָּלָה, דָּם לֹא יִשָּׁפֵךְ עוֹד בְּבֵיתִי, אַף אֶחָד לֹא יִקָּרַע מִמֶּנִּי, וְלֹא יֶאֱרַע יוֹתֵר שׁוּם צַעַר בְּמִשְׁפַּחְתִּי. אַל נָא תָּסֵר מִמֶּנִּי אֶת הַשְׁגָּחָתְךָ לְטוֹבָה, וְלֹא אֵדַע יוֹתֵר יוֹם מַר חָשׁוּךְ וְאֻמְלָל. וְלֹא צַעַר וְיָגוֹן.

שְׁמַע קוֹל בְּכִיָּתִי רִבּוֹנוֹ שֶׁל עוֹלָם, רְאֵה אֶת דִּמְעוֹתַי וְלִבִּי הַנִּשְׁבָּר, וּמַלֵּא אֶת בַּקָּשָׁתִי. אַתָּה מַכֶּה וְאַתָּה מַרְפֵּא. אַתָּה שֶׁבֵּרַתָּנִי בְּיוֹם זֶה, וְאַתָּה יָכֹל לְנַחֲמֵנִי. לָכֵן אֲנִי מְחַלֶּת לְךָ וְלָרַחֲמֶיךָ הָרַבִּים שֶׁתִּשְׁמַע קוֹל תְּחִנָּתִי, וְתִתְעוֹרֵר עָלַי זְכוּת הַנְּשָׁמָה הַקְּדוֹשָׁה שֶׁל [הקרבה] שֶׁנִּפְטַר/ה בְּיוֹם זֶה, וּזְכוּת הַמַּעֲשִׂים טוֹבִים שֶׁלּוֹ/ה יַעַמְדוּ לִי בְּיוֹם זֶה וּבְכָל יוֹם, אָמֵן.

אֲנִי מִתְפַּלֶּלֶת בִּשְׁפִיכַת הַלֵּב לְפָנֶיךָ הַשֵּׁם יִתְבָּרַךְ, שֶׁתִּתְעוֹרֵר רַחֲמֶיךָ לִזְכֹּר אֶת נִשְׁמַת [הקרבה] שֶׁנִּפְטַר/ה בְּיוֹם זֶה לְהַעֲלוֹתָהּ לְמַדְרֵגָה גְּבֹהָה, שֶׁתִּהְיֶה תַּחַת כִּסֵּא כְּבוֹדְךָ זוֹרַחַת וּמְאִירָה כְּזֹהַר הָרָקִיעַ, וְיִהְיֶה לָהּ מָקוֹם בֵּין הַנְּשָׁמוֹת הַקְּדוֹשׁוֹת שֶׁל הָאָבוֹת אַבְרָהָם יִצְחָק וְיַעֲקֹב, וְשֶׁל הָאִמָּהוֹת שָׂרָה רִבְקָה רָחֵל וְלֵאָה, וּבֵין כָּל הַנְּשָׁמוֹת הַקְּדוֹשׁוֹת שֶׁל הַצַּדִּיקִים וְהַצַּדְקָנִיּוֹת, וּתְהֵא נִשְׁמָתוֹ/ה צְרוּרָה בִּצְרוֹר הַחַיִּים לָנֶצַח. מְחַל נָא לְכָל מַה שֶּׁחָטָאָה, וּזְכֹר רַק אֶת מַעֲשֶׂיהָ הַטּוֹבִים. זְכוּת הַצְּדָקָה שֶׁאֲנִי נוֹתֶנֶת הַיּוֹם תַּעֲמֹד לָהּ לְהִתְרוֹמֵם מַעֲלָה מַעֲלָה וְתָשׁוּב לִחְיוֹת בִּתְחִיַּת הַמֵּתִים כְּשֶׁיָּבוֹא מְשִׁיחַ צִדְקֵנוּ בִּמְהֵרָה בְיָמֵינוּ אָמֵן.

וְאַתְּ נְשָׁמָה קְדוֹשָׁה וּטְהוֹרָה שֶׁאֲנִי מִתְפַּלֶּלֶת עָלַיִךְ הַיּוֹם, יְשַׁר הוּא שֶׁתִּתְפַּלְּלִי גַּם עָלַי וְתַעְתִּירִי לַקָּדוֹשׁ בָּרוּךְ הוּא. הֱיִי נָא מְלִיצַת יֹשֶׁר עָלַי

the patriarchs—Abraham, Isaac, and Jacob, and the matriarchs—Sarah, Rebecca, Rachel, and Leah, and among all the holy souls of the righteous men and women. May his/her soul be bound up in eternal life. Please forgive all of his/her wrongdoings, and remember only his/her good deeds. May the merit of the charity that I give today stand in his/her favor, to lift the soul ever higher, and may he/she be restored to life at the resurrection of the dead, when our righteous Messiah comes, may it be speedily in our days. Amen.

And you—holy, pure soul for which I pray this day—it is only fair that you pray for me, too, and plead before the Holy One, blessed be He. Speak up on my behalf, to uplift my fortune and the fortune of my husband and my children for long life, and to grant us health, sustenance, honor, and contentment, that we may be saved from illnesses, from cruel events, from all types of evil, and untimely death, heaven forfend.

You, holy soul—as I cared for you in life, so be faithful to me now, too, and to all of my loved ones. In the merit of the charity that I give, and in the merit of the prayer that I offer for you, may it be God's will that I be worthy of seeing you arise at the resurrection of the dead, may it come soon. Amen.

לְרוֹמֵם מַזָּלִי וּמַזָּל בַּעֲלִי וִילָדַי לַאֲרִיכוּת יָמֵינוּ, וּלְחָנֵּנוּ בִּבְרִיאוּת, פַּרְנָסָה, כָּבוֹד וְנַחַת, שֶׁנִּנָּצֵל מִמַּחֲלוֹת, מְאוֹרָעוֹת קָשִׁים, מַרְעִין בִּישִׁין וּמָוֶת שֶׁלֹּא בִּזְמַנּוּ רַחֲמָנָא לִיצְּלָן.

אַתְּ נְשָׁמָה קְדוֹשָׁה, כְּשֵׁם שֶׁהָיִית בְּאֶמְנָה אִתִּי בַּחַיִּים, כָּךְ הֱיִי נֶאֱמָנָה גַּם עַתָּה אֵלַי וְאֶל כָּל הַנִּלְוִים אֵלַי. בִּזְכוּת הַצְּדָקָה שֶׁאֲנִי נוֹתֶנֶת, וּבִזְכוּת הַתְּפִלּוֹת שֶׁאֲנִי מִתְפַּלֶּלֶת עָלַיִךְ, יְהִי רָצוֹן שֶׁאֶזְכֶּה לִרְאוֹתֵךְ עוֹמֶדֶת בִּתְחִיַּת הַמֵּתִים בִּמְהֵרָה אָמֵן.

PRAYER OF AN UNHAPPY WIFE

Fanny Neuda

"I am weary with groaning; I cause my bed to be watered
every night, I water my couch with my tears. My eye is
wasted for grief; it grows weak with all my troubles."

[PSALMS 6:6–7]

*B*ent under the weight of my anguish I stand before You, my God,
to open before You my heart filled with pain, to pour before You the
bitterness of my affliction and suffering. The heavy grief I dare not utter;
my anguish will not be assuaged if I speak of it; I shall hide it from all.
Only the eye of God, looking down, can perceive it.

I am a married woman, wife of the man whom You destined for me,
You—the All-Knowing. In Your Presence I committed myself to love; I
was betrothed in good faith. But a loving marriage—the heart of a woman
and of her husband suited to one another, their aspirations matching those
of each other, a life of tranquillity and companionship—has not been
my lot. I have not been one of Your chosen ones. Love does not reside in
my home, nor do peace and friendship dwell in it. Rather, a gloomy air
of friction, a spirit of hurt and misunderstanding and all such ill feeling
surrounds and prevails over it.

My God, what is life without love, life devoid of blessed companionship?
What [good] is this unsown path, which You have not lined with delicacies
and apples; a path that leads to a home in which there is no rose among the
thorns? What is a home in which there is no love that covers up—softly,
gently—misdeeds and mutual mistakes, and uplifts and crowns with a

תפילת הרעיה האומללה

פאני נוידא

"יָגַעְתִּי בְּאַנְחָתִי אַשְׂחֶה בְכָל־לַיְלָה מִטָּתִי, בְּדִמְעָתִי עַרְשִׂי אַמְסֶה:
עָשְׁשָׁה מִכַּעַס עֵינִי עָתְקָה בְּכָל־צוֹרְרָי"

[תהלים ו 7-6]

בְּרֶגַע מֻטָּל הַיָּגוֹן עוֹמֶדֶת אֲנִי לְפָנֶיךָ, אֱלֹהַי, לִפְתֹּחַ בְּפָנֶיךָ אֶת לִבִּי
הַמָּלֵא בִכְאֵב, לִשְׁפֹּךְ לְפָנֶיךָ אֶת מַר סִבְלִי וּכְאֵבִי! הַתּוּגָה הַכְּבֵדָה – אָסוּר
שֶׁתַּעֲלֶה עַל דַּל שְׂפָתוֹתַי, יְגוֹנִי לֹא יֵקַל אִם אֲשִׂיחֶנּוּ, אַסְתִּירֶנּוּ מִכֹּל. רַק עֵין
אֱלֹהִים בְּהַשְׁפִּילָה מַבָּטָהּ תּוּכַל הָבֵן.

אֵשֶׁת אִישׁ אֲנִי, הָאִישׁ שֶׁיָּעַדְתָּ לִי, אַתָּה הַיּוֹדֵעַ כֹּל. לְעֵינֶיךָ נָדַרְתִּי אֶת
נִדְרֵי הָאַהֲבָה, בֶּאֱמוּנִים אֲרַשְׂתִּי; אַךְ נִשּׂוּאֵי אַהֲבָה, לְבָבוֹת אִשָּׁה וְאִישָׁה
הַהוֹלְמִים זֶה עִם זֶה, מִשְׁאֲלוֹת־לֵב הָעוֹלוֹת בְּקָנֶה אֶחָד, חַיִּים שֶׁל שַׁלְוָה
וְאַחֲוָה, מְנָת־חֶלְקִי לֹא הָיוּ. לֹא הָיִיתִי עִם בְּחוּרֶיךָ. בְּבֵיתִי לֹא שׁוֹכֶנֶת
אַהֲבָה, אֵין מִתְגּוֹרְרִים הַשָּׁלוֹם וְהָרֵעוּת: רַק רוּחַ רִיב קוֹדֶרֶת, רַק רוּחַ
נִכְאִים וְאִי־הֲבָנָה וּבְנֵיהֶם סוֹבְבִים וְשׁוֹלְטִים בּוֹ.

אֱלֹהַי, מָהֶם חַיִּים בְּלֹא אַהֲבָה, חַיִּים נְטוּלֵי אַחֲוָה מְבֹרֶכֶת? מַהִי דֶרֶךְ
לֹא־זְרוּעָה, שֶׁלֹּא סָמְכוּהָ בָּאֲשִׁישׁוֹת וּבַתַּפּוּחִים, דֶּרֶךְ הַמּוֹבִילָה לְבַיִת שֶׁאֵין
שׁוֹשַׁנָּה בֵּין חוֹחָיו? מַהוּ בַּיִת שֶׁאֵין בּוֹ אַהֲבָה, הַמְּכַסֶּה – בְּרָכוֹת וּבְעֶדְנָה –
עַל פְּשָׁעִים וּטְעָיוֹת הַדַּדְיוֹת, וּמְרוֹמֶמֶת וְעוֹטֶרֶת בְּנֵזֶר שִׂמְחָה וְהַצְלָחָה
מְשֻׁתֶּפֶת, בַּיִת שֶׁאֵין בּוֹ אַהֲבָה שֶׁל הַקִּרְבָה הַדַּדִית וְכֹחַ וְאֹרֶךְ־רוּחַ? בְּבַיִת
חֲסַר אַהֲבָה דָּרִים רַק הִרְהוּרֵי חֵטְא, תַּאֲווֹת קוֹרְעוֹת וּמְעַוְּתוֹת לֵב, וּנְשָׁמָה
הַמִּצְטַמְּקֶת לְנֹכַח הָרוּחַ הַקְּפוּאָה וְהַקָּרָה כַּקֶּרַח שֶׁל הָאֲדִישׁוּת.

373

garland of joy and mutual prosperity; a home that lacks the love of mutual self-sacrifice, and strength, and patience? In a home that is devoid of love there reside only sinful thoughts, desires that tear apart and distort the heart, and a soul that shrivels in the face of the frozen, ice-cold wind of uncaring.

Woe to me, I who am groaning, I who suffer this fate. With bitter weeping my laments rise up to You, my God. Have mercy upon Your maidservant, merciful Father; forgive me if I have sinned and transgressed, and remove my suffering, the bitterness of my fate. Before Your Presence I vow to guard myself from evil deeds and from evil thoughts. In order for You to cause love, companionship, peace, and friendship to dwell between us, I am quite ready to sacrifice my pleasures: to perform the household chores without a murmur, and patiently to fulfill my obligations; to receive bitter rebuke—the biting and hurtful words—softly and gently, and to capture my husband's heart.

*M*y God in heaven, bless the intentions of my heart, and grant me the strength and perseverance to bring them to realization. Let my spirit not fall helpless in battle, and let my hopes not become mired. May my goal always stand before me, so that I may proceed toward it with courage, and may success and happiness reward my efforts. God of the heavens— You Who direct hearts like streams of water—turn our hearts toward each other, so that they may meet in love and compatibility, and flow toward each other. You, Who know the secrets inside of us—allow the walls of our longing hearts to ascend with song that has been made whole. Let all ill feeling dissipate, so that tranquillity may return and spread its canopy over our home, and let mutual respect and trust serve as its steady basis. Then my mouth shall be filled with laughter and my tongue with song. I shall give thanks to You with happiness and rejoicing, and praise Your Name at all times. Amen.

אֹויָה לִי, אֲנִי הַנֶּאֱנַחַת, אֲנִי שֶׁזֶּהוּ גּוֹרָלִי. בִּבְכִי מַר עוֹלוֹת אֵלַיִךְ תְּלוּנוֹתַי, אֵלַי. רַחֵם עַל אֲמָתְךָ, אַב הָרַחֲמִים, מְחַל לִי אִם אָשַׁמְתִּי וְחָטָאתִי וּמָרֵק אֶת יִסּוּרַי, אֶת מַר־גּוֹרָלִי. לְנֹכַח פָּנֶיךָ אֲנִי נוֹדֶרֶת לְהִשָּׁמֵר מִמַּעֲשִׂים רָעִים וּמֵהִרְהוּרִים רָעִים. וּכְדֵי שֶׁתִּשְׁכֹּן בֵּינֵינוּ אַהֲבָה וְאַחֲוָה וְשָׁלוֹם וְרֵעוּת, אֲנִי מוּכָנָה וּמְזֻמֶּנֶת לְהַעֲלוֹת לְקָרְבָּן אֶת הֲנָאוֹתַי; לִשְׁקֹד עַל מְלֶאכוֹת הַבַּיִת בְּשֶׁקֶט, וּבְאֹרֶךְ־רוּחַ לְמַלֵּא אֶת הַחוֹבוֹת הַמֻּטָּלִים עָלַי. בְּרָךְ וּבְעֶדְנָה לְקַבֵּל אֶת הַתּוֹכָחָה הַמָּרָה, אֶת הַמִּלִּים הַמָּרוֹת וְהַפּוֹגְעוֹת, וְלִכְבֹּשׁ אֶת לֵב בַּעֲלִי.

אֵלִי שֶׁבַּשָּׁמַיִם, בָּרֵךְ אֶת כַּוָּנוֹת לִבִּי, וְתֵן לִי כֹּחַ וְהַתְמָדָה לְמַמֵּשׁ אוֹתָן; שֶׁלֹּא תִּפֹּל רוּחִי בְּמַאֲבָק חֲסַר־אוֹנִים, וְשֶׁלֹּא יִשְׁקְעוּ תִּקְווֹתַי בַּמְּצוּלוֹת, שֶׁתָּמִיד תַּעֲמֹד לְנֶגֶד עֵינַי מַטְּרָתִי, שֶׁבִּאֹמֶץ אֶצְעַד לִקְרָאתָהּ, וְהַצְלָחָה וַאֲשֶׁר יִהְיוּ שָׂכָר לְמַאֲמַצַּי. אֱלֹהֵי הַשָּׁמַיִם, אַתָּה הַמַּטֶּה אֶת הַלְּבָבוֹת כְּנַחֲלֵי מַיִם, הַטֵּה אֶת לְבּוֹתֵינוּ זֶה לְזֶה, שֶׁיִּפָּגְשׁוּ בְּאַהֲבָה וּבִתְמִימוּת דֵּעִים, וְיִזְרְמוּ זֶה אֶל זֶה. אַתָּה הַיּוֹדֵעַ אֶת מִסְתְּרֵי קָרְבֵּנוּ, תֵּן לְקִירוֹת לִבֵּנוּ הַהוֹמִים לַעֲלוֹת מַעְלָה בְּקוֹל שִׁירָה שֶׁחָבַּר לוֹ יַחְדָּו. עֲשֵׂה שֶׁכָּל קַדְרוּת תָּמוּג, שֶׁהַשַּׁלְוָה תָּשׁוּב וְתִפְרֹשׂ חֻפָּה מֵעַל בֵּיתֵנוּ, וְכָבוֹד וְאֵמוּן הֲדָדִי יְשַׁמְּשׁוּ לָהּ מִשְׁעֶנֶת אֵיתָנָה. אָז יִמָּלֵא שְׂחוֹק פִּי וּלְשׁוֹנִי רִנָּה. בְּשִׂמְחָה וְצָהֳלָה אוֹדֶה לְךָ וַאֲשַׁבֵּחַ בְּכָל עֵת אֶת שְׁמֶךָ, אָמֵן.

PRAYER FOR *AGUNOT*

Shelley Frier List

*C*reator of heaven and earth, may it be Your will to free the captive wives of Israel when love and sanctity have fled the home, but their husbands bind them in the tatters of their *ketubbot*. Remove the bitter burden from these *agunot* and soften the hearts of their misguided captors. Liberate Your faithful daughters from their anguish. Enable them to establish new homes and raise up children in peace.

Grant wisdom to the judges of Israel; teach them to recognize oppression and rule against it. Infuse our rabbis with the courage to use their power for good alone.

Blessed are you, Creator of heaven and earth, who frees the captives.

In 1991, Shelley Frier List composed this prayer in English for an *agunah*, a woman chained to her marital status because her husband's whereabouts are unknown or because he refuses to give her a *get*.

תְּפִלָּה לַעֲגוּנוֹת וּלְמְעוּכָּבוֹת גֵּט

שלי פרייר ליסט

יְהִי רָצוֹן מִלְּפָנֶיךָ שֶׁיִּמָּלְאוּ רַחֲמֶיךָ לְהַתִּיר נְשׁוֹת יִשְׂרָאֵל הַשְּׁבוּיוֹת בִּידֵי בַּעֲלֵיהֶן וּקְשׁוּרוֹת בְּכַבְלֵי כְּתוּבּוֹתֵיהֶן, אַךְ קְדֻשָּׁה וְאַהֲבָה כְּבָר סָרוּ מִמְּעוֹנָן.

הָסֵר נָא מֵעֲלֵיהֶן אֶת עֹל הַמַּר וְרַכֵּךְ אֶת לִבָּם הַמֵּאָן שֶׁל שׁוֹבֵיהֶן. פְּתַח חַרְצֻבּוֹת רֶשַׁע וּשְׁלַח בְּנוֹתֶיךָ חָפְשִׁי לִבְנוֹת בַּיִת בְּיִשְׂרָאֵל וּלְגַדֵּל יְלָדִים בְּאַהֲבָה וְאַחֲוָה, בְּשָׁלוֹם וְרֵעוּת.

הָשִׁיבָה שׁוֹפְטֵינוּ כְּבָרִאשׁוֹנָה וְיוֹעֲצֵינוּ כְּבַתְּחִלָּה וְתֵן בְּלִבָּם רוּחַ חָכְמָה וּגְבוּרָה, רוּחַ עֵצָה וְתוּשִׁיָּה לְהַצִּיל עָשׁוּק מִיַּד רוֹדֵף וְאִשָּׁה מִשְּׁבְיָהּ. בָּרוּךְ אַתָּה, מַתִּיר אֲסוּרִים.

VII

PRAYERS

for

PEACE

and

REDEMPTION

AT RACHEL'S GRAVE

I pray You, O King Who is full of mercy: Behold, I come this day to prostrate myself upon the grave of our matriarch, Rachel, so that the good deeds that she performed throughout her life may be counted in my favor. For the sake of her merit, her righteousness, and her prayer, which You remembered unto her when she was barren, and You opened her womb—as it is written, "God remembered Rachel and God heard her, and He opened her womb," and for the sake of her righteousness of heart toward her sister, Leah, in conveying the secret signs to her so that she would not be humiliated by the deceit of Laban, her father, so may You remember unto us her merit and her righteousness—for me and for all of Your nation, Israel, and accept our prayer and hear our cry for what we ask of You, and fulfill the desires of our hearts for the good, and grant us a remembrance of salvation and mercy from the heavens of old. Let Your

---

The Torah recounts that Rachel died and was buried in Bethlehem, as Jacob and his family journeyed from Paddan-Aram to Canaan. Rashi (Rabbi Shelomo Yitzhaki, 1040–1105) explains that God chose this specific location ". . . so that she could come to the aid of her children when they were exiled by Nebuzaradan. When they passed by there on the way (being led out of their land by the same route that Jacob had used in his return), Rachel emerged from her grave and wept, pleading

תפילה מיוחדת לקבר רחל אמנו

אָנָּא מֶלֶךְ מָלֵא רַחֲמִים, הִנְנִי בָּאתִי הַיּוֹם לְהִשְׁתַּטֵּחַ עַל קֶבֶר רָחֵל
אִמֵּנוּ. שֶׁתִּזְכְּנִי מַעֲשֶׂיהָ הַטּוֹבִים שֶׁעָשְׂתָה כָּל יָמֶיהָ וּלְמַעַן זְכוּתָהּ וְצִדְקָתָהּ
וּתְפִלָּתָהּ שֶׁזָּכַרְתָּ לָהּ בִּהְיוֹתָהּ עֲקָרָה וַתִּפְתַּח אֶת רַחְמָהּ, כְּמוֹ שֶׁנֶּאֱמַר,
וַיִּזְכֹּר אֱלֹהִים אֶת רָחֵל וַיִּשְׁמַע אֵלֶיהָ אֱלֹהִים וַיִּפְתַּח אֶת רַחְמָהּ. וּלְמַעַן
צִדְקַת לְבָבָהּ אֲשֶׁר עָשְׂתָה עִם אֲחוֹתָהּ לֵאָה, שֶׁמָּסְרָה לָהּ הַסִּימָנִים כְּדֵי
שֶׁלֹּא תֵבוֹשׁ מֵרַמָּאוּת לָבָן אָבִיהָ. כֵּן תִּזְכּוֹר לָנוּ זְכוּתָהּ וְצִדְקָתָהּ עָלַי וְעַל כָּל
עַמְּךָ יִשְׂרָאֵל. שֶׁתְּקַבֵּל אֶת תְּפִלָּתֵנוּ וְתַאֲזִין שַׁוְעָתֵנוּ מַה שֶּׁאֲנַחְנוּ מְבַקְשִׁים
מִלְּפָנֶיךָ, וּתְמַלֵּא מִשְׁאֲלוֹת לִבְבֵּנוּ לְטוֹבָה, וּפָקְדֵנוּ בִּפְקֻדַּת יְשׁוּעָה וְרַחֲמִים
מִשְּׁמֵי שְׁמֵי קֶדֶם, וְהַטֵּה אָזְנְךָ וּשְׁמָע, פְּקַח עֵינֶיךָ וּרְאֵה שׁוֹמְמוֹתֵינוּ וְהָעִיר
אֲשֶׁר נִקְרָא שִׁמְךָ עָלֶיהָ, כִּי הָיִינוּ לַעַג וָקֶלֶס בַּגּוֹיִים וְאוֹמְרִים אֵין תּוֹחֶלֶת
וְתִקְוָה. וְאִם לֹא לְמַעֲנֵנוּ, לְמַעַנְךָ פְּעַל, עַד מָתַי יִהְיֶה עֻזְּךָ בַּשְּׁבִי וְתִפְאַרְתְּךָ
בְּיַד צָר:

---

for mercy for them, as it is written, "A voice is heard in Ramah …" Her supplication is answered: "There is a reward for your toil, says God, and the children will return to their borders."

Today, Rachel's grave remains a popular pilgrimage site, and the prayer that appears here is traditionally recited when visiting it.

ear listen and hear; let Your eyes be opened to see our desolation, and the city named after You, for we have become a source of scorn and mockery among the nations, who declare that there is no hope for us. If not for our sakes, act for Your own sake; for how long will Your might languish in captivity, and Your splendor in enemy hands?

Behold, the tradition that we have from our Sages, of blessed memory, teaches that when our patriarch Jacob buried our matriarch Rachel on the way, and did not bring her to Bethlehem, he did so in accordance with a divine command, in order that she would be an aid to her children. When Nebuzaradan exiled them and they passed by there, our matriarch Rachel rose up from her grave and pleaded for mercy for them, as it is written: "A voice is heard in Ramah, the sound of bitter weeping; Rachel is weeping for her children, refusing to be comforted for her children, for they are gone." And You, Lord God, answered her—as it is written: "So says the Lord: Withhold your voice from weeping and your eyes from tears, for there is a reward for your toil, says God, and they shall return from the enemy's land. And there is hope for your end, says God: The children shall return to their borders." How can we speak and what shall we say? If over the first exile, which lasted only seventy years, our matriarch Rachel caused the world to tremble, what can be said now of this bitter and violent exile? For a thousand and nine hundred years we have been in one place after another, scattered and forsaken in the four corners of the world, subject to kings and ministers, we ourselves lowly and despised, regarded by them like thorns cut down, with each day more cursed than the previous one. Their principal goal has been to threaten our souls and force us to abandon the teaching of our holy Torah, so that the name of Israel will no longer be remembered. They have set their eyes even upon young children, scheming how to separate them from their faith, handed down to them from their ancestors. What can you say, our matriarch Rachel? How can you rest in

וְהִנֵּה כַּאֲשֶׁר קִבַּלְנוּ עַל יְדֵי חֲכָמֵינוּ זִכְרוֹנָם לִבְרָכָה, שֶׁאָבִינוּ יַעֲקֹב שֶׁקָּבַר אֶת רָחֵל אִמֵּנוּ בַּדֶּרֶךְ וְלֹא הֱבִיאָהּ לְבֵית לֶחֶם, הָיָה עַל פִּי הַדִּבּוּר, כְּדֵי שֶׁתִּהְיֶה לְעֶזְרָה לְבָנֶיהָ. כְּשֶׁהִגְלָה אוֹתָם נְבוּזַרְאֲדָן וְהָיוּ עוֹבְרִים דֶּרֶךְ שָׁם, יָצְאָה רָחֵל אִמֵּנוּ מִקִּבְרָהּ וּבִקְשָׁה עֲלֵיהֶם רַחֲמִים, כְּמוֹ שֶׁנֶּאֱמַר, קוֹל בְּרָמָה נִשְׁמָע נְהִי בְּכִי תַמְרוּרִים רָחֵל מְבַכָּה עַל בָּנֶיהָ מֵאֲנָה לְהִנָּחֵם עַל בָּנֶיהָ כִּי אֵינֶנּוּ. וְאַתָּה יְיָ אֱלֹהֵינוּ, הֲשֵׁבֹתָ לָהּ, כְּמוֹ שֶׁנֶּאֱמַר, כֹּה אָמַר יְיָ מִנְעִי קוֹלֵךְ מִבֶּכִי וְעֵינַיִךְ מִדִּמְעָה כִּי יֵשׁ שָׂכָר לִפְעֻלָּתֵךְ נְאֻם־יְיָ וְשָׁבוּ מֵאֶרֶץ אוֹיֵב. וְיֵשׁ־תִּקְוָה לְאַחֲרִיתֵךְ נְאֻם־יְיָ וְשָׁבוּ בָנִים לִגְבוּלָם. מַה נֹּאמַר וּמַה נְּדַבֵּר, אִם עַל גָּלוּת רִאשׁוֹן שֶׁהָיָה רַק לְשִׁבְעִים שָׁנָה הִרְעִישָׁה רָחֵל אִמֵּנוּ אֶת הָעוֹלָם, מַה תֹּאמַר עַתָּה בְּגָלוּת הַמַּר וְהַנִּמְהָר הַזֶּה אֲשֶׁר זֶה אֶלֶף וּתְשַׁע מֵאוֹת שָׁנָה שֶׁאֲנַחְנוּ בְּגָלוּת אַחַר גּוֹלָה מְפֻזָּרִים וְנִדָּחִים בְּאַרְבַּע כַּנְפוֹת הָאָרֶץ תַּחַת עַל מְלָכִים וְשָׂרִים, וַאֲנַחְנוּ שְׁפָלִים וְנִבְזִים וּבְקוֹצִים כְּסֹחִים אָנוּ בְּעֵינֵיהֶם, וּבְכָל יוֹם, קִלְלָתוֹ מְרֻבָּה מֵחֲבֵרוֹ, וְעִקָּר כַּוָּנָתָם לַעֲמֹד עַל נַפְשֵׁנוּ לְהַעֲבִיר דַּת תּוֹרָתֵנוּ הַקְּדוֹשָׁה, וְלֹא יִזָּכֵר לָהֶם שֵׁם יִשְׂרָאֵל עוֹד, גַּם עַל תִּינוֹקוֹת שֶׁל בֵּית רַבָּן נָתְנוּ עֵינֵיהֶם הֵיאַךְ לְהַעֲבִירָם מֵאֱמוּנָתָם הַמְחֻזֶּקֶת לָהֶם מֵאֲבוֹתֵיהֶם, מַה תֹּאמְרִי רָחֵל אִמֵּנוּ, אֵיךְ תּוּכְלִי לָנוּחַ בְּקִבְרֵךְ? הָקִיצִי וּתְעוֹרְרִי לִישֵׁנֵי חֶבְרוֹן וּמֹשֶׁה רַעְיָא מְהֵימְנָא וְכָל אֲבוֹתֵינוּ הַקְּדוֹשִׁים, עִמְדִי נָא, הִתְיַצְּבִי נָא, חַלִּי נָא פְּנֵי כְבוֹדוֹ יִתְבָּרַךְ בְּעַד שְׁאֵרִית פְּלֵטַת בֵּית יִשְׂרָאֵל, הַנֶּאֱנָחִים וְהַנֶּאֱנָקִים, בְּדוּדִים וּשְׁדוּדִים. שְׁפָלִים וְנִבְזִים. נְתוּנִים בְּסֵתֶר הַמַּדְרֵגָה, עַד מָתַי אֱלֹהִים יְחָרֶף צָר, יְנָאֵץ אוֹיֵב שִׁמְךָ לָנֶצַח! עַד מָתַי רְשָׁעִים יַעֲלֹזוּ. וּבָנֶיךָ בּוֹז יָבוֹזּוּ! עַד מָתַי לֹא תְרַחֵם עַל יִשְׂרָאֵל עַמְּךָ וְעַל אַרְצְךָ יְרוּשָׁלַיִם עִירֶךָ וְעַל צִיּוֹן מִשְׁכַּן כְּבוֹדֶךָ! הִנֵּה זֹאת תּוֹרַת הַבָּיִת. הֵיכַל וְהַר הַבַּיִת הָיָה לְשַׁמִּיר וָשָׁיִת. עָלָה כֻּלּוֹ קִמְּשׂוֹנִים. כָּסוּ פָנָיו חֲרוּלִים, שׁוּעָלִים הִלְכוּ בוֹ [וְאוֹיְבֵנוּ פְּלִילִים וּבָאוּ בוֹ פָרִיצִים וַיְחַלְּלוּהוּ, בְּבֵית תְּפִלָּה, כָּל עָרֵל וְטָמֵא נוֹתֵן תִּפְלָה]. וְהָעִיר הַקְּדוֹשָׁה רַבַּת הַמַּעֲלוֹת עִיר אֱלֹהִים סֶלָה הִנֵּה הִיא עַתָּה שַׁמָּה וּשְׁאִיָּה, וְאִם אֲנַחְנוּ בַּעֲווֹנוֹתֵינוּ וַעֲווֹנוֹת אֲבוֹתֵינוּ

your grave? Arise and waken those who slumber in Hebron, and Moses, the loyal shepherd, and all of our holy forefathers. Stand up, I pray you; please present yourself, please turn the countenance of the blessed, glorious God toward the remnant of your nation, the house of Israel, who sigh and groan, alone and ravaged, lowly and despised, regarded with contempt. How long, God, will the tormentor abuse us; will the enemy forever insult Your Name? How long shall the wicked rejoice, while Your children are mocked and scorned? How long will You have no mercy upon Israel, Your nation, and upon Your land, and Jerusalem—Your city, and Zion—the dwelling place of Your glory? For this is what has become of the Holy Temple: The Sanctuary and the Temple Mount have become hewn stones and thistles; they are overgrown with thornbushes. They are covered with brambles; foxes roam over them (our enemies passed judgment on us; they invaded and violated it; in the House of prayer every uncircumcised and defiled person offers prayer). And the holy city of many virtues, the city of God, Selah—behold, it is now desolate and ruined. If we, through our transgressions and those of our forefathers, have caused all of this—are You not the merciful One? Will You forsake us and remain angry for all eternity? "You shall arise and comfort Zion, for it is time to pardon her."

Therefore we come before You—our heads bowed, our spirit submissive, humbled and brokenhearted, that You may remember unto us the merit of our holy forefathers and the merit of the righteous Rachel, our matriarch, and grant atonement for all of our sins and transgressions and wrongdoing which we have committed before You, and help us to return to You in complete repentance, and lengthen our days in goodness and our years in pleasantness upon the land—the holy land. Remove from us all of the obstacles that distract us from divine service, in order that we may study and teach, observe, perform, and fulfill all the words of Your Torah's

גָּרַמְנוּ אֶת כָּל אֵלֶּה, הֲלֹא אַתָּה בַּעַל הָרַחֲמִים, הַלְעוֹלָמִים תִּזְנַח וְתֶאֱנַף
לָנֶצַח! אַתָּה תָקוּם תְּרַחֵם צִיּוֹן כִּי עֵת לְחֶנְנָהּ:

לָכֵן בָּאנוּ לְפָנֶיךָ בִּכְפִיפַת קוֹמָה וּבְהַכְנָעַת רוּחַ וּבְשִׁפְלוּת הַנֶּפֶשׁ
וּבִשְׁבִירַת לֵב, שֶׁתִּזְכֹּר לָנוּ זְכוּת אֲבוֹתֵינוּ הַקְּדוֹשִׁים וּזְכוּת הַצַּדְקָנִית רָחֵל
אִמֵּנוּ, וּתְכַפֶּר לָנוּ אֶת כָּל חַטֹּאתֵינוּ וַעֲוֹנוֹתֵינוּ וּפְשָׁעֵינוּ, שֶׁחָטָאנוּ וְשֶׁעָוִינוּ
וְשֶׁפָּשַׁעְנוּ לְפָנֶיךָ, וְתַעַזְרֵנוּ לָשׁוּב בִּתְשׁוּבָה שְׁלֵמָה לְפָנֶיךָ, וְתַאֲרִיךְ יָמֵינוּ
בְּטוֹב וּשְׁנוֹתֵינוּ בַּנְּעִימִים עַל הָאֲדָמָה אַדְמַת הַקֹּדֶשׁ. וְתָסִיר מֵאִתָּנוּ כָּל
הַמְּנִיעוֹת הַמְּבַלְבְּלִים אוֹתָנוּ מֵעֲבוֹדַת הַקֹּדֶשׁ. כְּדֵי שֶׁנּוּכַל לִלְמֹד וּלְלַמֵּד
לִשְׁמֹר וְלַעֲשׂוֹת וּלְקַיֵּם אֶת כָּל דִּבְרֵי תַלְמוּד תּוֹרָתְךָ וּמִצְוֹתֶיךָ בְּכַוָּנָה
שְׁלֵמָה וּרְצוּיָה בְּלִי שׁוּם טִרְדָּה, וְתָסִיר מִמֶּנּוּ וּמִכָּל עַמְּךָ בֵּית יִשְׂרָאֵל
כָּל מִינֵי חֳלִי [וּבִפְרָט מֵחוֹלֶה פב"פ] וְתֵן לָנוּ כֹּחַ וּבְרִיאוּת הַגּוּף, שֶׁנּוּכַל
לַעֲבֹד אוֹתְךָ יוֹמָם וָלַיְלָה בְּלִי רִפְיוֹן, וְתֵן לָנוּ פַּרְנָסָה טוֹבָה וְגַשְׁמֵי בְעִתָּם,
שֶׁתְּהֵא הַשָּׁנָה הַזֹּאת מְבֹרֶכֶת בְּכָל מִינֵי תְבוּאוֹת וְכָל מִינֵי פֵרוֹת וְכָל
מִינֵי יְרָקוֹת, וְתֵן סִפּוּקֵנוּ לְכָל אֶחָד וְאֶחָד דֵּי מַחְסוֹרוֹ, וְלֹא יֶחְסַר לָנוּ כָּל
יְמֵי חַיֵּינוּ, וּתְזַכֵּנוּ לְגַדֵּל אֶת בָּנֵינוּ [וּבִפְרָט פב"פ] וּתְזַכֵּנוּ לִשְׁמֹעַ בְּשׂוֹרוֹת
טוֹבוֹת מִבָּנֵי שֶׁתַּצְלִיחַ לָהֶם בְּכָל מַעֲשֵׂה יְדֵיהֶם, וְהִנְנִי בְּלִי נֶדֶר נוֹדֶבֶת שֶׁמֶן
לְמָאוֹר לְעִלּוּי נִשְׁמַת רָחֵל אִמֵּנוּ, וְנִשְׁמַת רַבִּי מֵאִיר בַּעַל הַנֵּס, וְנִשְׁמוֹת
כָּל הַצַּדִּיקִים וְהַחֲסִידִים [וּלְהַצְלָחַת בְּנֵי פב"פ וְכוּ']. שֶׁיַּאֲרִיכוּ יְמֵיהֶם
וּשְׁנוֹתֵיהֶם וְלֹא יָמוּת שׁוּם אֶחָד מִבְּנֵיהֶם בְּחַיֵּי אֲבִיהֶם וְאִמָּם. וְיִזְכּוּ לְבָנִים
צַדִּיקִים וּכְשֵׁרִים בְּכָל מִדּוֹת טוֹבוֹת. וְתַזְמִין לָהֶם זִוּוּג כָּשֵׁר וְרָאוּי לָהֶם, וְלֹא
יֵרָאֶה וְלֹא יִשָּׁמַע שׁוּם שֶׁמֶץ פְּסוּל בְּזַרְעֵנוּ וּמִשְׁפַּחְתֵּנוּ. וְנִזְכֶּה לִרְאוֹתָם יַחַד
בְּקִבּוּץ גָּלֻיּוֹת וּגְאֻלָּה שְׁלֵמָה בַּעֲגָלָא וּבִזְמַן קָרִיב, אָמֵן סֶלָה. יִהְיוּ לְרָצוֹן
אִמְרֵי פִי וְהֶגְיוֹן לִבִּי לְפָנֶיךָ יְיָ צוּרִי וְגֹאֲלִי.

teaching and Your commandments with perfect and proper intention with no disturbance. Remove from us, and from all of Your nation, the house of Israel, all manner of illness (and particularly with regard to the patient [insert patient's name], son/daughter of [insert name of patient's mother]). Grant us strength and bodily health, that we may serve You day and night without weakening. Grant us good sustenance and rains at their proper time, so that this year may be blessed with all manner of produce and species of fruits and vegetables. Provide for each one of us in accordance with his needs, that we may never be wanting for as long as we live. Grant us the gift of raising our children (and in particular [insert child's name] son/ daughter of [insert name of child's mother]), and let us hear good reports concerning our children—may You grant them success in all of their endeavors. Without making a formal vow, I hereby pledge oil for lighting, for the elevation of the soul of our matriarch Rachel, and the soul of Rabbi Meir, who wrought miracles, and the souls of all the righteous and pious ones (and for the success of my children [insert children's names], sons/daughters of [insert name of children's mother]). May their days and years be lengthened, and may none of their children die during their parents' lifetimes. May they be granted children who are righteous and commendable in all positive attributes. Appoint good and worthy spouses for them, so that no hint of any taint will be seen in our descendants and our family, nor spoken of them. May we be worthy of seeing together the ingathering of the exiles and the complete redemption, swiftly and soon. Amen, Selah. May the words of my mouth and the thoughts of my heart find favor before You, Lord, my Rock and my Redeemer.

THE PRAYER OF GLÜCKEL OF HAMELN

Germany

Great and only God,

I ask of You from the depths of my heart that You pardon me [...]

And so the matter must be entrusted to the hands of God, blessed be He, remembering that all the world is vanity, a passing shadow.

You, the great Lord, know how immersed I was, in earlier times, in great anxiety and grief.

I was a wife, and I took refuge in the departed one—my pious husband, who protected me like the apple of his eye. But following his death, all of my wealth and glory left me; it is over this that I weep and keen all the days and years of my life, even though I know that it is weakness on my part, and a great flaw, to always be sorrowful and wailing. It would be better were I every day to bend down on my knees and give praise and

We conclude this book of prayers with the innocent supplication of Glückel of Hameln. Glückel was born in Hamburg, Germany, in 1645 and died in Metz in 1724. She was married at the age of fourteen and bore fourteen children (two of whom died before she did). According to her own testimony, she worked with her husband in commerce and he took no step without first consulting her. After his death, the burden of earning a livelihood for the family fell to her shoulders. In her widowhood, Glückel wrote: "When his soul left him, I lost all my wealth, all my splendor, all my glory." Further on in the same composition, which addresses the meaning of life, the will to live, and her strength to survive, she writes: "But what could I do? ... To earn a livelihood for my orphans to the extent that it was in the faint power of a weak woman, full of sorrow and distress, to do."

אֵל גָּדוֹל וְיָחִיד,

אֲנִי מְבַקֶּשֶׁת מִמְּךָ מֵעֹמֶק לִבִּי כִּי תִּמְחַל לִי...

וּבְכֵן, צָרִיךְ לִמְסֹר אֶת הַדָּבָר בִּידֵי הַמָּקוֹם בָּרוּךְ הוּא וְלִזְכֹּר כִּי כָּל הָעוֹלָם הֶבֶל הוּא וְצֵל עוֹבֵר.

אַתָּה הָאֱלֹהִים הַגָּדוֹל יוֹדֵעַ אֵיךְ שֶׁהָיִיתִי שְׁקוּעָה בִּזְמַנִּי בִּדְאָגוֹת גְּדוֹלוֹת וּבְתוּגַת לֵב.

אִשָּׁה הָיִיתִי וּבַעַת, בַּעֲלִי הֶחָסִיד, חָסִיתִי, וְהוּא הָיָה חָס עָלַי כְּמוֹ עַל בָּבַת עֵינוֹ, אֲבָל אַחֲרֵי מוֹתוֹ חָלַף כָּל עָשְׁרִי וּכְבוֹדִי, וְעַל אֵלֶּה אֲנִי בּוֹכִיָּה וּמִתְיַפַּחַת כָּל יְמֵי חַיַּי וּשְׁנוֹתַי, אַף עַל פִּי שֶׁאֲנִי יוֹדַעַת כִּי זֹהִי חֻלְשָׁה מִצִּדִּי וְחִסָּרוֹן גָּדוֹל לִהְיוֹת תָּמִיד עֲצוּבָה וּמְיַלֶּלֶת, יוֹתֵר טוֹב הָיָה אִלּוּ הָיִיתִי בְּכָל יוֹם כּוֹרַעַת עַל בִּרְכַּי וּמְהַלֶּלֶת וּמוֹדָה לֵאלֹהֵי הַחֶסֶד בְּעַד הַחֶסֶד שֶׁהוּא עוֹשֶׂה עִמִּי, שֶׁאֵינִי רְאוּיָה לְכָךְ.

But Glückel also did something else. In addition to seeing to the sustenance of her family, she shared with us one of the most genuine, heartfelt, and touching documents to have been preserved from all of Jewish history. To alleviate her loneliness and as a living will to her children, Glückel set down her memories, allowing us a glimpse of European Jewry at the time. Her work opens a window onto late-seventeenth- and early-eighteenth-century Jewish life in Germany. The story of Glückel's eventful life is influenced by the *musar* literature of the time, particularly those works addressed to women, as well as by various stories, legends, and biblical sources.

thanks to the God of kindness for the kindness that He performs toward me, although I am unworthy of it.

Even today, I still sit at my own table, eat to my heart's content, and lie down at night in my own bed. I still have a shilling or so in my pocket to spend, for as long as it pleases the blessed God.

And if my children do not always enjoy good fortune to the extent that I might have hoped, we are nevertheless still alive, thank God, and we thank our Creator.

How many people there are in the world who are more righteous and more pious than we, yet they have not enough food even for a single meal. There are even some whom I have known personally, who were completely righteous.

How many thanks I owe my Creator for all the kindness that He does for us even when we are not worthy of it—as I have mentioned. If only we sinful and pitiful mortals would acknowledge His many mercies: The great Creator formed us from matter and inspired us with the knowledge of His holy and awesome Name. Therefore we must serve our Creator wholeheartedly [...].

Therefore, my beloved children, be comforted and bear your suffering with fortitude. Serve the Almighty Lord with a perfect heart, even when—heaven forfend—you do not enjoy good fortune. Even when it seems to us that the suffering is unbearable, we must know that the blessed God does not burden His servants with more than they are able to bear. Happy is the man who bears his own suffering, or that of his children, accepting it all with love.

And this I ask of the Creator: that He grant me forbearance, for everything that happens in the world is in accordance with our deeds, and [therefore] we are obliged to bear it. And "just as one blesses [God] for the good, so one blesses [Him] for the bad."

עוֹדֶנִּי גַם הַיּוֹם יוֹשֶׁבֶת עַל־יַד שֻׁלְחָנִי, אוֹכֶלֶת כְּאַוַּת נַפְשִׁי, שׁוֹכֶבֶת בַּלַּיְלָה בְּתוֹךְ מִטָּתִי שֶׁלִּי. יֵשׁ לִי בְּכִיסִי עוֹד אֵיזֶה שִׁילִינְג לְהוֹצָאָה כָּל זְמַן שֶׁיִּהְיֶה בִּרְצוֹן הַשִּׁי"ת.

וְאִם גַּם לִבְּנֵי הַיְקָרִים לִפְעָמִים לֹא כָּךְ הַשָּׁעָה מְשַׂחֶקֶת כְּמוֹ שֶׁהָיִיתִי רוֹצָה, בְּכָל זֹאת חַיִּים אָנוּ ב"ה וּמוֹדִים לְיוֹצְרֵנוּ.

כַּמָּה יֵשׁ בָּעוֹלָם אֲנָשִׁים יוֹתֵר צַדִּיקִים וְיוֹתֵר חֲסִידִים מִמֶּנּוּ, וְאֵין לָהֶם אֲפִלּוּ מְזוֹן סְעוּדָה אַחַת, וְגַם אֵלֶּה שֶׁאֲנִי בְּעַצְמִי הִכַּרְתִּי שֶׁהָיוּ צַדִּיקִים גְּמוּרִים.

כַּמָּה אֲנִי צְרִיכָה לְהוֹדוֹת אֶת יוֹצְרִי בְּעַד כָּל הַחֲסָדִים שֶׁהוּא עוֹשֶׂה עִמָּנוּ גַּם אִם אֵינֶנּוּ כְּדַאִים לְכָךְ, כְּמוֹ שֶׁכָּתַבְתִּי, אִם רַק אֲנַחְנוּ בְּנֵי־אָדָם הַחֲטָאִים וְהָעֲנִיִּים נַכִּיר אֶת רַחֲמָיו הַמְרֻבִּים שֶׁהַבּוֹרֵא הַגָּדוֹל יָצַר אוֹתָנוּ מֵחֹמֶר וְנָתַן בְּלִבֵּנוּ לְהַכִּיר אֶת שְׁמוֹ הַקָּדוֹשׁ וְהַנּוֹרָא, וּלְפִיכָךְ עָלֵינוּ לַעֲבֹד אֶת יוֹצְרֵנוּ בְּלֵב שָׁלֵם...

וּלְפִיכָךְ, בָּנַי הָאֲהוּבִים, הִתְנַחֲמוּ וּשְׂאוּ אֶת יִסּוּרֵיכֶם בְּסַבְלָנוּת וְעִבְדוּ אֶת ד' הַכֹּל יָכוֹל בְּלֵבָב שָׁלֵם גַּם בְּשָׁעָה שֶׁאַתֶּם מְקַבְּלִים ח"ו אֶת הָרָעָה, וְגַם כְּשֶׁנִּדְמֶה לָנוּ כִּי הַיִּסּוּרִים קָשִׁים מִנְּשֹׂא, אָנוּ צְרִיכִים לָדַעַת כִּי הַשִּׁי"ת אֵינֶנּוּ שָׂם עַל עֲבָדָיו מַשָּׂא יוֹתֵר מִמַּה שֶׁהֵם יְכוֹלִים לָשֵׂאת, וְאַשְׁרֵי הָאִישׁ הַנּוֹשֵׂא אֶת הַיִּסּוּרִים שֶׁבְּגוּפוֹ אוֹ שֶׁבְּבָנָיו, הַכֹּל מְקַבֵּל בְּאַהֲבָה.

וְעַל זֶה אָנֹכִי מְבַקֶּשֶׁת מֵאֵת הַבּוֹרֵא שֶׁיִּתֵּן בְּלִבִּי סַבְלָנוּת, כִּי הַכֹּל מַה שֶּׁיְּקָרֶה בָּעוֹלָם הוּא לְפִי מַעֲשֵׂינוּ וְחַיָּבִים אָנוּ לִסְבֹּל, "כְּשֵׁם שֶׁמְּבָרְכִים עַל הַטּוֹבָה כָּךְ מְבָרְכִים עַל הָרָעָה".

ACKNOWLEDGMENTS

I received a great deal of help from a number of people during the course of my global exploration of women's prayers. Librarians, scholars, collectors, and translators provided significant assistance; women "conveyors" shared their childhood experiences with me, students shared their life stories, and the women members of my extended family—in all corners of the globe—became active researchers.

I was propelled toward my first meeting with Bill Gross, a collector of Judaica, by an inexplicable longing. It was as though I had some sense of the secret that had awaited me there for many years. Lisa and Bill opened their home to me and took me in as one of the family, and Bill's sound advice and extensive international connections were of great assistance.

A special thank-you to Professor Avigdor Shinan, from the Department of Hebrew Literature at the Hebrew University in Jerusalem. His readiness at all times to lend a helping hand put my mind at rest.

Professor Sam Lehman-Wilzig, chairman of the Department of Political Science at Bar-Ilan University, provided moral support and professional assistance, both greatly appreciated.

Special thanks are owed also to Dr. Yael Levine, my academic adviser for the original publication in Hebrew, for sharing her knowledge and expertise in this field and for directing me to forgotten prayers. Her rare assiduity enhanced the work in its entirety.

I owe much to my teacher, friend, and colleague Malka Pietrokowsky, whose knowledge and wisdom—along with the questions with which she challenged me—goaded me on to find worthy answers.

My thanks to Rabbi Dr. Benny Lau for his insightful comments and his willingness to help throughout the project.

My colleagues at the Kolech Religious Women's Forum were a steady source of collective support and advice. Their familiarity with religious texts made them a reliable and efficient resource.

I am indebted to the entire staff of Yedioth Ahronoth Publishers for their guidance and molding of the book in Hebrew, *Tefillat Nashim*. Director Dovi Eichnold believed in the book and its importance from the moment I first approached him, and became an enthusiastic advocate.

The translation of the prayers, supplications, and liturgical poems posed a complex challenge, but from the very outset of my voyage of discovery I knew that the book must appear in English, too, for the sake of many people who want to pray and to read but are unable to do so in Hebrew. After an entire year of seeking the right person for the task, I found Kaeren Fish. From our very first telephone conversation I knew that my search had ended. It was one of those rare moments in life when knowledge strikes with the power of dormant memory. We later discovered that it had been her husband's family (before they were married) that had adopted my husband and me when we arrived in Durban, South Africa, exactly twenty years ago, to serve as *shlichim* (emissaries) for the Jewish community there. Coincidence? Surely not.

My heartfelt thanks to Kaeren for her stirring translation of this book. Her devoted and exacting effort reflects her wholehearted aspiration to produce a work that would inspire in English the spirit of the Hebrew original, our mother code.

The English translation was made possible through a grant from the Keshet Foundation (www.keshet.org). My thanks to its members for their faith in this project, for their support and cooperation during the long process of the translation, and for making it possible for the vast English-speaking public to reconnect with the forgotten feminine traditions of generations gone by.

Our desire to preserve the authenticity of the prayers while ensuring that the texts would speak to women and men living in the twenty-first century presented no small challenge. A veritable army of friends, colleagues, and experts volunteered their valuable time and helped to resolve translation issues. They are too numerous to mention by name; below are just the major contributors, but each and every question answered, comment offered, and help rendered is truly appreciated.

Thanks to my teacher Harold Fleishman, who grew up in South Africa, was educated in England, worked internationally ... and accompanied me, insightfully and sensitively, throughout the translation of this book, allowing me glimpses into the life of the wandering Jew. Special thanks also to my friend Holly Nosatzki, who accompanied me from start to finish.

My wonderful agent, Deborah Harris, believed in this book and its importance from the outset. At our first meeting, she told me, "There are many people in the world who are waiting for this book." Her determination to find the right publisher for the English translation, and the right people to work with, bore blessed fruit. Thanks, too, to Phillipa Brophy, Deborah's coagent in New York, for taking me and this book under her generous patronage.

My thanks to the entire Spiegel & Grau team, and especially to Julie Grau, who asked the right questions and guided the translation in the right direction, so as to give voice in English to the life stories of Jewish women poets and liturgists throughout the generations. I am deeply grateful to Hana Landes, who devoted herself wholly to the task of grasping the book's delicate texture and molding it in the best possible way. Thanks also to Gretchen Koss and Lauren Lavelle, for their sensitivity in publicizing the book and their far-sighted commitment to its dissemination, and to Kirk Reed, who was most helpful throughout the tranlation process.

To my dear family: My mother and father, Miriam and Menashe Mashiah, were involved in my work from the very first speculative conversations and became enthusiastic supporters; my father-in-law, David, and my mother-in-law, Dina—my other parents—explored with me the forgotten customs of Libyan Jewry. I am grateful to all four of you for your support of our family throughout the years. To my sister, Dr. Rivka Tuval-Mashiah, for encouraging me to write (separately) about my path to the prayers—to record the life stories of the people I met, to describe the appearance of the rare prayer books preserved in private collections that excited my imagination and the secrets that were revealed by accident. To my brother, Avi Mashiah, my brother-in-law and sisters-in-law, to my tribe—my thanks for all the understanding, the love, the togetherness.

To our beloved children—Yarden, Arbel, Dror-David, and Amit-Hanna: This book is yours; it is for you. The discussions with you, the deliberations, and—especially—your reactions were a source of inspiration to me. This book is part of my unceasing effort to convey to you some of the Jewish experience that has molded me since childhood and that has accompanied me throughout my adult life.

To my husband, Tzuriel—for everything. More than anything else, for your support and love; for being with me at every stage, even though at first you didn't understand. In the end it was you who introduced me to the beautiful prayer of Perl, wife of Rabbi Levi Yitzhak of Berditchev.

396

NOTES

PREFACE

xvii   "It is possible": G. H. Cohen, "Prayer and Modern Man" [Heb.], *Jewish Prayer: Continuity and Innovation* (5738).

xvii   newspaper interview: Anat Meidan, *Yedi'ot Aḥaronot*, September 15, 2002, Yom Kippur supplement.

xix   "her countenance was": *Emunah u-Vitaḥon*.

xxv   "When the Ba'al": Legend recounted by Gershom Scholem.

I. MOMENTS IN A WOMAN'S LIFE

2   "Lady Urania …": Avraham Grossman (5761).

3   Avraham Grossman's conclusions: Ibid.

4   "the venerable matriarch": Sperber (1998).

5   details about first translation of Haggadah: Yael Levine, "The Woman Who Translated the Haggadah into Italian: The Story of Flora Randegger Friedenberg" [Heb.], *Kolech* (5763): 67.

6   "May He, in His mercy": Grossman (5761).

8–9   Biographical details for Freiha: see Levine (5763), 2, 93–94; Sheetrit (5740); S. Kaufman, G. Hasan-Rokem, and T. S. Hess (1999).

12–15   Text of "A Mother's Early Morning Prayer": The text of this prayer and background information are reprinted with the author's kind permission: Pinhas Cohen (1995).

17   "My sister—may you become": Genesis 24:60.

17   The second alternative version: from the library of the Jewish Theological Seminary, New York, MS 8255. My thanks to art historian Evelyn M. Cohen for her helpful information.

17   The third alternative: Gili Zivan, "The Time Has Come for a New Prayer Book: Preliminary Thoughts" [Heb.], paper presented at the International Congress (2005), in Cohen and Lavie (2005).

17   Yehuda Henkin's solution: Yehuda Henkin (5765).

24   "God—fill my mouth": Psalms 126:2.

24   "Let my heart": Psalms 131:1.

24   "Until I find": Psalms 132:5.

24   "For there God commanded": Psalms 133:3.

25   Information about Hamitovsky: Mr. Hamitovsky is a lecturer in the Department of Land of Israel Studies, Bar-Ilan University.

26   "Hear my cry": Psalms 18:7.

30   Information in Mishnah Nidda, 6.

30   The Ben Ish Hai's ruling: Rabbi Yosef Haim (the "Ben Ish Hai"), *Laws of the First Year, parashat* Re'eh 17.

31   Rabbi Yitzhak Nissim's ruling: Yitzhak Nissim (5724), 1–5. Also quoted in an article by A. Arend, "The Bat Mitzvah Celebration in the Rulings of Rabbi Nissim" [Heb.], in Friedland Ben-Arza (2002), 109–15; Genesis 24:60.

31   "Now our responsibility": Yehiel Yaakov Weinberg, *Seridei Eish* Responsa, Jerusalem edition (5759), 2, 39.

32–35 Information about and the text of the prayer reprinted with the kind permission of Aharon Cohen, ed., *Zeved ha-Bat;* Mr. Cohen also brought to our attention the custom of reciting Deborah's Song.

36–37 "wife of Heber the Kenite": Judges 4:21.

54–55 Text of "Prayer to Find a Worthy Match": Salman Mutzafi (5752).

57   Text of prayer and its source: Some prayers of the Breslov Hassidim contain references to the writings of Rabbi Nahman; this prayer does not refer to any specific source.

58–59 Text of prayer: Yoel Bin-Nun (5765) by courtesy of the author.

60–61 The Maharal's elaboration: Maharal, *Be'er ha-Gola, ha-be'er ha-sheni.*

II. BARRENNESS AND FERTILITY

75   "Jacob's anger is": Leibowitz (1989).

76–77 Text of "Prayer for Childless Couples": Salman Mutzafi (5752).

78–81 Text of "Prayer of a Childless Woman": *Sefer Tehinot ha-Shalem,* courtesy of Simhonim Publishers.

92–93 Text of "Upon Admission to the Hospital": Zakkai (5748).

96–99 Text of "The Birth" and commentary: This prayer, along with the other prayers taken from *Shevet Musar,* appear in Italian manuscripts of women's prayer books. My thanks to Yael Levine for this reference. E. Ha-Kohen (5723).

100–1 Midrash citing Elijah's apparent questioning: *Pirkei de-Rabbi Eliezer,* 28.

101   Custom during the Middle Ages: Sperber (1998).

101   The custom originated: Babylonian Talmud, Tractate Sanhedrin 32b.

102–5 Text of "Prayers Following Childbirth": E. Ha-Kohen, *Shevet Musar:* Gross family collection.

106–9 Text of "Offering of Prayer": *Sefer Tehinot* ha-Shalem, courtesy of Simhonim Publications.

110–11 Text of "*Mi Sheberakh* Prayer for a New Daughter": Ya'ari (5718).

124–28 Formula for celebration: This is the version of the She'erit Yisrael congregation of the Spanish-Portuguese synagogue in New York from Aharon Cohen, ed., *Zeved ha-Bat*, reprinted with his kind permission.

III. PRAYERS FOR MOTHERS

136–39 Text of "Upon Bringing Her Child to the *Melamud*": *Sefer Tehinot ha-Shalem*, courtesy of Simhonim Publishers.
150 "than seven sons": Ruth 4:15.
150 "Daughter shall rise": Micah 7:6.

IV. WOMEN'S *MITZVOT*

154 "Both men and women": Maimonides, Laws of Shabbat in *Mishneh Torah*, 5, 3.
154 "Remember the Shabbat": Exodus 20:8.
154 "Observe the Shabbat": Deuteronomy 5:12.
154–55 The Talmud's explanation: Babylonian Talmud, Shabbat 119a. "Rabbi Hanina used to wrap himself [in a prayer shawl] and stand, as it grew dark on Shabbat eve, and say, 'Let us go out to greet the Shabbat Queen!' Rabbi Yannai, dressed in special Shabbat garb, used to say, 'Come, bride; come, bride!'"
156–58 Text of *tekhineh*: *Sefer Tehinot ha-Shalem*, courtesy of Simhonim Publications. The parts of the prayer are recorded there in a different order.
166–69 Formula for blessing for the candles: This formula of the blessing is mentioned in testimonies given before the Inquisition, starting from 1543; see Sluschetz (5692).
174 Details about source of custom: Y. Ta-Shma, *Minhag Ashkenaz ha-Kadmon* (Jerusalem: magnes, 5752), 128, note 12. My thanks to Moshe Halamish for bringing this source to my attention.
174–79 Text of "Prayers for the Household": This material is recorded in Aharon Zakkai, ed., *Sefer Segulot u-Tefillot* (Jerusalem: Yeshivat Or Yom Tov, 5748).
180–83 Text of "Friday Prayer": Freund (1879).
186–87 Text of "Prayer Upon Separating Challah": *Sefer Tefillat Hanna* (1995).
190 Origin of "Blessing Over a Tithe": Sluschetz (5692).
196 Source of prohibition: The prohibition against sexual relations is found in Leviticus 20:18.
197 Maimonides's comments on menstruation: Maimonides, *Guide to the Perplexed*, part III, chapter 47.
200–1 Text of "Blessing Upon Immersing in a *Mikveh*": Scribe: Meshulam Zimmel of Polna, Vienna, 1751; from the collection of The Jewish Museum of Budapest, MS 64.626. My thanks to Sharon Liberman Mintz, Curator of Jewish Art at the library of the Jewish Theological Seminary, for drawing my

attention to this item. Another, almost identical, version is to be found in the collection of the Israel Museum, Jerusalem, MS 180/6; scribe: Aaron Wolf Herlingen, Vienna, 1739.

209   Rabbi Nina Beth Cardin: Rabbi Nina Beth Cardin. *Out of the Depths I Call to You.* Northvale, N.J.: Jason Aronson, 1995.

212–13   Text of "Prayer at Menopause": Sa'ad (2004; not published).

V. FESTIVALS AND HOLY DAYS

218   "The honorable Lady Sara": Avraham Grossman (5761).

219   Talmudic legend: Babylonian Talmud, Shabbat 119a.

220–23   Text of the blessing for a daughter according to Aharon of Berakhia: *Avodat Yisrael* prayer book, Redelheim Publishers (1951).

222   Rabbi Yehuda Henkin's blessing: Yehuda Henkin (5765); see also Levine (5763), 1.

224   Details about adorning synagogues: Milano (1992).

224–25   Text of prayer "For Beautifying the Synagogue": Luzzatto (1966).

226   Details about synagogues' women's section: Grossman (5761).

226–27   Information about language of prayers: Grossman (5761). "But in our times, with most of our sons and daughters—owing to our many sins—speaking the language of Edom and Arabia and Greece, according to the languages of the nations, where even most of the men do not know Hebrew, how shall we propose that the women should understand the language written in the Gemara?" So writes Mordekhai, son of Yitzhak Ibn Kimhi, who lived in southern France in the thirteenth century.

226–29   Text of "Opening the Gates": Wunder (5752).

231   Hebrew text of "At the Conclusion of the Shabbat": Translation courtesy of Shemuel Refael, Naime and Yehoshua Salti Center for Ladino Studies, Bar-Ilan University.

233   Malka Pietrokowsky's suggestion, 2002.

234–37   Text of "Prayer for the Eve of the New Moon": *Tehinah Rav Peninim* (1964).

234–35   Information about Sara Bat-Tovim: According to the testimony of Hanna Safrai. My thanks to her for her good advice and for her support throughout my research.

238–43   Text of "Matriarchs' Supplication": *Sefer Tehinot ha-Shalem,* courtesy of Simhonim Publications. Wunder (5752) features a different prayer for the blessing over the new moon that is likewise attributed to Rabbanit Sheril (Sarah Rivkah Rachel Leah) Horowitz.

246–47   Text of "Paschal Prayer": Morpurgo (5650), 107.

247   Dr. Yael Levine's proposal: Yael Levine, "'*Ko katva ha-tze'ira min ha-tzon*': Concerning the *Mi Sheberakh* Prayer by Rachel Morpurgo," *Hatzofeh,* March 19, 2004, Sofrim u-Sefarim supplement, 11, 14.

250–53   Text of "I Shall Sing Like the Song of Moses and Miriam": Elnekaveh (5753).

250–51 Custom of reciting a *tikkun*: Shatrog and Shmama (5633).

254–55 "It Was the Middle of the Night": Yael Levine, *Midreshei Bitya bat Pharaoh: Iyyun Nilveh ha-Seder*, Jerusalem, 40 Levine, 5764, pp. 54–58 (self-published). The Hebrew text with an English translation was published in several places, including in Joel B. Wolowelsky, *Women at the Seder: A Passover Haggadah* (New York: Ktav, 2005), pp. 90–91. The background information for this prayer was provided by Yael Levine.

256 Toby Trackletaub's Haggadah: I am grateful to Sahara Blau of the institute for bringing this item to my attention and for helping me to obtain a copy of it.

258 The five catastrophes that occurred on the ninth of Av: Babylonian Talmud, Ta'anit 26.

260–69 Excerpts from *The Supplication of the Mothers for the Rebuilding of the Temple*: For the complete Hebrew text, see Yael Levine, *Teḥinat ha-Nashim le-Ninyan ha-Mikdash* (Tel Aviv: Eked, 1996). See further: Yael Levine, "*Teḥinat ha-Nashim le-Ninyan ha-Mikdash*: The Supplication of the Mothers for the Rebuilding of the Temple: Excerpts and Commentary," *Nashim* 9 (2005): 126–34; Yael Levine and Chava Weissler, "*Teḥinat ha-Nashim le-Ninyan ha-Mikdash*: A Conversation," *Nashim* 9 (2005): 135–43.

270–71 Biographical information about Osnat: See further: Levine (5763), 2.

270–73 Text of "Women's Lamentations for *Tish'ah be-Av*": The eulogies that appear here were conveyed by Gorgia Avraham-Avishur. Avraham-Avishur (5741).

271 Information about *Tish'ah be-Av* in Iraq and Kurdistan: A book of lamentations of the women of Kurdistan for the eve of *Tish'ah be-Av*, known as *Leil Huza*, was recently published.

272 Commentary on "Eulogy for the Slaughterhouse": Ibid.

274 "day of sounding": Numbers 29.

274 "day of remembrance": Leviticus 23.

274–75 "conveys a veiled message": Maimonides, *Laws of Repentance*, chapter 3.

275 It was on this day: Midrash Tanḥuma, *Ki Tisa*, 31.

276–77 Biographical information about Rabbinit Sheril Horowitz: Wunder (5752).

286–89 Text of Yiddish *tekhineh*: Ibid.

290–91 Excerpt from Ovadia of Bartenura's letter: Hartum and David (5757).

293 "You shall rejoice": Deuteronomy 16:13–15.

294–97 Text of "Following Candle Lighting on Sukkot": Reproduced with the kind permission of Simhonim Publications.

294 "On that day:" Amos 9:11.

298–303 Text of "Upon Taking Up the Four Species": Hartum and David (5757).

308 "The prayer for rain": Leah Shakdiel (Ḥeshvan 5763). Prayer for Rain [Heb.], *Amudim* (668): 2, 4–5.

335 "When the Messiah": Maimonides, *Mishneh Torah*, Laws of *Megilla* and Hanukkah, 2, 18.

336–39 Text of "Qeen Esther's Plea": The introduction to the Hebrew Transtalion of *Targum Shani*, titled *Patshegen Haketav*, includes the following words: "*Targum Shani* on *Megillat Esther*, in Hebrew that is easily understandable for all those of our nation who do not know the language of the *Targum* (Aramaic) ... and in order ... to carry out "the wish of each and every individual," for those who do not understand ... as well as for the women, I set out ... the words of this *Megilla* in Ashkenazi language ..." Aharon, son of Mordekhai of Tribetch (Vilna, 5630).

VI. TIMES OF CRISIS

VII. PRAYERS FOR PEACE AND REDEMPTION

BIBLIOGRAPHY

Adelman, H. "Finding Women's Voices in Italian Jewish Literature." In J. R. Baskin
  (ed.), *Women of the World: Jewish Women and Jewish Writing*. Detroit: Wayne State
  University Press, 1994.
Alendaf, A. *Seridei Teiman*. Jerusalem: Zukerman Press, 5688.
Ashkenazi, S. "Mahbarot Piyyutim, Tehinnot u-Tefillot," *Mahanayim* (5727): 109.
Avishur, Y. *Mehkarim ve-Toldot Yehdei Irak u-ve-Tarbutam*. Or Yehuda: Babylonian Jewry
  Heritage Center, 5751.
Bar-Ilan, M. *Some Jewish Women in Antiquity*. Atlanta, Ga.: Scholars Press, 1998.
Bashan, E. *Neshot Hayil Yehudiyot be-Maroco*. Tel Aviv: Aretz, Tel Aviv University, 2003.
Baskin, Y. "Mabat Hadash Al ha-Isha ha-Yehudiya be-Ashkenaz be-Yemei ha-
  Beinayim," in R. Levin-Melamed (ed.), *Harimi be-Koah Kolekh*. Tel Aviv: Lamaskel,
  5764.
Ben-Pazi, Y. "Al Minhagan Shel Benot Mishpahat ha-Ben Ish Hai be-Amirat Tikkun
  ba-Layl." *Mikra'ei Shabbat u-Mo'ed*. Ashkelon Academic College: Department of
  Core Studies, vol. 9, 5764.
Ben-Yaakov, A. *Kehillot Yehudei Kurdistan*. Jerusalem: Ben Zvi Institute, 5721.
———. *Yehudei Bavel mi-Sof Tekufat ha-Geonim Ad Yameinu*. Jerusalem: Kiryat Sefer, 5731.
Ben-Yekutiel Rossi, M. *Sefer ha-Tadir*. New York: Moshe Yehuda HaKohen Blau, 5752.
Buber, M. *Or ha-Ganuz, Sippurei Hassidim*. Tel Aviv: Schocken, 1979.
Cardin, N. B. *Out of the Depths I Call to You*. Northvale, N.J.: Jason Aronson, 1995.
Cohen, A. (ed). *Zeved ha-Bat*. Jerusalem: Kanah, 5750.
Cohen, G. H. *Ha-Tefilla ha-Yehudit: Hemshekh ve-Hiddush*. Jerusalem: Institute for
  Contemporary Judaism and Philosophy, 5738.
Cohen, T., and A. Lavie (eds.). *Lihyot Isha Yehudiya* (To Be a Jewish Woman), third
  anthology. Jerusalem: Kolekh, 2005.
Cohen, Y. *Nashim be-Hanhagat ha-Tzibbur*. Jerusalem: Ha-Kibbutz Ha-Dati (Tenu'at
  Ne'emanei Torah ve-Avoda), 5751.
Davidson, Y. *Otzar ha-Shira ve-ha-Piyyut, Mi-Zeman Hatimat Kitvei ha-Kodesh Ad Reishit
  Tekufat ha-Haskala*. New York: Rabbinical Council of America, 1970.
Epstein, Y. M. *Kitzur Shenei Luhot ha-Berit*. Jerusalem: Ha-Tehiya Press, 5720.
Falaji, Haim. *Mo'ed le-Khol Hai*. Izmir, siman 30, ot 7, 352a-b, 5621.
Friedland Ben-Arza, S. (ed.). *Bat Mitzva*. Jerusalem: Matan, 2002.

Gavra, M. *Encyclopedia le-Hakhmei Teiman*. Benei Berak: Institute for the Study of Yemenite Scholars, 5761–5763.

Gellis, Y. *Encyclopedia le-Toldot Hakhmei Eretz Yisrael*. Jerusalem: Mossad ha-Rav Kook, 5735.

Girondi, Y. *Iggeret ha-Teshuva*. Printed together with *Sefer ha-Yir'ah*, and printed together with *Iggeret ha-Mussar* as *Dat ha-Nashim*, by Rabbi S. Alami (Berlin, 1713).

Goldschmidt, D. "Minhag Benei Roma," in S. D. Luzzatto, *Mavo la-Mahzor Benei Roma*. Tel Aviv: Devir, 5729.

Gonen, R. *El Kivrei Tzaddikim: Aliyot li-Kevarim ve-Hilulot be-Yisrael*. Jerusalem: Israel Museum, Hemmed Books, 1998.

Grintz, Y. *Yehudit: Tahzurat ha-Nussah ha-Mekori be-Tziruf Mavo, Peirushim u-Maftehot*. Jerusalem: Bialik Institute, 5717.

Grossman, A. *Hassidot u-Mordot: Nashim Yehudiyot be-Eiropa bi-Yemei ha-Beinayim*. Jerusalem: Zalman Shazar Center for Jewish History, 5761.

Haberman, A. M. "Nashim Sofrot, Mehabrot u-Madpisot," *Mahanayim* 98 (5725): 76.

Hagag-Liluf, Y. *Toldot Yehudei Luv*. Bat Yam: S. M. and the Institute for the Study and Research of Libyan Jewry, 2000.

HaKohen, A. (Malonil). *Orhot Hayim*. Jerusalem: Yosef Dov Shtitzberg Edition, Laws of Tish'a be-Av, 5716.

Harlow, J. *Pray Tell: A Hadassah Guide to Jewish Prayer*. Woodstock, Vermont: Jewish Lights, 2003.

Hartum, A., and A. David. *Me-Italia li-Yerushalayim: Igrotav Shel R. Ovadia mi-Bartenura me-Eretz Yisrael*. Ramat Gan: G. G. Communications Jerusalem Project, Department of Land of Israel Studies, Bar-Ilan University, 5757.

Hazzan, A., and A. Elbaz. *Sefer Tehilla le-David: Kovetz Shirato Shel Rabbi David Ben Hassin—Paytana Shel Yahadut Maroco*. Lod: Orot Yahadut ha-Magreb, 5759.

Henkin, Y. H. (Rabbi). Shu't Benei Vanim, part IV. Jerusalem: self-published, 5765.

Herman, D. *Ma'agal ha-Hagim ve-ha-Mo'adim ba-Bayit ha-Yehudi*. Jerusalem: Prologue, 5764.

Hozeh, S. *Toldot ha-Rav Shalom Shabazi*. Jerusalem: published by Yosef Hassid and the author, 5733.

Hyman, P. *Ha-Isha ha-Yehudiya bi-Sevakh ha-Kidma*. Jerusalem: Zalman Shazar Center for Jewish History, 1995.

Jacobson, Y. *Netiv Bina*. Tel Aviv: Sinai, 1964–1972.

Kalfon, H. *Lanu u-le-Vaneinu: Ma'agal Hayei ha-Kehilla ha-Luvit*. Netanya: Yad la-Gibborim Synagogue, 1986.

Kapah, Y. *Halikhot Teiman*. Jerusalem: Ben Zvi Institute, 5721.

———. "Kotvei u-Ma'atikei Sefarim be-Teiman," *Mahanayim* 106 (5726): 152–57.

Kasher, M. M. *Torah Sheleima, Megillat Ester*. Jerusalem: Noam Aharon Press, 5754.

Kaufman, S., G. Hasan-Rokem, and T. S. Hess (eds.). *The Defiant Muse: Hebrew Feminist Poems from Antiquity to the Present: A Bilingual Anthology*. Translated by Peter Cole. New York: Feminist Press at the City University of New York, 1999.

Kislev, S. "Zeved ha-Em," in M. Shilo (ed.), *Lihyot Isha Yehudiya*, pp. 222–29, Jerusalem: Urim, 2001.

Kook, T. Y. (Rabbi). "Kohah Shel ha-Isha be-Seder ha-Min ha-Enoshi," in B. T. Rosenfeld (ed.), *Ha-Isha ve-Hinukha*. Kfar Saba: Amana, 5740.

Langleven, L. "Nashim Yehudiyot me-Hungaria be-Aushwitz-Birkenau be-1944,"
  Da'at 7: Merkaz Limudei Yahadut, 5759; Jewish Studies Center Web site: www.
  daat.ac.il/daat/kit/.

Lau, Y. M. (Rabbi). *Yahadut Halakha le-Ma'aseh.* Tel Aviv: Modan, 1978.

Lavie, A. "Kemo Malka," *Kolekh* 55–56 (5762).

———. "Nashim Gedolot" (Great Women), in Y. Mishali (ed.). *Pirkei Imahot.* Tel
  Aviv: Yedioth Aharonoth, 2002.

Leibowitz, N. "Ha-Tahat Elohim Anokhi," *Ha-Penina: Ha-Isha ha-Yehudit ba-Hevra, ba-
  Mishpaha u-ve-Hinukh.* Jerusalem: Benei Hemmed, 1989.

Levine, Y. "Bein Megillat Rut le-Mizmor Eshet Hayil," *El Asher Telkhi: Iyyunim bi-
  Megillat Rut,* Jerusalem: Mishpahat Raviv, 5762, pp. 101–9.

———. *Midreshei Bitya Bat Paro: Iyyun Nilveh le-Leyl ha-Seder,* Jerusalem: Y. Levine, 5764,
  pp. 54–58.

———. "Nashim Ortodoksiyot bi-Zemaneinu ki-Mehabrot Teillot li-Khlal Yisrael,"
  in M. Shilo (ed.), *Lihyot Isha Yehudiya.* Jerusalem: Urim, 5763, 1.

———. "Nashim Ortodoksiyot bi-Zemaneinu ki-Mehabrot Teillot li-Khlal
  Yisrael—Iyyun Histori," *Kenishta* 2 (5763): 2.

———. "Tehinnat ha-Nashim le-Vinyan ha-Mikdash: Midrash Hadash ve-Tekst
  Liturgi le-Tish'a be-Av," in M. Shilo (ed.), *Lihyot Isha Yehudiya.* Jerusalem: Urim,
  5761.

———. "Va-Titpalel Hanna: Al Parshat Hanna u-Tefillata be-Liturgiya," *Massekhet* 4
  (5766): pp. 81–111.

———. "Va-Yehi be-Hatzi ha-Layla," in: *Midreshei Bitya Bat Pharaoh: Iyyun Nilveh
  le-Leyl ha-Seder,* Jerusalem, 5764, pp. 54–58.

Levine Katz, Y. "Nashim Lamdaniyot bi-Yerushalayim," *Mabu'a* 26 (5754).

———. *Tehinnat Nashim le-Veit ha-Mikdash.* Tel Aviv: Akad, 5756.

Levine-Melammed, R. "Judaizers and Prayer in Sixteenth-Century Alcazar." In B.
  D. Cooperman (ed.), *In Iberia and Beyond: Hispanic Jews Between Cultures,* pp. 273–95.
  Newark: University of Delaware Press, 1998.

Levine, Yael. "The Woman Who Translated the Haggadah into Italian: The Story of
  Flora Randegger Friedenberg" [Heb.], *Kolech* (5763): 67.

Levinsky, Y. *Encyclopedia Shel Havay u-Massoret.* Tel Aviv: Devir, 5730.

Liedloff, J. *The Continuum Concept.* New York: Perseus Books Group, 1986.

Luzzatto, S. D. *Igrot Shadal,* part VII, pp. 978–79. Cracow: Yosef Fisher Press, 5651.

———. *Mavo Shadal le-Mahzor Benei Roma.* Tel Aviv: Devir, 1966 (Livorno, 1856).

Mack, H. *Mavo le-Tefillot Yisrael.* Tel Aviv: Ministry of Defense, "Broadcast University"
  Library, 2001.

Malovitzky, A. (ed. and trans.). *Sefer Tehinnot ha-Shalem.* Jerusalem: Simhonim, 5758.

Meikoff, M., and S. H. Mizrahi. *Ha-Neshek ha-Adin: Teillot li-Rega'im Gedolim u-le-Sha'ot
  Ketanot.* Jerusalem: Nahalat Tzvi Institute, 1999.

Meizlish, S. "Bein Yael li-Yehudit," *Al Mah: Ketav Et le-Kiddum Ma'amad ha-Isha,* 2001.

Melamed, A. and R. Levin Melamed, "Ha-Rabbanit Osnat—Rosh ha-Yeshiva be-
  Kurdistan," *Pe'amim* 82 (5760): Journal published by Israeli Ministry of Education,
  Culture and Sport.

Meyuhas, G. A. *Yehudim, Anusim ve-"Notzrim Hadashim" bi-Sefarad*. Tel Aviv: Ministry of Defense, "Broadcast University" Library, 1999.

Milano, A. *Ghetto Roma: Temunot min he-Avar*. Tel Aviv: Ma'ariv, 1992.

Murporgo, Rachel. *Ugav Rachel*. Cracow: Ed. Rabbi Yitzhak Castileone, 5650.

Mutzafi, B. *Olamo Shel Tzaddik: Hayav u-Fo'alo shel ha-Mekubal ha-Tzaddik R. Salman Mutzafi*. Jerusalem: published privately at the Keter Press, 5736.

Mutzafi, S. *Orah Tzaddikim, Tefillot u-Vakashot*. Jerusalem: Yeshivat Benei Tzion, 5752.

Nahman mi-Breslav. *Sefer Likkutei Etzot*. Jerusalem-Benei Berak: Breslov Chassidic Foundation, 5737.

Offenberg, A. K., E. G. L. Schrijver, and F. J. Hoogewoud (eds.). *Bibliotheca Rosenthaliana: Treasures of Jewish Booklore*. Amsterdam: Amsterdam University Press, 1994.

Pieterkowsky, M. "Rosh Hodesh—Haggan shel ha-Nashim," in S. Friedland Ben-Arza (ed.), *Bat Mitzva*. Jerusalem: Matan, 2002.

Pinhas Cohen, H. *Masa Ayala*. Tel Aviv: Ha-Kibbutz ha-Me'uhad, Ritmus Series, 1995.

Rabinowitz, A. Z. *Zikhronot Glukl*. Tel Aviv: Devir, 5689.

Refael, S., and M. Bakhar. Para *Mujos Aniyos—Seder Rosh ha-Shana be-Ladino*. Ramat-Gan: Bar-Ilan University and "Hemshekh" Association, 2002.

Rosenthal, D. S. (ed.). *A Joyful Mother of Children*. Spring Valley, N.Y.: Feldheim, 1988.

Ross, T. "Ha-Od Mesuggalot Anu Lehitpallel le-Avinu she-ba-Shamayim?" in N. Ilan (ed.), *Ayin Tova: Du-Siah u-Fulmus be-Tarbut Yisrael*. Tel Aviv: Ha-Kibbutz ha-Me'uhad, 5759.

Rut, B. *Ha-Yehudim be-Tarbut ha-Renaisans be-Italia*. Jerusalem: Bialik Institute, 1962.

Sefer Yehudit (The Book of Judith). Jerusalem: Bialik Institute, Yehoshua M. Grintz Edition, ch. 16, 5717.

Sefer Yossipon (The Jossipon). D. Plosser Edition [original version, copy of manuscript with additions]. Jerusalem: Zalman Shazar Center, 1978.

Seri, S. (ed.). *Bat Teiman: Olamah shel ha-Isha ha-Yehudiya*. Tel Aviv: A'aleh be-Tamar Organization, undated.

Shamrock, H. "Ha-Soferet ha-Yehudit ha-Rishona be-Polin—Rivka Bat Meir Tiktiner ve-Hibbureiha," *Gilad—Ma'asaf le-Toldot Yahadut Polin*, 5739. Published privately.

Shatrog, Y., and Y. Shmama (eds.). *Dinei Shehita u-Vedika bi-Leshon Aravi*. Livorno: Piyyutim, 16b, 5633.

Sheetrit, Y. "Freiha Bat Yosef—Meshoreret Ivriya be-Marocco be-Me'ah ha-18," *Pe'amim* 4 (5740): 84–93.

———. "Freiha Bat Yosef—Meshoreret Ivriya be-Marocco be-Me'ah ha-18," in Y. Sheetrit (ed.), *Piyyut ve-Shira be-Yahadut Maroco: Asufat Mehkarim Al Shirim ve-al Meshorerim*. Jerusalem: Center for Jewish Languages and Literature, Hebrew University of Jerusalem, Bialik Institute and Ashkelon Regional College, 5759.

———. "Freiha Bat Yosef—Nosafot al Meshoreret Ivriya mi-Maroco be-Me'ah ha-18," *Pe'amim* 55 (5753).

Shiloh, M. *Ha-Kol ha-Nashi ha-Yerushalmi: Kitvei Landaniyot min ha-Me'ah ha-19*. Jerusalem: Dinur Center, 5764.

Sluschetz, N. *Ha-Anusim be-Portugal*. Tel Aviv: Devir, 5692.

Sperber, D. *Minhagei Yisrael: Mekorot ve-Toladot*. Jerusalem: Mossad ha-Rav Kook, 1998.

Steinzaltz Even Yisrael, A. *Ha-Siddur ve-ha-Tefilla—Madrikh li-Me'ayen u-le-Mitpallel.* Tel Aviv: Lamaskel, 1994.

Strikowsky, A. (ed.). *Nashim ve-Limmud Torah.* Jerusalem: Torah Culture Department, Israeli Ministry of Education, 5753.

———. *Sifrut Yiddish be-Polin.* Jerusalem: Magnes, 5741.

Tarnor, N. *A Book of Jewish Women's Prayers.* Northvale, N.J.: Jason Aronson, 1995.

Ushpizai, D. Minhagim be-Rosh Hodesh. Ph.D. thesis submitted to Bar-Ilan University, Ramat Gan, 5757.

Weissler, C. *Voices of the Matriarchs.* Boston: Beacon Press Books, 1998.

Wunder, M. *Ateret Rivka.* Jerusalem: Institute for the Commemoration of Galician Jewry, 5752.

Ya'ari, A. *Masa'ot Eretz Yisrael.* Tel Aviv: World Zionist Organization, Division for Youth Affairs, 5706, pp. 289–90.

———. "Tefillot Mi Sheberakh: Hishtalshelutan, Minhageihen ve-Nus'haoteihen," *Kiryat Sefer* 33 (5718).

———. *Toldot Hag Simhat Torah.* Jerusalem: Mossad ha-Rav Kook, 5724.

Yosef Haim. *Keter Malkhut—Ateret Tiferet.* Jerusalem: Rabbi Ben-Tzion Mutzafi Edition, 5741.

———. *Sefer Hukkei ha-Nashim.* Jerusalem: Yeshu'a ben David Salem, 5757.

———. *Sefer Leshon Hakhamim,* 5769.

Zakutinski, R. (ed.). *Techinas: A Voice from the Heart: "As Only a Woman Can Pray."* New York: Aura Press, 1992.

Zuaretz, P., and P. Tayer (eds.). *Se'u Zimra.* Tel Aviv: Council of Libyan Communities in Israel, 5739.

PRAYER BOOKS, HOLIDAY PRAYER BOOKS (*MAHZORIM*), AND BOOKS OF CUSTOMS

Abuhbut, M. *Siddur Ketav-Yad Ishi,* including unknown *piyyutim* written by the compiler. Livorno: Gross family collection Az/011/001, 1740.

Alnekaveh, Y. (ed.). *Siddur Sha'arei Komemiyu.* Jerusalem: Sha'arie Komemiyut, 5753.

Avodat ha-Lev: Ma'alat ha-Tefilla ve-Inyana. Jerusalem: Devar Yerushalayim, 5741.

Bar-Da, Rabbi Y. *Siddur Tefillat Hanna.* Ramat Gan: Ryb'd Publishers, 5746.

Bar Moshe, R. Yosef. *Lekket Yosher.* Berlin: Yaakov Freiman Edition, Yoreh De'a, 5664.

Berakhia of Modena, Rabbi Aharon. *Ma'avar Yabbok.* Mantova: Siftei Renanot, ma'agar 3, 5386.

Bin-Nun, Rabbi Y. "Za'aka u-Tefilla," *Ha-Tzofeh.* 19 Tevet 5765, 31 December 2004, supplement.

Doron, R. *Ha-Siddur ha-Meforash Kavvanat ha-Lev le-Vat Yisrael.* Petah Tikva, 5762.

Eliyahu, Rabbi M. *Kol Eliyahu.* Jerusalem: self-published 5757.

Freund, Y. *Siddur Tefilla li-Neshot u-Venot Yisrael.* Breslau: Wilhelm Yaakovson, 1879.

Girondi, Rabbi Yona. *Iggeret ha-Teshuva, derush* 3.

Haim Sofer, Rabbi Yaakov. *Shulhan Arukh Orah Haim, Im Sefer Kaf ha-Haim,* part IV. Jerusalem, siman 363; ot 34, 37a.

Ha-Kohen, Rabbi A. *Shevet Musar*. Jerusalem: Yaakov Rubinstein, 5723.

Ha-Kohen Kook, Rabbi A. Y. *Olat Ra'aya*. Jerusalem: Mossad ha-Rav Kook, 5723.

Hartum, M. A. (trans. and ed.). *Maḥzor Minhag Italiyani*, vol 1: Weekdays—Shabbat—Various Festivals—Fasts. Rome: Caracci, 5750.

Hefetz, D. *Sefer Sha'arei Hefetz*. Jerusalem: self-published, 5707.

Horowitz, Rabbi Y. *Shenei Luḥot ha-Berit*. Amsterdam: Massekhet Tamit, 258b, 5009.

Ibn Tzur, Y. *Et le-Khol Hefetz*. Egypt: Pereg Haim Mizraḥi Press, 5655.

Kol Bo. Siman 62, Laws of 9th of Av and the Order of Prayers, and the Law Concerning the Four Fasts, 5250.

Maharam, son of Rabbi Barukh of Rothenburg. *Sefer Minhagim*. New York: Yisrael Shenhav Alpenbein Edition.

Mualem, Aharon Tzion Hakham Barukh: *Sefer Toldot Aharon u-Moshe*. Jerusalem: self-published, 5752.

Mussaiouf, A. *Siddur Hukkat Olam ha-Shalem*. Jerusalem: Mantzur, 5751.

Neuda, F. *Hours of Devotion: Book of Prayer and Ethical Teachings for Jewish Women and Girls, for Public and Private Prayer, and for Any Moment in a Woman's Life* (Yiddish). Prague: Breslau, 1855.

Nissim, Rabbi Y. "Al Birkat Barukh She-Petarani," *Noam*, Book VII, 5724.

Nussaḥ ha-Tefilla shel Yehudei Paras. Jerusalem: Shelomo Tal, 5741.

Rabbi, T. *Siddur Avodat Hashem ha-Shalem le-Vat Yisrael Im Sefer Tehillim*. Holon: self-published, 5758.

———. Siddur Bat Yisrael Nezer ha-Kodesh. Petah Tikva, 5752.

Reverends Handbukh. *Siddur le-Ḥazzanim Kolel Kol ha-Tefillot ve-ha-Berakhot ve-Khol Minei Matzevot ve-gam Luaḥ Al Me'a Shanim*. New York: S. Druckerman, 1918.

Seder Korban Minḥa. Im Ivri Teitch Yashan. Lvov, Tel Aviv: Gross family collection, 1888.

Seder Tefillot mi-Kol ha-Shana (Tamim). Amsterdam: Gross family collection, three volumes, 5749–5759.

Sefer Tefillat Hanna. New York: Cohen Publication, 1995.

Sefer Tefillat Nashim. Ketav Yad Likhvod Sara Eshet K. Hizkiya Levi. Tel Aviv: Gross family collection, 5574.

Sefer Teḥinot. Jerusalem: Miller, 5762.

Seder Teḥinot u-Vakashot. Zoltzbakh: Gross family collection, 5536.

Sharabi, M. *Lekket Ma'asiyot, Tefillot, Segulot, Musar*. Jerusalem: Beit Midrash Or ha-Shalom.

Shinan, A. *Siddur Avi Ḥai*. Tel Aviv: Sifriyat Hemmed, 5760.

Teḥinah Rav Peninim. Tel Aviv: Sinai, 1964.

Yanai, Rabbi. *Maḥzor Piyyuti le-Torah u-le-Mo'adim*. Tel Aviv: Tzvi Meir Rabinowitz Edition, vol. 1, 5745.

Yosef, Rabbi O. *Hazzon Ovadia*. Jerusalem: Ohr va-Derekh, 5750.

———. Siddur Bat Tzion ha-Shalem Im Tehillim. Jerusalem: Betzalel, 5757.

———. Siddur Or ve-Derekh "La-Bat Yisrael." Jerusalem: Midrashiyat Rachel, 5748.

———. Siddur Tefillat Rachel le-Vat Yisrael. Jerusalem: Yeshvat Hazon Ovadia Press, 5758.

Zakkai, A. *Sefer Segulot u-Tefillot*. Jerusalem: Yeshivat Or Yom Tov, 5748.

AUTHOR INDEX

ABOUT THE EDITOR

DR. ALIZA LAVIE is a lecturer in the Department of Political Science at Bar-Ilan University in Israel. Her fields of research include gender, public communications, multiculturalism, and Jewish women's prayers. She is also a presenter and editor of television programs on Jewish culture, and is active in a number of social initiatives promoting tolerance, equality, and empowerment. She lives in Netanya, Israel.

ABOUT THE ENGLISH TYPE

The English text of this book was set in a digital version of Centaur. Centaur was created in 1914 for the Metropolitan Museum by the noted type and book designer Bruce Rogers (1870–1957). The cut of the letters is based on Venetian old-style typefaces by the fifteenth-century printer Nicolas Jenson. Centaur has a beauty of line and proportion that has been widely acclaimed since its release.

ABOUT THE HEBREW TYPE

The Hebrew text of this book was set in a digital version of Koren. Koren was designed in the mid-twentieth century by Eliyahu Koren (1909–2001) for his series of siddurim created in the 1980s. His objectives in designing the font were legibility, beauty, and maintaining the traditional characteristics of the letters.

Composed by Rina Ne'eman

Hebrew Language Services

East Brunswick, New Jersey

Printed and bound by RR Donnelly

Crawfordsville, Indiana